Equity, Income, and Policy

edited by
Irving Louis Horowitz

The Praeger Special Studies program—
utilizing the most modern and efficient book
production techniques and a selective
worldwide distribution network—makes
available to the academic, government, and
business communities significant, timely
research in U.S. and international economic, social, and political development.

Equity, Income, and Policy
Comparative Studies in Three Worlds of Development

PRAEGER SPECIAL STUDIES IN INTERNATIONAL POLITICS AND GOVERNMENT

Praeger Publishers   New York   London

Library of Congress Cataloging in Publication Data

Main entry under title:

Equity, income, and policy.

(Praeger special studies in international politics
and government)
  Includes index.
  1. Equality—Addresses, essays, lectures.
2. Income distribution—Addresses, essays,
lectures. 3. Poverty—Addresses, essays,
lectures. I. Horowitz, Irving Louis.
HM146.E67   301.5'1   76-2904
ISBN 0-275-56570-X

PRAEGER PUBLISHERS
200 Park Avenue, New York, N.Y. 10017, U.S.A.

Published in the United States of America in 1977
by Praeger Publishers, Inc.

789   038   987654321

ACKNOWLEDGMENTS

This book originated in a series of panels I had the privilege to organize for the 1976 annual meetings of the American Political Science Association on the broad theme, "America: A Bicentennial Critique." The series of panels on the special question relating to income, equity, and policy is my own doing. Perhaps I should add "undoing," since when political scientists hear the word *income,* they assume the problem belongs to the American Economic Association. In truth, when economists hear the word *equity*, they assume that this is a special preserve of the American Sociological Association. And, of course, when sociologists are faced with policy issues, they often return the compliment to the American Political Science Association. This completes the cycle of intellectual buck-passing to the detriment of some very basic issues in normative theory and empirical research alike.

The ever-present dangers of interdisciplinary efforts notwithstanding, I must first register my appreciation to the participants and panelists who came from many parts of the nation and the world to contribute their efforts. These are fine contributions, pushing the discussion of basic normative issues on equity, income, and policy as far as empirical analysis permits. Since each author is identified by name and affiliation, no further acknowledgement is due. Beyond that of the participants, the vision of two people, Frances Fox Piven of Boston University and Seymour Martin Lipset of Stanford University, proved central to this enterprise. Their foresight and energy in serving as program chairpersons was crucial to the completion of the panels and papers. Additional sources of technical support cannot go unnoticed. Alan Gold provided that rare form of copyediting that transcended the boundaries of a craft and involved invaluable intellectual inputs for nearly every chapter. And Stanley DeViney provided a superb index, and in the process served to highlight the major threads that made this rich garment of ideas hang together.

CONTENTS

LIST OF TABLES

LIST OF FIGURES

This is one instance when the subtitle, *Studies in the Three Worlds of Development,* equals in importance the title, *Equity, Income, and Policy.* For the organizing concept of these chapters is undoubtedly the unitary character of the developmental process. While the break-up of chapters is clearly in terms of the three worlds (at least with respect to the character of international political economy), the thirst for development, as a mechanism for staying ahead or for catching up, is universal.

Beyond that point, the beliefs that divide are nearly as important as those which unite these chapters. For even though the concept of equity is universally held as an ultimate value in the developmental process, it is defined in nearly as many ways and takes into account as many different measures, as the number of chapters themselves. The multiple ideologies of development, and hence the drive toward equity, are congruent with different social systems. This congruence is clearly a focus of discussion within these chapters.

There is a sense of connection between developmental ideologies and equity goals. Uniformly, they are viewed as isomorphic with policy making and the instrumentalities for achieving distributive justice. Both the common concern for equity and the differing means of achieving equity through a developmental standpoint must be appreciated in the light of the types of national societies in which the developmental process is being carried out. These chapters address themselves to this issue.

The obstacles to equity are a source of greater divergency of opinion than the goals of equity. While there remain clear epistemological differences as to the nature of equity, these pale in consequence to the sociological differences. These can be located either internal to the system, whether it be class, status, or military factors, or external to the system, having to do with the economic imperialism of the West (First World) or the political imperialism, or what the Chinese prefer to call the "social imperialism," of the Soviet orbit (Second World). Hence, where one places emphasis on the source of inequity is perhaps a truer benchmark of the ideological persuasion underlying these chapters than the common core of accepted shibboleths concerning equality.

The first cluster of chapters deal primarily with problems of the First World. The chapters by Lampman, Hewlett, and Ritzer, while differing markedly in their emphasis, or for that matter even appreciation for what the market economy of the First World can provide, each address themselves to economic problems central to those types of societies dominated by a free market, and representing political processes characteristic of open societies. The main problem in this First World would seem to be how growth and development is to be maintained within a capitalist structure of rewards for incentive and innovation and yet provide for distributive justice.

The processes described represent a sense of advocacy and not simply information. The efforts of Lampman and Ritzer at least are clearly intended to support a concept of equity within a framework of achieving further capitalist development. A curious factor at work in those people supporting this position, and at the same time a recognition of this as a negative feature of capitalist democracy in the chapter of Hewlett, is that the sources of policies intended to establish equity lay not only or primarily within the state, but among other segments of society: factory, community, neighborhood, and voluntary associations. Ritzer's study of industrial democracy in Sweden, for example, emanates exclusively from management-labor impulses. There is little federal or governmental involvement taking place in this process, beyond minimal regulatory functions. Ritzer's own conclusions coincide with the findings of the team sent to Swedish auto plants by United Automobile Workers: The United States should go slowly in adopting Swedish methods of factory management, since adoption of these methods also means absorption of much greater state regulation, which American auto workers clearly view as outside their dream of greater union democracy.

The empirical researches indicate that the concept of policy formation in search of equity goals is viewed as taking place apart from the state or state power. For Hewlett the very centrality of the state is artificially minimized by the capitalist process of growth. Capitalist systems do so because the nature of the private enterprise system tends to minimize, as do all market systems, the role of private property as a prime source in the uneven and unequal distribution of wealth. Hence, the search for solutions directly within the framework of the economy, and outside the framework of the state, only intensifies the drive toward monopolistic and oligopolistic tendencies that maximize profit. The hidden hand of auto regulation based on self-interests institutionalizes a sort of hierarchial premise and clearly weighted property relationships that make the search for equity an eternal goal, and perhaps the solution to the equity problem an eternal impossibility.

What is virtue for those who advocate First World solutions turns out to be vice for those who are critical of such approaches. There does not seem to be much argument with the benthamite credo that capitalism properly understood is a society in which the best state, if one can call it that, is one which rules least, not most. The issue thus becomes empirical. First, does the state exercise a greater degree of control than the self-management people would allow for? Second, does the state in effect direct the market economy to the point where the hidden hand of Smith becomes the overt hand of Keynes, and hence, presumably the oppressive hand of Marx? The chapters in this section well appreciate that policy formations within capitalist systems are restricted to a view of equity as one of opportunity and access to the market, rather than equity as limitations on the class, racial, or sexual differences between individuals and collectivities. The ongoing confusion between policies aimed at achieving equity often rest on such different assumptions in economic philosophies.

The Second World of socialism, as presented in the chapters by Connor, Minkoff, and Turgeon, clearly show, and even take for granted, the central role of state power and centralism as a method of policy formation. In such a system, equity goals are defined not in terms of self-management or bootstrap economics, or monetarist pump primings, but rather the capacity of the state in imposing its will on all phases of government to produce equity programs. This imposition on all phases of social living produces not only equity for citizens but presumably strong support for the state by recipients. Indeed, some researchers have argued that social security more than social revolution accounts for regime support in socialist societies.

Once again, this time with the proverbial shoe reversed, the very emphasis on the state over society as a mechanism for achieving equity, seems to result in new sources of inequity by generating new elite forces that have nothing to do with the original purposes for which the state intervenes. The general welfare measures are real: The production of education, medical care, and welfare measures exist. However, the emergence of new classes or privileged occupational strata are also real. The public economy exists within a world of higher incomes for privileged people, and a world of special punishment for deviant people who do not accept the rule of the elite, the party, or its benificent institutions. The Second World, which replaces the concept of the good society with that of the good state, suffers the obverse problems. Namely, it acts as a stimulant to new forms of inequitable social relations and new measures of power control and rules. These serve to produce new kinds of status inequity in the very process of liquidating older varieties of class inequity. The chapters in this section stand in strategic opposition to each other. This is a function of emphasis on whether economic or sociological "evils" are worse. Minkoff-Turgeon see the relative and real advantages of state regulation in eliminating class competition. Connor sees the relative and real disadvantages of state regulation in stimulating status competition. The mixed blessings of the two systems, the tradeoffs rather than the resolutions of fundamental questions of equity, has resulted in the Third World being slow, even reticent, to accept policies for dealing with equity as they currently exist within the First and Second Worlds.

As the chapter by Portes and Ferguson makes clear, most Latin American countries remain within the capitalist economic structure. Despite this, they display differing forms of state power and social ideology. Hence, despite the existence of capitalism, they have evolved exceedingly differing policies to achieve equity goals. The differing policy potentials within established economic modes is made evident in the discussion by Bar-Yosef and Greene in their respective analyses of Israel and Tanzania. Both countries, to varying degrees, have socialist systems of economy and yet have little in common with Second World statist systems, or for that matter with Western-styled party systems. Both contain high mixtures of market-type incentives and large-scale mass political inputs. Both have political systems differing from each other and more profoundly from either the First or Second Worlds. This is illustrated by the high degree of mobilization of participation within the Israeli kibbutzim and similarly in the villagization processes in Tanzania. And still, neither of these two Third World democracies have anything to do with each other.

What we have is not only a changing response to structure, but changing historical tempos. The First World of capitalism developed "naturally"; that is, the bourgeois economies of Western Europe and the United States evolved prior to any political systems appropriate to the form of capitalism that now exists. The liberal democratic thrust, which is now denounced as caretaker regimes of capitalism, in fact came into being as a response to working-class demands to curb the bourgeoisie and to limit the degree of monopolization. The special character of democracy within the First World has always been the sense in which the "social" polity represents a creative tension with the "natural" economy. The role of the state as an agency of the society as a whole, instead of any one class within the economy, is the central reason why the conservatives have argued against state intervention, federal interference, and central government growth. Whatever else, the First World of development is primarily an economic world. That is why it has chafed under any and all forms of political imposition that aimed at producing equitable results by unnatural, policy-directed means.

The Second World came into existence as a result of direct, political-party intervention, and not merely from a mystical (or scientific) belief in the inevitability of socialism. The vanguard party precedes in time the actual existence of such systems. Socialism is a system of society, dedicated to the achievement of full economic development through the magic lever of state power. By operation no less than by ideology the role of the party, the state, and the bureaucracy is geared and mobilized to achieve the ends of equity. Built into the socialist claim is that capitalism, by its class-bound nature to maximize profits rather than welfare, makes equity impossible. From this perspective, the intervention of state power is not artificially produced by bureaucrats in need of work, but is a necessary concomitant of the policy of equity as such. Classlessness rather than opportunity becomes the ultimate expression of the dream of equity. That new classes have come into Second World existence, sometimes of a type and nature more oppressive and extreme than the economic classes left behind in the First World, does not obscure the continuing socialist goal of achieving equity through the political processes, that is through the state as a civilian party apparatus. Admittedly, this is a far cry from the original Marxist concept that a classless society would axiomatically signify a stateless society.

But the obvious increase of state power in the socialist bloc clearly leaves such theorizing behind.

The Third World being very much a mid-twentieth-century phenomenon, has what Furtado properly calls a "shopping basket" approach to social systems. It could do this because Third World revolutions and anticolonialist movements alike were largely spearheaded by military or paramilitary guerrilla movements. Hence, economic and political forms were largely determined by the special character of the military origins of the Third World. That this vanguard enterprise of spearheading revolutions for national independence should fall to the military was a consequence of the absence of well-defined class formations within much of the Third World. In nation after nation the military became, more by default than design, a unique expression of the overall national will. The military rather than any one economic class or political party, became the physical and human embodiment of patriotism and nationalism: the one element beyond the parochial grip of classes, sections, ethnic, and tribal rivalry.

The military of the Third World, despite its own caste and bureaucratic constraints, was in itself an expression of equity, of mass mobilization, self-improvement programs, and officers rising from the ranks—universalistic criteria for promotion and advancement. But more, in the very processes of being the mediator of the economic claims of the marketplace and the political claims of the bureaucracy, the military were guarantors of equity demands. This mediator role between the marketplace and the bureaucracy meant that the economy of the Third World remains largely capitalist, while the polity remains largely socialist or dominated by a single-party regime. One had Keynesian free-market economies combined with one-party systems. But neither the economy nor polity were able to exercise a dominant influence over the other. Both, either through direct appeal or through the absence of power, as signified by an autonomous mass or class constituency, turned to the military to solve the problem of social management.

However awkward the military, however filled and fraught with tendencies toward arbitrary persuasion and autocratic distemper, it appeared to be the only section of the society within the Third World capable of producing equitable outcomes. It is hardly an accident that there is hardly a regime within the Third World that does not have either an overt military leadership or a barely covert military leadership. There are a few exceptions, perhaps Tanzania in Africa is one of them (and hence an interesting model to examine unto itself in relation to this volume); Venezuela in South America is another, and Israel in the Middle East is a third. In all candor one would have to examine closely even those civilian democracies of the Third World to see how close to the surface military power comes in exerting real authority. After all, the main shock of the Chilean debacle is less the overthrow of a democratically elected regime than the use of the military to do so in what had, up to 1973, been imagined as a nation exempt from the "laws" of military participation in the political and economic processes.

Finally, whether we are dealing with the economism of the First World, the politicism of the Second World, or the militarism of the Third World, the universal cry for equity as justice, for equality in both opportunities and outcomes has grown to astronomical proportions. Few leaders—be they civilian or military, capitalist, socialist, or a mixture of both—dare violate the notion of the right of equity between races, sexes, tribes, and ethnic groups. That this also happens to be a century that has seen the most extraordinary violation of equity demands through the arbitrary termination of life, for all manner and sizes and shapes of groups—that is, through genocidal and regicidal practices—should not blind us to the impact of policy on equity: a world in which the process of nationalism is defined by achieving developmental goals and in which the touchstone of such goals is defined by the achievement of equity.

August 23, 1976
Irving Louis Horowitz
Rutgers University

1

SOCIAL WELFARE, STATE POWER, AND THE LIMITS TO EQUITY
Irving Louis Horowitz

U.S. society presents a major inconsistency: a near unanimous belief in the value of equity and a constant of income and occupational differences. The support of communications had a corresponding decline in fixed class distinctions, accelerated by a rise in service industries and a fall in productive activities. The gap between values and effect, while not any larger than it was in the past, has been viewed as more intolerable. Hence, much more pressing demands for equity practices and procedures have now been registered, along with the termination of all forms of inequity to the extent that that is possible.

THE STATE AS GUARANTOR OF EQUITY

Before taking up subjects of the limits of equity, and the possible handicaps and curbs, it is important to register how the rugged individualist form of the competitive society has broken down. First, many Americans have begun to realize that the limits of geographical frontiers have finally been reached and that consequently the corresponding ideology of striking it rich through land acquisition has come to an end. Second, as society itself has become more politicized, the population has become less patient with inequality, especially as the political demands have come upon an increasing awareness of the bureaucratic and corporate obstacles that make for powerlessness rather than power. Finally, the affluence stimulated by the end of World War II enabled many Americans to raise their incomes to a point where they were no longer concerned only with making ends meet. As a result, new expectations emerged, not only for a higher standard of living, but also for gains in the quality of life and in the control of one's own destiny.

In addition to these precipitating factors of equity demands, there have been structural changes within U.S. society that give force and urgency to the concept of equity. Foremost of these structural changes is the size, role, and legitimation of state power. The U.S. government has grown from a small organization to a large, complex network of organizations, and most growth has taken place in the twentieth century. The very rapidity of bureaucratic growth itself contributed to demands for equity, since hiring practices, social relations, and ideological demands are all made in terms of the federalist credos rather than in terms of the old capitalist ethic with its implicit neo-Darwinian struggles for survival.

Growth and size alone do not explain the structural basis of equity demands. The changing role of the state, connected as it is to the changing base of legitimation, must also be taken into account. The major role of the federal government in the nineteenth century was to provide a favorable environment for business activity. The state, within this framework, was Hamiltonian, involved with the stabilization of currency and the steady legal pattern that insured the rights of exchange in contracts. In addition to the support for business activity, government came to provide for services and facilities in economic areas that individuals and corporations could not provide for themselves. Hence, everything from national roadways and waterways to the development of the National Aeronautics and Space Administration required government support in order to be remotely successful. The idea of government support at this level was still directly linked to commerce or, better, to those areas in which the public sector could perform with far greater rationality than could the private sector. This type of legitimation for federal involvement in the affairs of society might be viewed as a legal, rational level. It insures that the state provides for a stable and predictable environment for the growth of commerce and capital. The government legitimated the expansion of its own state power by presenting its activities as a favorable approach in support of the economic system. Calvin Coolidge put the matter bluntly when he said that "the business of America is business." This was carried further by the General Motors president, Charles E. Wilson, when he declared that "what is good for General Motors is good for America." The state, in other words, grew by assisting the business and commercial activities of society. Anti-Trust legislation was first intended to check the evils of monopoly in order to make sure business activities flowered.

But then, in American society as in other types of advanced, postindustrial systems, the role of the state began to take on an autonomy quite apart from assistance to business and commerce. Anti-Trust legislation, for example, which began by checking the evils of monopoly, ended by checking the evils of commerce itself. The state changed its role slowly but surely from defending entrepreneurial interests to creating some sort of balance between classes that would permit no one class to rule. By default, if for no other reason, with the change of role the state became even more powerful, albeit different in character in the late twentieth century from that during previous stages of capitalist and socialist development.

With the Depression and the New Deal the role of government began to change dramatically. In its new guise the government sought to improve not only business conditions but the condition of the population as a whole, even if this meant a curb on profits. The state began to intervene more directly into the economy for the purpose of creating upward mobility and greater participation, thereby insuring that the stratification system would not harden or calcify. Some of the early activities in this area were the recognition of labor unions as a co-partner with business associations in the conduct of commerce. It did this through a series of legislative measures favorable to union activities. Another indicator of this changing attitude toward equity was the growth of social welfare programs, which began during the New Deal but was accelerated under the Fair Deal, the New Frontier, and the Great Society. All these actions were presumed necessary, not because individuals failed to take advantage of opportunities of the capitalist system but as a consequent belief that the bourgeois economy made equity as such impossible. In this way, the state legislated itself not only in terms of business needs but in terms of improving the status of all groups.

In the process of presenting its goals in these terms, the state inevitably increased the pressure for new demands far beyond the economic realm envisaged by policy makers in the New Deal "Brain Trust." The state inexorably and increasingly became involved not simply in matters of economic equity, but also racial, ethnic, and sexual parity. The state presented itself, and was perceived by the wider public, as the source of law, and hence the ultimate recourse for those who had legitimate demands. No longer was the archetypical struggle waged between workers and bosses: It was between interest groups mediated by the force of law embodied in the power of the state.

The black movement of the 1960s can be considered important in this general revitalization of equity issues in two fundamental ways: First, the methods of the movement involved a direct appeal to law and the government for a restitution of civil rights; second, the demands were different from those of earlier periods. Methods used by the black movement differed considerably from those of the trade-union movement in that they were directed more to the government, particularly on the federal level, rather than to the entrepreneurial groups and corporations. In this way, the black movement attempted to bring the federal government and state power directly into play to insure equity. Whatever it took (federal troops in Little Rock or Supreme Court decisions in Washington), there was a belief that the government was that unique institution that had to support the black demands for equity or stand ideologically bankrupt.

The second factor in the black movement involved a sense of rising expectations that again could only be assuaged by federal support and intervention. Early victories by blacks and the raised level of educational and cultural institutions and, equally, of public accommodations, only stimulated the sense of equity. This was followed quickly by demands for similar pay for similar work and for open housing without local ordinance restrictions or banking prejudice, by voting-rights pressures that led to a great number of black public officials and all the way to community control, and by affirmative action, which one might say led to the complete turn of the screw, since what started as a demand for equity ultimately terminated as a demand for pluralism, or the right to be different. Separate but equal, once again became a factor, this time at the urgings of black rather than of white groups.

The utilization of the state by the blacks led in quick succession to the same approach by women and by ethnics. In the hierarchy of the women's rights movement, the similarity to the black model is self-evident. First, there is the pluralist model, which anticipates a society in which racial, religious, and ethnic differences are retained and valued for their diversity, yielding a heterogeneous society in which it is hoped that cultural strength is increased by the diverse strands making up the entire society. Second, the older alternative model, which anticipates a society in which minority groups are ultimately absorbed into the mainstream by losing their distinguishing characteristics and acquiring the language, occupational skills, and lifestyles of the majority, does not vanish but remains a leitmotif. Finally, a hybrid model emerges, in which there is a change in both the ascendant group and the minority groups, so that changes take place not only among blacks, women, and ethnics, but among the dominant racial, sexual, and religious groups.

Although the equity model becomes ascendant within vast social movements, the curious fact is that the government, far from being feared through intervention on the side of the opposition, is strongly encouraged to intervene. The assumption of "oppressed" groups is that legitimate or judicial review or lobbying involve potentials for higher equity rather than for more repression. This is clearly a departure from the traditional role of the state as a supporter either of the status quo or of the business community.

The old view of the state is that its role and function are in the service of privileged and wealthy classes. The new view of the state is that its role and function are in blunting, if not eliminating, differences of class and status. The distribution and the quality of public services effect the absolute and relative well-being of individuals. Although inconsistencies exist between classes with respect to income and resources, the state is charged with the task of minimizing such inconsistencies. The whole gamut of social services and health, education, and welfare is viewed as the federal "hidden hand," intervening on the side of the poor and the downtrodden to create an equal starting point for all concerned, whatever different outcomes may yet occur. The state becomes a service organization, whereas political power becomes the level that measures permissible levels of inequality and freedom.

What began as a nonideological effort to increase the efficiency and rationality of governance, terminates with a new ideological concept and struggle: the state as exclusive guarantor of the democratic promise. Samuel P. Huntington has referred to the new role of the state as "democratic distemper." His definition of what the 1960s brought about stands as a succinct reminder that the effort to end ideology actually resulted in the reemergence of new and more vigorous status ideology:

> The 1960's also saw a marked upswing in other forms of citizen participation, in the form of marches, demonstrations, protest movements, and "cause" organizations (such as Common Cause, Nader groups, environmental groups). The expansion of participation throughout society was reflected in the markedly higher levels of self-consciousness on the parts of blacks, Indians, Chicanos, white ethnic groups, students, and women, all of whom became mobilized and organized in new ways to achieve what they considered to be their appropriate share of the "action" and its rewards. In a similar vein, there was a marked expansion of white-collar unionism and of the readiness and willingness of clerical, technical, and professional employees in public and private bureaucracies to assert themselves and to secure protection for their rights and privileges. In related fashion, the 1960's also saw a reassertion of equality as a goal in social, economic, and political life. The meaning of equality and the means of achieving it became central subjects of debate in intellectual and policy-oriented circles. This intellectual concern over equality did not easily transmit itself into widespread reduction of inequality in society. But the dominant thrust in political and social action was clearly in that direction (Huntington 1975: 17-18).

So much has the role of the state as the guarantor of equity become central to a new ideology, the raging debates of the 1970s involve precisely the role of federal intervention and state power in the affairs of the citizenry. The new conservatism holds that further centralizing authority, far from insuring equity, leads to disorder and a breakdown of community. The government becomes the only center of gravity between the individual and the monolith. In its more advanced versions, the public sector itself becomes subject to ideological attack. Thus, the commercial sector, which at the beginning of the century was serviced by the state, has come to view the state as the enemy of its class interests. Private enterprise has developed a strong defensive posture with respect to any furtherance of state power. The bourgeois state of the nineteenth century has turned into the antibourgois state of the twentieth century. With this phenomenon, the whole notion of the role of government in relation to economy becomes subject for profound review.

WEAKENING OF THE PUBLIC SECTOR:
RETURN TO MALTHUSIANISM

The Stevensonian call for a "revolution of rising expectations," which began in the mid-1950s, is now resolving itself as an equally urgent appeal for a "revolution of falling expectations." Universal boosterism has yielded to a particularistic pessimism. Now the cry is for "the end of progress" (Renshaw 1976: 7-19). Time does indeed march on, but in directions so diverse and disarrayed that charting the marchers, much less participating in the events, has become a major undertaking whose outcome is highly uncertain. Nothing is more dangerous than to presume that the models of the world that we create are either more perfect or less elegant than the imperfections we find about us in nature and society alike.

This observation is prompted by dismay at how thoroughly unprepared the social sciences were to receive the so-called energy crisis of the 1970s. Less prepared yet were social scientists to cope with the consequences of this new state of affairs. Social science in the United States has grown up in a neo-Keynesian (or, better, Galbraithian) world of abundance. The only admissable problems faced by the technostructure concern the allocation of resources, not their availabilities. But the hoary demons of neo-Malthusianism have struck back, and the shared contempt that orthodox Keynesians and unorthodox Marxists alike held for the Malthusian scenario of war, famine, and plague as a "solution" to poverty and population has turned upon them.

Industrial societies in general, and U.S. society in particular, have fed the hopes and illusions of millions concerning the royal road to upward social mobility. Equity is a right guaranteed to all by democratic constitutions, but it is underwritten by an economic apparatus that from nursery school to graduate school assumes that the path to success is work: occupation and specialization. The road to failure is departing from this well-trodden formula. At the present time, many themes in U.S. culture have conspired to shake loose inherited Enlightenment assumptions that social welfare and economic mobility march into the future in step and hand in hand. Work and welfare have become opposite expressions of the American ethos. Energy and equity have both been subject to cost-benefit analysis that all but cancels out moral visions of the good society. We are confronted by new forms of social relations and hence new forms of social antagonisms. This study is a first effort to come to terms with what is new and old in society and, by extension, what is living and dying in social science.

The first point that strikes a novel chord about the 1970s is that in the ebb and flow of cost-benefit analysis, the present tilt clearly favors costs (and work) rather than benefits (and welfare). The concern is currently with the economy as a whole, and not simply with federal budgetary processes (Mishan 1976: 416-49). There has been a precipitous shift away from a sociological and social-welfare orientation toward what might be termed an econometric and accountability model. The most pervasive fact of the United States at every level, in every sphere, is that systems of measurement have been established to evaluate the cost and quality of performance. Questions are raised about productivity of labor and only secondarily about welfare benefits for those who do not toil. This represents a profound decennial shift in U.S. society. There is a more sober and modest estimate of potentials for growth through public or governmental sectors and a marked return to potentials for growth through production or private-sector modalities.

What might be considered a derivative of this changed American view is the further recognition that the 1970s is a decade of finite resources. In several dramatic forms, heightened to a fine point by the domestic energy crisis and foreign oil embargo, a new awareness has taken root that resources are limited and therefore that growth is limited. This is no mere ideological preference for a zero-growth model in either the economy or demography, but a response to the limits of natural wealth of any country. An acute awareness now exists that without mineral resources, the entire concept of economic growth is menaced. Beyond that, the "dependency model" applies not only to the developing nations of the Third World but also the more developed nations of the capitalist and socialist worlds.

To indicate the novelty of this shift, as late as 1972 reports were being issued by leading economists at the Hudson Institute that by 1980 Japan would be the world's first or second leading industrial power in the capitalist orbit. There was slender awareness among most forecasters of the major problems of scarce resources, the more than merely routine problems of allocating abundance. Our economic obtuseness largely derived from an inherited world-view, both Marxian and Keynesian, or sometimes a combination of the two, which persists in assuming that the central problem is product allocation rather than resource availability. We are living through the shock of a change in economic paradigms in which resource availabilities once again become significant in our collective cogitations. We have come to rediscover a Malthusian-Ricardian world in which problems of famine, pestilence, shortages, and subsistence become mechanisms to stabilize and rationalize economic systems through gradual population reduction, if not through outright military competition for dominating such scarce resources.

These developments represent the end of what might be called the "optative mood" Americans have imbibed. Progress has become problematic. "Built-in controls," "the search for control in the face of license," and "prudent restraint" have become familiar refrains cautioning those who simply identify progress with freedom (Bennett 1976: 852). The exceedingly high pessimism is a result, in part at least, of the recognition that resources are finite. With this has come a growing polarization within each of the dominant structures of the world economic system.

Within the capitalist world system the contradictions between the United States and Western Europe have become intense, heightened by different political and military strategies to gain necessary resources for continued high industrial and consummatory growth. Within the socialist bloc there is intense rivalry between the Soviet Union and the PRC, propelled by similar drives to maximize production outputs. Within the Third World there is a growing divergence among nations with oil and food resources that allow them to penetrate the advanced economies, at least as junior partners, and those nations in a Fourth World that remain poor in both food and energy resources. There is a geographic component to this Malthusian drive that intensified the polarization and breakup of world systems and empires. We witness a divergence not only between colonies and empires but between empires and nations that presumably share similar economic and cultural systems.

The redistribution of wealth leads to a different image of the world. In the past it took international warfare to bring about major redistribution of wealth. World War I and World War II both produced dramatic shifts in power and economy—but did so among those established European and Asian nations that by the turn of the twentieth century had already achieved high levels of productivity. While warfare remains a constant problem, armed conflict has mainly been conducted at subnational and regional levels. Hence, the process of redistribution of wealth has changed from a military to a diplomatic struggle. Game-oriented decisions have been employed to bring about wider redistribution of wealth, with a more telling effect than had the moral-persuasion arguments of earlier decades.

Nations such as the Middle Eastern cluster, as well as select nations within Latin America and Asia, have managed to participate in the market economy as recipients no less than as donors of real wealth. As a result, there is a shrinkage of resources among the wealthy industrial countries. Making do with less has become a way of life in Western Europe, and now North America is compelled to follow suit—against its cultural will, as it were. New slogans bombard us on all sides: Small is beautiful; growth is limited; resources are finite. Instead of an unreflective appeal to giganticism, there is the emergence of a miniaturization process most notable in relation to automobiles, housing, and other aspects of social life in the advanced nations.

Changing attitudes toward size, greater utilization of commodities already available, is a function of the redistribution of wealth. Such redistribution occurs without the warfare usually accompanying massive changes in ownership of wealth. As a result of these tendencies within the U.S. economy, there have been corresponding rebellions against big government, which is reputed to be the source of inflated budgets and systems of welfare established without a recognition of the high cost factors involved. More specifically, the charge is made that a level of government expenditures has been reached that assumed continuing levels of economic growth that can no longer be either sustained or realistically forecast.

An essential way in which this redistribution process has manifested itself is the sharpening gap between private enterprise and the public sectors. Although the private sector has recovered from the recession of 1973, the public sector clearly has not. As a result, those involved in the public-sector end of the economy continue to feel the burden of the 1970s recession—perhaps in fuller measure now than when it was underway. Almost every major indicator of economic growth—housing, new private starts, automotive production, consumer durable expenditures, number of people employed, corporate profits after taxes—would indicate that the recovery of the private sector has been fulsome, whereas the illness of the public sector has remained severe, even chronic (cf. Juster 1976:3-5). In consequence, the politics of this period reflect a genuine belief that if a choice has to be made between lower profitability and continuing measures to insure the welfare of the citizenry, it is the latter that will have to be sacrificed rather than the former.

What lends weight to this decision of the private-sector elites to weaken the public sector is its support by the proletarian cluster employed in the private sector, particularly the trade-union movement. What sometimes is euphemistically referred to as a taxpayer's rebellion is in fact a working-class discontent with a system of federal expenditures that equalizes the high end of the welfare package and the low end of the working package. This rebellion from below, whether it takes the form of a taxpayer's rebellion or trade-union discontent with government schemes for increasing the welfare package, reflects itself in the virtually instinctual patterns of negative voting with respect to any increase in taxation that would raise levels of federal expenditures or bureaucratic management. As a result, various programs of affirmative action, whether in education or other areas of the public sector, come hard upon tenure and seniority systems that cannot be overcome in a situation of relative economic stagnation.

U.S. society provides a spectacle of a pincer movement: an industrial rebellion against the public sector from above and below. Commercial elites and proletarian unions join together in negating any effort on the part of the government to increase the welfare package for marginal and under classes. Such changes have served to accommodate the new era of energy shortages with a minimal disruption to the private sectors. They may have created the conditions for new types of upward mobility in the form of demands for higher levels of participation in the workforce and lower levels of tax payouts to the welfare rolls. There is no mistaking the harshness and bluntness of this antagonism: Neo-Malthusiasm joins forces with neo-Darwinianism to satisfy the claims of proletariat and bourgeoisie against the marginal underclasses. Work versus welfare becomes more critical than inherited class and race antagonisms.

Paul Neurath (1975:296-97) recently called attention to this return of Malthusianism, and gave a pessimistic reading of the energy and food shortages. His own call for a serious standpoint somewhere between pessimism and optimism, while well taken, remains to be worked out in practice. For the issues are quantitative at one level (How much of a reduction in living standards can advanced social sectors accept?) and qualitative at another (What amount of growth is the U.S. public willing to sacrifice to retain present standards of liberty and equity?).

LIMITED ENERGY RESOURCES AND EQUITY DEMANDS

The velocity with which new realities have emerged can perhaps be gauged by the fact that only a decade ago the phrase "Third World" was considered an innovation and an idiosyncracy. It has now become a commonplace, and in fact a new paradigm has come into being: the "Fourth World." Now a nation may be rich in energy and rich in food; rich in energy and poor in food; poor in energy and rich in food; or, lo and behold, poor in energy and poor in food. While the United States numbers itself among the more fortunate nations on earth, in the first category and still very much the center of the First World, it too has had to cope with the shock of recognition that resources are finite and that problems of allocation are nastier and more brutish when one allocates shortages.

Simple aggregate data themselves reveal the implausibility of continuing the present scenario into the future. In the First World, some 20 percent of the world's inhabitants concentrated on 10 percent of the world's land mass currently absorb 80 percent of the world's resources (van Dam 1975:11). Under such circumstances, the question of diminishing natural resources must take on a grim aspect even for the most affluent country in the world. Especially telling is the fact that although resources are reduced, or withheld, as in the case of oil, expectations for the United States continue unabated, and interest-group politics becomes the operational guideline for all citizens on the margins of society. Appeals for government relief of inequities continue at a heated pace. Statistical measures of inequality—whether by blacks in relation to life expectations, women in relation to occupational mobility, youth in relation to quality of life, the aged in relation to security and health measures, earnings gaps between different regions of the nation—are often pressed by subgroups and cross cuttings. Whenever resources shrink, demands increase. The ideology of equality becomes more pronounced as the capacity of U.S. society to fulfill demands for equality becomes strained.

It would be profoundly erroneous to assume that such demands for equity are without merit. A recent report issued by the Council of Economic Advisors (Shanahan 1974:10) noted that the bottom 20 percent of all families had 5.1 percent of the nation's income in 1947 and almost the same amount, 5.4 percent, in 1972. At the top of the economic ladder there was a similar absence of significant change. The richest 20 percent had 43.3 percent of the income in 1947 and 41.4 percent in 1972. Thus, while the incremental wealth of Americans continued to rise during the post-World War II economic cycle, the ratio of wealth to poverty hardly budged. This is not to deny that notable gains were made on a sectoral basis; for example, the median income of black families went from 57 percent of that of white families in 1959 to 76 percent in 1972. On the darker side, however, people who are defined as poor are now poorer in absolute terms when compared to the rest of the U.S. population. In 1959 those defined as poor had about half as much income as the typical family; in 1972 they had only a little more than one-third as much. And these statistics were compiled prior to the recession that shook the United States between 1973 and 1975. Even were we to accept the premise that U.S. society can fulfill the main prerequisites of the drive toward equality for large population clusters, such as working women, black males, or minorities whose native language is not English, there remains a darker side to equity demands: They are unending and ubiquitous. As David Donnison reminds us:

> There are in fact so many different patterns of inequity in a complex urban society that to call for more (or less) equality without specifying which pattern concerns you is a pretty vacuous appeal. The main patterns are as follows: *The life-time cycle of incomes* producing for all social classes, successive periods of relative poverty and affluence during childhood, early adult life, early parenthood, middle age, and retirement. *Spatial inequalities,* due to (a) interregional, (b) urban-rural and (c) intra-urban differences in opportunities and living standards. The patterns of *social stratification* within urban, industrial, bureaucratic societies which produce social classes with differing bargaining strengths and differing inheritances (material, cultural, physical and intellectual). Social *discrimination* which benefits or handicaps particular groups on grounds of sex, religion, ethnic origin, accent or other characteristics (Donnison 1975:424).

The demands for parity by short people, fat people, handicapped people, or whomever become increasingly plugged into the general interest-group models that U.S. society has substituted for older class models. Demands for black psychiatrists raise counter demands for Italian psychiatrists. Research into cancer brings forth appeals for basic research into the causes of diabetes. All of these demands are perfectly reasonable; none save those who are without human compassion could deny the legitimacy of such demands. All utilize the very model that U.S. society has made the test for political participation—namely, articulating interests in a legal manner, and withholding political support if necessary to achieve such interest.

When one measures that cacophony of equity demands against the shrinking resources base, the problem of the U.S. commonwealth as it moves toward the twenty-first century becomes increasingly apparent. For it is no longer reasonable to expect other nations to permit the United States of America to resolve its own domestic tensions and prevail in the world at large with resources supplied by them. The demands for a new economic order must be taken seriously. Even if one could muster a philosophical argument along the lines of Rudyard Kipling, that along with the white man's burdens come the white man's prerequisites, no one out there is listening anymore; there are few whites who would care to make such arguments. Thus, the deadly equation of shrinking resources and rising expectations must unquestionably meet in a head-on collision that will test the mettle of U.S. society as never before in a peacetime context.

Addressing himself to the central issue, the relationship between continued inequality and a limited growth model, Karl W. Deutsch asks, somewhat rhetorically: "What is the probable effect if the world is now told to expect more scarcity, not less, and not for a short period but for a long one, and perhaps even in permanence?" His answer essentially is that a revolution of falling expectations "risks a new age of international conflicts that in the end may prove fatal to all of us." Indeed, he urges a prevention of such "a drift toward catastrophe." Among the mechanisms he recommends are the following:

> National and international stockpiling, an international system of reserves of food and fuel, the opening up of new agricultural acreages and mineral deposits, the improvement of technologies, the development of substitute materials and energy sources, the transition to less heavy but more sophisticated equipment (e.g., to transistors and printed electronic microcircuits)—all these may help to stave off a "revolution of falling expectations" and thus to buy more time for mankind to become truly joined "for better or worse, for richer or poorer" in the unity of the human race (Deutsch 1975: 381-98).

These are by all odds meliorative measures, which at best "buy time" to stave off disaster by rationing available resources, and imply no alteration in essential current inequalities. The question remains: Precisely why is it that a revolution in falling expectations cannot, or even ought not, take place? Indeed, one must argue that, contrary to Deutsch's view, persistent and increasing inflation and unemployment within industrialized nations serve precisely to accelerate a revolution of falling, or at least stable expectations, and provide mechanisms for accommodation to lower or "sustainable" standards of living that will insure the larger survival of the political and social systems as a whole.

Early efforts at futurology, based as they were on mechanistic frameworks and models that simply assumed the continuance and extension of current ratios of international resources make no sense. If social research proved inept at anticipating the current energy crisis, even though the crisis was initiated as a boycott inspired by political considerations, what is one to make of research estimates predicated on events a quarter-century in the future? To deal with the future implies an understanding of the present, and that also signifies a sense of how current dilemmas can be resolved with currently available techniques. It is more than a tautology to assert that problems of resources can only be resolved at this point by technology, whether the prevailing technology, harnessing atomic energy for industrial use, or a counter-cultural, counter-technology based on harnessing bigger and better windmills. Energy resources and their discovery is after all a problem for physical science, engineering, and technology generally. At this level we are dealing not so much with the possibility of expanding resources but with a timetable for that expansion that realistically continues to satisfy rising social expectations. If the problem of technology is the allocation of resources, the problem of bureaucracy becomes the allocation of scarce resources. The bureaucratic prerequisites of the moment are to harness available resources and to allocate them in such a way as to prevent an explosive civil war, a race war, a class war, or warfare generally. Thus, in point of fact, the bureaucratic problem has little to do with the limits of growth because to talk in such terms is simply to freeze present inequities into the social system.

Those urging a position based upon the "limits to growth," such as Jay W. Forrester (1971) have argued that the question is not, Can science remove the physical limits to growth? Rather, we should ask, Do we want science to remove the physical limits? Forrester observes that to assert an argument in favor of continued growth "is equivalent to saying we want growth to be arrested by social stress alone" (Forrester 1975:110-11). Nowhere in this position is the thought entertained that corking scientific and technological mechanisms of expansion might actually cause social stress. In this framework, stress is caused by growth whereas tranquility is insured through stagnation. But surely one might at least raise serious objections to this reversal of independent and dependent variables, this unexamined assumption that growth causes stress, rather than that social stress may result from increased demands for a technological halt. The recognition that stress may increase from a zero-growth policy has led to the emergence of a middle-ground view based on slow growth. But the question still remains: How slow should growth be, and who must slowdown most and/or least?

To freeze the developmental process at this time is intolerable for all marginal groups currently making their equity demands upon the society as a whole. The object in bureaucratic terms, and in human terms as well, is not the freezing of growth at present levels to create a new stasis but rather the reallocating of whatever wealth and resources are available, whatever their absolute size, so that the pie is distributed in a more equitable manner. The American people have proven quite capable of accepting a smaller pie. They are probably not capable of accepting a smaller pie in terms of present ratios of haves and

have-nots (Curtin 1976). The present imbalance of earnings and incomes characteristic of classes in the twentieth-century United States as a whole will only
exacerbate questions of redistributive justice, since the total pie will clearly be
reduced by virtue of international factors beyond the control even of the
wealthy. The data on redistribution that would open the stratification and
participation networks are not encouraging to those who want both economic
change and political order.

To enter a world of technology and bureaucracy is also to face a world of
technocrats and bureaucrats. It is to leave behind old formulas based on class
struggle along conventional lines of bourgeois versus proletarian. Old classes
attached to economic production shrink, whereas new classes attached directly
to the state apparatus grow exponentially. Nor do technocrats and bureaucrats
simply grow: They *become* each other, not merely *like* each other. They often
represent interchangeable parts in a commodities culture that serve to keep the
system intact. This introduces yet a more advanced problem, in addition to that
of responding to a world of shrinking resources and rising expectations: The
success of these tasks may imply a curb, if not an end, to the democratic political and social structure that Americans have been used to. As unpalatable as
Huntington's thesis on this might appear, his challenge is at least one that has to
be met with candor rather than with rancor:

> The vulnerability of democratic government in the United States
> thus comes not primarily from external threats, though such threats
> are real, nor from internal subversion from the left or the right, al-
> though both possibilities could exist, but rather from the internal
> dynamics of democracy itself in a highly educated, mobilized, and
> participant society (Huntington 1975:37).

Whatever else democracy is, whatever arguments can be mustered in its
behalf (and there are many), it is an expensive system. It involves a great deal of
deliberation, competition, conflict over goals, methods, making decisions based
upon humane considerations that are more political than economical. And such
decisions require high growth to cover new demands.

Here we come to the ultimate problem of the last portion of our century.
As I stated earlier, the issue is not only the survival of republic but its survival in
terms of a democratic framework that has come to be viewed as an extraordinary luxury in many other societies. It might well be that the allocation system
will work its magic ways. Technocrats and bureaucrats alike will attempt to
solve problems of shrinking resources and rising expectations, respectively. However, they do so increasingly at the cost of democratic politics, by resorting to a
policy-making state apparatus that is effective, efficient, and highly centralized.
We may be faced with a devil's dilemma: on the one hand, to save the republic
and lose its democratic essence; on the other, to continue preserving democracy
and seriously jeopardize the republic as it now exists.

The choice between the state as guarantor of equality and the community as guarantor of liberty is hardly a pleasant one. But it is a measure of the lines of future struggle that issues and institutions are perceived in this manner. Similar polarities are taking place in the world at large. Those who urge world peace, for example, often do so at the cost of continued world development; on the other hand, those urging world development often do so without much regard for the tranquility of the world as a whole. The proliferation of atomic capability is clearly only the most important and apparent of these dichotomies. Whatever the resolution, we can expect that the new revolution in U.S. society will be one of falling, not of rising expectations. Or, put in a more optimistic manner, as the United States becomes part of the world community, it must share the burdens of others. It must become more like the rest of that world in its lifestyles, consumption levels, and in the productivitity of its citizens. This is both for better and for worse.

It might well be that more sophisticated technology is related to decreases in productivity and that the current malaise in worker output, variously described as alienation and anomie in the workforce, is little more than an early warning that advanced industrial societies such as the United States are indeed drawing closer to the rest of the world. But there is a larger sense in which this growing similitude has dire potential consequences. At the level of political organization, only a few countries in the world—two dozen at the most—can still manage the luxury of democracy. To become part of that larger world may be to lose the luxury of democracy as well, unless it can be demonstrated once and for all that democracy and development go together, and not at the expense of the permanently poor. There are no cheap victories, no scenarios for a year 2000 that can spare us the tragedy of choice.

When one views future international relations as characterized by options based on interdependence, independence, or isolation, perhaps the most persuasive, if most evasive, solution is to choose all of them. There is always a combination of confrontation, subordination, and superordination in the affairs of states. The question at all times is the mix. Beyond that, whether such relationships are based on superordination, equality, or subordination depends on the national, subnational, or supernational units to which we refer. My own position is that the demands for economic equity and social parity that have pushed their way forward within the United States are now at work at the international level. Every person and each nation seemingly must take seriously the idea that all people (and all peoples) are created equal, or risk the perils of rebellion. The concomitant approach that nations, no less than people, can only count as one, will be a harder lesson for the powerful of the earth to absorb.

Equity has become the fundamental spinal cord organizing the relationships of the smallest national units with the largest national units: Albania with the Soviet Union, Puerto Rico with the United States, and, for that matter, Nicaragua with Mexico. "Sovereignty," like "the person" in Anglo-Saxon jurisprudence, is a legal entity. It demands liberty in relationships based on rather powerful constraints of law. This serves to underwrite and underscore a continuing tension between nationalism and individualism. Equity demands also compel a powerful drive toward various types of redistributive mechanisms that may prove to be undemocratic, a drive that certainly moves counter to traditionalist concepts of liberty. The dealings of nations with each other have increasingly been characterized by a cautionary but positive spirit. These impulses may in part be thwarted by other phenomena such as militarism—the prima facie strength of powerful nations with respect to weak nations. But if there are to be future international relations without war, then certainly equity is the touchstone and the hallmark of such a future. For the first time, the revolution of rising expectations in the Third World has been understood to entail a revolution in falling profits in the advanced nations of the First and Second Worlds. It remains to be seen whether the acquisition of basic equity demands also results in a parallel appreciation of the worth of individual liberty. The shock of recognition that benefits for some involve costs for others is a mark of maturation in international affairs, even though it may involve potential confrontation at a later stage of development. But as Arnold Toynbee long ago reminded us, this capacity to absorb new challenges and creatively resolve old dilemmas is the benchmark of surviving civilizations.

Equity and energy both involve issues of basic importance, since both entail the processes of distribution and programs for redistribution. While discussions among social scientists and environmentalists alike have focused on the distribution of income and resources, the core of the problem, in the proximate future at least, is more likely to involve questions of power, since those who control the flow of capital and resources are clearly the ultimate determinants of the extent to which equity concerns are realized. This may simply be a complicated way of asserting a simple truth of our times: Political considerations have largely come to prevail over purely economic factors.

But this insight, accurate as it may be, represents less than half of the story. By far, the bigger portion is the dialectic of equality and liberty. For as the state continues to underwrite programs to guarantee equity through social welfare it has been compelled to enlarge the character and scope of its own administrative apparatus. Thus, as income and wage differentials decline under the watchful and baleful eyes of the federal bureaucracy, the gap between government and citizens must clearly widen. The very success of equity-oriented programs, involving mandated restrictions on class differentiations, serves to widen power differentiations. As authoritarian regimes have made patently and repeatedly clear, the price of social welfare is political anomie for the masses. The equation that emerges is as painful as it is incontestable: libertarian goals tend to vanish as the range of federal social welfare programs expand.

For those living under Third World or internal colonial conditions of economic impoverishment, talk of political liberty has been placed on the policy back-burner. The largely military regimes of these vast areas of Africa, Asia, and Latin America have begun to play the role of political surrogates, harnessing national economies to the achievement of social equality. The past inabilities of the economic system of these areas of guaranteed equity through maximum participation or the political machinery to assure liberty through mass participation, has made the task of the military relatively simple. But as Third World societies become increasingly sophisticated and differentiated, the military role becomes less viable, serving more to disguise than to correct historical grievances and imbalances. In this sense, the attempts of nations such as Tanzania and Israel (and perhaps Venezuela in Latin America) become extremely interesting for their exceptionalist features, for their attempts to deal with problems of equality and liberty in a direct and forthright manner. They deserve close attention as possible alternatives to military paths of development, and options to the dire choice between equity and liberty.

For the First World and Second World no such postponements of the key issues are possible. The very successes of industrialization under conditions of both capitalism and socialism make the issue of political rights and participation far more volatile in the developed than in the developing regions. It is no accident that the achievement of a large measure of social equality, far from creating a new political consensus, has only fueled concerns over the political direction of "postindustrial" societies. Just as the idea of equality, once announced by the Enlightenment, could not be controlled, so too the idea of liberty becomes central in defining the ground rules under which the dispensation of goods and services are to take place. Thus, the very success of the idea of equality: who gets what, and why, rekindles at a new level long-standing issues of liberty: Who rules whom, and why.

REFERENCES

Bennett, John W. 1976. "Anticipation, Adaptation, and the Concept of Culture in Anthropology." *Science* 192, no. 4242 (May 28):847-53.

Curtin, Richard I. 1976. "Perceptions of Distributional Equity: Their Economic Bases and Consequences." Unpublished dissertation, University of Michigan.

Deutsch, Karl W. 1975. "On Inequality and Limited Growth: Some World Political Effects." *International Studies Quarterly* 19, no. 4 (December):381-98.

Donnison, David. 1975. "Equality." *New Society* 34, no. 685 (November 20):422-24.

Forrester, Jay W. 1971. *World Dynamics.* Cambridge, Mass.: Wright-Allen Publishers.

——. 1975. "Limits to Growth Revisited." *Journal of the Franklin Institute* 300, no. 2 (August):107-11.

Huntington, Samuel P. 1975. "The Democratic Distemper." *The Public Interest* 41 (Fall): 9-38.

Juster, F. Thomas. 1976. "The Recovery Gathers Momentum." *Economic Outlook* (USA) 3, no. 2 (Spring):23-25.

Mishan, E. J. 1972. *Economics For Social Decisions: Elements of Cost-Benefit Analysis.* New York: Praeger.

——. 1976. *Cost-Benefit Analysis*, 2d edition. New York: Praeger.

Neurath, Paul. 1975. "Zwischen Pessimismus und Optimismus." In *Wissenschaft und Welt-bild (Festschrift für Hertha Firnberg)*, edited by Wolf Fruhauf. Vienna: Europaverlag, 289-312.

Renshaw. Edward F. 1976. *The End of Progress: Adjusting to a No-Growth Economy.* North Scituate, Mass.: Duxbury Press.

Shanahan, Eileen. 1974. "Income Distribution Found Little Changed Since War." New York *Times*, February 2, p. 10.

van Dam, Andre. 1975. "A Simpler Life for the Advanced Countries." *Progress International* 2 (November):10-12.

2

CONCEPTS OF EQUITY
IN THE DESIGN OF SCHEMES
FOR INCOME REDISTRIBUTION

Robert J. Lampman

Equity issues arise at almost every stage in the design and redesign of schemes to redistribute income. Such schemes, by definition, take *from* somebody and give *to* somebody else. Both those taken from and those given to are concerned that the taking and the giving be fair or just or equitable. However, it seems that equity, like beauty, is in the eye of the beholder. One famous economist said that in matters of tax equity we are at sea without rudder or compass. Another concluded that equity is the mother of confusion. Still others have reasoned that economists could play a part in resolving distributional questions only if noneconomists provided them with a social-welfare function. Some texts represent horizontal equity—equal treatment of people in equal positions—as being of a different order from vertical equity—unequal treatment of people in unequal positions—and hence more amenable to consideration by the skilled economist.*

Despite all these caveats, academic economists have been active in the design and review of income redistribution schemes, and this chapter discusses some of the equity issues that have arisen in the past ten years of debate over the negative income tax (NIT). In particular, it contrasts the equity assumptions

---

Supported in part by funds granted to the Institute for Research on Poverty at the University of Wisconsin by the Department of Health, Education and Welfare, pursuant to the provisions of the Economic Opportunity Act of 1964.

*Richard A. Musgrave (1959:20) says that ". . . the implementation of distributional considerations raise difficulties of a technical sort. It is by no means obvious how to measure the relative positions that are to be adjusted." He also says (1959:160, 164) that an "objective index of equality or inequality" is needed to translate the principle of horizontal equity into a specific tax system, and that ". . . the choice of the index of equality is a question of social value."

implicit in categorical assistance and in certain in-kind and job-creation programs with those of the NIT, and shows how these different viewpoints were expressed in legislative proposals and enactments during the past decade. This history reveals growing awareness of the complexity of the equity issues involved and a pragmatic tendency to blend the several points of view and the programs they inspire.

The controversies stirred up by academic economists have been aired in the halls of Congress and in presidential campaigns. Recent proposals put forward by Caspar Weinberger, secretary of Health, Education and Welfare, and by a subcommittee of the Joint Economic Committee of Congress (JEC) chaired by Representative Martha Griffiths assure us that these controversies are still alive.* During this same period, numerous measures of tax reform and provision of cash and in-kind benefits have been adopted, including Medicare and Medicaid, tax deductions and welfare deductions for child-care expense, a nationwide food stamp program, Supplemental Security Income for the aged and disabled, an earned-income credit for low-income families, and emergency public service employment.

THE NEGATIVE INCOME TAX AS PART OF A WAR ON POVERTY

President Johnson's declaration of a war on poverty in 1964 opened up the question, who are the people below some arbitrarily set income-poverty lines? These lines were set in terms of annual money income adjusted for family size and, hence, reflected some concern for vertical and horizontal equity issues. It was not long before questions were raised about what U.S. income-maintenance institutions were doing to reduce income poverty and how they could be redesigned to do more in pursuit of that goal.†

---

*The staff background paper for the HEW position is Barth et al. (1974). The JEC plan is presented in U.S. Congress (1974). This report follows 19 volumes of staff studies, entitled *Studies in Public Welfare*.

†My first published effort along this line was a paper presented to the National Tax Association in September 1964, in which I suggested that people be refunded 14 percent of their unused income tax exemptions and deductions. I repeated this suggestion, which would have cost about $2 billion, at the American Economic Association in December of that year. Harry G. Johnson was one of the discussants of that paper, and he appeared to be urging a much larger-scale NIT, on the order of $25 billion. In light of this, I was bemused by his 1973 paper inveighing against "analytically weak or unsupported recommendations for policy, such as remedying inequality by giving large sums, taken from those who currently have high incomes to those who have not" (Johnson 1973:55).

One incongruity that stood out from the data on the poor was that most of those who were poor did not receive cash income-maintenance benefits. This was because eligibility was set in categorical terms. Yet most poor people were not in families headed by aged, blind, or disabled persons, nor were they in families broken by death or desertion. On the contrary, most were unattached individuals or were in intact families headed by non-aged, nondisabled men. Much of the cash benefits, which then totalled $35 billion, went to people who were not poor prior to receipt of benefits. Obviously, the system was not targeted efficiently on those in income poverty.

Public assistance was the most target-efficient part of the system and had a much higher score in this regard than the social insurances (particularly, Unemployment Compensation) or the status programs (for example, veterans' benefits). Nonetheless, economists singled out public assistance, particularly Aid to Families with Dependent Children (AFDC), as the devil in the piece and proceeded to advocate, as a substitute for it, "welfare reform" in the shape of a negative income tax. An equally plausible response to the exclusion of the noncategorical poor would have been to add a new program specifically for the excluded group and to improve AFDC and other categorical benefits in the lowest-paying states. Some so argued. What formed the powerful movement for negative income taxation, however, was the vision of a universal scheme to replace all the categorical assistances at one blow. This movement challenged the concept of equity in public assistance on the grounds of reasonable classification, asserting that income poverty was a basis for discrimination more relevant to the public interest than was the traditional categories.* It also challenged assistance on the grounds that its 100-percent implicit tax rates, or benefit-loss rates, were both unfair and inefficient.

The NIT movement picked up momentum and gathered new equity issues as it went, challenging existing practice in virtually every corner of the income-maintenance field, and eventually going so far as to suggest revising the whole structure and rate schedule of the individual income tax. It was rather like a new religion sweeping out of the desert to set right inequities perpetrated in pursuit of false gods that had dominated earlier efforts against poverty, insecurity, and inequality.

---

*This is an interesting example of how a specific income distribution measure appeared to serve as a road map for social intervention (Lampman 1973). For a good brief discussion of the importance of "reasonable classification" to horizontal equity, see Groves (1964:15-16). He says that "a levy that is unimpeachable in its objective is none the less vulnerable if it cannot be defined so that those in essentially similar circumstances contribute alike. Discrimination is the essence of tax wisdom, but it sheds its curse only when it is proved to rest on genuine differences, the recognition of which is required by the public interest."

The reference point in the quest for equity was the federal individual income tax, which was seen as embodying the ideals, if not the practice, of vertical and horizontal equity.* Public assistance, with its multijurisdictional administration and with discretion in the hands of the case worker, was pictured—in sorry contrast—as intolerably unfair and self-defeating. Few were willing to stand up and defend the old-time religion of public assistance,† and prophets of NIT found themselves in a complex political alliance of "welfare reformers," not all of whom pursued the same goals, although they did share a lack of appreciation for public assistance.

The pure NIT idea was to achieve vertical and horizontal equity by simply turning the income tax upside down. While that might be acceptable as a way to redistribute a relatively small amount of money, as would follow from a 14-percent negative tax rate against unused exemptions and deductions, it would not be acceptable if the guarantee were set near public-assistance levels and the negative tax rate were set near 50 percent. The latter course would require new decisions about the definition of income (what about transfer income and other tax-exempt income?), the family unit (what about members of a nonpoor family filing separate returns?), the income accounting period (what about the reasons that public assistance uses a one-month period?), and the method of paying benefits (should tax withholding have a symmetrical counterpart in prepayment of benefits and reconciliation of the account at the end of the year?). The concern for symmetry led some to advocate changes in the income tax. They asked, if it is fair to insist on, say, compulsory joint filing for NIT people, why not insist on it for positive taxpayers? It is doubtless because of this preoccupation with symmetry that few early writers had anything to say about child care and other work expenses and most assumed a single tax rate for all types of income of 50 percent or less. Few discussed a work test.

THE 1967 AFDC AMENDMENTS
AND NEW IN-KIND BENEFITS

While designs were being drawn for noncategorical schemes of NIT, there were interesting developments in public assistance. The 1967 amendments to

---

*See Pechman and Okner (1974). Of particular interest to this discussion is Chapter 5, "Variations in Tax Burdens among Population Subgroups." They find (p. 82) that the overall tax system favors homeowners, rural-farm residents, families with transfers as a major source of income, and large families. It hits hardest at single persons and those families whose major source of income is property or business.

†One writer belabors social workers for not defending public assistance in this debate (Mahoney 1975).

AFDC carried a clear signal that Congress was changing its expectations about work by women who head families. This was revealed by, among other things, the lowering of the nominal tax rate on earnings from 100 to 67 percent and, simultaneously, the mandating that work expenses were to be deducted from countable income in calculating benefits. It was consistent to say that if women are to be urged to work, then their expenses of working must not unduly diminish their stay-at-home income. However, these and other changes raised break-even levels of income and thereby contributed to the explosion of the welfare rolls.

Contemporary NIT literature reflected little awareness of these amendments and of their uneven implementation. Perhaps it is fair to say that few contributors to that literature had much detailed knowledge of how public assistance actually worked. However, later writings show concern about a new "inequity" arising, in part, out of these amendments, in the form of relatively high total incomes (including reimbursements for child care) of some people on welfare.* NIT was advocated as a way to bring this and other "excesses" under control.

Other significant developments on the income redistribution front in the 1960s include the introduction of Medicaid (1965), legal services for the poor (1965), direct provision of federally supported child care (1965), and major changes in the food stamp program (1967 and 1969). Medicaid eligibility (in some states) was noncategorical, but benefits were income conditioned. The same thing was true of legal services, child care, and food stamps. Some of these new in-kind programs, following the tradition of public housing, had remarkably high guarantees and high breakeven points, often restrained only by highly inequitable notches in the benefit schedules. A pattern often followed was to set guarantee levels equal to "need" as the latter is envisioned by experts in health care or legal services or housing or child care and to follow with breakeven points well beyond poverty lines. This generous pattern is then offset by an appropriation that will fund—or a method of administration that will enroll— only a small percentage of all those nominally eligible. By NIT standards this is highly inequitable, but in-kind defenders say it is better to do "enough" for one than to do a trivial amount for a score. Do the best you can for a select few— that is fair if the cause is just—as opposed to doing an inadequate and ineffective job for a thankless mass. These few words are enough, perhaps, to indicate that

*Representative Griffiths in her foreword to the JEC report, says: "We found that the woman on welfare did better in every city than the woman who worked at the median wage. The theory of comparing what is given in welfare with what is needed is foolish. 'What is needed' is a phony standard set up by a paternalistic middle class. The real standard is what similar people earn, and how they are treated. Few have ever asked what those who work need" (U.S. Congress 1974:vi).

some in-kind promoters start from a concept of equity quite opposed to that of NIT. We shall refer to this concept later when discussing public-service employment (PSE).

Again, it was quite a time before NIT advocates caught on to the significance of in-kind programs and to the need to confront their competing ethic.

NIXON'S WELFARE-REFORM EFFORT, 1969-72

It seemed to some in August 1969, when President Nixon outlined his welfare-reform scheme, that he had picked up the NIT flag and would carry it over the top, and with it, the NIT concepts of vertical and horizontal equity. However, by 1972, after two passages through the House and two redesigns by the Senate Finance Committee, the notion that cash benefits should be available to all, with only adjustment for income and family size, was lost in a maze. The product was mostly based upon the principles of AFDC as modified by the 1967 amendments. The House did adopt from NIT advocates the idea of a national minimum, the idea of dropping federal matching grants to the states, and the idea of extending cash benefits to intact families headed by employed persons. However, numerous categorical assistance principles were reaffirmed. For one thing, there were categories: the adult (aged, blind, and disabled) category, the noneligible category of single persons and childless couples, and the family category. Families with children, whose per capita benefits were to be about one-half those of the adult category, were further divided with regard to expectations to work. A work test was to be required of most adult members of families, including female heads whose youngest child was under the age of six— or three—years (a provision further strengthened by the Talmadge Amendment, enacted in 1971). Failure to meet the work test would be followed by a reduction of the guarantee. Plans were offered to couple the work test with child care, training, and job creation. As the legislation proceeded, more money was to be appropriated for noncash benefits than for cash. The original Family Assistance Plan (FAP) guarantee was raised by $800 through the cashing out of food stamps. To offset the cost of the higher guarantee and to keep the breakevens from going too high, the tax rate was raised from 50 to 67 percent. The particular combination of tax rate and day-care expense deductibility yielded less monetary incentive for work by mothers than did AFDC. Some members of the Senate Finance Committee pointed out that the combined guarantees and tax rates of FAP, in addition to Medicaid and public housing and directly provided child care, were so high as to leave little pecuniary advantage to work. Income other than earnings was to be taxed at 100 percent, and nonsupporting fathers were to be pursued across state lines and subjected to loss of other federal benefits.

In spring of 1972 Senator McGovern offered a combined welfare- and tax-reform scheme, which seemed to ignore most of the points raised in congressional acts and debates since 1964. He proposed a scheme to replace public assistance and the income tax. It featured a $1000 guarantee per person, and a flat tax rate of 33 percent against all income with no exclusions, exemptions, or deductions. Three critical equity issues in this loosely sketched plan had to do with the elimination of certain tax preferences, the variation of tax credits with family size, and the amount of tax relief for high salary earners (Lidman 1972).

The lack of political support for the McGovern plan—and his own denial of it—may have been one of the reasons for the failure of the Congress to pass Nixon's FAP (Burke and Burke 1974; Bowler 1974). Just as there were strange political bedfellows in the early days of NIT advocacy, so were there in the shooting down of FAP. The National Welfare Rights Organization opposed it because it would have cut back benefits for AFDC in the North. Similar difficulties were noted by governors and mayors in high-benefit states. There seemed to be little political mileage in adding benefits for men, since such benefits would not give states and local governments relief for their treasuries. What are the lessons there with respect to concepts of equity?*

Although FAP was not enacted, the other big part of Nixon's welfare reform, namely, Supplemental Security Income (SSI) for the aged, blind, and disabled, did become law in 1972 and went into effect in 1974. This program contains relatively high guarantees, a 50 percent tax rate on earnings, and an end to relative responsibility and to lien laws, a generous assets test, and no work test. Nonearned income is taxed at 100 percent. However, it leaves the way open for supplementing states to vary the guarantee with respect to dependents, essential persons, and living arrangements.

RECENT DEVELOPMENTS, 1972-75

Congress has recently made a number of other remarkable departures with respect to income redistribution. These include a liberalization of income tax deductibility of child care and homemaker expense (1972), a doubling of food stamp benefits (1973), a big breakthrough in public service employment (1971 and 1974). Also, the "work bonus," or earned-income credit, pushed by Senator Russell Long was incorporated in the tax reform of 1975. Each of these moves is, of course, based upon its own concept of equity, but they all reflect a concern

---

*This query invites a line of study about indirect beneficiaries of change in income-maintenance arrangements. While shifting and incidence of taxes are much studied, little has been written about incidence of benefits.

that was at the forefront of the NIT involvement ten years ago, namely, the exclusion from benefit eligibility of the noncategorical poor. The food stamp program, an in-kind NIT, may be seen as meeting two goals of FAP. First, it raised benefits for AFDC recipients in the low-income states, and, second, it extended benefits to those not eligible for AFDC. The earned income credit is an interesting variant of negative income taxation. It features a guarantee of zero, with the benefit rising to $400 at $4000 of earnings and then falling to zero at $8000 of earnings. This design is rather like that of British Family Income Supplement of 1971.

PSE is also addressed to the latter goal but is subject to complaints of inequity along the lines we noted earlier with respect to certain in-kind programs. It offers a high "benefit" (average pay in PSE in 1975 was around $8000) but rations a relatively few jobs among a large number of potentially eligible persons. Neither vertical nor horizontal equity can be carefully observed in the administration of the several billions of dollars appropriated. Clearly, a different standard or concept of equity is involved. A PSE advocate might respond to that line of criticism with the countercharge: "Any inequality you don't like is an inequity." Here, again, we can identify a "movement" competitive with the NIT movement and informed by a set of unique purposes.

I referred at the outset of this chapter to the current HEW and JEC proposals for "welfare reform" (incidentally, that term is now disavowed by both groups). These carefully worked-out plans symbolize a kind of winding down of the NIT movement. They reflect an informed concern for recent changes in AFDC, in the several in-kind programs, and in PSE. Whereas ten years ago NIT schemes could react solely to perceived inequities of categorical-assistance cash benefits, now they must react to a much more complex system of cash and in-kind benefits, welfare deductibilities, and payroll tax and income tax provisions.

Perhaps this point can be illustrated by a quick look at the JEC scheme. It would cover all individuals and families except aged, blind, and disabled adults, who would remain under SSI. It offers a guarantee of $3600 for a two-adult family of four. This comes in two parts: One is refundable tax credits, which would replace income tax exemptions and minimum standard deductions in the income tax; the other is a cash benefit called an Allowance for Basic Living Expenses (ABLE). The tax rate is 50 percent on earnings net of Social Security taxes paid and 67 percent on most nonearned income, including imputed income from assets. The tax rate on earnings is slightly reduced by a nonitemized work-expense deduction expressed as a percentage of earnings up to stated maximums. This deduction is markedly less generous than present AFDC and income tax deductions.

This plan would be administered by the Internal Revenue Service. No state would have to supplement any benefit after two years. There would be no work test. Food stamps would be cashed out and housing subsidy income would be taxed at 80 percent in calculating ABLE benefits. The plan calls for a low tax rate in the schedule of benefits in federally supported day care and in Medicaid or any substitute for it. The net cost to the federal government of this program is estimated at $15 billion. There would be 34 million people eligible for ABLE benefits, and other 4.8 million would enjoy income tax cuts. In the case of families of four, only those with incomes of more than $25,000 would pay higher taxes.

This complex package may be characterized as one set out to float against a tide. It would restrain the manifest wish of Congress to be generous to the broken family and to the consumers of publicly supported housing and day care. At the same time it would open the purse without a work test for the working poor and near-poor. It fights to preserve incentives to work, but it has to contend with the drag of unreimbursed work expenses and income conditioning of in-kind benefits. Cumulative tax rates are likely to be well above 50 percent for many ABLE beneficiaries. (For further discussion of the cumulative tax rate problem, see Lampman [1975].)

The JEC plan attempts to integrate and systematize much of the tax-transfer system. To do this it must take a stance on a range of interrelated vertical and horizontal equity issues. Each stance is taken in recognition of painful tradeoffs. For example, it trades less work-expense deduction for one-parent families in order to gain higher benefits for two-parent families. Highly refined concepts of equity are involved in such tradeoffs, and many readers will wonder whether the insights into equity questions from the income tax mentality are sufficient to resolve them. The authors of the JEC report are quite aware that efficiency as well as equity considerations are involved and that our knowledge of the ultimate outcomes of social policies is severely limited.* They are aware of what Boulding calls the pathologies of grantsmanship and, in particular, what he refers to as the "ignorance trap." A careful reading of the JEC report will make one empathize with the man on Boulding's welfare mountain, whose chief problem is to avoid falling off unmarked precipices (Boulding 1973).

This chapter reviews only one aspect of the recent history of income-redistribution policy. It does not touch on some of the more flamboyant equity

---

*Harry G. Johnson spells out his reasons for backing away from large-scale negative income taxation as follows: ". . . ethically-motivated social concern about inequality should focus on inequalities of opportunities and the knowledge and resources to explore them properly. It should not focus on the statistical facts of measured inequalities, which indiscriminately reflect both inequality of original opportunities and rational, voluntary choices among available opportunities intended to maximize individual self-fulfillment. Analysis and remedies that focus on the resultant income distribution—and attempts to correct it by redistributive . . . systems—will have (undesirable) side effects." He goes on to detail how such systems may burden those with socially desirable preferences and reward those with undesirable preferences and warns that "in the long run, social institutions and customs adapt to produce the kind of people favored by the fiscal system" (Johnson 1973:58).

issues in the income-redistribution field having to do with such matters as reducing intrastate variability in educational expenditures, compensatory education for those with learning disabilities, and affirmative action for equal opportunity in employment. Nonetheless, it does indicate a range of concepts of equity and their significance in one corner of the field.

REFERENCES

Barth, Michael C., George J. Carcagno, and John L. Palmer, with an overview paper by Irwin Garfinkel. 1974. *Toward an Effective Income Support System; Problems, Prospects, and Choices.* Madison, Wisc.: Institute for Research on Poverty.

Boulding, Kenneth E. 1973. *The Economy of Love and Fear.* Belmont, Calif.: Wadsworth.

Bowler, M. Kenneth. 1974. *The Nixon Guaranteed Income Proposal.* Cambridge, Mass.: Ballinger.

Burke, Vincent, and Vee Burke. 1974. *Nixon's Good Deed.* New York: Columbia University Press.

Groves, Harold M. 1964. *Financing Government,* 6th ed. New York: Holt.

Johnson, Harry G. 1973. "Micro-Economic Reflections on Inequality." *The Annals of the American Academy of Political and Social Science* 409 (September):53-60.

Lampman, Robert J. 1973. "Measured Inequality of Income: What Does It Mean and What Can It Tell Us?" *The Annals of the American Academy of Political and Social Science* 409 (September):81-91.

——. 1975. "Scaling Welfare Benefits to Income: An Idea That Is Being Overworked." *Policy Analysis* 1 (Winter):1-10.

Lidman, Russell. 1972. "Cost and Distributional Implications of a Credit Income Tax Plan." *Public Policy* 20 (Spring).

Mahoney, Michael. 1975. "The Challenge of Income Maintenance," paper delivered at the National Conference on Social Welfare, May 12. Mimeographed.

Musgrave, Richard A. 1959. *The Theory of Public Finance.* New York: McGraw-Hill.

Pechman, Joseph A., and Benjamin A. Okner. 1974. *Who Bears the Tax Burden?* Washington, D.C.: The Brookings Institution.

U.S., Congress, Subcommittee on Fiscal Policy, Joint Economic Committee. 1974. *Income Security for Americans: Recommendations of the Public Welfare Study,* 93d Cong., 2d sess., December 5.

3

INEQUALITY AND ITS
IMPLICATIONS FOR
ECONOMIC GROWTH

Sylvia Ann Hewlett

"Capitalism is the extraordinary belief that the
nastiest of men for the nastiest of motives will
somehow work for the benefit of us all."

—John Maynard Keynes

Despite the comforting and reassuring language of economic theory (which
abounds with phrases like "perfect competition," "stable equilibrium," and "the
harmony of interests") the dynamics of modern economic growth, can be, and
often are, extremely costly in social and political terms. Nothing shows this more
clearly than the question of equity.

How does one judge economic equity? To put it another way, how does
one evaluate the distribution of economic rewards in society?

The sentiments of the U.S. Constitution are distinctly egalitarian, but it
would be wrong to assume that ideologies have consistently advocated greater
equality as a desideratum towards which society should strive. The civilization of
ancient Greece was based on slavery, and the ethos of the early capitalist period
was extremely unegalitarian. The Protestant ethic—which emerged together with
Puritanism, Calvinism, and capitalism during the Industrial Revolution—condoned
and encouraged the quest for riches and wealth. In this value system reward
resulted from hard work and thrift and was an external manifestation of internal
goodness. The path to heaven was marked with signs of success, prestige and
high incomes; the poor were depreciated as a feckless lot, who squandered (most
likely on drink) what little money they had.

The Protestant ethic gave rise to a distributional theory that has been
labelled Social Darwinism, which dominated intellectual thinking on the subject

for much of the nineteenth century. The English philosopher Herbert Spencer
wrote in 1884:

> The command 'if any would not work neither should he eat', is
> simply a Christian enunciation of that universal law of nature under
> which life has reached its present height—the law that a creature not
> energetic enough to maintain itself must die.[1]

Spencer was even skeptical of private philanthropy, arguing against that "injudi-
cious charity" that permits "the recipients to elude the necessities of our social
existence."[2] In the United States William Graham Sumner voiced a similar point
of view:

> ... 'the strong' and 'the weak' are terms which admit of no definition
> unless they are made equivalent to the industrious and the idle, the
> frugal and the extravagent [;] ... a plan for nourishing the unfittest
> and yet advancing in civilization no man will ever find.[3]

Social Darwinism was unambiguous in that it laid the blame for economic
distress squarely on the shoulders of the individual. It bred a punitive attitude
towards poverty and was the source of a political slogan, "Pull yourself up by
your own bootstraps," both of which survive, in some measure, to this day.

INEQUALITY IN MODERN MARKET ECONOMIES

Contemporary views on the optimal distribution of economic rewards in
society are diverse and often contradictory. Two of the most commonly used
criteria are, on the one hand, the efficiency and, on the other, the equitability and
justice of the conditions of a distribution of income. These two ways of judging
distributional questions emanate from radically different perspectives of modern
society and often embody policy recommendations that are incompatible.

Arthur M. Okun has called U.S. society a "split-level structure."[4] And it is
true that a political framework premised on notions of political freedom and
equal justice inherited from eighteenth century humanistic doctrines of the
natural rights of man is juxtaposed with an economic system in which inequality
is functional. Market economies are based on inequality, inasmuch as differentials in income constitute a structural necessity serving as incentives, rewards,
and penalties that are instrumental in promoting efficiency in the use of resources
and contribute towards generating a great, and a growing national product.

All Western democracies are permeated with this contradiction, laying
claim to an egalitarian political and social system and simultaneously generating
glaring disparities in economic well-being through a market system that allows the
big winners to "feed their pets better than the losers can feed their children."[5]

Inequality is often thought of as an unfortunate flaw or weakness in modern market economies. Witness a recent statement by Robert L. Heilbroner:

> ... market mechanisms ... contain profound weaknesses that have been overlooked during the period of uninhibited capitalist expansion. One of these is its tendency to create extremely skewed distributions of income and property.[6]

It is my contention that inequality, rather than a "weakness," is functional to the workings of a market economy; in the United States, far from being "overlooked," it has been deliberately exacerbated during the 1970s, as part of an economic strategy whose prime aim has been the maintenance of growth rates in the face of unprecedented rates of inflation and a world recession.

But before examining the exact nature of the tradeoff between inequality and efficiency, it is essential to confront several thorny questions, concerning the meaning of economic equity, the relationship between equity and poverty, and our definition of *efficiency*.

LOCATING A DEFINITION OF INEQUITY

Modern economic theorists have not been a great deal of help in defining *equity*, a term that denotes the preferred shape of the distributional curve, or just distribution of economic resources in society. Harry G. Johnson has dismissed a concern for questions of equity in economics as a type of neurosis, attributing such misguided preoccupations to a "naive and basically infantile anthropomorphism."[7] Milton Friedman has discarded the goal of equity and substituted that of freedom:

> The heart of the liberal philosophy is a belief in the dignity of the individual, in his freedom to make the most of his capacities and opportunities according to his own lights, subject only to the proviso that he not interfere with the freedom of other individuals to do the same.[8]

But as R. H. Tawney has pointed out, "Freedom for the pike is death for the minnows."[9] The libertarian philosophy does not seem to get us very far with questions of social welfare.

As far as the mainstream of the discipline is concerned, much of contemporary welfare theory is concerned with issues that carefully avoid judgments on the distribution of economic rewards altogether.[10] Take the concept of Pareto optimality, which is after all a foundation stone of welfare economics. There is an infinite set of Pareto optimal points open to society; each point is characterized by a distinct distribution of income. The theory properly used does not tell

us how to distinguish between the various Pareto optimal points; it only guarantees that each point represents a position from which no change is possible, such
that someone could become better off without making someone else worse off.
As an illustration of the uselessness of Pareto optimality on the equity front, if
the lot of the poor cannot be made any better without cutting into the affluence
of the rich, the situation would be Pareto optimal despite the glaring disparities
between the rich and the poor: This conclusion hardly makes the air electric
with expectations when discussing distributional questions!

Another influential thread running through orthodox economics is the
conviction that the appropriate measure of social welfare is the level and rate of
growth of GNP. GNP is merely the money measure of the overall annual flow of
goods and services in the economy. It thus excludes much domestic labor (which
is often carried out by housewives and is unpaid), ignores the deleterious effects
of pollution (which is rarely costed), and, most importantly, because of its preoccupation with money yardsticks, failed to capture human need. GNP is concerned with money votes, and therefore it is possible to conceive of a situation
which the working classes (the bulk of the population) receive stagnant or falling
incomes but GNP continues to increase due to the enhanced prosperity of a rich
minority. This is precisely what has happened in the United States in the 1970s.
The global product is considerably larger in 1976 than it was in 1970, but the
majority of the population is no better off than it was at the beginning of the
decade.[11] The basic theoretical point is of course that maximizing the rate of
growth of GNP totally disregards the interpersonal distribution of the national
product, making GNP a useless criterion for the measuring or judging of equity.

One is left with the depressing feeling that conventional economics has
bypassed the equity issue fairly thoroughly. As Alice M. Rivlin has put it:

> In a truly amazing act of self-denial, economists of the past generation
> have taken themselves out of the theoretical-philosophical discussion
> of how income ought to be distributed.... They have not only
> stayed out of the argument, but devoted some of their most ingeni-
> ous intellectual efforts to explaining to each other why they had so
> little to say.[12]

We may rest assured, however, that the issue has not been ignored by some
collective slip of the memory. Ignorance is seldom arbitrary and the oversight
exists for some highly rational reasons. As Gunnar Myrdal has put it:

> People who are better off usually have done their best to keep their
> minds off the equality issue.... In every country there have been
> whole systems of psychological and ideological barriers protecting
> the well-to-do from knowledge of facts which would be embarrassing
> to them.[13]

Economists are not eager to remind the public that economic growth in market economies does not and cannot mean prosperity for all and, with few exceptions, have chosen to bury their heads in the sand on this uncomfortable issue.

Philosophers have done rather better. The best known, indeed almost "trendy," work on the subject is John Rawls' *A Theory of Social Justice.*[14] Rawls uses a Kantian framework to establish both the natural equality of men and the optimum distribution of income. He attempts to demonstrate that there is only one structure of economic rewards that everyone would be willing to accept. This is a distributional structure that maximizes the minimum prize (the maximin). The snag with the maximin principle is that it assumes that people are risk-adverse, that everyone acts on the assumption that he or she will come out at the bottom of the heap and thus wants to maximize the smallest prize. It also discounts envy. If people are, by and large, envious, then anything that lowers the incomes of the better-off people faster than it lowers the income of the worst-off individual obviously maximizes the minimum prize. This scenario would rapidly lead to zero incomes for everyone. An even more serious criticism is that it is extremely difficult to operationalize Rawls' vision of equity. His distinction between factual states and preference states creates a situation where the worst-off individual will be the person with the preference function that is hardest to satisfy and will therefore be the one to dictate the direction of change in society. Since it is precisely this individual that has the least economic and political power, such an outcome seems unlikely, to put it mildly.

Other attempts to define and make relevant concepts of equity have revolved around notions of the common good. For example, sociologists have often argued that social unrest, crime, riots, and other upheavals are caused by maldistributions of economic rewards and could be cured by improving the distribution of income between the various classes of society. Unfortunately, this theory rests on little or no empirical evidence. W. G. Runciman comes to the conclusion that

> . . . the relationship between inequality and grievance only intermittently corresponds with either the extent and degree of actual inequality, or the magnitude and frequency of relative deprivation which an appeal to social justice would vindicate.[15]

SCENARIOS FOR ECONOMIC EQUITY

After this brief and depressing survey of the extant theory in the academic disciplines, I would like to turn to what some practical scenarios might be if policy makers were actually trying to operationalize a greater degree of economic equity in U.S. society.

The statement, "I am for equality," is obviously open to many interpretations, but it is useful to group the implicit or explicit value judgments into clusters that can be seen to form distinct ideologies about the specific objectives of an egalitarian state.

The first scenario, and the one that has the broadest political appeal, revolves around the equality of opportunity ideal. The general aim is to erradicate illegitimate barriers to a higher standard of living, and it usually emphasizes a more equitable distribution of educational services, the taxing away of inherited privilege, and the elimination of extreme poverty in order to reduce the environmental barriers to equal opportunity. Since the equal-opportunity approach takes a market-oriented economy as a given, it merely attempts to ensure that all people have an equal chance of altering their income positions. Income differentials not only remain significant, but the degree of dispersion may be as wide as ever.

A second scenario can be called the "lessening inequalities," or "normative egalitarian" approach. The main objective is self-consciously to constrain differences in income levels, and in order to achieve this goal, its protagonists are prepared to place a firm upper lid on income and wealth, to upgrade the incomes of lower income groups, and to raise the level of basic welfare services. The assumption behind this second cluster of policy measures is that the market will continue to operate, but that considerable effort will be made, through the tax and transfer infrastructure, to modify the income effect of these market mechanisms. This approach begs a question of central concern to this chapter: Is it possible to regulate a capitalist system to achieve such a high degree of redistribution? For, if inequality is functional to the capitalist growth process, it presumably cannot be modified to the extent that it is deemed desirable by a "normative egalitarian."

A third scenario can be called "practicing egalitarianism."[16] This is based on the starkly simple premise that everyone should have the same income. Modifications to the principle of full equality are made to allow for the variation in personal need that may arise from factors such as age, health, and family size. However, such modifications are not meant to reward unequal talent or training unequally; they are meant rather to accommodate differences in individual circumstances.

Practicing egalitarianism is seen by most people as being incompatible with a capitalist framework, and therefore is not exactly a wildly popular ideology within the U.S. political establishment. Certainly, if one can demonstrate that normative egalitarianism requires a degree of redistribution likely to undermine the efficiency requirements of a market economy, then it would seem that practicing egalitarianism is not a realistic policy option for a capitalist state.

EQUITY AND POVERTY

In the early 1960s Peter Townsend argued:

> ... both 'poverty' and 'subsistence' are relative concepts and ...
> they can only be defined in relation to the material and emotional
> resources available at a particular time to members either of a
> particular society or different societies.[17]

His position is now the consensus: The degree of inequity present in society is important because poverty is a relative and not an absolute phenomenon. Government statistics recognize this fact: The poverty level is never defined as a physiological minimum, that is, the amount of income a person would need to have a perfectly balanced diet and the longest life expectancy that is medically possible.

Consider the cheapest balanced diet obtainable in the United States. By combining soybeans, lard, orange juice, and beef liver, a balanced diet can be created that costs as little as $154 per person per year (in 1974 prices).[18] Medically speaking this would constitute a better diet than most of us now eat, but what American would ever volunteer to eat it? This example merely serves to underline the general point that in advanced industrial countries "wants" have very little to do with physiological needs. As Lester C. Thurow puts it, "Anything to which we have grown accustomed and that is generally available becomes a necessity. Needs thus defined, grow right along with average incomes."[19]

Most goods produced in affluent capitalist economies are unnecessary in the physiological sense of that word: the sale of these goods is dependent upon induced demand.[20] We are not born needing, or even wanting, padded bras, bell-bottomed trousers, or deodorants; demand for such items is created by the elaborated battery of advertising techniques devised by our consumer society.[21]

Theoretically, induced wants are insatiable; in practice, people tend to confine their level of expectation to a reference group: neighbors, workmates, members of the same social class. For the most part it seem to be a question of "keeping up with Jones'," not one of "keeping up with the Kennedys."

The relative nature of the expectational calculus can be seen in Gallup polls that ask, "What is the smallest amount of money a family of four needs to get along in this community?" Lee Rainwater has shown that responses represent a rather consistent fraction of the average income prevailing at the time at which the question was asked. Since World War II families have tended to estimate their own needs to be a little more than half of the average family consumption of the day.[22]

We are left with the overwhelming conviction that the degree of inequality constitutes *the* important criterion, both in determining the incidence of poverty and in assessing welfare levels of the various groups within society. The dramatic increase in absolute income levels for all Americans since World War II has no positive implication for social welfare, unless these trends have been accompanied by a narrowing of income differentials. As Robert L. Heilbroner aptly puts it, ". . . each generation takes for granted the standard of living it inherits so that the psychic gains from growth are not cumulative."[23]

But before we come to the unambiguous conclusion that lessening the degree of inequity is synonomous with improving social welfare and reducing the incidence of poverty, we need to look at the costs of such a strategy. And thus we return to the big question mark of this chapter: Does improving equity, or narrowing the range of income differentials in society, impair efficiency? It does, but in no simple-minded sense. Efficiency is a surprisingly complex concept that requires rigorous analysis.

MARGINAL-PRODUCTIVITY THEORY

Modern economic theory has concentrated on efficiency questions almost as wholeheartedly as it has avoided the issue of equity. This is generally justified on the grounds that efficiency constitutes a value-free, noncontroversial goal, universally desired by society-at-large. After all, the idea that more is better would seem to be incontrovertible, and, as long as economic analysis concerns itself with producing more aggregate income, the equity question of who should get what can safely be left in the hands of political scientists, theologians, and citizens, groups that are presumably meant to feel more at ease with value judgments.

There are some logical flaws in this vision of reality. Means and ends are hopelessly scrambled. In market economies individual preferences (whether intrinsic or induced), which determine market demand for goods and services, are weighted by economic resources before they get to be communicated in the market. A destitute man or woman obviously has needs and desires but lacks the economic wherewithal to express them in the market. It is this confusion between needs and effective demand that has caused modern economists to gloss over the fact that distributional phenomena determine what is produced. The distribution of factors of production determines both what can be produced (through the supply of factors and the production-possibilities frontier) and what will be preferred (through the distribution of income and the preference system). The Brazilian economy, which has a particularly skewed distribution of income (in 1970 the richest 10 percent of the population appropriated 48 percent of national income[24]) provides an example of the interconnection between patterns of income distribution and the composition of production: Despite the fact that average income is around $500 per year, the most dynamic sector of the economy is that concerned with the production of luxury goods, such as automobiles, color television sets, and audio equipment. A comment on the degree to which inequality has conditioned demand and therefore production is the fact that in 1972 Volkswagen discontinued production of its cheapest model because demand was more "exuberant" for the more elaborate versions of the "beetle"[25]—in a country where 10 million people earn a mere $83 a year, and half the children die before they are five years old! More is better only if the additional goods enhance the welfare levels of the majority of citizens.[26]

The classical school of thought in economic theory was well aware of the linkage between distribution and production. Ricardo defined the laws that regulate income distribution as the "principal problem in Political Economy," not only because of the significance of distributional shares per se but because the theory of income distribution held the key to an understanding of the production system.[27] It is a pity that modern economics has failed to come to terms with this vital interconnection and frequently ignores the fact that unless societal norms about the distribution of factors of production are met, there can be no "correctness" to the resulting bundle of goods produced. (The "aberrant" Cambridge school of thought continues to stress this fundamental interconnection.[28]) As I have stressed before, distributional factors determine the production possibility frontier of an economy, the preference function of a society, and ultimately the composition of production.

It should now be obvious that the efficiency goal, conceived of in the conventional sense of getting the most out of a given set of resources, is far from being value free, in that it is highly dependent upon a previously existing state of equity. But, despite this unresolved theoretical problem, I intend to use the maximization of the rate of growth of production as a rough and ready approximation to dynamic efficiency. (My definition of *dynamic efficiency* differs from at least one common usage, that of Balassa, who uses dynamic efficiency to refer to differences in growth rates between societies with identical labor/leisure and consumption/savings ratios. In this case dynamic efficiency refers to the sources of growth other than increased inputs.[29]) I justify this approximation on the practical grounds that, the maximization of the rate of growth of GNP constitutes a prime goal of many governments. It is therefore extremely relevant from the policy-making point of view to examine the nature of the tradeoff between equity and economic growth.

First, we must be clear that maximizing the rate of growth of GNP is not the same thing as maximizing static efficiency. This distinction has often been ignored. Static efficiency is intimately connected with the perfectly competitive world of neoclassical analysis. In this context, when every factor is paid in accordance with its marginal product (its marginal contribution to the total supply of economic goods and services), and when marginal products are determined by competitive demand and supply conditions, then a market economy is functioning efficiently; that is, it is at a Pareto optimal point. To see what this scenario means for earnings levels and income differentials, we will take a concrete situation. An employer is supposed to take on such a number of workers so that the money value of the marginal product is equal to the money wage he has to pay; under these conditions, the real wage of each type of labor measures its contribution to national output. This situation is the "efficient" solution to the distributional question and gives "to each according to what he and the instruments he owns produces."[30]

This piece of orthodox wisdom has been bitterly criticized by the Cambridge school of thought in economic theory. As Joan Robinson has put it:

> The salary of a professor of economics measures his contribution to society, and the wage of a garbage collector measures his contribution. Of course, this is a very comforting doctrine for professors of economics, but I fear that . . . the argument is circular. There is not any measure of marginal product except the wages themselves.[31]

Aside from this tautological element to marginal-productivity theory, it is possible to refute it on factual grounds. Thurow has demonstrated that there is very little wage competition in the labor markets of advanced economies, and that theories involving labor "queues," random "walks," economic power, and societal norms are much more useful in explaining income differentials.[32]

Perhaps the most serious criticism of marginal-productivity analysis as an interpretation and justification of income differentials, is its absolute lack of implications for efficiency, unless one believes in the existence of, and the rationale for, perfect competition. This is particularly relevant when one is concerned with dynamic efficiency, in our specific sense of maximizing the rate of growth of GNP. A basic fact of modern economic life is increasing returns to scale in the production process. This is a key factor in explaining why, in a search to maximize profits and growth, the market structures of advanced nations have become increasingly concentrated and have moved further and further away from the competitive ideal of the textbooks. Increasing returns to scale violate one of the fundamental conditions of perfect competition: that price should equal marginal cost. And, unless all conditions are met, the whole edifice collapses and the theoretical link between efficiency and a specific distribution of income falls apart.

In short, there seems to be no convincing neoclassical construct that adequately links income differentials to questions of efficiency and economic growth, at least not one that is at all pertinent to the highly concentrated, oligopolistic world of the contemporary United States. Even if one accepts the relevance of marginal-productivity analysis to the static world of perfect competition (and at least one school of thought does not), it falls on its face when confronted with the momentum of oligopolistic economies and is a singularly inadequate tool to explain the interaction between inequality and economic growth. However, marginal-productivity analysis is the only coherent conceptual framework that economists have, and if we dismiss it, we are left with some rather weak propositions regarding savings as the only remaining theoretical thread linking inequality to efficiency.

A highly skewed distribution of income is assumed to produce a group of individuals with a high marginal propensity to save, and savings are obviously a prerequisite for growth. However, the logic of the argument tends to be less than compelling when confronted with the facts of the situation. Thurow finds that in 1973, 71 percent of all U.S. savings took the form of retained earnings and depreciation allowances. And if you subtract from the global savings figure those funds that go into residential housing, more than 99 percent of all industrial and commercial investment was internally generated. He comes to the conclusion that personal savings are "basically used to finance housing, and the business sector is self-financing."[33]

INEQUALITY AS A STRUCTURAL NECESSITY OF CAPITALISM

I rest my case for inequality being a necessary condition for economic growth in a modern market economy, on neither of the above factors. Marginal-productivity theory and savings-levels arguments are bedevilled by false premises and have been at least partially refuted by the available empirical evidence.

On a general level of reasoning, economic inequity can be seen as structural necessity of market economies. It is built into the property and production arrangements of capitalist societies as an integral part of the institutional framework. On a more specific level of reasoning, economic inequity can be seen as directly and immediately functional to the growth process: It enforces labor discipline, is a crucial ingredient in the incentive apparatus, and produces those levels of private profit that are essential to capitalist growth.

Let us examine inequality as a structural necessity.[34] In the first instance, inequality is a function of the property relations of capitalist systems. The severely unequal ownership of productive and financial resources accounts for much of the inequality in the United States in the 1970s. Although roughly three-quarters of total income is received in the form of wages and salaries, inequalities in labor income account for less than half of the total inequity. Of the residual, one quarter is attributed to inequalities in property income and one quarter is attributed to the fact that the large property and capital-gains income recipients also tend to receive handsome salaries. Inequalities in income from property can be statistically accounted for by two facts: First, property is very unequally owned; second, the returns to capital (rent, interest, dividends, profits) are also unequal, the large owners in general receiving a higher return on each dollar of property owned.

In short, the contribution of property income to overall income inequality follows from one of the basic institutional characteristics of capitalism: the private ownership of property.

A second structural feature of market economies that promotes inequality is the phenomenon of uneven development.[35] Rapid economic growth in some sectors, regions, or groups of the population often goes hand in hand with the stagnation and exploitation of other sectors. In the contemporary United States this characteristic can be most readily seen in the rapid growth of the corporate and the state sectors of the economy and in the stagnation of independent, entrepreneurial, and household production.

Uneven development is a result of the fact that there is little that is predictable or gradual about economic growth. It involves technological and organizational breakthroughs, the opening up of new markets, the development of new products, and the tapping of new sources of raw materials and labor. It is hardly surprising that it is the privileged minority—possessing capital and exerting political influence—that grows and prospers. Superiority of resources allows the big and the powerful to drive out small-scale opposition through market manipulation, coordinated organization and planning, ability to employ advanced and large-scale technology, and corresponding higher rates of capital accumulation. Those without these resources must merely wait for the results of economic progress to "trickle down."

We come next to structures of control in capitalist societies and their implications for inequality. The relations of production in advanced capitalism are characterized by bureaucratic organization and hierarchical lines of authority. An important consequence is a wide spread in pay scales, since hierarchical structures are based on the assumption that a superior must always have a higher salary than a subordinate, whatever the conditions of relative supply of the two types of labor. It is impossible to explain this organizational framework on technological grounds. Not only is there evidence that suggests that even within the confines of existing technology work could be organized on more egalitarian lines,[36] but several researchers have pointed to the "inefficiency of the hierarchical division of labor" as it denies "workers room for the employment of their creative power."[37] Why then their hierarchical structures? The prime reason lies in the need of the management class to maintain control over the workforce. Control over the production process requires the retention of decision making at the top; its maintenance is always problematic since, whenever possible, workers will attempt to gain some control over the terms and conditions of employment. Organizing production hierarchically divides workers on different levels against one another and reduces the independent range of control for each individual. Both of these factors weaken the solidarity of workers and serve to convince them of their personal incapacity to challenge the system.

This leads us to an associated function of hierarchical structures: the legitimization of inequality. The typical, mature, capitalist enterprise is organized so as to make the structure of authority (and reward) appear at best just, at least inevitable. The general cultural values of society are drawn upon to bolster and maintain the credibility of the system. Blacks and women are not generally placed above whites or men in the line of hierarchical authority; work roles are structured so that young people will not boss older people; educational credentials are extensively used as "objective" criteria in the hiring and promotion process. The importance of legitimacy cannot be overemphasized, as Rousseau puts it: "The strongest man is never strong enough to always be master, unless he transforms his power into right and obedience into duty."[38] Hierarchical organizations in capitalist enterprises ensure the retention and sanctioning of power in the hands of the management class, and provide the justification for a finely graded system of earnings differentials: all this is accomplished without the use of force.

Economic inequality emerges as a structural necessity of market economies because it is an integral part of the institutional framework. It is built into the property relations of capitalist systems, is an inevitable accompaniment of uneven development, and is a function of the imperatives of hierarchical control. These "background characteristics" of capitalist economies translate themselves into a more specific set of factors (labor discipline, the incentive apparatus, and the profit share) that link inequality directly and immediately to the growth process.

GOVERNMENT MANAGEMENT OF DEPRIVATION

Market economies have two attributes that make a system of labor discipline essential. In the first instance, capitalism makes unemployment contingent upon market demand. This means that in times of economic downturn or structural change significant portions of the laboring population may become redundant, sometimes to the extent of a generation of mass unemployment, distress, and disorganization. Second, there is the necessity of ensuring that millions of boring menial tasks are performed at minimum cost and with no overt political coercion. Despite the reasoning of Adam Smith, capitalism is undoubtedly a system in which "some men are made to do the harshest work for the least reward."[39] The degree of inequality and the incidence of poverty are important factors in forcing acceptance of both these phenomena. In short, the threat of increased relative deprivation is an important disciplinary tool.

The way in which the U.S. government has manipulated the public welfare system over recent decades is a good example of the disciplinary process at work. Frances Piven and Richard Cloward make an excellent case for the chief function of relief arrangements being the regulation of labor. When mass unemployment and structural change threatens the political order, welfare programs absorb enough of the unemployed to restore order. As turbulence subsides, the relief system contracts and, in a shrunken state, performs a labor-regulating role: "... expansive relief policies are designed to mute civil disorder, and restrictive ones to reinforce work norms."[40] The fact that relief policies are cyclical belies the popular supposition that the government's social policies have become progressively more humane and generous. Despite the rhetoric, welfare programs are shaped less by good intentions than by economic and political function.

The last decades of U.S. history have been marked by two major relief explosions: those of the Great Depression and of the 1960s. In 1935 20 million people were on the dole; this economic and social catastrophe provoked government action, but relief measures had less to do with humanitarian or Keynesian sentiments than with the rising surge of political unrest. Economic distress produced unprecedented disorder:

> Communist-led rallies and marches in New York City drew thousands
> of people who participated because they were hungry and wanted
> jobs. ... In Chicago, where half the working force were unemployed
> and Socialists and Communists were organizing mass demonstrations
> the Mayor pleaded for the federal government to send $150 million
> for relief immediately rather than federal troops later. ... Congress-
> man Hamilton Fish Jr., announced to the House of Representatives
> that "if we don't give under the existing system, the people will
> change the system. Make no mistake about that."[41]

In the 1960s the nation experienced a welfare explosion that was a response to the civil disorder caused by the dislocations of rapid structural change. The source, in large part, lay in the modernization of Southern agriculture, but black poverty had to turn to violence before local and federal governments reacted to its presence.

It is no coincidence that the Great Society programs accompanied the most serious outbreak of domestic disorder since the 1930s: the civil rights struggle, the widespread and destructive rioting in the cities, and the formation of militant grassroots movements to combat welfare restrictions. The anti-poverty programs of the Johnson administration placated the ghettos and appeased the underprivileged segments of U.S. society.

In 1976 we can see a definite lowering of the welfare profile: We are in the downswing of the relief-program cycle. By the early 1970s civil disorder has been contained, and it was time to reinforce work norms and remind labor of its proper place in society. Rising rates of unemployment and the differential impact of inflation on living standards have both served to reinforce the new docility of the laboring classes.

In summary, a fairly good case can be made for welfare programs being functional to the economic system. Market values and market incentives are presumably weakest at the bottom of the social order where individuals have

very little to lose and everything to gain by upsetting the status quo. Governments have therefore resorted to the manipulation of relief programs in order to
strike the "happy" balance between enforcing labor discipline and alienating
labor so completely as to jeopardize the capitalist framework.

If welfare programs provide one of the most clearcut examples of government management of relative deprivation to enforce work norms, the other
obvious example is unemployment. During the 1970s a high rate of unemployment has been one of the main weapons that the Nixon and Ford administrations have used to fight stagflation. The welfare infrastructure has only compensated the unemployed to the tune of one-third of their previous earnings levels,
and, the resulting increase in inequality has done much to decrease labor mili-
tancy.[42] As *Business Week* put it:

> ... many corporations are optimistic about 1976, "very few eco-
> nomic issues are going to precipitate a strike next year," says the
> personnel vice-president of one giant company. . . . [Many] industrial
> relations experts now believe that the nation can emerge from the
> 1976 negotiations with a non-inflationary wage pattern and without
> large numbers of strikes. . . . Instead of exploding, wage gains have
> surprisingly run behind inflation in the past 2½ years."[43]

I do not find this at all "surprising": Unemployment is running at its highest
level since the late 1930s.

The background characteristics of capitalist economies, discussed earlier,
are extremely important prerequisites for a system of labor discipline. To put it
in formal terms, they constitute necessary if not sufficient conditions for the
functioning of a disciplinary apparatus. The property relations of market economies are particularly important in this regard, for if property were equally
divided, workers, owning more than mere "labor power" would have greater
bargaining strength, especially in the face of unemployment. The hierarchical
organization of production is also significant in that this structural characteristic
explains the mechanism through which workers are actually controlled so that
they accept work norms rather than overthrow the system.

PECUNIARY INCENTIVES

I would now like to turn to an examination of the incentive apparatus. An
effectively functioning and growing capitalist economy needs both a disciplinary
and an incentive structure: in other words it requires the carrot as well as the
stick. This is particularly true in the era of the welfare state. Since it is no longer
possible to threaten the workforce with starvation, it follows that, to prevent
wholesale voluntary unemployment, it is necessary to create some positive
inducements to work.

Among the nonsupervisory workforce, which is after all the vast majority of all workers, the main incentive structure is pecuniary. This is a direct result of the degree of alienation among the modern workforce: Given the degree to which most manual workers are engaged in routine, repetitive tasks it is hardly surprising that the psychological as opposed to the monetary rewards are minimal. As one Lordstown assembly line worker put it:

> Every day I come out of there I feel ripped off. I'm gettin' the shit kicked out of me and I'm helpless to stop it. . . . I don't even feel necessary. . . . They could always find somebody stupider than me to do the job.[44]

The importance of the pecuniary incentive structure can most clearly be seen in the institutionalization of overtime. It is built into the pay structures of most manual occupations that no one will do any "extra" work (above and beyond the statutory work week) without being compensated for each hour of work done at a rate higher than the normal scale.

In the managerial echelons of the workforce, psychological rewards reinforce monetary incentives to a very large degree.[45] Status, responsibility, involvement in the production process, variety in type of task—all these increase along with salary level, and managerial career structures in mature capitalist enterprises are cleverly orchestrated so as to maximize the work effort that can be derived from a composite pecuniary/psychological incentive apparatus. Once again, the system of rewards appears to be counterintuitive, in that those with the highest salaries also enjoy the greatest degree of job satisfaction. Common sense, let alone notions of fair play would lead one to expect that those with boring menial jobs would need to be compensated with the highest salaries. To explain this apparent paradox we need to return to one of the background characteristics of market economies: hierarchical control. The hierarchical organization of capitalist firms constitute a necessary condition for the operation of an incentive structure that is heavily weighed in favor of the managerial class. The carrot waved in front of the workers is just big enough in terms of incremental material rewards to ensure that they do not opt to be unemployed; management appropriates all the other benefits and especially those that can be grouped under the general heading of psychological satisfaction. As we discovered in an earlier section, it is the bureaucratic organization and hierarchical lines of authority typical of large capitalistic enterprises that ensure (and legitimize) this type of control over the laboring classes.

CAPITALIST GROWTH AND PROFIT LEVELS

Profits in the private sector of the U.S. economy have risen substantially in the 1970s (from $39.3 billion in 1970 to $85 billion in 1974).[46] "Exuberant" profits have been accompanied by stagnant or falling wage rates in a period of productivity increases and moderate rates of real economic growth. The distribution of factor shares between labor and capital has thus moved unambiguously in favor of the latter. Recent administrations have chosen to move out of the economic doldrums of the 1972-75 period by squeezing labor, allowing corporations to keep a larger share of profits, and stimulating investment. Nothing shows this more clearly than President Ford's State of the Union message of January 1976. In this statement he gave corporate enterprise a clear mandate to increase profit levels, promised a range of incentives to boost private investment, and left labor to the mercies of the market. And if one accepts the goals of the Ford administration, these policies directives were undoubtedly sound. Given the economic conditions that prevail in 1976, economic growth can only be achieved at a cost, and that cost incorporates an increase in inequality and a stagnant or falling standard of living for large groups of lower-income Americans. As Andrew Glyn and Bob Sutcliffe have put it:

> Capitalism is a system of production dependent on private profit. It cannot operate without sufficient profits; they are the incentive which drives capitalists to invest, and they provide much of the finance for investment.[47]

In the U.S. context, 99 percent of industrial and commercial investment is dependent upon retained earnings and depreciation allowances: the private profits of firms. No wonder profit levels are thought to be an important ingredient of economic recovery!

That link between capitalist growth and economic inequality that revolves around the profit share, is most definitely related to the background characteristics of market economies. The existence and unequal distribution of private property, the phenomenon of uneven development, and the hierarchical structure of control are all necessary conditions that have to be met before a modern oligopolistic enterprise is capable of maximizing long-run profits. And profits are the moving force in the capitalist system, an essential if not sufficient condition for economic growth. The quest for profits involves eliciting a high level of output from a generally recalcitrant workforce. In practical terms it boils down to exacting from labor as much work as possible in return for the lowest possible wages. Hierarchical control and severely weighted property relationships are essential ingredients in this critical process, which rests upon advancing the interests of a minority (capitalists and managers) against the interest of a majority (the workers). In short, the hierarchical structure, bolstered by the property relationships of capitalism, constitutes a mechanism used by employers to control the work force in the interests of profits and stability. Uneven development is a rather specific prerequisite for oligopolistic growth, as explained in an earlier section, the dynamics of contemporary capitalism have Darwinian "survival of the fittest" overtones that tend to polarize society, producing great prosperity in some sectors and areas and stagnation in others.

Much of this chapter has been devoted to examining inequality as a structural necessity in market economies, with the general goal of explaining the apparent contradiction between the political and economic aims of U.S. society. I would like to end with the proposition that the important explanatory variables can all be subsumed under my final argument: the profit motive. All the background characteristics of market economies—property relationships, uneven development, hierarchical control—and even the more specific facts of the disciplinary and incentive systems are essential contributions to the quest for profits. Once this proposition is fully accepted, our paradox is resolved. Profits constitute the crucial link that makes inequality functional to the growth process. In the final analysis any capitalist system is geared to the imperatives of profit and domination rather than to human need. To quote Samuel Bowles and Herbert Gintis: "The undemocratic structure of economic life in the US may be traced directly to the moving force in the capitalist system: the quest for profits."[48]

Finally, it is important to remember that the inequality-efficiency relationship constitutes a tradeoff. The maximization of growth rates and a dramatic narrowing of income differentials would appear to be incompatible under capitalism, but precisely how much equity is sacrificed for how much growth is a political choice. The United States in the 1970s has clearly emphasized growth at the expense of equity, but there is nothing inevitable about this policy scenario. With a different structure of power, with less conservative administrations, the American people could have fared rather better.

NOTES

1. Herbert Spencer, *Social Statics: Man versus the State* (New York: Appleton, 1913), p. 151.

2. Ibid., p. 152.

3. William Graham Sumner, *The Challenge of Facts, and Other Essays* (New Haven: Yale University Press, 1914), p. 90.

4. Cf. Arthur M. Okun, *Equality and Efficiency: The Big Tradeoff* (Washington, D.C.: The Brookings Institution, 1975), pp. 1-31.

5. Ibid., p. 1.

6. Robert L. Heilbroner, *Business Civilization in Decline* (New York: Norton, 1976), p. 116.

7. Harry G. Johnson, "Some Micro-Economic Reflections of Income and Wealth Inequalities," *Annals of the American Academy of Political and Social Science* 409 (1973): 54.

8. Milton Friedman, *Capitalism and Freedom* (Chicago: University of Chicago Press, 1962), p. 195.

9. R. H. Tawney, *Equality* (New York: Harcourt, Brace, 1931), p. 220.

10. A useful discussion of this point is contained in Amartya Sen, *On Economic Equality* (Oxford: The Clarendon Press, 1973).

11. New York *Times,* October 30, 1975. Average earnings for "workers" fell from $102 per week in 1970 to $99 per week in 1975, while average compensation for "managers" rose at a rate of 9.4 percent per year between 1970 and 1975.

12. Alice M. Rivlin, "Income Distribution—Can Economists Help?" *American Economic Review* (May 1975):5-6.

13. Gunnar Myrdal, *Economic Theory and Underdeveloped Nations* (London: Duckworth, 1957), p. 123.

14. John Rawls, *A Theory of Social Justice* (Cambridge, Mass.: Harvard University Press, 1971).

15. W. G. Runciman, *Relative Deprivation and Social Justice* (London: Routledge & Kegan Paul, 1966), p. 337.

16. These and other categories of egalitarianism are treated in some depth in, for example, Martin Rein and S. M. Miller, "Standards of Income Redistribution," *Challenge* (July/August 1974):20-27.

17. Peter Townsend, "The Meaning of Poverty," *British Journal of Sociology* 13 (1962):210-27.

18. Victor E. Smith, *Electronic Computation of Human Diets,* M.S.U. Business Studies (East Lansing: Michigan State University, 1964), p. 20, cited in Lester C. Thurow, *Generating Inequality: Mechanisms of Distribution in the U.S. Economy* (New York: Basic Books, 1975), p. 27.

19. Thurow, op. cit., p. 46.

20. Some interesting discussion of induced demand is to be found in Richard J. Barnet and Ronald E. Muller, *Global Reach* (New York: Simon and Schuster, 1974), pp. 123-47.

21. John Kenneth Galbraith, in *Economics and the Public Purpose* (Boston: Houghton Mifflin, 1973), pp. 193-229, makes the interesting point that the only real limit to induced demand is the time involved in consuming. Without middle-class "homemakers" to perform a consumption management role, demand would be much less dynamic. Conventional theory has generally overlooked the fact that consumption takes both time and energy: It is not costless.

22. Lee Rainwater, "Poverty, Living Standards and Family Well-Being," Working Paper No. 10, Joint Center for Urban Studies of M.I.T. and Harvard, prepared for the Subcommittee on Fiscal Policy, Joint Economic Committee, U.S. Congress, June 1972.

23. Heilbroner, op. cit., p. 45.

24. See Carlos Geraldo Langoni, *Distribuicao da Renda e Desenvolvimento Economico do Brasil* (Rio de Janeiro: Editora Expressao e Cultura, 1973), pp. 63-64.

25. This example is cited in Sylvia Ann Hewlett, "The Dynamics of Economic Imperialism: The Role of Direct Foreign Investment in Brazil," *Latin American Perspectives* (Summer 1975):146.

26. Recently, there have been some attempts to replace the rate of growth of GNP goal with a composite index, incorporating the stressing the standard of living of the mass of the people. Chenery suggests a "poverty-weighted" index; see Hollis Chenery, Montek S. Ahluwalia, C.L.G. Bell, John H. Duloy, and Richard Jolly, *Redistribution with Growth* (Oxford: Oxford University Press, 1974), pp. 38-43.

27. Piero Sraffa, ed., *The Works and Correspondence of David Ricardo* (Cambridge, Eng.: Cambridge University Press, 1962), p. 5.

28. See Piero Sraffa, *Production of Commodities by Means of Commodities: Prelude to a Critique of Economic Theory* (Cambridge, Eng.: Cambridge University Press, 1960).

29. See Bela Balassa, *The Hungarian Experience in Economic Planning* (New Haven: Yale University Press, 1959), pp. 10-13.

30. Friedman, op. cit., pp. 161-62.

31. Joan Robinson, "The Second Crisis in Economic Theory," *American Economic Review* (May 1972):9.

32. Thurow, op. cit., pp. 75-129.

33. Ibid., p. 146. Thurow obtains his data from the U.S. Department of Commerce, "National Income and Product Accounts," *Survey of Current Business* 53 (1973):38.

34. The theme of inequality as a structural necessity is treated in some depth in Samuel Bowles and Herbert Gintis, *Schooling in Capitalist America* (New York: Basic Books, 1976), pp. 53-101.

35. See Stephen Hymer, "The Multinational Corporation and the Law of Uneven Development," in *Economics and World Order*, Jagdish N. Bhagwati, ed. (London: Macmillan, 1972), pp. 113-40.

36. One of the best researched examples is Katherine Stone's study of the development of the U.S. steel industry. She shows that the social organization of work arose not from technological necessity, but from the power relationships of steel production. See Katherine Stone, "The Origins of Job Structures in the Steel Industry," in *Labor Market Segmentation*, Richard C. Edwards, Michael Reich, and David M. Gordon, eds. (Lexington, Mass.: Heath, 1975), pp. 27-85.

37. Bowles and Gintis, op. cit., p. 80.

38. Quoted in Harold D. Hasswell and Abraham Kaplan, *Power and Society: A Framework for Political Inquiry* (New Haven: Yale University Press, 1950), p. 121.

39. Frances Fox Piven and Richard A. Cloward, *Regulating the Poor: the Functions of Public Welfare* (New York: Vintage Books, 1971), p. xv. Smith felt that "the wages of labour vary with the ease or hardship, the cleanliness or dirtiness, the honourableness or dishonourableness of the employment. Thus in most places . . . a journeyman tailor earns less than a journeyman weaver. His work is much easier." See Adam Smith, *The Wealth of Nations* (New York: Modern Library, 1937), pp. 100-106. This sentiment has great intuitive appeal, and yet we know that in modern market economies this relationship is reversed.

40. Ibid., p. xiii.

41. Ibid., p. 67.

42. See Edward M. Gramlich, "The Distributional Effects of Higher Unemployment," in *Brookings Papers on Economic Activity*, no. 2, Arthur M. Okun and George L. Perry, eds. (Washington, D.C.: The Brookings Institution, 1974), pp. 293-336.

43. *Business Week,* December 1, 1975, pp. 44-45.

44. Stanley Aronowitz, *False Promises: The Shaping of American Working Class Consciousness* (New York: McGraw-Hill, 1973), p. 21.

45. This theme is elaborated in Richard C. Edwards, "The Social Relations of Production in the Firm and Labor Market Structure," in Edwards, op. cit., pp. 3-27.

46. Figures were compiled from various issues of *Business Week.*

47. Andrew Glyn and Bob Sutcliffe, *British Capitalism and the Profits Squeeze* (Harmondsworth, Eng.: Penguin, 1972), p. 10.

48. Bowles and Gintis, op. cit., p. 54.

4

IMPLICATIONS OF AND BARRIERS TO INDUSTRIAL DEMOCRACY IN THE UNITED STATES AND SWEDEN

George Ritzer

This chapter is concerned with the policy implications for various units within U.S. society of the recent efforts to democratize work in Sweden. The democratization of the Swedish workplace has received widespread and highly favorable publicity in the United States. Some journalists have hailed it as a model for needed changes in work in the United States (for example, Norcross 1974), while others writing for popular magazines, such as *Time* and *Newsweek*, have supported this view by underscoring the problems of work in the United States and the need for reform. Widescale publicity has been accorded the General Motors plant in Lordstown, Ohio, which, after it speeded up its automobile assembly-line, became the symbol of what needed to be changed in work in the United States. Even a government-sponsored report has outlined the problems of work in the United States and urged that we resolve a "contradiction in our nation between democracy in society and authoritarianism in the work-place" by democratizing work, among other measures (HEW 1973:104). Thus, a societal consensus seems to be emerging about the problems of work in the United States as well as the solutions to them.

The irony of all this is that we really know very little about what has really taken place in the Swedish workworld. Furthermore, we have not really thought out the policy implications of following Sweden's lead. This chapter deals with those two issues. In the first part, we deal with five in-depth cases of Swedish efforts to democratize work. The discussion is based on the author's visit to many of the locations discussed, personal interviews with management, labor, and academicians involved in these projects, and published documents on these efforts. Following a discussion of these five cases, we turn to an analysis of the implications of these efforts for U.S. policy. In particular, we deal with the policy implications for government, business, and labor. We will be concerned with the policies that leaders of each of these entities should adopt in light of the Swedish experience.

Before we turn to the five cases of democratization of work in Sweden, we must make clear what we mean by our focal concern in this chapter, *work-linked* democracy. There are at least three types of workplace democracy (Trist 1974). First, there is the democracy that results from the adversary relationship between labor and management. Second, there is the type of democracy that occurs when workers are represented on joint labor-management committees. Finally, there is work-linked democracy in which workers influence, and sometimes even decide upon, how their own work is to be performed. Although the three types of democracy are not mutually exclusive and can be found in Sweden, our focus will be on work-linked democracy, which we regard as the most important Swedish innovation. In focusing on this type of workplace democracy, we are following Paul Blumberg's argument that "it is what happens at the lowest level . . . that matters most to the worker" (1968:3).

WORK-LINKED DEMOCRACY IN SWEDEN

There are a number of reasons why Sweden has been in the forefront of efforts to democratize work. One of the positive reasons for the development of work-linked democracy in Sweden was the long history of peaceful and cooperative labor-management relations that made it possible to try out new forms of work, each party having every expectation that the other party would cooperate. Against this positive background, a number of negative forces were impelling Swedish managers to take some form of action. First, turnover rates were averaging 30 percent per year, and in many companies the percentage was considerably higher. Such turnover rates severely disrupted the smooth functioning of many companies, and the costs were high, with each turnover costing the company approximately $2000. The structure of the benefit programs in Sweden allowed an employee to change companies without losing his rights (Salpukas 1974:31). Further complicating the turnover problem was the fact that there was (and still is) virtually no "industrial reserve army" in Sweden to draw upon for replacements. Unemployment in Sweden usually has run at about 1 or 1.5 percent, and many in this group have simply not been suited to the kinds of jobs that tend to become available. Until the early 1970s Swedish companies could rely on a ready supply of foreign workers (primarily Finns and Yugoslavs), but in 1971 pressure from the unions led to the passage of a law severely restricting the use of foreign workers. Worried about these problems, management almost panicked when the normally placid industrial scene in Sweden was shaken by a series of wildcat strikes.

On the workers' side, dissatisfaction was mounting against the extreme measures taken by Swedish management to streamline the production process: "An implicit respect for engineering and engineers, a passion for efficiency and hard work, a highly competititve situation in industry and the persistence of piecework along with highly rationalized mass production methods—all combined to heighten the pace of production and the consequent stress on the worker" (Bjork 1975:17). Working against these developments were the progressive liberalization of Swedish education, as well as of the society as a whole. Radically liberal social values were brought face to face in the workplace with radically efficient production principles. The clash of these value systems laid the groundwork for Sweden to become the country in which the most innovative efforts in work-linked democracy were undertaken. One of our theses is that Americans have tended to look at these changes too uncritically. The fact is that the Swedes themselves are well aware of the limitations of what they have done and see work-linked democracy as only a small part of a broad overall plan to cope with problems in the workworld. A discussion of the limitations of the Swedish efforts will give us a better idea of the degree to which work-linked democracy will be useful in the United States.

Although no one knows exactly how many programs in work-linked democracy are currently underway in Sweden (one estimate is more than 500; see SAF 1975), the undeniable fact is that there are many such efforts. They range from small-scale efforts at job rotation and job enlargement to the new Volvo plant at Kalmar, in which 110 million Swedish Crowns (about $30 million) have been invested in a plant that has been designed and built on the principles of work-linked democracy. Five major experiments in work-linked democracy have been chosen for discussion here; two at Swedish automobile companies (Volvo and Saab-Scania), one at a die-casting foundry (Granges), another at a manufacturer of small machinery (Atlas Copco), and the final one among white-collar workers in an insurance company (Skandia). From these five cases we can derive a number of insights into the nature and limitations of work-linked democracy as well as its policy implications for the United States.

Volvo

No company has been more active in the area of work-linked democracy than Volvo. The company's general manager has enunciated the company policy: "Here at Volvo, in fact all over Sweden, we are trying to create small groups of workers who develop into skilled and proud craftsmen, small groups under one large umbrella—craftsmen who set their own work pace, their own coffee breaks. It cost more, but there is evidence that it decreases the rate of absenteeism" (Norcross 1974:15).

This general policy has been implemented in different ways by the various semiautonomous units within Volvo. At the Torslanda plant a large-scale job rotation program has been undertaken: "One group will assemble fuel pipes on Monday; fit side windows on Tuesday; fit car interiors on Wednesday; assemble rear parts on Thursday; and fit fuel pipes again on Friday" (Mire 1974:6). Such a program is not unusual, but Volvo has gone further. At the Volvo Lundby-werken plant work-linked democracy has been implemented: "Groups of up to nine workers are given a work assignment and they decide for themselves who does what. The teams elect their own foremen—on a rotating basis—and they do their own training, with the cost of the training borne by the company. Production problems are discussed with management at monthly meetings" (Mire 1974:6). At Volvo Skövde "The assembly-line has been replaced by small 'work groups.' Built-in 'buffer zones' give workers and/or the work groups a chance to determine their own work pace as well as rest periods. The work groups are fully responsible for quality control, processing of raw materials, and tool inventories. Each work group takes care of transport of motors from one workshop to another" (Mire 1974:6). While these efforts to build work-linked democracy and replace the traditional methods of doing work are important, they can be seen as mere preludes to Volvo's most important contribution to work-linked democracy: its new plant at Kalmar.

The Kalmar plant was created on the basis of the following mandate from the corporate general manager: "Produce a factory which, *without sacrificing efficiency and economic result,* provides the possibility for the employee to work in groups, to communicate freely, to carry out job rotation, to vary the rate of work, feel identification with the products, to be aware of quality, and also be in a position to influence their working environment" (Salpukas 1974: 31; emphasis added).

After some effort, the designers brought the general manager plans for a fairly traditional assembly-line plant. The general manager rejected these plans and demanded a plant that did away with the traditional elements of an assembly plant proving so nettlesome to workers. In a very short period of time they returned with a plant design that was in many ways almost as revolutionary as Henry Ford's original assembly line.

Before discussing this plant, some preliminary warnings are needed. First of all, Volvo, unlike many of its admirers, does not consider the Kalmar plant to be the ultimate answer to workplace ills. Second, the factory was built with the clear directive from the general manager that efficiency *not* be reduced. Third, this development, like many others in Sweden, was the result of a management initiative aimed at coping with pressing problems, such as turnover, absenteeism, difficulty in recruiting young Swedes, and so on. The unions usually became involved in these efforts, but not until *after* management had started the project and set at least some of the guidelines. We will have occasion to return to these points later.

In order to get an idea of the significance of the Kalmar plant, two diagrams are presented. Figure 4.1 gives an overview of the plant, and Figure 4.2 gives a more detailed picture of one section of it. The star, or hexagonal, shape of the factory has a number of implications for the work that takes place within it. The center of the plant is devoted to material storage; the actual assembly of

FIGURE 4.1

Layout of the Volvo Plant at Kalmar

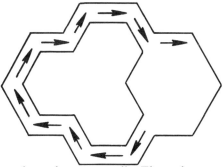

the cars takes place along the outer walls. Thus, the assembly work is done in close proximity to the numerous windows that allow sunlight in and give the workers a pleasant view of the surroundings. More important, the angular construction of the walls allows each group to have its own relatively well-defined area. Each angle represents the end of one group and the beginning of another. Each of these groups performs a different part of the general process: electrical system, instruments, safety equipment, and so on. Each team includes about 20 workers. The differentiation of function, along with the physical structure of the building, gives the members of each group the feeling that they are set apart from those groups that precede and succeeed them in the construction process. This sense of independent identity is enhanced by the fact that each group has its own entrance, changing room, rest rooms, coffee-break area, and even its own sauna. All of this is aimed at creating an environment in which autonomous or semiautonomous work groups develop. In other words, the goal is the creation of something akin to a set of old-style skilled workshops under the roof of one large factory. In so doing, the anonymous feeling of working in a huge impersonal setting is greatly reduced.

FIGURE 4.2

Detailed Look at One Portion of the Volvo Plant at Kalmar

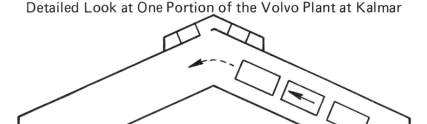

The atmosphere in the plant is remarkable. It is light, colorful, and airy. Great pains have been taken to reduce the noise level. It has none of the noisy dinginess that is characteristic of most U.S. automobile assembly plants. As one observer has noted, the plant generally looks like a large, modern supermarket.

It is not pleasant conditions that produces cars, of course. The structure of the plant, as well as the philosophy behind it, ruled out the possibility of an assembly line. To move the cars in the process of being assembled through the various stations, the Volvo engineers developed an electrically driven carrier system. Each car is on a separate carrier that can be controlled by either a central computer or manually by the workers as they work on the car. The workers in each group therefore have the ability to move the car through their work area in any way they decide. They can collectively work on the car as it stands still or moves slowly through their area, or they can set the carrier to move through their area at a set pace so that they can work on it as it passes in much the same way as they would on the traditional assembly line. The one major constraint on them is that they must produce a set number of cars per hour. The workers in each group have the possibility, if they want, of working quickly and filling up the two-car buffer zone that exists between them and the next group. If they can fill the buffer zone, they will have time for a ten-minute coffee break. Incidentally, the electric carriers have the ability to tilt the car at about a 90-degree angle so that the formerly odious task of working under the car is made far easier and can be done like all of the rest of the work.

The workers themselves have the ability to determine how the work within their group is to be done (there is ordinarily only one foreman for every two groups). They can decide to do a single task, rotate among a number of tasks, or assemble a car collectively. Basically, each group can either use the "straight assembly" or the "dock method." In the straight assembly method each individual works at a set station doing a particular task or set of tasks. This is much like the traditional assembly line in that the workers do their tasks as the carriers roll by. About 70 percent of the groups at Kalmar are, as of this writing, using this method. In the other technique, the dock method, the workers work on the car as a team. They can follow the car through the entire process in their area and when they are finished they return to the starting point and begin again on a new car. Although only 30 percent of the teams are currently using the dock method, the plant management feels that groups are moving increasingly toward this method because of the positive feelings many derive from the teamwork involved. In either case, the team is free to choose the method it prefers as long as productivity remains at the prescribed level.

The Kalmar plant clearly had problems in its initial year, but much of it was apparently the usual problems associated with a new plant. A rather novel set of problems was caused by the flood of visitors, many from the United States and Japan, who flocked to see the new development. Despite its initial difficulties, by mid-1975 the plant was running at the level hoped for by its designers.

Although foreigners were prone to see the "Kalmar concept" as the answer to workplace problems, the Volvo people do not share this exalted conception of what they have done at Kalmar. In fact, as a result of Volvo's decentralization, different parts of the company are doing very different things in an effort to cope with their particular problems. As one Volvo official involved in corporate planning puts it: "Today we find not one Volvo-model for socio-technical-administrative changes (as is often presumed) but a number of different models, or rather change processes. There is a wide-range of approaches with different strategies involved. We thus find different developments—and results—in each plant where factors such as environment and cultural traditions play a crucial role" (Jonsson 1975:3). Furthermore, the developments at Kalmar are but one element in the future planning at Volvo: "Within Volvo we look upon Kalmar as *the first step* to a new generation of production technology rather than the ultimate solution to assembly-work problems. At the moment we are using this as a base to make further development work to be implemented in old as well as in new plants" (Jonsson 1975:9; emphasis added).

Almost as a warning to overeager Americans, the Volvo people state: "We will fail when we try to uncritically copy solutions" (Jonsson 1975:4). Although most workers seem relatively satisfied with the new developments (perhaps because they are still new), others are already becoming dissatisfied with these new developments, and this dissatisfaction stands as still another warning to foreigners anxious to build Kalmars of their own. One Kalmar worker says: "This is certainly different from other jobs I've had. But there is a certain amount of monotony. It can't be avoided" (Salpukas 1974:31).

As if to underscore the limited applicability of the Kalmar concept to the United States, Volvo, in planning for its plant in Virginia scheduled to open in 1977, has decided against the hexagonal shape used in the Kalmar plant (although the electric carrier will be used).

Saab-Scania

Like Volvo, Saab has been engaged in democratization at various levels; we will focus in this discussion on work-linked democracy, however. Efforts at Saab to democratize work were begun in 1969 for many of the same reasons Volvo was forced to seek ways of reforming blue-collar work. Small scale experiments were begun in two departments (engine finishing and small-bore piping), and the success of these experiments led to the extension of its principles to many other groups in Saab's large multiplant facility at Soedertalje. The initial experiments were based on four principles. First, there would be small, knowledgable production groups with a real need to interact on the job. Second, each group itself was to take on much more responsibility for the quality of what it produced. Third, maintenance tasks were also to be integrated into the group. Finally, rotation between different tasks was to take place. As change progressed, these principles were adopted by some groups and not by others. In fact, the company policy was to avoid laying down a hard set of guidelines but rather to let changes evolve within each work setting gradually and spontaneously.

Saab is quick to point out that these efforts have not been an unqualified success. For example, in at least one location some employees were not carrying their share of the load, and this put intolerable pressure on the more conscientious members of the group. On the positive side, seven achievements were noted. First, productivity goals are met or exceeded. Second, unplanned stoppages were reduced. Third, costs averaged about 5 percent below budgeted costs. Fourth, fewer quality adjustments were needed after the production process was completed. Fifth, while job rotation did not work in all locations, where it did, it had the advantages of (a) greater variety of work, (b) opportunity to learn, (c) the ability to vary working positions, (d) the ability of the group to adapt more easily to absences, and (e) greater ease in adapting to changes in the tempo of work. Sixth, turnover was substantially reduced. Finally, absenteeism was lowered.

With this generally (*not* totally) positive experience, Saab used the principles evolved in these early experiments in the development of its new Saab 99 Engine factory opened in 1972. Since the building was a revamped older building, Saab could not undertake the massive changes that characterized the Volvo plant. Furthermore, there seems to be a feeling among Saab executives and planners that Volvo had gone too far at Kalmar. In any case, Saab did radically alter the assembly line on which the engines are assembled. Figure 4.3 is a diagram of the engine assembly-line at Soedertalje.

FIGURE 4.3

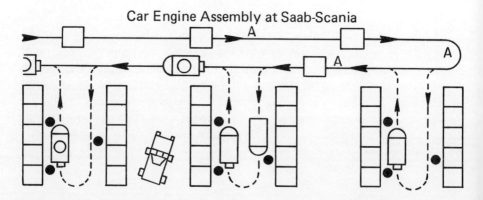

Car Engine Assembly at Saab-Scania

There are seven assembly groups in the section, with three to five members in each group (one of the lines is a training line for new employees). The basic engine blocks circulate on the oval conveyor belt (labelled A in the dark lines). When a group is ready to begin work on an engine, it routes one of the engine blocks into its area (engine blocks awaiting assembly circulate on the conveyor system until a group is ready to work on them). The group then has 30 minutes to assemble a completed engine, but how the work is done is up to the group to decide. The members can divide the tasks among themselves and then move the engine from station to station until all the tasks are completed. Of course, there are no more than five stations in each group, so even under this method each individual performs a number of tasks. There are other options including the possibility of a single person putting together an entire engine on her own (most of the workers are women). It is the group that decides which of the methods of engine assembly available will be used. The flexibility inherent in this system is particularly important in an area in which the employees are often not the primary providers in their families and are therefore prone to higher levels of absenteeism. Under the system employed a line can operate even if only one person shows up for work on a given day.

The company claims that the new methods have led to an increase in employee satisfaction. One woman had worked on a conventional line previously and was asked to evaluate the old and new lines.

> Yes, if I had to make a choice today I would choose this way, if only for the reason that you feel more like a human being working this way rather than sitting or standing at the same place year after year. Especially when you more or less see that you are doing more, when you can see what's turning out and when you can see the thing being finished (Norstedt and Agurén 1973:43).

Some notes of caution need to be added before this discussion of the Saab experience is closed. The majority of the Saab employees, and even most of those in the new engine factory, have not been markedly affected by these changes. Outside of the rather novel engine-assembly area, the rest of the engine factory looks surprisingly like any U.S. assembly plant. However, it should be noted that Saab has made an effort to make the plant look more pleasant, with colorful walls, cleanliness, and coffee-break areas. In many departments employees are given the option of developing more work-linked democracy, but the fact is that many evince little interest in changing the traditional way they do their jobs. Many seem to prefer simple, monotonous tasks. The Saab management feels that many people are simply unaware of the concept of workplace democracy and how they can gain from it. They feel that it is the company's obligation to educate its employees, as well as the general public, about the joys of industrial democracy. They do not feel that they will make much headway with this generation, so they pin their hopes on the next one. This is an interesting problem, especially given the claim by Swedish industry that they are reacting to the demands of the populace for more democratic work. It raises the question of where the initiative for industrial democracy actually comes from. Is it, as management claims, from the demands of increasingly dissatisfied workers? Or is it from management which is seeking a new device for coping with such mounting problems as turnover and absenteeism? Swedish management cannot have it both ways. They cannot simultaneously claim that the workers are demanding more democracy *and* that the workers are not willing to accept democratization.

Granges

The Granges foundry in Upplands Vasby was confronted in 1968 with an acute turnover problem: The rate was 46 percent, and by the end of the first half of 1969 it had grown to 61 percent. Turnover was an even more serious problem at Granges than at Saab or Volvo since foundry work requires workers with a good deal of training and experience. The high turnover rates created a less skilled workforce than was felt to be adequate, with the result that there were an undue number of production stoppages. Too much time was spent on setups and adjustments, and the unacceptably high defect rate of 4.8 percent in 1968 rose to 5.4 percent in the first half of 1969.

In order to cope with these problems, Granges decided in the summer of 1969 to shift from a piece-rate system of wages to fixed wages. At the same time, semiautonomous production groups were set up with the goal of creating more cooperation, group solidarity, and job satisfaction. However, these group changes never took hold, as problems arose almost immediately with the new wage system. Performance under the new system dropped considerably. In addition, turnover actually rose to 87 percent in late 1969. Although it dropped somewhat in 1970 (to 65 percent), it was still higher than before the change. These problems were caused, to a large extent, by the fact that the most skilled and productive workers resigned because their wages were reduced significantly by the new wage system. Work-linked democracy could not even begin in this first phase of the experiment in which a new wage system severely penalized those people on whom the company most relied. It is clear from this that work-linked democracy is inextricably tied to a variety of forces both inside and outside the immediate work setting. Its success or failure is often tied to changes in these factors.

Admitting the failure of the system, the company instituted another new wage system in 1971, in which the workers were paid fixed wages amounting to 70 percent of their pay, with the other 30 percent in a flexible premium to be shared by the members on the basis of the group's productivity. In addition, the company reinstituted the changes designed to create semiautonomous work groups. The results of the second half of this experiment were very positive: Productivity rose substantially; quality improved; the workforce was reduced; turnover dropped to only 18 percent in the first half of 1972; employee attitudes seemed to improve (Edgren 1974).

One problem that is clear in the second portion of the Granges experiment but is equally true of all such experiments in democratization is that of ascertaining exactly what factors have contributed to the positive results obtained. Without controls, no one can be sure that the changes occurred wholly, or even in part, as a result of the changes introduced. For example, a tightening in the labor market could be an important contributor to a number of the results obtained.

Another problem raised here is whether any "reasonable" change would lead to the kinds of positive results obtained (the first half of this experiment clearly entailed unreasonable changes). This is the so-called Hawthorne effect, which points to the fact that when a group is made the object of an investigation, its performance will improve as a result of its privileged status and not because of the specific changes that are introduced. This stems from the finding in the Hawthorne studies that productivity increased in an experimental group when the lighting in the room was improved, as well as when it was reduced almost to the level of moonlight. It was not the light that was causing the changes but rather the cohesion created in the group as a result of being the object of so much attention. It is not certain whether it was industrial democracy, or whether it was simply change, that led to the positive findings in the second half of the Granges study, as well as in a variety of other Swedish experiments.

Atlas-Copco

Although the term *experiment* has been used to describe the changes that occurred in the cases described above, the fact is that they are not really experiments in the scientific sense of the term. Rather, they were efforts by very practical people to cope with very mundane problems on the job. There were no experimental designs and no set experimental procedures. In the Atlas-Copco case, we have an example in which academicians have played a much larger role than in most efforts in Sweden. The Atlas-Copco case can be called an action experiment. Although it was more rigorous than the efforts already described, it too cannot qualify as an experiment in the strict sense of the term. The implication of this is that in the Atlas-Copco case, as in the others, we cannot be certain that the results obtained are due to the changes introduced. They may be partly or wholly the result of external changes. The researchers admitted "that changes . . . could not be measured precisely" (Bjork 1975:19).

The research was undertaken in a department of the Sickla works of Atlas-Copco engaged in the final assembly of rock-drilling equipment. A development group was formed composed of management and union representatives, an industrial engineer, a psychologist, and a social psychologist (later, two workers and a foreman were added). The goal of the project was to increase job satisfaction, although it was stipulated that the level of productivity had to be maintained. Each member of the development group had the right to veto any proposal it felt was opposed to its best interests. The general objective of the experiment was described by one member of the development group: "The objective of increased work satisfaction was intended to be achieved by changes aimed at giving the worker more opportunity to influence his own job, to take on responsibility, to solve problems and to advance his own development in the job. We were interested in learning whether such changes could in turn affect motivation to work and productivity" (Bjork 1975:19).

The department studied included 12 men and a foreman and operated on the traditional one man, one machine principle. There were various pay systems within the department, and this in addition to the structure of the work created a situation in which "the two workers on the assemblyline felt themselves most exploited: underpaid and bound to one location and to a flow of work they could not control" (Bjork 1975:20). Interviews led to the conclusion that most of the men wanted to do away with the assembly-line system. As a first step, there was substituted for the line a special table designed by the workers, where drills could be assembled at the workers' own pace. In this system productivity remained at the same level as previously, and work was freer and less monotonous. However, the heavy steel equipment proved hard to handle. The workers hit upon the idea of using the conveyer belt, in a modified form, simply as a source of transportation for heavy material. The pace of the conveyer could be controlled by the workers who were assembling drills on benches beside it.

The experiment in this modified use of the assembly line was begun in February 1971 with the following plan:

> The basic idea was that the workers in the department would constitute a single team, with equal pay. The team would be split up into groups of from two to four men, and each group would move through the department, carrying out the entire sequence of operations for a single lot, or batch, of drills. . . . The allocation of individual tasks within each group would be left up to the group to decide, as would the exact method of performing each operation. It was to be more than job rotation among previously designed jobs, since the old designs could be scrapped in favor of whatever methods the men found most convenient and satisfying (Bjork 1975:21).

The first half year was difficult since workers were involved in a great deal of new learning and adapting to new cooperative social relationships, and in trying to keep up their past level of productivity out of fear of losing their guaranteed pay and "partly to show that they could keep up the pace while working their own way" (Bjork 1975:21). Things settled down considerably in the second half of the experiment, and it then proceeded smoothly. As the experiment progressed, changes in some secondary roles were required. Staff personnel became more advisers to the workers, while the foreman was no longer engaged in close supervision and was freed for broader-range tasks.

The Atlas-Copco experiment was formally closed at the end of the year. All parties were apparently satisfied. Management wanted it to be the way work was carried out in the department, and the others agreed. Productivity rose 5 percent; much new learning took place; employees became more anxious to cooperate; the process became much less prone to disruption as a result of absenteeism, turnover, and so forth; the operation grew more flexible as employees became able to cope with and adapt to emergencies and changes. Absenteeism and turnover were low before the experiment and did not change as a result of it. Most workers preferred the new system and did not want to go back to the old one. However, even in this generally positive environment, some workers were less than enthusiastic. Said one, "I'd rather work alone than in a group. Then you worry about yourself and you don't have to depend on all the bull all over the department" (Bjork 1975:22).

One of the byproducts of this project was a rise in the expectations of the workers. One of them said, "In the future we want to be in on decisions on the department's budget" (Bjork 1975:23). This leads one to wonder in this case, as well as in the others, whether management has set in motion a process that it neither anticipated nor desired. That is, the logical end of this process is the total democratization of the organization.

Another unanticipated consequence is the creation of an almost insatiable desire for change. That is, once workers see that change is possible in a system they once thought unchangeable, there follows the exertion of greater and greater pressure for change in many other aspects of the working environment. In the Atlas-Copco experiment this occurred when at least some employees enjoyed the problem solving involved in the early phases of the project. Once the problems had been solved and the new system was set, these employees wanted to keep on solving problems and were unhappy that there was none. It is conceivable that these unfulfilled desires could create greater problems in the future than the company was trying to cope with in the first place.

Skandia

This experiment among white-collar clerical workers in an insurance company combines developments initiated at the local level with efforts worked out in coordination with professional researchers. The first effort began in a department of 200 employees where the manager was dissatisfied with the method of working and was troubled by the problems of high costs and inexperienced personnel. In addition, he felt that some way had to be developed to cope with the increasingly complex work. In the light of this and a general management policy supporting innovation at the local level, the following changes were undertaken:

1. The first and second line supervisory positions were eliminated, and 20 work groups without formal leaders were formed reporting directly to a management team composed of the section manager, functional experts, and consultants (the former supervisors).

2. Each work group was given a specialized function—for example, claims adjustment, records, and register control.

3. Each group appointed a representative for a two-month period. That person represented the group during that period with the management team as well as with other outsiders.

4. There was the possibility for job rotation between different groups.

5. The plan was basically a management plan, although the employees' ideas were solicited.

As is the case with many of the experiments in Sweden, hard data on the success or failure of this effort are hard to find. One clear fact, however, is that the number of employees in the section was cut from 239 in 1970 to 150 in 1975. Part of this drop is due to computerization; it is, however, the section manager's belief that about 50 fewer people are needed in the new system. None of these people has been fired; since the company is growing, they were absorbed into other departments. This points up a problem for Americans wishing to copy this experiment. If one's company is not expanding, then it would be necessary to lay off or fire employees, and these are always serious causes of disruption in an organization. Thus, in order to work well, the company, and even the economy as a whole, needs to be expanding.

The other experimental group was set up from the beginning with the advice of academic researchers and with the active involvement of employees. It began in January 1973 and ended late in 1974. The project was directed by a group composed of three management and three worker representatives. Researchers participated in the group but had no vote. Both management and workers had the power to veto proposals of the group. The plan developed by this group included the following elements: Group leaders were elected for two month terms; the employees were to be granted increased personal discretion; workers were given a greater say on such issues as transfers of employees and recruitment through ad hoc joint groups formed to deal with these issues. A broader joint union-management group was formed with two management and two worker representatives. The group made decisions on central issues, such as departmental budgets and budgetary goals, promotions and transfers, wage revisions, organizational development and changes in work organization, decisions regarding internal relations between work groups as well as on relations with other departments, and the department's involvement in systems development.

In their analysis of this research project and its results, the researchers are well aware of its limitations (Docherty and Stymne 1974). The limitations of the nature of the work set boundaries on the degree to which each individual could develop his own talents. The experimental situations are largely isolated from the rest of the organization, to say nothing of the rest of Swedish industry. The isolation of the experiments helped make them highly vulnerable to interference, and even curtailment, by powerful officers within the larger organization. In fact, one of the managers seemed fearful that top management would cut off the experiment at any moment. The isolation of the experiments have another impact. Since the rest of the organization is unchanged, its expectations of the changed departments remain the same even though things are done differently in the department. This sometimes results in pressure to revert back to old ways. Various vested interests in the organization have been threatened by the changes and this has led to resistance from various factions. Similar problems are likely to confront efforts to democratize work in the United States.

POLICY IMPLICATIONS

Given the experiences discussed, what are the policy implications for the United States of work-linked democracy in Sweden? Instead of attempting to answer this question globally, I will deal with the policy implications for three units in U.S. society—business, unions, and the federal government. Before I get to these implications, one general point deserves to be underscored. The Swedish business leaders who are in the forefront of efforts to democratize work are not romantic idealists interested in these efforts for humanitarian reasons. Rather, they are tough, profit-minded capitalists who view the democratization of work as a rational solution to the practical problems they face.

Traditional methods of organizing work in Sweden (for example, the assembly-line system) were proving to be inefficient. It was impossible to attract native Swedes to these jobs; turnover rates were high, as were the costs of replacing people; absenteeism and sabotage were additional problems to management. Replacing the traditional organization with work-linked democracy promised to be attractive to the Swedish workforce, to reduce turnover and the attendant costs, and to cut down on absenteeism and sabotage. Swedish management adopted work-linked democracy on rational grounds and we must assess its policy implications for the United States in the same way.

Management

On the basis of the available evidence, it would be unwise for U.S. managers to be misled by the media and adopt a policy of work democratization. There are a number of reasons for this. Of major importance is the fact that Swedish managers themselves have not adopted such a policy. Work-linked democracy is viewed by the Swedes as only part of a wide and varying range of programs needed to cope with a set of highly different problems. To Swedish businessmen, democratization may work on one problem, but an entirely different approach might be needed to cope with other problems. U.S. business leaders would be wise to follow the lead of their Swedish colleagues. If they want to experiment with work-linked democracy, let them find some specific settings in which the problems and the structure make democratization a reasonable solution.

Even in those Swedish organizations where we do find efforts at democratization (and there are many where we find no such programs), management has moved cautiously. Frequently, next to a department that has democratized are others that are operating on the basis of traditional principles. Democratization will only be extended if it works in the pilot setting, if it makes sense given the work in any given department, and if the workers in a department want it (and not all workers do). Another measure of Swedish caution, and one of particular importance to U.S. managers, is that Volvo is *not* building a Kalmar-style plant in Virginia. The company is simply not sure the U.S. workforce would accept such a work setting.

Another reason for U.S. managers to go slow is that there is no evidence in Sweden (or the United States) that a majority, or even a significant number, of workers really want democratized work. In fact, it appears that in the Swedish case, much of the initiative for democratization, at least in the cases described here, was management's and not the workers'. Swedish managers have fallen into the elitest trap of arguing that workers do not know that democracy is good for them and that what needs to be done is to educate them into accepting management's way of thinking. It is clear that there is no significant demand from U.S. workers for democratization. Furthermore, many workers may well prefer highly specialized, routinized kinds of work (Baldamus 1973). If U.S. managers are determined to democratize, it should be done in small pilot programs, and even then workers should be allowed to choose whether they want traditional or democratic work. In fact, a situation in which workers have this option is probably the ideal work setting.

U.S. managers would also be wise to go slow because of the lack of hard data in Sweden on how well these programs are working. In some cases the programs are too new to have yielded any reliable results. In many other cases, the Swedish managers seem to eschew data collection and instead rely on subjective judgments and feelings about how well work-linked democracy is functioning. Many of these judgments do not convince me, and I do not think they should convince U.S. managers. Furthermore, even if we accept the fact that these programs have been successful, they are too new to allow anyone to know what their long-term impact will be. Many observers of the Swedish workplace believe that as soon as the novelty of work-linked democracy wears off, such old problems as turnover and absenteeism will return. Before embarking on any large-scale reforms, U.S. management should wait for some long-term results.

Another set of reasons that U.S. managers should proceed cautiously arises from the different conditions that prevail in the United States and Sweden. We simply do not have many of the problems that bedeviled the Swedes. For example, we do not have the low unemployment rate that exists in Sweden. Thus, it is far easier, and cheaper, for U.S. organizations to replace workers who quit due to dissatisfaction with the nature of work. U.S. organizations do not have the same difficulties as Swedish organizations in attracting workers into traditional settings. Finally, we do not have the history of peaceful union-management relations that made it easy for Swedish managers to undertake these programs because they were sure the unions would go along. U.S. managers would not be assured of such cooperation.

Of related significance is the cultural differences between the United States and Sweden. What worked in Sweden in the early 1970s (if, indeed, it has worked) need not work in the United States in the mid- and late 1970s. There are obviously many cultural differences between the two countries, and these should be taken into account in considering whether to follow the Swedish model. Indeed, Volvo, as we have seen, in planning its Virginia plant, has been careful to adapt its structure to the U.S. scene. The structure of the Virginia plant will allow Volvo to run either a straight assembly line or democratic work groups, depending on what they find that U.S. workers want. Such caution should be emulated by U.S. managers.

There are a set of reasons that are internal to their own organizations that U.S. managers should consider in developing a policy on democratization. Managers must be willing to support such a program very vigorously. They would have to emulate the general manager of Volvo whose strong advocacy of democratization was necessary to overcome resistance from many quarters. In addition to the union, U.S. managers can also anticipate opposition from vested interests within their organization. Foremen and skilled craftsmen are likely to be particularly resistant, since many of their jobs will be eliminated. In addition, old-timers throughout the organization who are resistant to any change will certainly fight an innovation of this magnitude.

U.S. managers should realize that once such a program is set in motion, it may well have a number of unanticipated consequences. Even if it is begun in only a few departments, it may well spread rapidly, since other departments will want to be part of the innovation. New developments like this look very attractive, even if those who want it do not fully understand its significance. As in Sweden, work-linked democracy may become a self-fulfilling prophecy. Once begun by management, it may lead to a desire for it on the part of the workers, a desire that was not there in the first place. The workers may come to demand democracy, get it, but then find that they really did not want the added work and responsibility. This, by the way, was the reaction of workers from the

United States who have worked in Swedish organizations. They felt that they were being asked to work harder and take on more responsibility for no increase in pay.

Finally, U.S. managers should consider the cost of democratizing work. Is it a worthwhile investment? Might not the money be better spent on something else? It might be better to automate some of the most dismal jobs in the factory so that they can be eliminated, leaving more meaningful work for the rest. Swedish managers have plans to automate many jobs, when and if the efforts to democratize fail.

In sum, I am very doubtful that U.S. management should adopt any large-scale policy of work-linked democratization. In my view, the evidence that this is really going to improve the lot of many workers is highly dubious. Of course, U.S. managers are far more interested in higher profits than improving the lot of U.S. workers, but even here there is little evidence that democratization will lead to greater profitability.

Unions

If anything, U.S. unions should be even more cautious than management about adopting a policy of democratization. They certainly are not impelled in the direction of adopting such a policy by the demands of their members. Workers and unions seem much more concerned with the historical interests of U.S. labor-pay, job security, reduced unemployment, and so on.

Although U.S. unions will not take a public stance against democratization (such a position would be ideologically impossible), they are likely to oppose it covertly for a variety of reasons. If it comes, work-linked democracy will be a management initiative aimed at increasing the rationality of the workplace. Management, not labor, will therefore be the one to gain from this development.

One threat to the union stems from the autonomous work groups themselves. If successfully developed, they could come to be competitors to the formal union structure—competitors that could well destroy many unions that have grown distant from the needs and interests of the workers. Although we might like to see such unions destroyed, they are not going to sit idly by and allow such a development to take place.

U.S. unions may well oppose democratization because of the similarities between the modern Swedish version and the old (and hated) human relations movement. In fact, there are numerous similarities. The only thing that really sets the Swedish developments apart is the willingness to restructure the technology and even build new plants on the basis of a design that will enhance the possibility of the development of autonomous work groups. The Swedish efforts are clearly manipulative. They are surrendering only a minimal amount of power, and then only on the condition that productivity not suffer. It is a long way from true democracy, and U.S. union ideologues would do well to recognize this. This last thing Swedish (and U.S.) capitalists want is true workplace democracy. They will allow only enough democratization to increase their profitability. U.S. unionists should clearly recognize that work-linked democracy is nothing but another device to buttress the system of capitalist exploitation. Swedish management makes no bones about this: "We cannot, or will not, introduce reforms which are inimical to capitalism" (Karllson 1973:179). Ramondt observes: ". . . a striking feature of these forms of consultation is that they tend to reinforce power rather than to bring about a redistribution of power" (1973: 241).

Unions have a number of other reasons to be hesitant about adopting a prodemocratization policy. Work-linked democracy may well be used by management to speed up production, cut workers, and eliminate the union. It will adversely affect the current cozy relationships unions now have with management. Unions should be concerned about the adverse effects such changes will have on older workers who will find it hard to adapt to the new system and skilled craftsmen whose jobs will be eliminated.

Overall, U.S. unions are ill-advised to adopt a prodemocratization policy. It is loaded with dangers for unions as independent institutions as well as for the interests of the members. If true democratization of the workplace was intended by these reforms, then it might be possible to urge unions to support them, but it is clear that work-linked democracy is not designed to lead to an overall democratization of work. Indeed, it seems as if management is adopting this limited program to forestall total democratization.

Government

There is far less to be said about the U.S. government's policy toward this issue. Even in Sweden, the government played only a small role in democratization. Given the vagaries of the program, it would be wise for the government to stay out of this issue. In any case, such a development, even if it was desirable, cannot be legislated. If management decides to democratize, then the government may be drawn into the issue by, for example, the hostile reactions we can anticipate from the unions. It is not an ideal governmental role, but my guess is that it should take only a reactive role on this issue.

CONCLUSIONS

As should be clear throughout this chapter, I am at best highly ambivalent about the efforts at work-linked democracy in Sweden. We must not romanticize these efforts. The Swedes have not embarked on a program of complete democratization and humanization of work. They have rather adopted a policy of limited democracy that will forestall broader changes while increasing their profits in the short run. U.S. management, should it decide to follow the lead of the Swedes, will have similar goals in mind. It is highly doubtful that we should support limited programs that will only serve to impede the development of far more meaningful reforms in work in the United States. Swedish-style workplace democracy sounds good at first, but a careful examination indicates that it is fraught with problems.

REFERENCES

Baldamus, W. 1973. "Tedium and Traction in Industrial Work." *Men and Women in Modern Britain,* edited by David Weir. England: Fontana, pp. 78-84.

Bjork, Lars. 1975. "An Experiment in Work Satisfaction." *Scientific American* 232:17-23.

Blumberg, Paul. 1968. *Industrial Democracy: The Sociology of Participation.* New York: Schocken.

Docherty, Peter, and Bengt Stymne. 1974. "Office Worker's Participation in Organizational Development: An Experiement in a Swedish Insurance Company." Stockholm: Stockholm School of Economics.

Edgren, Jan. 1974. *With Varying Success—A Swedish Experiment in Wage Systems and Shop Floor Organization.* Stockholm: Technical Department, SAF.

U.S. Department of Health, Education and Welfare. 1973. *Work in America.* Cambridge, Mass.: MIT Press.

Karllson, Lars Erik. 1973. "Industrial Democracy in Sweden." In *Workers Control: A Reader on Labor and Social Change,* edited by Gerry Hunnius, David Garson, and John Case. New York: Vintage, pp. 176-92.

Jonsson, Berth. 1975. "Strategy towards Flexible Production Design." Paper presented at the Conference of Equilibrium Technology, Salzburg, Austria.

Mire, Joseph. 1974. "Improving Working Life—The Role of European Unions." *Monthly Labor Review* 98:3-11.

Norcross, Derek. 1974. "Sweden's Newest Export—Industrial Democracy." *Parade* (December 15):15.

Norstedt, Jan Peder, and Stefan Agurén. 1973. *The Saab-Scania Report.* Stockholm: SAF.

Ramondt, J. J. 1973. "Personnel Management and Shop Floor Consultation." *Participation and Self-Management,* vol. 4. Zagreb, Yugoslavia: Institute for Social Research.

Salpukas, Agis. 1974. "Swedish Auto Plant Drops Assembly Line." New York *Times*, November 12, p. 31.

Swedish Employers' Confederation (SAF). 1975. *Job Reform in Sweden.* Stockholm: Technical Department, Swedish Employers' Confederation.

Trist, Eric. 1974. "Work Improvement and Industrial Democracy." Paper presented to the Conference of the Commission of European Communities on "Work Organization, Technical Development and Motivation of the Individual," Brussels, Belgium.

5

COMPARATIVE IDEOLOGIES
OF POVERTY AND EQUITY:
LATIN AMERICA AND THE
UNITED STATES

Alejandro Portes
D. Frances Ferguson

> Everyone who hath will be given more; but from the man who hath not, even what he hath will be taken away.
>
> —Luke 19:26

> Under the names of the poor and the weak, the negligent, shiftless, inefficient, silly, and impudent are fastened upon the industrious and prudent as a responsibility and a duty.
>
> —William Graham Sumner

The existence of social inequalities and the need to explain their origins have been recurrent issues confronting human societies. Sociologists of the functional school, on the one hand, will classify the problem as one of integration: the need to reconcile a sense of "oneness" and solidarity in the society with the reality of vast and persistent differences in life chances. Critiques of ideologies of inequality in the Marxist tradition have stressed, on the other hand, their role as that of explaining poverty to the poor. Since Weber (1965), however, we know that these ideologies have the additional function of explicating poverty to the nonpoor. In his sociology of domination Weber noted that those in positions of well-being wish not only to enjoy their situation but to feel morally justified in doing so. To accept that one's situation is maintained only through the exploitation and suffering of others creates dissonance and promotes defection of the young, petty bourgeois intellectuals, and other potentially "charismatic" groups from the existing order (Roth 1975).

The term *ideology* is used throughout this chapter in a relatively loose manner that does not correspond to "tighter" interpretations, for example, the written ideologies of political parties and codified religious doctrine. The present use is not incompatible with Mannheim's (1966) definition of ideology as "an integrated set of ideas for systematically ordering and evaluating social reality." Still, in relation to the problem of inequality, our definition more appropriately centers on widely accepted interpretations of the origins of this situation that, in turn, has consequences for policies of the state and other political agencies toward the groups affected. This loose usage of the term, however, immediately raises two questions. First, what are the specific social loci among which these interpretations are "widely diffused?" Second, what is the relationship of such general interpretations with scientific and intellectual "theories" of inequality?

The following account of ideologies of poverty does not propose to be exhaustive of all those advanced or embraced by different groups. Rather, we focus on those interpretations that, at specific points, have gained wide acceptance among key sectors, especially intellectuals and government officials. Such ideologies generally underlie or are reflected in the policies of government during more or less extended periods; they also provide the basic framework--as a set of assumptions taken for granted—within which scientific research and learned writing on the problem take place. It should be clear, however, that an ideology labelled "dominant" in the above sense need not be understood or accepted among other social sectors, including the poor themselves.

It is by now a commonplace that dominant ideologies reflect the interests and concerns of dominant groups. Ideologies do not tend to challenge common knowledge; rather, they place different weights on its different truths. By stressing and elaborating some and neglecting others, they offer an image of society comfortable to the needs of economic and political elites.

Followers of Mannheim have pursued the argument by stressing the "abstract" character of ideological tenets that renders them impermeable to empirical evidence. This is another sense in which general ideology is said to differ from specific theories. While the evidence assembled below agrees with this basic correspondence between class and power arrangements and dominant ideologies, it also shows that such interpretations must cope with structural constraints imposed by the existing situation. Dominant groups are not entirely free in their choice of ways of justifying inequality, for ideologies of poverty must relate in plausible ways to the actual situation of the poor.

The counterpoint between different interpretations of poverty and different structural conditions has been the topic of writings in both the United States and Latin America. In each case, however, analyses tend to be limited to the particular national phenomena and use, as points of comparison, domestic historical experiences. For this reason, critical writings on "subculture of poverty" in the United States and on "marginality" in Latin America have pointed out linkages between dominant class interests and dominant ideologies of poverty but generally have failed to note the manner in which such ideologies are conditioned by the very situation they are called on to interpret.

An explicitly comparative perspective between a "central" capitalist country like the United States and the countries of Latin America is useful because it helps maximize variance along historically significant dimensions. This brings forth aspects in the development and diffusion of ideologies of poverty that are obscured when one concentrates solely on the separate experiences of each region.

More preliminary groundwork must be covered. This involves three aspects: (a) the factors conditioning reemergence of poverty as an "issue" in contemporary Latin America and the United States, (b) the theoretical range of interpretations available for the explanation of inequality, and (c) the actual conditions of poverty requiring interpretation.

THE ISSUE OF POVERTY

There has always been poverty, but the problem of explaining inequality has not always possessed the same urgency. For extensive periods in the history of the United States and Latin America poverty faded from public consciousness as the poor themselves disappeared into an "invisible landscape" (Hardoy 1972a). It can be argued that the characteristic of properly legitimized social systems is precisely the reduction of inequality to the status of a nonissue. It is the function of dominant ideologies of inequality to transform these differences between men from contingencies into historical necessities that become progressively more acceptable to rich and poor alike.

It would be presumptuous to attempt here a systematic account of all the factors that could lead to reappearance of the poor in the visible landscape. Nevertheless, a general and perhaps obvious guiding principle is that poverty becomes an issue when objective circumstances render previous interpretations increasingly untenable. Such ideological "breakdown" means that dominant viewpoints become unconvincing to important sectors, including elites and the poor themselves.

The United States and Latin America share two important parallels in regard to this general issue. One has to do with the ideological heritage that legitimized inequality before the onset of the contemporary situation. The other refers to structural developments that account for the current reemergence of poverty as a problem. In this section we outline both trends, for they constitute a common framework within which specific ideological developments must be understood.

The Ideological Heritage

Both regions of the Americas inherited a set of ideas grounded on the European experience with feudalism and Christianity and its subsequent transformation into a capitalist-industrial order. From Europe flowed two ideological themes that were to have an impact in the new societies from colonial days to the present.

The first is identified with the notions of hierarchical order and "life destiny." The ideology, dominant throughout Europe in feudal times and extending in most nations well into the eighteenth century, conceived a stable society in which individuals had preordained places. Such "mandated" positions had transcendental roots and hence were to be accepted with humility, regardless of whether they entailed a situation of super- or subordination. The existence of the poor was in the nature of things. The poor raised themselves in the eyes of society and of God not by climbing to higher positions, but by fulfilling their mandated tasks. The Catholic ideology did not preach mere resignation by the weak and humble; rather, it preached positive fulfillment and rejoicing for the proper behavior in one's life destiny.

The wealthy and powerful were enjoined to be charitable and protective toward the weak, but violation of this prescription did not justify disobedience by the latter. Society, as a stable pyramid of authority and honor, reproduced the order of heaven; positions in it were filled by family inheritance rather than by individual achievement. Questioning poverty would be no less absurd than questioning wealth since both were necessary parts of a transcendental design. While the poor could aspire to improvements in their situation, attempting to break out from it or attacking those in positions of power was a breach against divine law.

The "Iberic" heritage of Latin America is often described in terms that reproduce the above conceptions of society (cf. Vivas 1945; Ramos 1963; Anderson 1967). It is true that these tenets constituted the earlier dominant interpretation of inequality in the region. But while it can be accepted that such ideology became more important in Spanish- than in British-colonized territories, its role in the latter was by no means insignificant. At the very least, the ideas of preordained social strata and of birth-determined life destinies permeated the justifications for exploitation of nonwhite races both in the pre- and postslavery periods (Warner and Srole 1945; Greeley 1971; Blauner 1972).

The second, and better known, common theme arose in the nineteenth century as the need grew to justify early industrial capitalism. It revolved around the notions of the ultimate benefits of free markets and the evolutionary requirement of selection. The first notion dated back to classic economics and evolved around the more humanitarian view that, in the long-run, operations of the market would yield the greatest benefit for the greatest number. The second notion, usually tied to Spencerian sociology, fitted better the harshness of the era: Unlike earlier Catholic ideologies of inequality, which did not explain poverty by blaming something or someone, poverty in the new laissez-faire society was squarely blamed on the poor.

Our epigraph from William Graham Sumner reflects the thoughts on the matter of an entire generation of British and U.S. scholars. The tenets of this new ideology—evolutionary selection, survival of the fittest, organicism, and so on—are sufficiently well known to deserve further comment. As will be seen, the style they initiated, that of placing responsibility for injustice on its victims has persisted up to the present time.

Writers on poverty in the United States have identified this conception of the "undeserving poor" with the rise of industrial capitalism in the "core" or central countries (Rainwater 1967; Wachtel 1973). This represents the same shortcoming, in reverse, as that of writers on the "Iberic" corporatist heritage. While it is true that laissez-faire ideologies became dominant during the development of the United States and other central industrial nations, they were by no means unknown in Latin America. Students of nineteenth century ideologies in the region (Izquierdo 1968) and observers of more recent trends (Hirschman 1961) can attest to the importance that this doctrine has had as Latin American elites attempted to integrate into a changing world situation and move away from the earlier Catholic feudal *weltanschauung.*

Reemergence of Poverty as a Problem

The rediscovery of poverty in Latin America and the United States after the mid-twentieth century is associated with similar processes of rural-urban migration. This is not to say that cities in both regions had not known migration in the past. Internal migration to Spanish-American cities had existed since the late sixteenth century; in fact, reception patterns that had crystallized in earlier periods provided definite continuity to those confronting migrants in the twentieth century (Portes and Walton 1976). Nevertheless, until the mid-nineteenth century, landowners throughout Latin America appeared sufficiently strong to hold the rural poor to the land and even to force a relative net "ruralization" of the population in many countries (Morse 1975). In the United States coastal cities were, of course, well-acquainted with the phenomenon of immigration and in time became net exporters of labor in the form of would-be homesteaders to the rural periphery (Rothstein 1966).

Despite the "select" character of migrants relative to the original populations and other nuances uncovered by recent demographic research (cf. Balan et al. 1973), the basic fact remains that contemporary internal migration represents a massive transfer of poverty from rural and quasi-urban areas to major cities. Formal similarities with previous internal migrations and the experiences of foreign immigrants should not hide the fact that contemporary population shifts in the two parts of the continent represent a truly unique structural transformation.

For our purposes, what the process has mainly accomplished is concentration in a restricted, highly visible space of a previously dispersed population. Marx (1967 ed.) and later theorists (Lipset 1963; Arendt 1965) have noted the dual importance that numbers and density have in promoting consciousness of an objective structural situation. Concentration in the city not only promotes awareness among impoverished masses of a common life situation; it also creates "consciousness" among intellectuals, officials, and other elites of the existence of the poor.

Poverty reemerges as a social issue in the city because it is there that it acquires sufficient visibility to burst into public consciousness and there that it has sufficient permanence to stay visible. Rural poverty, no matter how abysmal, is too dispersed to challenge dominant interpretations. Massive migration of the poor means the impossibility of dispersal and hence the eventual concentration and partial control by these groups over neglected urban areas. These "cities of the poor"—inner-city slums and "barrios" in the United States, squatter settlements, "conventillos," "mesones," and the like in Latin America—constitute a highly visible and permanent feature of the urban landscape that confronts society with evidence of its own contradictions.

There is an additional common feature of internal migration relevant to the nature of emerging interpretations of poverty. The class distinctiveness of migrants in both regions is reinforced by other accidental characteristics. In the United States, the migrant and the poor have overwhelmingly been the native Southern blacks, Spanish-speaking blacks and mulatto Puerto Ricans, and the Spanish-speaking mestizo Mexicans. The class issue of poverty has become inseparable from the ethnic issues of skin color, language, and culture. That the poor are also the nonwhite and the Spanish-speaking have both enhanced their visibility and reinforced the barriers and estrangement from established urban quarters.

In Latin America absolute levels of misery are reflected in the outward characteristics of the poor: barefoot children, ragged clothing, the low stature and physical deterioration caused by malnutrition. Race, though perhaps less salient than in the United States, has also been important in many countries. Association of poverty with the "cholos" in Peru, the "negros" in the Colombian coast, or the "cabecitas negras" in Buenos Aires reproduce the linkage between class and color and reinforce the separateness of the poor from elites and middle urban groups (Solaun and Kronus 1973).

Physical density and increased visibility set the stage during several decades, but they did not suffice for the emergence of poverty as an "issue."

It is impossible to systematize all "accelerating factors" leading to this outcome into a set of neat theoretical categories. The passage of the poor from invisibility to a relatively central social stage is not a sudden event but a cumulative process of confrontation, reaction, and compromise. In the United States the populist marches and protests of black and other racially based movements and, especially, the urban ghetto explosions of the 1960s played the decisive role in focusing public attention on the plight of the poor (Turner 1969).

In Latin America, the process has been, if anything, more complicated. It has involved, among others, the alarm spread by journalists, demographers, and others at the size of urban-bound migration; widespread land invasions and the consequent partial breakdown of capitalist, regulated land markets; public pronouncements and agitation by political parties, such as the MIR and the Communists in Chile, ANAPO in Colombia, the Odria and Apra organizations in Peru, and the different splits of the Justicialista movement in Argentina; demand making and public protests by organizations of the poor themselves, such as the now extinct Federation of Favela Dwellers (FAFEGH) in Brazil (A. Leeds 1974) and the National Association of Land Invaders in Colombia (Hardoy 1975); the often decisive electoral power brought to bear by favelas, barriadas, and poblaciones in local and state elections, and their growing impact on national ones (E. Leeds 1972; Cornelius 1975).

Poverty as a reemerging concern brings about a critical examination of previous theories and an urgent search for new interpretations and policies adapted to the new public mood. The range of contemporary ideologies and the situations they are called on to interpret are discussed next.

STRUCTURAL CONSTRAINTS

The demise of magical and religious explanations has left accredited "scientific" theories as the major source of legitimation for new ideologies. Within this context, we find a third feature common to the United States and Latin America: In both areas recent interpretations of poverty have ranged along the same ideal-typical continuum. At one extreme, causes of poverty are attributed to features characteristic of the poor. Such interpretation has two major variants: (a) ideologies that trace the origins of poverty to individual shortcomings and (b) those that assign blame to the collective style of life or "subculture" in which the poor must live.

At the opposite extreme stand those who define poverty as a consequence of existing arrangements of power and resource distribution. Such structural interpretations also have two subtypes: (a) "mild" viewpoints, which describe poverty as an unnecessary product of social neglect, a "dysfunction" in an otherwise viable system, and (b) "full" structural interpretations, which define poverty as intrinsic and necessary for maintenance of the existing social order.

The applicability and effectiveness of different ideologies of inequality is not independent from the situation in which they are advanced. Similarities between the United States and Latin America end here, for while the former and most of the latter are part of the same capitalist "world economy" (Wallerstein 1974), their forms of integration into it are very different. The purpose of this section is to outline the major differences as a necessary prelude to discussion of ideological trends. There is no possibility or intention of documenting in detail the characteristics of poverty in the United States and Latin America. The data presented below serve rather as illustration and reminder of trends already documented by the specialized literature in the field. The differences to which we wish to call attention are of two types: (a) regarding the numbers of those characterized as poor and (b) regarding the life conditions encompassed by the term.

Number of Poor in the United States and Latin America

Poverty in the United States, especially urban poverty, is a quantitatively limited phenomenon. Available census data show that the proportion of individuals and families below the official poverty level represents a relatively small percentage of the urban (metropolitan) population. The data presented in Table 5.1 indicate, for example, that the percentage of families below the poverty line at the time of the last census did not exceed 10 percent in any of the 20 largest U.S. metropolitan areas. Percentages ranged from a high of 9.8 in Houston to a low of 4.6 in Minneapolis-St. Paul. The unweighted average was 7.16 of urban families living in poverty, as defined. Even allowing for the usual underestimation in official statistics, a situation of poverty can not be said to exceed, in any case, one-fifth of the urban population.

Not only are the poor fewer than the nonpoor, but they are perceived as such by both defenders and detractors of the existing order. That the poor can be labeled "minorities" represents a definite symbolic advantage for those interested in preservation of the status quo. Critics, on the other hand, have repeatedly stressed the theme of the injustice done to these minorities when denied access to what is considered normal and decent by the rest of the population. Urban poverty in the United States is generally perceived as an "enclave" phenomenon—sizable but isolated groups—in the midst of a relatively affluent society.

No such perception of urban poverty can be plausibly advanced in most of Latin America. Table 5.2 presents estimates of the size of the urban settlements, inner-city slums, and other precarious dwelling arrangements in Latin America. These residential estimates tend to underestimate the magnitude of the phenomenon, because while most individuals living in these areas can be safely assumed to be poor, many others live in more "respectable" quarters and hence are less easily identified (A. Leeds 1974). Even taking present estimates at

TABLE 5.1

Percent of Poor Families in 20 Largest U.S. Cities, 1969

City (SMSA)	Percent of Families below Low-Income Level*
1. New York, N.Y.	9.3
2. Los Angeles-Long Beach	8.2
3. Chicago	6.8
4. Philadelphia	7.3
5. Detroit	6.5
6. San Francisco-Oakland	7.2
7. Washington, D.C.	6.1
8. Boston	6.1
9. Pittsburgh	7.2
10. St. Louis	8.1
11. Baltimore	8.5
12. Cleveland	6.9
13. Houston	9.8
14. Newark	6.8
15. Minneapolis-St. Paul	4.6
16. Dallas	8.6
17. Seattle-Everett	5.2
18. Anaheim-Santa Ana-Garden Grove	5.2
19. Milwaukee	5.7
20. Atlanta	9.1

*Low-income level for a nonfarm family of four, male-headed, was $3745 per year in 1969.

Source: U.S. Bureau of the Census, *City and Country Data Book*, Washington, D.C.: U.S. Government Printing Office, 1972.

face value, we find that from 20 to 80 percent of the relevant urban populations are poor. On the basis of these figures and the accounts of knowledgeable researchers, we estimate that poverty in its diverse forms comprises more than half the population in most primary as well as secondary cities.

Such poverty does not easily tolerate definition as an "enclave" phenomenon. Even when limited to highly visible slum compounds and precarious squatter settlements, their extension throughout the city core and especially the urban periphery negates every definition as an "exceptional" or isolated problem in an otherwise established population.

TABLE 5.2

Numerical Estimates of the Urban Poor in Latin America

Source	City or Country	Year	Relevant Figure
ECLA I	Arequipa	1961	40 percent of the city's population living in barriadas
Labadia Caufriez	Brasilia	1969	200,000 persons, or 50 percent of the city's population, living in favelas
ECLA I	Buenaventura	–	80 percent of the city's population living in tugurios
Ministry of Public Health	Buenos Aires	1965	423,824 persons in the metropolitan area (central city excluded) living in villas miseria
Abrams	Cali	1962	30 percent of the city's population living in barrios de invasion
Abrams	Caracas	1962	Rancho inhabitants numbered 263,000 according to official figures. Unofficial estimates put the number at 400,000, or 35 percent of the city's population
ECLA II	Chile	1960	321,863 dwellings with a total population of 1,507,841 in urban marginal areas. These figures represent 34.3 percent of the dwellings and 31.1 percent of the urban population
ECLA I	Chimbote	1961	70 percent of the city's population living in barriadas
Presidency of the Republic	Iquitos	1968	64.7 percent of the city's population living in barriadas
Rosenbluth	Lima	1960	394,263 persons or 24.43 percent of the city's population living in 154 barriadas
ECLA I	Lima	1961	21 percent of the metropolitan population living in barriadas
DESAL I	Lima	1961	21 percent of the metropolitan population living in barriadas
Abrams	Maracaibo	1962	50 percent of the city's population living in marginal settlements

(continued)

(Table 5.2 continued)

Source	City or Country	Year	Relevant Figure
Turner	Mexico City	1965 (approx.)	1.5 million people, or approximately one-third of the city's population, living in colonias proletarias or barrios paracaidistas
Harth Deneke	Mexico City	1966	2 million people living in colonias proletarias. By 1970 the colonias would cover 40 percent of the area of the Federal District
Presidency of the Republic	Peru	1967	804,878 persons, or 24.1 percent of the population in 11 major cities, living in barriadas
ECLA I	Recife	1961	50 percent of the city's population living in favelas
ECLA I	Rio de Janeiro	1961	900,000, or 38 percent of the city's population, living in favelas
Gonzalez Polio	San Salvador	1974	66 percent of the metropolitan population living in mesones, tugurios, and colonias ilegales
ECLA III	Santiago	1960	135,150 "irregular" or marginal dwellings with total population of 633,856. These figures represent 33 percent of dwellings in the metropolitan area and 29.8 percent of its population.
Abrams	Santiago	1962	25 percent of the metropolitan population living in marginal settlements
Rosenbluth	Santiago	1962	120,000 persons, or 18 percent of Santiago's municipal population, living in a single settlement: the Jose Maria Caro area
ECLA I	Uruguay	1963	30,000 urban dwellings in conventillos, cantegriles, and rancherios with a total of 100,000 inhabitants
ECLA II	Venezuela	1960	34.6 percent of the urban population living in ranchos

Sources for Table 5.2

Abrams, Charles. 1965. *Squatter Settlements: The Problem and the Opportunity.* New York: AID.

Cuevas, Marco Antonio. 1965. *Analisis de Tres Areas Marginales de la Ciudad de Guatemala.* Guatemala City: Ministerio de Educacion.

DESAL (Center for Social and Economic Development of Latin America) I. 1969. *Marginalidad en America Latina.* Barcelona: Herder. Ch. 2.

DESAL II. 1968. "Encuesta sobre Familia y Fecundidad en Poblaciones Marginales del Gran Santiago," vol. 1. Santiago. Mimeographed.

ECLA (United Nations Economic Commission for Latin America) I. 1969. Report to the First Pan-American Conference on Population, Cali, 1965. Reported in Luis M. Morea, "Vivienda y Equipamiento Urbano." In *La Urbanizacion en America Latina,* edited by Jorge E. Hardoy and Carlos Tobar.

ECLA II. 1965. "La Participacion de la Poblaciones Marginales en el Crecimiento Urbano." Santiago. Mimeographed.

ECLA III. 1965. "Los Servicios Publicos en una Poblacion de Erradicacion." Santiago. Mimeographed.

Gonzalez Polio, Egardo. 1974. "Informe Preliminar sobre la Situacion de la Poblacion Urbana Marginada de El Salvador." San Salvador: Fundacion Salvadorena de Desarrollo y Vivienda Minima. Unpublished document.

Harth Deneke, Jorge. 1966. "The Colonias Proletarias of Mexico City: Low Income Settlements on the Urban Fringe." Master's Thesis, Department of City Planning, Massachusetts Institute of Technology, Cambridge, Mass.

Labadia Caufriez, Antonio. 1972. "Operacion Sitio: A Housing Solution for Progressive Growth." In *Latin American Urban Research,* vol. 2, edited by Guillermo Geisse and Jorge E. Hardoy. Beverly Hills, Calif.: Sage, p. 203.

Ministry of Public Health. 1965. *Diagnostico Sanitario Aglomerado Bonaerense.* Buenos Aires. Quoted in Carlos Tobar, "The Argentine National Plan for Eradicating Villas de Emergencia." In *Latin American Urban Research,* vol. 2, edited by Guillermo Geisse and Jorge E. Hardoy. Beverly Hills, Calif.: Sage, 1972, p. 226.

Presidency of the Republic, Oficina Nacional de Desarrollo de Pueblos Jovenes. *Incidencia de la Urbanizacion Acelerada en Ciudades con Poblaciones de 25000 y mas Habitantes.* Quoted in Jorge E. Hardoy, "Urbanization Policies and Urban Reform in Latin America." In *Latin American Urban Research,* vol. 2, edited by Guillermo Geisse and Jorge E. Hardoy. Beverly Hills, Calif.: Sage, 1972, p. 35.

Rosenbluth, Guillermo. 1962. "Problemas Socio-economicos de la Marginalidad y la Integracion Urbana." Santiago, University of Chile. Mimeographed.

Turner, John F. C. 1968. "Uncontrolled Urban Settlement: Problems and Policies." *International Social Development Review* (UN), no. 1:107-30.

Life Conditions of Poor in United States
and Latin America

Differences in the nature of poverty are also qualitative. That the poor in Latin America live worse than the poor in the United States is a generally accepted fact. It is convenient, however, to examine briefly the magnitude and character of these differences. The data to be presented compare nations as a whole rather than urban areas. Reasons for this are twofold: First, national data are generally more available than data on individual cities; second, while poverty is rediscovered in cities, the issue tends to carry to a concern with all forms of poverty, rural ones included. For this reason, no ideology of inequality is strictly limited to its urban forms, but rather attempts to explain it as a global issue.

Table 5.3 presents recent data on GNP per capita for the U.S. and Latin American countries and its distribution. As of 1973, the U.S. per capita GNP stood at U.S.$5829, a figure more than nine times larger than that of Latin America as a whole (U.S.$620). Individual country comparisons ranged from five times the GNP of Argentina and Venezuela to more than 50 times that of Haiti. More than aggregate economic levels, what is of interest for present purposes is their distribution. The data illustrate the greater inequality with which already scarce resources are distributed in Latin America. Whereas in the United States the richest 5 percent of the population appropriates 16 percent of total income, available figures in Latin America range from 18 percent (Uruguay) to 36 percent (Brazil and Honduras), with most countries doubling the U.S. figure.

Similar conclusions emerge if the top 20 percent of the population is considered. The U.S. population in this bracket receives 41.4 percent of total income; comparable data for Latin America range from 47 percent (Uruguay) to 74 percent (Ecuador). At the other end of the distribution, no Latin American country exceeds the 5 percent of total income received by the bottom 20 percent of the U.S. population, nor the 17 percent received by the bottom 40 percent. Such differences are reflected in the independently computed Gini indexes of inequality (Table 5.3).

The data in Table 5.4 make these differences more apparent. In 1970 14 percent of the U.S. population was defined to have incomes below the poverty line; their approximate yearly per capita income was $500. By this definition the vast majority of Latin American populations would be considered poor. Adopting a more appropriate standard for the region, a recent UN study defined poverty in Latin America as comprising yearly incomes below U.S.$75 per capita. By this definition (less than one-sixth the mean poverty income for the United States) still 9 percent (Costa Rica) to 38 percent (Honduras) of the population in Latin American countries is poor. For most countries for which data are available, the percentage of the population at this level of poverty clearly exceeds that of the United States at a much higher yearly income.

TABLE 5.3

GNP per Capita and Its Distribution
in the United States and Latin America

Country	GNP per Capita 1973[a] (1972 dollars)	Income Shared Received by Population (percent)[b]				Gini Index of Income Inequality[c]
		Poorest 20 percent	Poorest 40 percent	Top 20 percent	Top 5 percent	
United States	5829	5.4	17.3	41.4	15.9	12.2
Argentina	1138	–	–	–	–	15.7
Bolivia	199	–	–	–	–	–
Brazil	539	3	12	63	36	36.4
Chile	792	5	15	56	30	37.1
Colombia	364	4	12	60	33	–
Costa Rica	638	–	12	59	–	29.3
Cuba	716	–	–	–	–	–
Dominican Republic	420	–	–	–	–	–
Ecuador	335	–	7	74	–	–
El Salvador	305	–	11	52	–	37.4
Guatemala	405	–	–	–	–	48.8
Haiti	116	–	–	–	–	–
Honduras	277	3	8	68	36	33.0
Mexico	774	4	14	57	29	–
Nicaragua	470	–	–	–	–	–
Panama	930	–	9	59	–	–
Paraguay	327	5	10	62	30	31.9
Peru	548	2	11	60	34	39.8
Uruguay	850	4	18	47	18	14.5
Venezuela	1290	–	8	65	–	48.7
Latin America	620					

[a]*Source:* U.S. Department of State, *World Military Expenditures and Arms Trade 1963-1973*, U.S. Arms Control and Disarmament Agency Publication no. 74, (Washington, D.C.: Government Printing Office, 1974).

[b]*Sources:* U.S. Bureau of the Census, *Current Population Reports,* series P-60, no. 400; United Nations, *1974 Report on the World Social Situation—Social Trends in the Developing Countries, Latin America and the Caribbean,* U.N. Document E/CN.5/512/Add. 1, 1974. Data are for years ranging from 1967 to 1972. Figures are approximate, since definitions of the total universe vary from country to country and with sources.

[c]*Source:* C. Taylor and M. Hudson, *World Handbook of Political and Social Indicators* (New Haven, Conn.: Yale University Press). Data are for years ranging from 1960 to 1965.

TABLE 5.4

Poverty Status of the Population, United States and Latin America (U.S. dollars)

Country	Mean per Capita Income of the Poor	Percent of the Population
United States, 1970	498.00	13.7
Latin America, 1969	<75	17
Brazil	<75	20
Colombia	<75	27
Costa Rica	<75	9
Ecuador	<75	59
El Salvador	<75	18
Honduras	<75	38
Mexico	<75	18
Panama	<75	11
Peru	<75	26

Note: U.S. figures were calculated by dividing mean income of families below poverty level by their average size. In comparison with figures for unattached individuals, these figures are a conservative (low) estimate of the mean income of the poor.

Sources: U.S. Census Bureau, *Summary of the 1970 Census,* Table 106; United Nations, *1974 Report on the World Social Situation—Social Trends in the Developing Countries, Latin America and the Caribbean,* U.N. Document E/CN.5/512/Add.1, 1974.

The meaning of these income differences becomes clearer when translated into data on nutrition, health, infant mortality, and other standard-of-living indicators. Data in Table 5.5 present nutritional indicators for the United States and Latin America. Taking a figure of 2750 calories per day as adequate intake, we find that available per capita calories in the United States far exceed this figure, but that in Latin America only Argentina and Uruguay exceed it. Other countries fall below the norm, with figures ranging from 2730 in Paraguay to 1760 in Bolivia. Note that these data represent average caloric availability, including consumption by middle- and upper-income sectors. Since nutrition reflects, at least in part, the profound inequalities in income detected above, the caloric intake in the poorer sectors should be considerably below these inadequate averages. Similar results emerge when protein consumption is considered.

Recent data on infant mortality documents some consequences of the above differences. Deaths per 1000 children under one year of age were 20.1

for the United States in 1970. This rate is more than doubled in Uruguay (42.6) and Venezuela (48.7), tripled in Costa Rica (61.5) and El Salvador (66.7), and quadrupled in Chile (78.8) and Guatemala (87.1) (UN 1973).

The meaning of poverty in Latin American countries is given both by absolute difficulties in food, health, and other living conditions and by the insecurity in which most workers find themselves. Aside from kinship and other informal networks (Lomnitz 1974), the situation is one of abandonment of most of the working population by public and private social security systems. Relevant data are presented in Table 5.6. While in the United States close to 90 percent of the economically active population is covered by social security, in Latin America only Chile, Argentina, and Uruguay exceed half this figure. The dismal situation in this area is punctuated by figures for Haiti (1.0 percent), Honduras (4.8 percent), Bolivia (8.4 percent), Paraguay (9.6 percent), and the Dominican Republic (9.7 percent). Even relatively "advanced" countries like

TABLE 5.5

Nutritional Indicators for the United States and Latin America

Country	Available Calories per Capita per Day	Available Proteins (grams) per Capita per Day
United States	3290	97
Argentina	3170	103
Bolivia	1760	46
Brazil	2540	63
Chile	2520	65
Colombia	2190	50
Costa Rica	2230	56
Dominican Republic	2080	46
El Salvador	1880	47
Guatemala	1950	49
Honduras	1930	49
Paraguay	2730	68
Peru	2200	52
Uruguay	3020	106
Venezuela	2490	66

Note: Average daily caloric requirements: 3200 for males, 2300 for females. Average daily protein requirement: 60 grams. Figures recommended by UN Food and Agriculture Organization. (See FAO, Nutritional Studies no. 15, 1957.) Figures were later reviewed and approved as accurate by Joint FAO/World Health Organization Expert Committee on Nutrition. (See FAO/WHO Technical Report Series no. 377, 1960.)

Source: United Nations, Statistical Yearbook, 1971. Data are given for 1966-69.

TABLE 5.6

Social Security Coverage in Latin America
and the United States, 1969

Country	Percent of Economically Active Population Covered by Social Security
United States	89.4
Argentina	67.6
Bolivia	8.4
Brazil	31.4
Colombia	14.4
Costa Rica	37.4
Chile	67.5
Dominican Republic	9.7
Ecuador	16.1
El Salvador	10.2
Guatemala	29.4
Haiti	1.0
Honduras	4.8
Mexico	20.9
Nicaragua	14.9
Panama	34.3
Paraguay	9.6
Peru	27.8
Venezuela	22.9

Sources: Statistical Abstracts of the United States, 1974; Economic Commission for Latin America, *Economic Survey of Latin America 1973*, Part 3, United Nations Document E/CN.12/974/Add.3, 1974. U.S. data refer to population covered by OASDHI. Latin American data refer to population contributing to security systems that cover major risks.

Mexico, Brazil, and Venezuela do not have one-third of their economically active population covered by social security.*

---

*A recent detailed study of security systems in Peru demonstrates how existing arrangements contribute to increase rather than meliorate the gap between relatively privileged groups and the masses of the poor. Thus, while the military, government officials, and white-collar employees are 100-percent protected by social security, only half the workers are. Independent workers and family workers without pay (which exceed the combined number of white- and blue-collar workers) are only covered from 2 to 10 percent. The author concludes: "Workers with the best social security protection are the ones which least need it, while those that need it the most, lack access to it" (Mesa-Lago 1973:24).

The data summarized in this section should bring forth differences between a relative level of poverty and one defined by basic issues of survival. To call poverty "relative" in the United States is not to dismiss the human suffering and frustration that this situation entails. It is rather to note that the problem in this case takes, as point of reference, the high living standards of the majority. Having transcended for the most part the problem of survival, poverty in the United States is defined essentially by the issue of inequality. It is the deprivation of lacking access to what is considered "normal" by the dominant standards of the society.

In Latin America, by contrast, what is "normal" is frequently to be poor, and the problem of poverty takes its meaning less from relative inequalities than from requirements for the preservation of life. This will be termed *absolute* poverty, though it should be clear that all such definitions are also relative to consenually held values. In the contemporary world, the term *absolute* is applicable to a situation in which workers earn less than what is necessary to provide for basic necessities, in which significant proportions of children die prematurely or are permanently damaged by malnutrition, and in which most of the economically active population is excluded from access to minimal social protection in times of need.

The above sketch of enclave versus widespread conditions of urban poverty and of poverty defined by relative inequality versus absolute need can only be taken as an approximation to empirical reality. Inevitably, it represents an abstraction from actual situations that frequently depart from such traits. Still, the fundamental cleavage that these concepts attempt to capture is one to which ideological interpretations must respond. Having covered the necessary background of concepts, we can now examine the interplay between types of poverty and types of interpretations of poverty—structural traits and cultural themes.

U.S. IDEOLOGIES

Social Darwinism during the nineteenth and beginnings of the twentieth century was reinforced by its "scientific" explanation of poverty by a gestalt of cultural and structural features that contributed to its stability. In a society where hard work and diligence were expected to reward the individual, those who remained poor were found to be in violation of societal values. Hence, to the evolutionary necessity of their eventual disappearance was added the moral scorn of a society that saw them as inferior and undeserving.

Structurally, the most visible enclaves of poverty in major cities were those composed of immigrants. Immigrant groups, especially those from Eastern and Southern Europe, were regarded as racially inferior. This inferiority accounted for their situation, an argument which fitted neatly with "survival of the fittest" interpretations. In addition, whatever sense of social responsibility existed toward the poor was diluted in this case by the very foreignness of these groups.

As newcomers, they did not possess a "claim" against the society (Handlin 1951; Warner and Srole 1945). Their decision to come was assumed to be a free one and to entail acceptance of whatever life conditions were found in the land (Gordon 1964).

The policy toward poverty flowing out of social Darwinism and Calvinist moralism was essentially no policy at all. Still the landscape of social action was not entirely barren. A philosophy of private charity—paternalism and good works—gained impulse from populist and progressive movements' attacks on unrestricted laissez-faire (James 1972). With some misgivings, states had begun to legislate rudimentary welfare programs. Workmen's compensation was the most widespread welfare measure, with all but four states having enacted appropriate legislation by 1929 (Cohen 1970).

Still, the major characteristics of policies toward the poor in this period are the lack of involvement of the federal government to any significant extent in welfare programs and the domination of the field by private and philanthropic interests. As evidenced by such efforts as the Charity Organization Societies and, in part, the Settlement House movement, private initiatives reflected well the spirit of the era: the need for "improving the indigent's moral standards, removing him from the influence of depraved family life, and subjecting him to the knowledge and counseling skill of an experience worker or skilled upper-class volunteer" (Kravitz 1969:53).

From such beginnings, ideologies of inequality and related policies have evolved during the past four decades. Poverty as a social issue in the United States and concomitant ideologies have followed a characteristic cycle during this century. In essence, individualistic and culturalistic interpretations are rendered periodically untenable by sudden, quasi-cataclysmic events. At these points, structural interpretations come to the fore, with milder versions becoming dominant. These portray the situation as a temporary crisis in a basically viable system. The problem is approached in a matter-of-fact fashion with solutions defined as "adjustments" rather than as transformations of the existing order. Once the crisis is over, either because remedial measures worked or because purely accidental factors intervened, the earlier viewpoints reemerge. Arguments are, of course, never the same; rather, they are modified to accord with the latest scientific fashion.

The perennial return to characteristics of the poor as explanations of inequality evidences an "exceptionalist" cultural approach toward the problem. Reflecting the structural characteristics of "enclave" poverty, such an approach views the condition in normal times as happening "to specifically-defined categories of persons in an unpredictable manner. . . . Their problems are unusual, even unique; they are exceptions to the rule, they occur as a result of individual defect, accident, or unfortunate circumstance" (Ryan 1971:17).

The first major structural confrontation to challenge such views in this century was the Great Depression. The rhetoric of laissez-faire and of undeserving (usually foreign) poor died through exposure to masses of well-bred Americans thrown out of work through no apparent fault of their own. The New Deal marked the first massive intervention of the federal government in the field of individual and family welfare. Policies of the new Keynesian state were to insure the permanence of such intervention through regular artificial injections of demand and routine federal aid to certain categories of the poor.

New Deal policies explicitly recognized that there was more to poverty than the demerits of the poor. Something was wrong with the existing social and economic structure and, hence, there was a need for significant readjustments. Yet the Keynesian state was still capitalist and, hence, carried certain obligations toward dominant groups. One of them was to insure industrial labor discipline and a continuous work incentive among the labor force. This created a dilemma: While unemployment was now acknowledged to have structural causes, the unemployed could not be so legitimatized and economically rewarded as to lose the drive to engage in low-paying occupations (Rainwater 1967).

The dilemma is apparent in the ideologies of poverty and related welfare programs that emerged after the crisis period. Poverty could no longer be attributed to immorality and negligence, but at the same time it could not be defined as a permanent and widespread consequence of capitalism. The latter alternative would have implied either the need of drastic structural transformation or the requirement that the government subsidize all the poor in an adequate and permanent basis.

The solution was accomplished by redefining the boundaries of poverty. Whereas previously all poverty had been, in some sense, "deserved," under the new interpretation two kinds were recognized. Undeserved poverty, due to causes over which victims had no control, involved two categories: (a) the permanently handicapped, such as the old, the blind, and the disabled and (b) the temporarily unemployed, victims of cyclical economic downturns.

Poverty with legitimate claim to state aid thus involved a relatively small sector of the population on a permanent basis and a potentially much broader sector on a temporary basis. It did not involve the category of the nonhandicapped and the long-term unemployed, who were still left in the second kind of "deserved poverty" and out of protection from the government.

This arrangement was translated into policy in the Social Security Act of 1935 and its subsequent amendments. The act subsumed two sets of provisions: (a) a program of social insurance benefits, according to which workers earn the right to old-age pensions and unemployment compensation purchased with their own contributions, and (b) public assistance for groups designated as needy, for example, dependent children, the blind, and the handicapped. Neither program was aimed at the "hard-core" unemployed, but rather at workers subject to spells of enforced idleness and at "deserving unemployables." Moreover, in both cases, assistance was generally limited to a minimal income (Levitan 1969).

The ideology and related policies of the New Deal proved effective for the following 25 years; they accomplished, at once, three goals. First, they provided renewed legitimacy to existing inequalities by bring involuntary victims under the protective wing of government while denying it to "undeserving" individuals. Second, they made it fiscally feasible for government to assume its new role by limiting it to short-term emergency periods and to the permanent protection of relatively small numbers. Third, they preserved the work incentive among the labor force by penalizing long-term unemployment. This included both the hard-core unemployed and those currently employed, but subject to the threat of temporary compensation if work was lost.

Roughly until the end of the 1950s, New Deal policies and World War II had effectively pushed poverty back to the status of a nonissue. We have noted the role that massive urban-bound migration played in the public rediscovery of poverty. For other urban sectors, the new enclaves of the poor posed the dilemma of a phenomenon that was both increasingly visible and increasingly foreign: a population whose social remoteness increased with physical nearness. In time, these new enclaves also took an active part in challenging established views via political protests and open confrontations.

The "new" poor did not fit neatly into categories inherited from the New Deal. Their significance in relation to the latter's ideology of inequality was this: They made obvious how large the category of the "undeserving poor" could be. Far from being a deviant sector, the poor who were not handicapped and were not temporarily unemployed comprised a significant portion of the population. They made clear, moreover, that one need not be unemployed to be poor in U.S. society—an insight that, though obvious at present, did not form part of the New Deal's interpretive categories. The marginally employed—menial and unskilled workers—formed the core of the new enclaves of poverty. The dichotomy, employed/unemployed, thus ceased to suffice as a framework for dealing with the problem.

The history of ideologies of poverty in the United States since the early 1960s and its policy implications is essentially the history of a second encounter between forces that advocate a mild structural interpretation of inequality and those that propose a refurbished way of blaming poverty on the poor. As during the first encounter in post-Depression days, the latter interpretation has emerged dominant after the initial crisis and threats subsided. "Break the cycle of poverty" and "Power to the People" have stood as the two apparently nonantagonistic rallying cries during this period. Origins and implications of each viewpoint need to be briefly outlined.

Subculture-of-Poverty Interpretations

The "enclave" character of inner-city slums and their racial-ethnic distinctiveness made the concept of an isolated subculture immediately attractive. Born in Mexico City but quickly naturalized in the United States, Oscar Lewis' notion of subculture of poverty transferred blame from the individual to his group, offering an interpretation that overcame most of the shortcomings of its predecessors. The comparative advantage of the new interpretation is apparent in three aspects.

First, it focuses not on the individual but on his immediate surroundings. Thus, the poor are not blamed directly; they are seen as victims of their own group. Second, it has the advantage over earlier categorizations between "deserving" and "undeserving" poor in that it explains permanent poverty among large sectors of the population who are neither handicapped nor temporarily unemployed. Unlike idiosyncratic individual traits, a culture can involve, affect, and mold many. Third, the new concept offered an interpretation of poverty as an integral way of life, a form of perceiving the world. It accounted for the problem in terms of processes normal and known to the rest of the society; one could be socialized into a culture of poverty, as easily as one could into the dominant culture. In passing, the comforting suggestion was offered that many of the poor may be accustomed to their way of life and actually resist trading it for another (Valentine 1969; Rainwater 1968).

Though intellectually superior to their predecessors, subculture-of-poverty interpretations partook of the same formal ritual of taking consequences of poverty—outward manifestations and rational adaptations by the poor—as causes of the problem. The popularity of the view soon permeated policy circles where "the vicious circle of poverty" became the enemy to be battled by new public programs. Figure 5.1 reproduces a representation of the "poverty cycle," as conceived in 1963 by John F. Kennedy's Council of Economic Advisers.

FIGURE 5.1

The "Poverty Cycle" of
Subculture-of-Poverty Interpretations

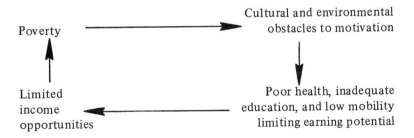

Structural Interpretation of Poverty

The structural interpretation that emerged at about the same time conceived poverty not as a consequence of individual or cultural shortcomings, but of the lack of power of relegated groups to participate in a pluralist society (Blauner 1972). Inner-city slums were as they were and the poor lived as they lived because they could not demand and gain access to a larger share of societies' resources. Such a position found support in some inner governmental agencies. For example, the President's Committee on Juvenile Delinquency (PCJD) during the Kennedy administration explicitly committed itself to support "those actions aimed primarily at changes in the social arrangements affecting target area youth rather than change in the personalities of the individual delinquent" (Helfgot 1974:487).

Note that this view did not amount to a full structural interpretation of poverty as intrinsic, necessary, and recreated anew by a capitalist order. In comparative terms, it was not much more "radical" than the marginality ideology advanced by Christian Democrats in Latin America (discussed below) and clearly less so than early Justicialism in Argentina and similar populist doctrines. Its message was not structural revolution, but reform; its concern was with consumption and distribution, not with control of the means of production.

Ghetto revolts of the 1960s and the pressure of organized, racially based groups compelled the government to revise the official New Deal poverty doctrine and initiate new programs. New policies could not tolerate a fully structural interpretation, but they could accept, at least in theory, an ideological range from individual-cultural interpretations to mild structural arguments. The initial year of the War on Poverty did in fact see some form of compromise between these two positions. The first budget of the newly created Office of Economic Opportunity (OEO) was apportioned as shown in Table 5.7.

Youth Programs and Work Experience items of the budget roughly reflected a cultural interpretation of poverty and the need for breaking its "vicious circle" through individual education and training. The Job Corps, the mainstay of the Youth Program, consumed nearly half of this item ($183 million) to "rehabilitate" the poor through occupational training. The Neighborhood Youth Corps, another subentry in this area, addressed the unemployment problem among teenagers in the slum (Levitan 1969). Finally, "work-experience" programs aimed primarily at rehabilitating the hard-core unemployed. In subsequent years, this effort was to be expanded through the various Manpower training agencies.

Allocation for community action programs (CAP) corresponded only in very rough terms to the opposite philosophy of communal organization for demand making. Provisions for the program included the controversial assertion of "maximum feasible participation" by the poor themselves on policies affecting them (Moynihan 1969). Though in an incomplete and confused manner, the

TABLE 5.7

1965 OEO Budget
($ millions)

Program, by Title	Congressional Authorization
Youth programs	412.5
Community action programs	340
Rural assistance	35
Small loans	0
Work experience	150
VISTA and administration	10

Source: Sar A. Levitan, *The Great Society's Poor Law* (Baltimore: Johns Hopkins University Press), 1969.

CAP entry preserved the notion that one of the avenues of overcoming poverty was to give a "voice" to organizations of the poor in political exchange and decision making. Such reformist viewpoint was termed "radical" by friends and enemies alike and quickly raised the opposition of entrenched middle-level and petty local welfare bureaucracies.

Having recognized poverty as a major social concern and committed itself financially to act in this field, the government approached the problem in a pragmatic, matter-of-fact fashion. Elimination of poverty was seen essentially as a technical problem, not too different from that, for example, of placing men on the moon. Governmental planning committees in the early 1960s "believed with fervor that a combination of refined intellectual understanding . . . mixed with political 'clout' and new funds would be the magic ingredient in the war on delinquency" (Kravitz 1969:56).

Again, the "professionalization of reform" (Moynihan 1968) could only occur because the government saw poverty as a problem caused by the poor or, at best, as a partial social dysfunction to be overcome by fiscal appropriations. Poverty as a technical rather than a structural issue led to the formation of stable bureaucracies that promptly inclined the balance toward manipulating the poor rather than to confronting the structure. This occurred because such organizations acquired primary interests in their own preservation. Survival could be seriously jeopardized by confrontation with older welfare agencies and other parts of the existing order. Rather than fighting them, the new "reform organizations" chose to join them and engage in manpower training and similar programs as their own "antipoverty" strategy.

TABLE 5.8

Selected Budget Categories and Expert Staff of a Reform Organization (Mobilization for Youth) in Different Periods
(percent)

	Phase I, Militant, 1962-65	Phase II, Transitional, 1966-68	Phase III, Manpower Training, 1969-72
Budget category			
Work Programs	21	27	53
Economic Development	0	<1	9
Individual and			
Family Services	23	22	16
Community Action	10	6	0
Total ($ millions)	14.14	17.86	8.45
Expert staff, by discipline*			
Sociology	51 (139)	33 (99)	20 (27)
Psychology	36 (102)	42 (126)	57 (78)
Economics	3 (8)	9 (26)	12 (17)

*Raw frequencies given in parentheses.

Source: Joseph Helfgot, "Professional Reform Organizations and the Symbolic Representation of the Poor," *American Sociological Review* 39 (August 1974):475-91.

The Nixon years marked the definitive end of community organization programs and a complete shift toward training the poor for coping with the society as it is. Data in Table 5.8 present the history of this change, as experienced by a reform organization in the New York area. It moves from early War on Poverty years, when community action existed but took only 10 percent of the organization's budget, to a transitional phase where the organization was confronted with orchestrated protest for its "communist" activities, to a final phase, in which such pressure plus changes in federal funding, determined complete abandonment of community organization programs.

This evolution coincided with changes in the "expert" staff of this organization: from sociologists and sociologically oriented social workers to psychologists and psychologically oriented social workers (Table 5.8). The latter implemented a strategy that shifted from social service to research on industrial psychology and behavior modification (Helfgot 1974:481).

The hundreds of millions of dollars spent in the professional attack on poverty have, of course, not solved or significantly reduced the problem in the

United States. They have, however, provided well-paid employment for large numbers of educated middle-class persons. Most important among them are those of black and other minority backgrounds, who have been rushed into attractive positions in existing organizations. This "symbolic representation of the poor" (Helfgot 1974) in poverty bureaucracies and the accompanying elimination of potential leadership for deprived groups may well have been an unexpressed goal of governmental strategy. If this was the case, it has in fact been associated with a reduction in explosions of discontent.

Whatever the accuracy of the above statements, it remains nevertheless true that the experience of recent years reasserts the dominance of "exceptionalist" ideologies of inequality in the United States. As in the past, poverty programs have decisively veered toward facilitating adaptation by the poor to the U.S. system, rather than toward changing it. The structural situation that makes this possible is one in which the poor are enclaved in a population generally considered nonpoor and in which the nature of the problem is defined by inequality and not survival. Neither characteristic is present in Latin America, where despite resistance by political and economic elites, ideologies of poverty have evolved in a different direction.

LATIN AMERICAN IDEOLOGIES

Hospicio Cabañas, the huge orphanage in the midst of Guadalajara, houses some of the most impressive frescos by Clemente Orozco. One of them, decorating the main chapel, represents the Mexican people turning away from preaching politicians and demagogues and toward the Church. The Church, however, offers only consolation for the misery and a gospel of resignation. A second fresco atop the chapel portrays a Spanish friar praying over the body of a dying Indian. His message and prayer is for the soul and the other life, while the Indian's mortal existence is given away to agony.

Remnants of the traditional Catholic heritage and its ideology of inequality are still to be seen in Latin America. Deprived of earlier religious overtones, the sense of ultimate justifiability of a hierarchical social order and of the positions of different classes within it remains among many of the poor and rich alike. Such an attitude, we believe, is not foreign to the repeated findings of empirical research on the limited aspirations of the urban poor, the absence of a "why not me" attitude toward lifestyles of the higher classes, and the tendency to blame particularistic events rather than the social order for one's poverty (Mangin 1967; Ray 1969; Cornelius and Dietz 1973). The basic feature of this "corporatist" ideology (Malloy 1973; Dietz 1975), as opposed to newer interpretations, is the absence of focused blame on any social actor or class for the existence of inequality.

Still, the spatial concentration of the poor in cities, the rapid growth of the physical manifestations of their misery, and the breakdown of earlier paternalistic, charitable arrangements to cope with their situation have prompted an urgent search for new interpretations. Laissez-faire ideologies, diffused throughout the continent since the late nineteenth century, offered an alternative. Yet, while upper groups may cling tenaciously to the notion of the "undeserving poor," it is difficult indeed to believe that only the shiftless and the negligent condemn themselves to poverty when the label must be applied to the hundreds of thousands.

The very extensiveness of poverty and its absolute character has made it difficult in Latin America to evolve explanations based on individual shortcomings. Few persons can be said to "deserve" to live as the poor must live in these cities. Accounting for their situation in terms of "deviations" from the mainstream fails to cope with the fact that in many cities the poor represent a significant proportion, if not the majority, of the population.

Nor have cultural interpretations of poverty found much acceptance in Latin Amerca. To assign responsibility to a "vicious circle of poverty" generated through socialization in a particular subculture assumes, first, that the poor need not live in this situation and, second, that their condition is somehow unique and restricted. In Latin America there was less need of critics like Charles Valentine (1969) and others to debunk this interpretation, for its assumptions ran straight against the evidence. The poor were not a rarity in the city, but rather the norm in vast areas. Whatever their values and subcultures, they could not live differently from the way they did, for this was determined for them by the scarce and unstable employment situation, the minimal wages, inflation, and a profit-regulated housing, food, and health market.

In essence, exceptionalist ideologies of poverty have not been convincingly "sold" in Latin America. Despite programs of international agencies, predicated on these theories, and the prestige of imported intellectual products, tales of individual and subcultural pathologies have not succeeded in explaining poverty. The structural situation imposed constraints on credibility that no amount of intellectual prestidigitation could overcome.

A variant of the ideologies that blame poverty on the poor did acquire, however, considerable diffusion in Latin America. This view was developed in Latin America mostly by a group of Catholic scholars and emerged under the name "marginality." The intellectual leader of the group was a Belgian Jesuit priest, Roger Vekemans, whose name has been progressively lost to students and critics of marginality.* Based in the Jesuit Centro Bellarmino in Chile and writing

---

*See, for example, the otherwise valuable critique of the marginality concept by Lisa R. Peattie (1974), where there is no single reference to Vekemans' work, nor any to those of his collaborators who launched and developed this orientation in Latin America.

in its magazine, *Mensaje,* Vekemans became a potent ideological force in Latin America during the early 1960s.

The theory of marginality was soon adopted as the official viewpoint on urban (and rural) poverty by Christian Democratic parties in the region. With the advent of the Frei government in Chile, it was elevated to state doctrine. The prestige of the Chilean Christian Democratic party and the vigor of its proponents spread the thesis throughout Latin America. As often happens with popular notions, its origins soon became lost and marginality acquired the appearance of a spontaneous, consensually developed viewpoint.

In discussing marginality, we will concentrate on the original Vekemans and DESAL* publications, for they presented and elaborated the positions much more eloquently than subsequent writings. Marginality as an interpretation of poverty is a mix of collective blaming of the poor with a mild structural argument. The poor are marginal because they are not integrated into the normal economic, social, and political life of the society. This occurs for two reasons: First, the poor lack certain cultural orientations, aspirations, and skills necessary for participating in modern society; second, the society itself has neglected the poor, creating the serious problem of profound urban and rural inequalities. The solution is then to alert elite groups to the needs and demands of the poor and to "promote" the latter into skills and orientation necessary for life in the modern world.

Unlike harsher culture-of-poverty interpretations, the victim-blaming component of marginality does not describe the poor as immersed in a lumpen environment of crime and apathy, but rather as well-meaning groups too ill-prepared to cope with modern reality:

> There is a concordance between historical conditioning and the incapacity of the affected to overcome by themselves the situation of marginality.... The marginal is, in a sense, "a different man," with different values and attitudes; with aspirations, yes, but acting on the basis of mechanisms completely ineffective to attain them. He is a diminished man, not in his moral values which are frequently heroic, but in his initiative and capacity to act individually and collectively.... Those who do not belong or do not participate are not only non-modern, under any definition of modernity, but are traditional since they represent the current projection of earlier pre-Columbian and pre-industrial situations (Vekemans and Silva Fuenzalida 1969:50,59).

---

*Center for Social and Economic Development of Latin America, Vekemans' organization based in Chile until the advent of the Unidad Popular government.

The state and society are reprimanded for rejecting and further marginal-izing the poor. Their past indifference is denounced, and the need for reform is repeatedly stressed:

> After long struggles to integrate himself into society, the urban marginal comes to attain a measure of group solidarity and to over-come his intrinsic individualism and distrust. But society rejects him and finally turns him into a passive being, dominated by an indiffer-ence projected into his community and his work. . . . The inequality in goods and services between the participating society and the urban marginals prevents the spontaneous development of the latter. There is an increasingly evident need for promotion, an external impulse (Hoffmann et al. 1969:364-65).

The newness and persuasiveness of the theory, its scientific ring, and the safe character of its appeals for reform attracted international agencies and governments, which began to pour resources into marginality studies and pop-ular promotion programs. "Popular Cooperation" under Belaunde Terry in Peru, "Popular Promotion" under Frei in Chile, and the various "community-development" programs in Central America and under COPEI in Venezuela trace their origins, in more or less direct fashion, to this ideological movement in Latin America.

The gradual demise of marginality as a viable interpretation of poverty has been due to three major factors. First, empirical investigations consistently revealed "marginals" to be far more dynamic, rational, and capable of taking advantage of opportunities than initially portrayed. In capacity to deal with their life situation, the poor did not appear to be inferior to other urban sectors. Their problem did not lie in cultural inability to take advantage of opportunity, but in the nonexistence of opportunities (cf. Ray 1969; Cornelius 1975; Portes and Walton 1976).

Second, another set of studies convincingly disproved the notion of marginality as lack of participation in the ongoing society (Quijano 1967; Roberts 1973; Peattie 1974). Despite their spatial and ethnic distinctiveness, the urban poor remain an integral part of the system, no more tangential and no less necessary than other groups. It is precisely their form of integration, the way in which they are forced to participate, not their lack of participation, that is reflected in their situation. As sources of cheap labor and as consumers, voters in elections, and users of urban services, the poor are an inextricable part of the urban structure in Latin America.

Third, and perhaps most important, marginality suffered from confron-tation with its own application in reality. "Promotores," full of youthful ideal-ism, were disseminated throughout squatter and other settlements in the continent. In most cases, they discovered that they had very little to promote.

The language of ideology in which they had been trained did not jibe with the language of reality. Whereas the former spoke of value changes and the need for an abstract integration into society, the latter spoke of strategies for job hunting and resource sharing, legal codes affecting land tenure, the means of manipulating local politics for personal and collective advantage, and the techniques for securing water and electricity when not legally available.

Those to be promoted often turned out to be far more adept at dealing with urban life than their promoters. The latter found that what was really needed they could not begin to provide: stable jobs, higher incomes, credit and housing opportunities, educational and health facilities. Their roles were used and their salaries paid essentially to implement a modernized version of Christian charity.

To our knowledge, large investments in popular promotion and community development in Latin America have not yielded anything beyond melioristic initiatives and have certainly not changed the conditions of poverty in any country. With the advent of the Allende government in Chile, the Promocion Popular program vanished without pain or glory. In other countries of Latin America, Community and Popular Development agencies have been incorporated into traditional ministries serving mainly as sources of employment for educated middle-class groups.

In a sense, marginality represented the last sophisticated attempt to avoid obvious structural facts. While still entrenched in official bureaucracies, this interpretation has ceased to be dominant among important intellectual sectors and even several governments. They have progressively turned to an interpretation which runs contrary to dominant economic interests.

The structural interpretation, as advanced by recent dependency writers (Quijano 1967; Sunkel 1972) and others (cf. Hardoy 1972b), cannot be said to be dominant throughout Latin America, but it has acquired an increasing momentum. Though formulations and schools vary, the general argument in relation to the problem of inequality consists of three major tenets. The first is that the existing conditions of poverty—its spread to vast sectors of the population and the abysmal life conditions it implies—are consequences of the existing political and economic order. The second is that such poverty is, to a large extent, necessary for maintenance of the existing structure (Nun 1969). Vast differences in wealth and life chances are intrinsic to capitalism, especially its "dependent" kinds, both as logical consequences of processes of accumulation and as conditions for the continuous generation and appropriation of an economic surplus (Frank 1967; Yujnovsky 1976). The third is that reduction of existing inequalities and elimination of poverty as known today in Latin America cannot occur without transfer of control of economic and political power to new social groups.

Once accepted, the above tenets cannot but run directly against past political and economic arrangements. It is in fact remarkable the extent to which this interpretation has managed to gain acceptance in such a hostile environment. Vis-a-vis conventional theorizing on the impermeability of ideology to objective facts, the current historical experience in Latin America offers an important corrective.

There are few who would publicly question at present that urban poverty in Latin America is intrinsic to the existing social order and, hence, that the remedy lies in changing the structure. Economic elites and political and military ruling groups in some of the major countries have opted, instead, for a different strategy. This interpretation does not deny conditions or determinants of poverty; it argues that the solution lies in rapid economic development within a capitalist framework. Extensive and immediate redistribution would eliminate the "motor" of economic growth provided by private profit incentives. The poor should sacrifice themselves at present, for in the long run the fruits of growth would filter down to them (Garrastazu Medici 1973).

The importance of contemporary ideologies of economic development ("desarrollismo") for the present topic is this: They do not attempt to buttress traditional interpretations of inequality, but rather shift ground and justify continuation of massive poverty as the price to pay for national growth. The promise, sustained in opposition to empirical evidence (Jencks et al. 1973), is that accumulated wealth will eventually and naturally flow from the rich to the poor. Economic growth and redistribution are not considered integral parts of the same developmental strategy; they are set in opposition to each other as separate stages of a process that must "take its time" to take its course.

SUMMARY

Departing from similar European origins, dominant ideologies of inequality in the United States and Latin America have evolved in relatively different directions in recent times. The basic theme underlying the outline of the process in this chapter is that the social situation conditions the emergence and diffusion of the different theories that pretend to explain it. This occurs not only through the interests of dominant groups and their attempts at legislation, but also through the forms that inequality takes and the conditions of poverty. These conditions set limits to the acceptability of different interpretations.

In both Latin America and the United States, the structural phenomenon forcing reemergence of poverty as a social issue has been massive processes of migration of the poor to cities. The urban visibility of poverty has been insured by the twin phenomena of numbers and density; they have resulted in a changed urban ecology where spatial concentration and consequent political actions by the groups involved have been too visible to be ignored. The distinctiveness of the poor in urban space has been reinforced by the association of class with physical features: race in the United States, and race plus the outward manifestations of misery in Latin America.

Ideological processes in the United States during this century can be described as a cycle in which "exceptionalist" views are periodically interrupted, at times of crisis, by mild structural overtures. The continuing viability of individualistic and culturalistic ideologies and the weakness of full structural interpretations are based on a situation where the poor can be plausibly labelled "minorities" and where poverty is defined by relative inequality rather than by basic need.

In Latin America, ideologies can be portrayed as evolving in a linear rather than in a cyclical fashion. From earlier "corporatist" doctrines, tainted by the end of the last century by laissez-faire theories, attempts were made to institutionalize the equivalent of a subculture-of-poverty interpretation. Structural circumstances of widespread and absolute poverty conspired against such view. Instead of alternations between individualistic and mild structural ideologies, the movement in this case has been from an uneasy mix of the two—marginality theory—to the full structural interpretations advanced by dependency and similar writings. Current ideological alternatives to this interpretation have been based on the themes of nationalism and rapid economic development. Both are presently used by different Latin American elites and governments to justify postponement of redistributive measures and to bypass logical consequences of a structural explanation.

Vulgar Marxism has seen ideologies entirely as "superstructure": epiphenomena mechanically developed and modified in response to changes in the economic order. The situation is far more complex, for reality is not entirely permeable to apologists of the existing order. Moreover, once diffused and accepted, ideologies play back on society, defining the interests of men, the limits of their normal relationships, and the causes to which they assign responsibility for their situation.

Accepted ideologies that justify existing social arrangements or see the need for "minor" adjustments define a situation drastically different from one in which "counterideologies" have become dominant. Desertion of sectors belonging to the dominant classes and a progressive self-denial of legitimacy among elite groups—these are likely consequences to follow. The diverging paths of ideologies of poverty described above signal the likelihood of continued amelioristic policies toward the U.S. poor, but they may well offer a prelude to significant transformations in Latin America.

REFERENCES

Anderson, Charles W. 1967. *Politics and Economic Change in Latin America: The Governing of Restless Nations.* Princeton, N.J.: Van Nostrand.

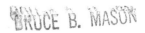

Arendt, Hannah. 1965. *On Revolution.* New York: Viking Press.

Balan, Jorge, Harley L. Browning, and Elizabeth Jelin. 1973. *Men in a Developing Society; Geographic and Social Mobility in Monterrey, Mexico.* Austin: University of Texas Press.

Blauner, Robert. 1972. "Colonized and Immigrant Minorities." In *Nation of Nations: The Ethnic Experience and the Racial Crisis,* edited by Peter Rose. New York: Random House, pp. 243-58.

Cohen, Wilbur J. 1970. "Government Policy and the Poor: Past, Present, and Future." *Journal of Social Issues* 26 (Summer):1-10.

Cornelius, Wayne A. 1975. *Politics and the Migrant Poor in Mexico City.* Stanford, Calif.: Stanford University Press.

———— and Henry A. Dietz. 1973. "Urbanization, Demand-Making, and Political System Overload: Political Participation among the Migrant Poor in Latin American Cities." Paper presented at the meetings of the American Political Science Association, New Orleans, September.

Dietz, Henry A. 1977. "Bureaucratic Demand-Making and Clientelistic Participation: The Urban Poor in an Authoritarian Context." In *Authoritarianism in Latin America,* edited by James Malloy. Pittsburgh: University of Pittsburgh Press.

Frank, Andre G. 1967. *Capitalism and Underdevelopment in Latin America.* New York: Monthly Review Press.

Garrastazu Medici, Emilio. 1973. *Nosso Camino.* Brasilia: Departamento de Imprensa Nacional.

Gordon, Milton. 1964. *Assimilation in American Life: The Role of Race, Religion, and National Origin.* New York: Oxford University Press.

Greeley, Andrew. 1971. *Why Can't They Be Like Us? America's White Ethnic Groups.* New York: Dutton.

Handlin, Oscar. 1951. *The Uprooted: The Epic Story of the Great Migrations That Made the American People.* Boston: Little Brown.

Hardoy, Jorge. 1975. "City and Countryside in the Historical Development of Latin America." Cycle of lectures offered at the Institute of Latin American Studies, University of Texas at Austin.

————. 1972a. "El Paisaje Urbano de America del Sur." In Jorge Hardoy, *Las Ciudades en America Latina.* Buenos Aires: Paidos, pp. 121-60.

————. 1972b. "Politica Urbanistica y Politica del Suelo Urbano y Surburbano en America Latina." In Jorge Hardoy, *Las Ciudades en America Latina.* Buenos Aires: Paidos, pp. 49-69.

Helfgot, Joseph. 1974. "Professional Reform Organizations and the Symbolic Representation of the Poor." *American Sociological Review* 39 (August):475-91.

Hirschman, Albert O. 1961. "Ideologies of Economic Development in Latin America." In *Latin American Issues,* edited by Albert O. Hirschman. New York: Twentieth Century Fund, pp. 3-42.

Hoffmann, Rodolfo, Nicolas Garcia, Olga Mercado, and Francisco Uribe. 1969. "La Marginalidad Urbana." In *DESAL, Marginalidad en America Latina; un Ensayo de Diagnostico.* Barcelona: Herder, pp. 285-374.

Izquierdo, Gonzalo. 1968. *Un Estudio de las Ideologias Chilenas; la Sociedad de Agricultura en el Siglo XIX.* Santiago de Chile: Center for Socio-economic Studies, University of Chile.

James, Dorothy B. 1972. *Poverty, Politics, and Change.* Englewood Cliffs, N.J.: Prentice-Hall.

Jencks, Cristopher, et al. 1972. *Inequality: A Reassessment of the Effect of Family and Schooling in America.* New York: Harper Colophon.

Kravitz, Sanford. 1969. "The Community Action Program: Past, Present and Its Future." In *On Fighting Poverty*, edited by James Sundquist. New York: Basic Books, pp. 52-69.

Leeds, Anthony. 1974. "Housing-Settlement Types, Arrangements for Living, Proletarianization, and the Social Structure of the City." In *Latin American Urban Research,* vol. 4, edited by Wayne A. Cornelius and Felicity M. Trueblood. Beverly Hills, Calif.: Sage.

Leeds, Elizabeth. 1972. "Forms of 'Squatment' Political Organization: The Politics of Control in Brazil." Masters thesis, Department of Government, University of Texas at Austin.

Levitan, Sar A. 1969. *The Great Society's Poor Law.* Baltimore: Johns Hopkins University Press.

Lipset, Seymour M. 1963. *Political Man.* New York: Doubleday.

Lomnitz, Larissa. 1974. "The Social and Economic Organization of a Mexican Shantytown." In *Latin American Urban Research* vol. 4, edited by Wayne A. Cornelius and Felicity M. Trueblood. Beverly Hills, Calif.: Sage, pp. 135-55.

Malloy, James. 1973. "Authoritarianism, Corporatism, and Mobilization in Peru." Department of Political Science, University of Pittsburgh. Unpublished.

Mangin, William. 1967. "Latin American Squatter Settlements: A Problem and a Solution." *Latin American Research Review* 2 (Summer):65-98.

Mannheim, Karl. 1966. *Ideology and Utopia.* Translated by Louis Wirth and Edward Shils. New York: Harcourt, Brace, and World.

Marx, Karl. 1967. "The General Law of Capitalist Accumulation." In *Capital, A Critique of Political Economy*, vol. 1. New York: International Publishers, Ch. 25.

Mesa-Lago, Carmelo. 1973. "Estratification y Desigualdad en la Seguridad Social Latino-americana: Peru." *Estudios Andinos* 3:17-48.

Morse, Richard M. 1975. "The Development of Urban Systems in the Americas in the Nineteenth Century." *Journal of Interamerican Studies and World Affairs* 17 (February): 4-26.

Moynihan, Daniel P. 1969. *Maximum Feasible Misunderstanding.* New York: Free Press.

————. 1968. "The Professors and the Poor." In *On Understanding Poverty*, edited by Daniel P. Moynihan. New York: Basic Books.

Nun, Jose. 1969. "Superpoblacion Relativa, Ejercito de Reserva y Masa Marginal." *Revista Latinoamericana de Sociologia* 5 (July):178-236.

Peattie, Lisa R. 1974. "The Concept of 'Marginality' as Applied to Squatter Settlements." In *Latin American Urban Research*, vol. 4, edited by Wayne A. Cornelius and Felicity M. Trueblood. Beverly Hills, Calif.: Sage, pp. 101-9.

Portes, Alejandro, and John Walton. 1976. *Urban Latin America: The Political Condition from Above and Below.* Austin: University of Texas Press.

Quijano, Anibal. 1967. "La Urbanizacion de la Sociedad en Latinoamerica." *Revista Mexicana de Sociologia* 39 (October):669-703.

Rainwater, Lee. 1968. "The Problem of Lower-Class Culture and Poverty-War Strategy." In *On Understanding Poverty*, edited by Daniel P. Moynihan. New York: Basic Books, pp. 29-59.

————. 1967. "Neutralizing the Disinherited: Some Psychological Aspects of Understanding the Poor." Pruitt-Igoe Occasional Paper no. 30. St. Louis: Washington University Press.

Ramos, Samuel. 1963. *Profile of Man and Culture in Mexico.* New York: McGraw-Hill.

Ray, Talton F. 1969. *The Politics of the Barrios of Venezuela.* Berkeley: University of California Press.

Roberts, Bryan. 1973. *Organizing Strangers: Poor Families in Guatemala City.* Austin: University of Texas Press.

Roth, Guenther. 1975. "Socio-historical Model and Developmental Theory." *American Sociological Review* 40 (April):148-57.

Rothstein, M. 1966. "Antebellum Wheat and Cotton Exports: A Contrast in Marketing Organization and Economic Development." *Agricultural History* 41:91-100.

Ryan, William. 1971. *Blaming the Victim.* New York: Vintage Books.

Solaun, Mauricio, and Sidney Kronus. 1973. *Discrimination without Violence–Miscegenation and Racial Conflict in Latin America.* New York: Wiley.

Sunkel, Osvaldo. 1972. *Capitalismo Transnacional y Desintegracion Nacional en America Latina.* Buenos Aires: Nueva Vision.

Turner, Ralph H. 1969. "The Public Perception of Protest." *American Sociological Review* 34 (December):815-31.

United Nations. 1973. *Demographic Yearbook.*

Valentine, Charles. 1969. *Culture and Poverty: Critique and Counter Proposals.* Chicago: University of Chicago Press.

Vekemans, Roger, and Ismael Silva Fuenzalida. 1969. "El Concepto de Marginalidad." In *DESAL, Marginalidad en America Latina; un Esayo de Diagnostico.* Barcelona: Herder, pp. 15-63.

Vivas, Elisio. 1945. "The Spanish Heritage." *American Sociological Review* 10:184-91.

Wachtel, Howard M. 1973. "Looking at Poverty from Radical, Conservative and Liberal Perspectives." In *The Poverty Establishment,* edited by Pamela Ruby. Englewood Cliffs, N.J.: Prentice Hall, pp. 18-90.

Wallerstein, Immanuel. 1974. *The Modern World System, Capitalist Agriculture and the Origins of the European World Economy in the Sixteenth Century.* New York: Academic Press.

Warner, W. Lloyd, and Leo Srole. 1945. *The Social Systems of American Ethnic Groups.* New Haven: Yale University Press.

Weber, Max. 1965. "The Fundamental Concepts of Sociology." In *Max Weber; The Theory of Social and Economic Organization,* edited by Talcott Parsons. New York: The Free Press, pp. 87-157.

Yujnovsky, Oscar. 1976. "The Urban Spatial Configuration and Land Use Policies in Latin America." In *Current Perspectives in Latin American Urban Research,* edited by Alejandro Portes and Harley Browning. Austin: Institute of Latin American Studies and University of Texas Press, Ch. 2.

6

EGALITARIANISM, PARTICIPATION, AND POLICY MAKING IN ISRAEL
Rivka W. Bar-Yosef

> "It is just because the pressure of events tends always
> to the destruction of equality that the force of legis-
> lation should always be directed to maintaining it."
>
> —Rousseau, *Social Contract*

Equality and participation are issues as old as the social system itself. The allocation of scarce resources is necessary for any collectivity, and likewise dividing the desired items and choosing those to make the decisions on allocation. The sociological literature treats these problems under the title of stratification, probably the most discussed top of sociological theory. Classical and neoclassical literature abounds in scholarly treatises on the phenomenon of social inequality resulting from unequal distribution of such diverse items as wealth, political power, social prestige, education, and occupations. Unequal distribution is the core feature of the most important comprehensive models of society. Max Weber (1946; 1947), Joseph Schumpeter (1951), W. Lloyd Warner et al. (1949), Talcott Parsons (1951), and T. H. Marshall (1964) are the most outstanding representatives of the vast number of scholars endeavoring to unravel the causes, results, and dynamics of inequality in societies. In some of these models inequality is seen as merely unavoidable, whereas in others it is considered essential to the proper functioning of a society. Kingsley Davis (1945; 1953), Melvin Tumin (1953; 1963), and Wilbert Moore (1963) in their famous discussion on functionality or disfunctionality of stratification did not resolve the issues that emerged with new vigor in the last decade.

Most stratification theories concentrate on inequality. Equality is viewed through the perspective of the existing inequalities. It is mentioned mostly as a negation of inequality but not as the central issue. The reason for this bias may be ideological as well as methodical. Modern societies are stratified, and studies based on empirical data tend to use frequency distributions of various social attributes to find the order and generality of the latter and to explain their maintenance, cause, and congruence. An additional reason may be the belief in the functionality of stratification. This belief is subsequently proved by the theoretical modes and by the empirical data.

The awakening of the theoretical interest in equality is undoubtedly the result of changing ideology in the intellectual community. An interesting example of this change is provided by a recent paper of Talcott Parsons (1970), whose theories on integration through legitimate inequalities seems to represent the core idea of functional stratification: "This paper attempts to bring up to date the author's conception of social stratification as set forth in . . . previous general papers . . . and to broaden the field of consideration by giving special attention to the forces pressing toward equality in various respects, as well as the bases of inequality." The main ideas developed in the paper are the following:

1. "All societies institutionalize some balance between equality and inequality." Both tendencies are essential aspects of the "social order."
2. Consequently, both trends have to acquire justification in terms of the dominant value system.
3. "The principal contexts in which the equality-inequality problem arises . . . [in a] pluralistic modern society . . . are to significant degrees independently variable."
4. Participation is implied in egalitarianism.
5. The balance between egalitarianism and stratification depends on "mechanisms which are functionally specified in the relevant modes of integration."
6. There is no single pattern of integration—and Parsons sketches four such models.

These are important steps toward a sociology of egalitarianism, although they may raise many critical thoughts concerning both the basic assumptions and the resulting analysis.

Parsons' model is obviously deduced from an ideal type of U.S. society; nevertheless, it is similar in its essence to stratification models based on the analysis of the socialist-communist societies:

> In socialist society we find opposite tendencies in the realm of distribution of values representing important status characteristics—education, income and social prestige. Either tendency is connected with different socialist principles. One tendency, the congruence of status characteristics, is connected with the principle "to each according to his work." The other tendency is associated with egalitarian ideals and leads to a decomposition, at least partial, of status characteristics . . . (Wesolowski 1969:477).

The equality-inequality problem is nearly always interwoven with normative approaches. Whatever the perspective of the scholar, the treatment of the issue hinges on the question of the desirability of equality. The most extensive treatment appears in connection with the concept of social justice, the assumption being that justice is seen by some as having both an egalitarian and a humanitarian element—the very same elements that were analyzed by Parsons (1970) and by Wlodzimierz Wesolowski in 1969. The social-justice perspective prescribes these two orientations purely because of their moral value: "All men are to be treated as equals, not because they are equal in any respect but simply because they are human. . . . [T]his equal treatment must be qualified in the light of certain principles: the recognition of contribution and desert . . . nonimpoverishment and perhaps the provision and improvement of opportunity . . ." (Frankena 1962:19, 23).

From the political point of view egalitarianism is part of the democratic value complex, logically connected with the idea of freedom, and hence that of political justice (Gewirth 1962). Besides the ideological imperative of egalitarianism, political analyses try to enlighten the structural needs of democracy and the relative importance of equality of rights, participation, and the stratification of authority and elite positions. In some models democratic stability is considered as depending on equality (Lindsay 1962). In others, it is assumed that in modern democracies equality may cause instability (Thompson 1970).

The most often discussed aspect of egalitarianism is the economic or distributive justice. Any economic policy interferes with the distribution of resources and thus takes a stand on equality and inequality: "To have no government programs for redistributing income is simply to certify *de facto* that the existing market distribution of incomes is equitable. One way or another, we are forced to reveal our collective preferences about the 'just' distribution of economic resources" (Thurow 1973:57). Lester Thurow defines equity as the "acceptable degree of inequality," which degree is influenced and justified—without being fully determined—by economic merit, the common good, the rules of fair play, and consensus about individual preferences.

Each of these ideas is discussed by various philosophers and economists as possible explanations or justifications of inequality. Economic theory being the most formalized among the theories of social behavior, problems of economic equality tend to be more thoroughly defined and centered on the measurable effects of egalitarian policy.

Obviously, since a model of society that includes both the egalitarian and the stratificatory aspect has to cover all the social institutions, it follows that each of the perspectives mentioned above have some relevance. Parsons has attempted such an integration, and similar multiinstitutional approaches have been taken by others who have endeavored to build more egalitarian models of societies (Galbraith 1973; Gans 1974).

The policy maker looks to the social theories to provide either programs or justifications. Theories and ideologies may be equally useful to the policy maker in justifying policy decisions. In most modern societies the idea of some balance between egalitarianism and stratification will be willingly accepted as a basis for policy making. But the crucial questions are the operative ones, and these involve the type of balance, the measuring of aspects of equality and equity and the effects of various measures of intervention. The commitment to egalitarianism often serves as a common platform for the social scientist and the policy maker: "In a welfare system . . . policy makers . . . often think of the social sciences as a rationale required for any projected change estimated to be in the social interest" (Horowitz 1970:39). For the social scientist these needs of policy making create opportunities for research focused on equality. Both the policy maker and the social scientist are expected to provide answers to some elementary questions about the dynamics of equality: What kind of equality is socially relevant? How can we measure or evaluate it? What are the conditions of change? How do equality and inequality affect the functioning of various institutions? And what are the limits of equality and of inequality?

Israel is a convenient place for the study of egalitarianism. The smallness of the country, the relatively new institutional system not yet legitimized by tradition, the lack of well-crystallized social classes, and the tendency toward social experimentation make Israel a quasi-laboratory type of society. There is in Israel a certain social transparency: Structures and their working have high visibility, and initiated changes produce many immediate effects. The streak of egalitarianism in the short and tumultuous history of the state is easily discernible. The social scientist can observe many aspects and variations of the problem of equality and a wide range of successes and failures of those coping with it. I shall use some aspects of the Israeli society as "cases" that serve to illuminate the dynamics of egalitarianism. The topic of the discussion will be economic or distributive equality, and I will deal with the distribution of income and services, occupational differentiation, and standards of living. The analysis will be anchored at three points: (a) the ideological approach toward equality and participation, (b) the macrosocial governmental policies, and (c) the subcultures of egalitarian communities. It must be emphasized that the dominant theme of this chapter is egalitarianism; participation will be treated mainly through the perspective of equality.

EGALITARIAN IDEOLOGY IN ISRAEL

In the ideological history of Israel egalitarianism and democracy were major "motifs" around which many of the political controversies revolved. The Jewish national renaissance movement known as Zionism combined cultural and political ideas with social ideology from its very beginnings a century ago. The aim of returning from the Diaspora to the historical homeland of the Jewish people was inseparably connected with the desire to establish a just society. The formulation of such a model was not only an intellectual and emotional need; it had the practical purpose of providing the immigrants with workable answers to questions concerning their daily lives. Many of the pre-statehood immigrants were young Eastern European intellectuals from middle-class families. From their perception of Zionism as a social and cultural revolution that would result in the normalization of the Jewish social structure they developed the ideology of "productivization," meaning the restructuring of the occupational distribution by countermobility, from middle-class white-collar occupations to agricultural and industrial blue-collar occupations. Their social program was imbued with an appropriate value system in which physical work was seen as a major value, the generator of intrinsic satisfaction and of social prestige. The self-imposed proletarianization was not regarded as downward mobility. This new working class perceived itself as the carrier of the principal social and national values and naturally demanded to be recognized as an elite. It was more or less inevitable that such groups should feel an affinity with the socialist movements of Central and Eastern Europe and be influenced by them. Indeed, each wave of immigrants brought with it elements of the then-current socialist ideology. In the nineteenth century early Russian socialism could be detected; in the early twentieth century some Tolstoyan ideas were redefined; later came the programs of the second and third Internationals, and the Marxist-Leninist orientations were reflected in the development of the Israeli socialism (Eisenstadt 1967:13-31). None of these ideologies was accepted in its original version. The mainstreams of Zionist socialism were intentionally trying to formulate their special brands of socialism, whether in its more dogmatic Marxist approach or in the various forms of socialism and social democracy. The common basis for all was the belief in the necessary interdependence between socialism and Zionism: "It is a queer and disconcerting idea that some people should want to establish an autonomous state based on the principles of social inequality and free competition. The Jewish state, if it will be realized in the near future, has to be by necessity socialist, in order to become the ideal of all the Jewish people, the ideal of the Jewish workers, of the varieties of proletarians, of the middle classes, of the Jewish intelligentsia and the ideologues" (Sirkin [1898] in Hertzberg 1970).

   Zionist socialism was essentially different from both the Marxist Communist and the Social Democratic parties of Europe. Whether in the pre-statehood period or after independence, the orthodox Marxist communism did not succeed in capturing the votes and the support of the citizens of Israel. While fully legal, the Israeli communists did not receive at any time more than 2 to 3 percent of the ballot.

The distinguishing characteristics of the various Zionist socialist parties are fairly conspicuous: (a) they placed primacy on such national goals as security, the absorption of immigrants, and development; (b) they emphasized the importance of the agricultural sector, especially the collective and cooperative settlements; (c) they were committed to the democratic form of government and hence to "reformism" rather than to "proletarian revolution"; (d) they were in readiness for coexistence with private enterprise; (e) they were committed to welfare legislation and governmental control so as to ensure a certain level of equality; (f) finally, they sought to maintain Histadrut, a powerful organization of the working class that functions as a federation of trade unions, a provider of welfare services, a holding company of financial and production enterprises, and in certain cases a federation of the labor parties. Working-class membership as defined by the Histadrut is a position in the labor market, and it does not depend on the content of the occupation. On the membership card of the Histadrut it is stated: "The Histadrut is an association of all the workers . . . who live from their work and do not exploit the work of others. . . ." In practice this means that all the wage and salary earners and the self-employed are entitled to membership in the Histadrut.

The agreement about these major principles did not lead to their unified consensual interpretation. Various ideological groups have different ideas on each of the issues. There are more and less radical opinions about the acceptable level of inequality, the desired extent of welfare legislation, the depth of government intervention in the economy, the status accorded to the communal settlements and the Histadrut, and so forth. Predictably, the actual policy decisions are not determined by ideology, but values and beliefs have an undeniable influence on policy.

The two levels of social organization to which this chapter will refer are anchorage points for two different ideological orientations (political socialism and collectivist socialism), which may be (but are not necessarily) integrated into a unified program.

Political Socialism

Political socialism is primarily aimed at the macrosocial level. It envisages a socialist, planned economy, and a moderately unequal society. The tolerance for inequality does not apply uniformly to all its sources. A certain level of inequality is deemed acceptable, according to some versions even desirable, if it is the result of differential rewards of occupations, educational level, and seniority. Much more sensitivity is shown for inequality linked with country of origin, the major cleavage being between the immigrants originating from Moslem countries and those coming from Christian cultures. The separation of these two types of inequality is difficult because of overlapping characteristics of origins and the other status dimensions. The immigrants from Moslem countries have a disproportionately large share among the low-income, low-education, and low-prestige occupations. Thus, the inequality that could be tolerated or even legitimized on the basis of achievement-oriented meritocratic values becomes illegitimate because of its linkage to an ascribed, seeming stratification. While there are no overt ideological variations in the condemnation of inequality connected with origins, there are variations concerning the balance of economic equality and inequality, and the relative standing accorded to the private enterprise and the competitive market versus the public entrepreneurship and planned economy. Political socialism is expected to ensure the socialist character of Israel through the political mechanism of a democratic government controlled by the labor parties, which maintain close cooperation with a powerful Histadrut. All the governments in the 28 years of the state have been coalition governments, in which the labor parties, while constituting the majority, had to share power with nonsocialist parties. Nonetheless, egalitarianism is avowedly one of the directing values of each government, as it is often stated in the programmatic addresses of prime ministers and other members of the governing elite. It is also regularly stated with the occasion of the yearly presentation of the national budget to the Knesset (parliament) and the discussion by that body.

Participation does not have similar standing, either in the dominant ideology or in the principles of policy. In general, the democratic system of government is seen as sufficiently guaranteeing popular participation. Moreover, there is latent elitism in the labor parties, presumably the heritage of the early pioneering ideals. The organized foci of power, the government, the labor parties, and the Histadrut, see themselves as the carriers of the socialist values. As the elites of these bodies are circulating among the top positions of each of these, there is no communication gap between the government, the Histadrut, and the labor parties. The labor elite can be seen as a group that represents the general consensus as well as the ideological variations. The old elite assumed responsibility for the maintenance of the ideological and power dominance of socialism and it distrusted the possible results of more active popular participation. But with the emergence of a younger, more heterogeneous elite, the ideological charisma of the leadership is paling, and at the same time the public pressure for more participation is increasing. The new elites tend to a more pragmatic self-definition and do not claim the position of ideological leadership.

Political socialism in Israel, in spite of a certain dogmatism, is a dynamic ideology. New problems and new ideas are absorbed and old ideas are reevaluated. There is no central dogma or universally accepted social philosophy. The most important ideological changes since the establishment of the state were the result of the necessity to adapt the doctrines to the demands of institution building in a newly established state and to the desire for rapid economic growth. It seems that British welfare socialism had the one recognizable major impact on ideas and programs. The ideas of W. H. Beveridge (1936; 1942), G. D. H. Cole (1943; 1957), C. A. R. Crosland (1956), and Richard Titmuss (1948; 1968) were superimposed on the older influences of Marx, Engels, and the Marxist Zionist Ber Borochov (1937). In the past two decades the ideological orientation weakened, and the pragmatic, programmatic aspects were emphasized. A general tendency of deradicalization is also evident, although lately there are signs of a revival of ideological concern, especially among the young intellectuals.

It is not to be expected that in a democratic system with a coalition government the ideology of the ruling party will shape the social and economic policy. Indeed, governmental policy is not outright socialist, nor quite egalitarian, nor typically Western capitalist. Egalitarianism, apparent in several spheres of policy making, is presumably the product of a multitude of forces: of ideological commitment, political interests, the pressure of the Histadrut, and in some cases the public and others. Lacking a proper instrument for the measurement of the relative level of equality as compared to inequality, I shall confine this discussion to some attributes of macrosocial policy, which can be considered as indicators of egalitarian tendencies. Three such indicators are suggested: (a) the allocation of public funds for a wide range of welfare payments and services, (b) constraints on ownership and income, which limit the range of possible inequality, (c) publicly avowed concern and accountability of the government for furthering equality.

Welfare Policy

National Insurance. By any of the customary definitions, Israel is a welfare state: "The essence of the welfare state is government-protected minimum standards of income, nutrition, health, housing and education, assured to every citizen as a political right, not as charity" (Wilensky 1975:1). The idea of "minimal standard of living" as part of the universal rights of the citizen preceded the establishment of the state.

The Histadrut maintained for its members an elaborate welfare scheme on a voluntary basis, and in this scheme can be found the origins of state welfare legislation. The first plans for a comprehensive state welfare system were indeed prepared in 1947 immediately after the UN decision on the establishment of the state of Israel and before the declaration of statehood.

The sponsors of this plan were experts, mostly from the Histadrut, among them the future director of the National Institute for Social Insurance. In 1948, while the country was still fighting the concerted attack of all its neighbors, the provisional coalition government proclaimed its commitment to a welfare system. The Histadrut continued to be an important factor, but in order to ensure the universal legitimacy of the idea it had to be promoted by the newly established foci of political power. The second plan was worked out by an interoffice committee; the Histadrut nominated the head of its Social Security Department as chairman. In 1953 the law of National Insurance was promulgated; at that time it provided a flat-rate universal old-age pension and survivors benefit, maternity grants, and work-injury insurance (Doron 1975). Because of the reluctance of the Histadrut to allow the nationalization of its large-scale sick-insurance services, the national insurance did not include health care, but various arrangements were made with the existing sick-insurance funds.

Since then, the functions of the national insurance were much enlarged. At present the following schemes are in operation (Nizan 1973):

(1959)   Old-age and survivors insurance for all Israeli citizens
(1953)   Maternity benefit for employed and self-employed women and maternity grant to cover confinement and layette expenses
(1953)   Work-injury compensation for the insured employed and self-employed, covering temporary and permanent disability (partial or total) and rehabilitation/retraining payments
(1959)   Family allowances for each child (the first two children get flat-rate allowance, while the allowance for each additional child increases; thus, in a family with nine children the total allowance is 18 times the allowance for one child)
(1970)   Unemployment insurance for insured persons in the workforce
(1972)   Alimony payment for divorced persons having obtained a court order for alimony
(1974)   Disability pension, treatment and rehabilitation for all citizens

Besides the national insurance there are additional welfare payments designated for the ensurance of a minimum income. But by far the most important

TABLE 6.1

Composition of Transfers, Israeli Welfare Payments, 1969

Type of Transfer	Percent
Old-age	34.9
Family	32.5
Survivors	5.8
Disability	1.8
Others	1.3
Total national insurance	76.3
Other welfare payments	23.7

Source: Jack Habib, *Poverty in Israel before and after Receipt of Public Transfers* (Jerusalem: National Insurance Institute, 1974), p. 11.

TABLE 6.2

Old-Age and Survivors' Pension Rates as Percentage of National Average Monthly Income of Employed Persons

	Rate
No dependents	28.9
One dependent	38.4
Two, three dependents	43.4
Widow or widower aged 40 to 50	28.9

transfers are effected by the national insurance, specifically through the old-age and family-allowance schemes (see Table 6.1). Some of these schemes serve to cushion the effects of sudden crisis, while others are mainly intended to redress chronic inequality. Old-age pension and family allowances have the strongest effect on family income. Table 6.2 shows the proportion of income provided by the welfare insurance. If we define the poverty line at about 25 percent of the average national income, then old-age payments alone maintain the aged population somewhat above the poverty line. Jack Habib states that "Forty one per cent of families with aged heads were removed from poverty [;] . . . as a result, after transfers the share of the aged among the remaining poor decreases. . . . Among the aged the reduction of poverty is greater for male than female family heads and is particularly high in families whose head is employed" (Habib 1974:32).

There is in Israel a strong correlation between family size and poverty (Derber 1970:185-201). The typical poverty syndrome is characterized by low income, low education, and large family, hence the special importance of the family allowance and its effects. Seventy-five percent of the poor children are from large families: "The incidence of poverty rises consistently with the number of children. . . . The incidence more than doubles from 6% among families with 1-2 children to 14% among families with three children . . . rising to 25.6% among families with 4-5 children then rising steeply up to 52.9% among families with 6 or more children" (Habib 1974:80). The effects of the welfare transfers are about the same for each subgroup. An average of 25 percent of the children and families with children and about 40 percent of families without children are taken out of poverty, according to 1969 data (Habib 1974:83).

Three large areas of welfare policy—health, education, and housing—are part of separate systems. Health insurance covers 93.2 percent of the total population (somewhat less among the poor). It seems that health care will not be nationalized, but a law for compulsory health insurance is in preparation. It must be emphasized that the working poor are already insured with the Histadrut. Insurance rates being progressive, the payments due from low-earning groups are minimal. For the nonworking poor special arrangements are being made with the existing sick-insurance funds.

Since educational equality is a very complex problem, it will be only cursorily mentioned in this chapter. Israel provides ten years of compulsory and free education: nine for the 6-to-15-year age group in a six-plus-three-year system of elementary and middle school, and one-year preschool education for the five- to six-year-olds. The regular school plan is enriched by programs for under-privileged groups such as two additional preschool years for the three- to five-year-olds, longer school days, remedial teaching, and special "enrichment" projects. High school and university are not free, but youngsters from low-income families are entitled to scholarships. A preacademic preparatory year enables gifted young people who do not have a matriculation examination to enter the university.*

In Israel as in many other modern countries it was expected that universal education will successfully ensure equal opportunities and equalize the chances of various immigrant groups. The failure of the school system, its explanation, and the search for solutions is the most discussed issue by politicians and social scientists (Eisenstadt 1967:261-84; Weller 1974:50-77).

Housing Policy. Housing policy is an eminently noticeable action for the reduction of inequality in residential status. It is also the most immediately effective and is highly loaded with emotions. Acquiring a home has great psychological importance in a country of immigrants. It symbolizes safety, stability, and gives a feeling of property. It is also a much coveted status symbol. Possibly this is the explanation of the very strong desire of the Israelis to own their dwelling and their reluctance to live in rented homes. The typical Israeli dwelling is an apartment in a condominium. About 70 percent of the population owns a home.

In the Israeli circumstances, owning a home or even living at the present standard would be an impossible objective for a large part of the population left to its own means. Israel does not have a reserve of dwelling, and in general the supply does not meet the demand. Rentals are scarce and buying requires large sums of ready cash for down payment. Housing is de facto recognized as part of the welfare service. It is a selective service, officially of the residual type.† Projects are planned for specific groups, each having a particular criterion of eligibility. But the number of projects is so large that a considerable percentage of

---

*Israeli universities ask for a matriculation certificate and an entrance examination. Success in the preparatory year replaces both.

†Wilensky and Lebeaux define *residual social welfare* as those institutions "which should come into play only when normal structures of supply, the family and the market, break down" (1958:138).

the population has enjoyed, at some period of its life, the benefits accruing from the housing policy. Thus 64 percent of all owned dwellings and about 55 percent of the rented apartments have been obtained with some government aid. The major housing aid projects are housing for immigrants, housing for married couples, slum clearing and replacement of substandard or overcrowded dwellings (more than three persons per room), and popular saving schemes based on low monthly payments.

As shown in Table 6.3, up to 1972 about half of the public building was for new immigrants; about 20 percent was for saving schemes, and smaller percentages were for the other projects. After 1972 the allocation for young married couples and for replacement of substandard dwellings increased, but no accurate data are yet available.

The majority of the dwellings in these projects are akin to those of the free market (that is, flats in condominiums), but the buildings are on the outskirts of the cities or in newly built suburbs. The flats can be rented with option to buy, when the rent paid up to that time becomes a down-payment. The projects are heavily subsidized by the government. The prices are much below the market price, and long-term, low-interest loans and mortgages are given to the eligibles. Subsidies are also given to the builders in the form of allocation of public land, loans, and credit. Given the continuous inflation and the rising prices of real estate, the investment in housing is the best way to maintain the value of savings or government-provided benefits. When the homes are bought, they become the property of the owner and can be sold on the open market, the only restriction being that the land remains public property and is leased to the owners

TABLE 6.3

Public Construction of Permanent Dwellings (Completed)
in Israel, by Type, 1949-72

Type	Percent
Immigrant housing	51.5
Popular housing-saving schemes	19.5
Building in rural areas	14.6
Slum clearance	3.2
Housing in development areas (for veteran settlers)	3.1
Young marrieds	1.9
Miscellaneous*	6.2

*Includes the clearing of temporary dwellings in immigrant camps.
Source: Israel, Ministry of Housing, Programming Department, Population and Building in Israel, 1948-1973 (Jerusalem: the Ministry [in Hebrew] 1975), p. 88.

TABLE 6.4

Israeli Households, by Type of Ownerships and Size of Household, 1971
(percent)

Size of Household	Owner Resident	Private	Rented Government	Total	Not Owned and Not Rented
1 person	46.1	24.8	20.4	45.2	8.7
2 persons	67.1	15.1	14.4	29.5	3.4
3 persons	68.4	13.3	15.4	28.7	2.9
4 persons	75.6	11.1	10.6	21.7	2.7
5 persons	71.9	8.1	15.6	23.7	4.4
6 persons and more	58.1	6.5	26.6	33.1	8.8
Total	64.6	12.8	17.7	30.5	4.8

Source: Israel, Central Bureau of Statistics, *Survey of Housing Conditions, 1971* (Jerusalem: the Bureau, 1971), p. 112.

for 99 years at a nominal rent. Subsidized housing practically means the transfer of capital from public funds to private persons. Although the recipient is forced to save as part of the transaction, he becomes nevertheless the possessor of valuable, convertible wealth.

Considering ownership and lack of crowdedness as measures of residential status, the distribution of housing is more egalitarian than the distribution of income. Table 6.4 shows the relationship between size of household and housing position. More than half of the population owns its own home, which besides some wealth also bestows stability and security. Among the single-person households and large families ownership is somewhat less frequent; about 20 percent of the population lives in apartments rented by the government. These do not have the same capital value, but they offer the same measure of residential security.

Comparing the poor with the nonpoor, the 1969 data show that 35.1 percent of the poor families were owners, compared with 66.9 percent of the nonpoor. Another 52.2 percent of the poor families are tenants in rent-controlled apartments, compared with 27.5 percent of the nonpoor.

Density as a measure of the quality of housing (Habib 1974:124) is highly correlated with family size. The Israeli standard of overcrowdedness is defined as three or more persons per room. In 1969, 7.9 percent of the nonpoor were overcrowded, versus 16.2 percent of the poor. However, while in 1957, 24.2 percent of the families lived in high-density dwellings, in 1974 there were only 5.2 percent.

Constraints on Ownership and Income

Welfare was defined as a cluster of consumption rights bestowed upon the citizens by their government. As such it is not exclusively an instrument for the reduction of inequalities. Nevertheless, the available evidence shows that welfare programs have some equalizing effect, at least by raising the status of the weakest groups (see Table 6.5).

The lowest income group is the recipient of about one-third of all transfers, which more than doubles its income. But the other low-income groups have much lesser shares. The relative value of the services varies with the income. Evidently the most "valuable" welfare investment is for the three lower deciles, where each percentage of the total transfer corresponds to 4.4, 1.9, and 1.3 percent, respectively, of the pretransfer income, as opposed to the three higher deciles, where the welfare investments are devaluated and correspond to entirely negligible quantities of the deciles income (0.4 to 0.2 percent).

Seen from a purely economic point of view this means that at least 20 percent of the expenses on transfer are misspent, but from a different perspective this is the price of universal as against selective services, and of the unmeasurable social benefits accruing from it to the lower-income groups.

An indirect egalitarian effect of the welfare system is the redistribution of incomes necessary for carrying the cost of welfare policy. Obviously, taxation is

TABLE 6.5

Transfers by Income Deciles

| Decile | Transfers | |
	As Percent of Pretransfer Income	Percent Distribution
Lowest	144.3	32.4
2	18.9	9.9
3	11.6	9.2
4	8.9	8.9
5	5.3	6.8
6	4.0	6.4
7	2.5	5.1
8	2.8	7.0
9	2.2	7.2
Highest	1.2	7.1
Total	5.2	100.0

Source: Jack Habib, *Poverty in Israel before and after Receipt of Public Transfers* (Jerusalem: National Insurance Institute, 1974), p. 13.

TABLE 6.6

Effect of Taxes and Transfers on Distribution of Income among Deciles and on Gini Inequality Index, 1969 (percent)

Decile	Pretransfer Income		Posttransfer Income		Posttax Income	
	Average Income as Percent of Overall Average	Decile's Share of Total Income	Average Income as Percent of Overall Average	Decile's Share of Total Income	Average Income as Percent of Overall Average	Decile's Share of Total Income
Lowest	12.7	1.2	23.9	2.2	28.5	2.6
2	31.5	2.8	36.5	3.3	43.0	3.9
3	45.3	4.1	48.3	4.5	55.6	5.1
4	58.1	5.2	60.3	5.4	68.1	6.2
5	71.8	6.8	72.2	6.9	79.6	7.5
6	87.6	8.5	86.7	8.5	93.0	9.0
7	106.7	10.5	104.3	10.3	108.2	10.7
8	131.2	13.2	127.8	12.8	128.6	13.1
9	170.7	17.5	165.7	17.0	158.2	16.0
Highest	284.5	30.2	274.4	29.2	237.2	25.9
Ratio between lowest and highest	22.4		11.48		8.32	
Gini index	0.428		0.397		0.349	
Percent decline in Gini index			7.3		18.6	

Source: Jack Habib, *Poverty in Israel before and after Receipt of Public Transfers* (Jerusalem: National Insurance Institute, 1974), p. 14.

not the invention of the welfare states, but usually its rate depends on the level of public expenditure. Wilensky (1975) assumes that welfare programs "are typically financed by regressive contributory and tax schemes." But Habib shows with Israeli data that at least in our case the opposite is true. Both transfers and taxes are progressive, the latter being more progressive than the former, but there are regressive areas. Thus, "the bottom decile pays a higher tax rate than either the second, third or fourth decile" (Habib 1974).

The combined effect of welfare and taxation shortens the stratification pyramid and reduces the "gaps" between the groups (see Table 6.6). The table shows the considerable shortening of the range of differences; the ratio of 22.4 between the lowest and the highest decile is reduced by transfers and taxes to 8.32. Similarly, the Gini index declines from 0.428 to 0.349. In both cases taxes have a much stronger egalitarian effect as measured by the Gini index but a lesser effect on the highest/lowest ratio, which is influenced mostly by the transfers.

In the Israeli egalitarian ideology the concept of "gaps," meaning the distance between the strata, is the core of many recurrent issues. Although deciles are not meaningful social strata, measuring the distance between each pair of deciles does reveal an interesting aspect of the dynamics of welfare transfers compared with taxes (see Table 6.7). In the initial pretransfer situation the lowest decile is far removed from all the others. The distance between the second and the third decile is much lower but still seems to be distinctive. From here on there is an even rise on the scale, with one more large gap removing the highest decile from the previous one. The transfers affect the lower part of the ladder, especially the two lowest deciles, and do not have any influence on the top. The taxes are complementary with little overlapping. They cause only negligible changes in the lower decile, but draw the upper two deciles nearer to the average.

Government Concern for Furthering Equality

Welfare policy and the progressive taxation system act as mechanisms of equalization, and as such they are at least de facto instruments of political

TABLE 6.7

Effects of Transfers and Taxes on Ratios between Adjacent Pairs of Deciles of Average Income as Percent of Overall Average

Decile	Pretransfer Income	Posttransfer Income	Posttax Income
Lowest to 2	2.78	1.53	1.51
2 to 3	1.44	1.32	1.29
3 to 4	1.28	1.24	1.22
4 to 5	1.23	1.20	1.17
5 to 6	1.22	1.20	1.17
6 to 7	1.22	1.20	1.16
7 to 8	1.23	1.23	1.19
8 to 9	1.30	1.30	1.23
9 to Highest	1.66	1.66	1.49

socialism. They have a social-control function, acting as correctives that reduce inequality but do not affect the initial relationship. At the beginning of this chapter, I pointed out that by definition inequality occupies a wide range on the equality-inequality scale, while equality is an end point. Hence, equality is an extreme and exceptional situation. The data on transfers and taxation show that their effect is more equality, but how good is this new level of inequality as compared with the initial level? The pretransfers ratio of the lowest decile to the highest is 1/25 and that of the lowest third to the highest third 1/7.5. After the interventionary policy they decrease to 1/10 and 1/4.5, respectively. For planners, politicians, and social reformers the practical question is the degree of equality to which the policy maker should aim. In the words of the first director of the National Insurance Institute:

> One of the impediments to communication is the lack of an agreed scale of values. Such a scale might serve as a yardstick to some of the authorities and experts as well as to the public at large, so as to indicate the degree of inequality that is "bearable" or that which is absolutely intolerable, and which of the "social evils" must be either overcome immediately or suffered, for the time being. It is true that it will be difficult to arrive at such an agreed scale of values . . . (Lotan 1972:19).

Lacking such a yardstick, the government of Israel has been eager to prove from time to time that it is moving toward more equality. In 1963 and in 1971 the government in cooperation with the Histadrut appointed a committee of experts "to examine the developments of incomes and their distribution, and in social inequality during the past decade" (Committee on Income Distribution 1971).

The documents touch on several interesting problems of the measurement of equality which, although apparently technical, do in essence affect the final conclusions. The committee tried to be painstakingly objective and precise. The Lorenz curve (Gini index) was chosen as the general measure of equality, and the data were those of various surveys conducted by the Central Bureau of Statistics. The committee found (a) "a trend of decreasing inequality," "an improvement in the relative position of the lower income brackets," and (c) "during the economic recession (1966-1967) . . . inequality in the distribution of incomes increased" (1971:4).

The discussions of the committee revealed many conceptual problems in the operationalization of equality and its measurement. In spite of the rigorousness of the approach, there was no escape from value discussions, and the social philosophy of the participants impinged on the choice of techniques, the evaluation of ambiguous data, and so on. The committee did not try to answer the overt value questions. It did not evaluate the meaning of the drop in the Gini index from 0.346 to 0.332. It "did not regard as its function to determine what is the poverty line since the definition of poverty is . . . a value judgment on the part of society influenced by various economic and social factors" (Committee on Income Distribution 1971:51).

For the policy maker and the bureaucrat it would be comfortable if the level and the character of economic equality could be codified in a manner similar to political equality. In a nondogmatic, democratic political system this does not seem possible. The limits of tolerance of inequality are unstable, and diverse agents demand from time to time the reevaluation of the situation. In each such case the legitimacy of the existing standards is questioned. The appointment of committees of prestigious experts is one way used by the policy maker for the establishment of new standards. The committees may be seen as gestures of participation, through which the government proves its receptivity to public opinion, mobilizes the support of the academic community, and shows its special concern for some key, value-laden questions. Among several important committees, the most influential ones dealt with a comprehensive tax reform and important changes in the salary system of the civil service. In general these are ad hoc committees and the majority of the members are drawn from the faculties of the universities. Although the mandate of the committees emphasizes their advisory status, the conclusions, once published, exert a powerful influence. The members of the committees, once their official task is finished, regard it as their duty to defend their conclusions and to mobilize public opinion, thus enhancing the participatory character of the process.

It seems proper to close this section with a glance at that most succinct declaration of the policy makers' intentions: the national budget. Until the 1960s the budget reflected the orientation toward economic growth and development, the appropriate item being the largest. In the past decade the social services became predominant, even though Israel went through three wars and its defense expenditures doubled. Wilensky (1975:74-80) proposes the hypothesis that "war and welfare have become mutually subversive." Although he states that "Israel is a special case," he finds nonetheless proof for his hypothesis:

> The case of Israel is ambiguous. Because of three short wars involving large-scale mobilization, the timing of changes in Israeli welfare-warfare spending bears little relationship to the cold war peaks and valleys of the countries. . . . Nevertheless, welfare and warfare in Israel appear to be antithetical. When military spending as a proportion of GNP dropped after the 1949 war, social security spending climbed. When military effort during and after the 1956 war increased fivefold—from 3 percent in 1955 to 14.2 percent in 1964—social security effort remained almost static (6.2 percent to 6.9 percent). When military spending dropped from 1964 to 1966 social security effort climbed again (Wilensky 1975:79).

His last data are from 1966. Since then there were three more wars, the military spending increased further, but welfare spending went up, too. Obviously, the dilemma was not always formulated as "guns *or* butter," but as "guns *and* some butter": The question was "What kind of butter?" Up to the 1960s priority was given to economic growth and state investments in it. From the late 1960s on, social services were given preference. Three illustrative budgets of these periods are shown in Table 6.8.The largest part of the welfare expenditure reaches the citizen in the form of services and a relatively small part only as downright payments. The 1975 allocations are shown in Table 6.9.

Prediction of future trends is difficult at this point. While the security needs remain as high as at present, it does not seem possible that the welfare services could be further expanded. But there can be changes in the utilization of the available funds, which may affect the existing balance of equality. We must remember that at present the major political problem is not equality in general but those pockets of inequality where ascriptive attributes—for example, country of origin of the individual and the geographic location of a community in Israel—overlap with status characteristics.

In this discussion of political socialism I have tried to show some aspects of the interrelationship between equality and inequality. It was suggested that the policy makers' concern with equality finds its expression in corrective measures, which reduce inequality mainly through welfare and taxation. Thus, the relevant policy problem concerns the proper balance between equality and inequality, the adjustment to changing limits of tolerance and the dimensions of the standard of living germane to the accepted concept of equality. The egalitarian tendencies of the Israeli policy are not directed by predetermined conceptions of the social ideal. Inequalities not only result from the imperfection of the system, they correspond to value conceptions that are widely accepted, including those of the labor movement, which represents the differential wage

TABLE 6.8

National Expenditures of Israel
(percent)

	1961	1970	1975
Security	17.80	33.91	37.84
Economy	34.83	13.77	11.63
Social services	22.60	20.33	23.95
Administration	9.71	12.36	4.40
Municipalities	1.60	2.86	3.20
Other, debts	13.46	16.77	18.98

TABLE 6.9

Social Welfare Expenditures in Israel, 1975 National Budget (percent)

	Social Welfare Expenditures	Total Expenditures
Education	31.10	7.45
Housing	25.07	6.00
Payments	14.39	3.44
Health	13.54	3.24
Price stabilization	12.46	2.98
Others	3.44	0.84

demands of various occupational groups. The justice and desirability of some kind of equity is contested only by small groups. The ideological negation of equity as a principle is the basis of the collectivist ideology.

Collectivistic Socialism

Collectivist socialism is at present not proposed as an alternative of political socialism but rather as complementary to it. The collectivist ideology envisages the ideal society as a participatory democracy, composed of self-managing egalitarian workers' communities (Kramer 1972). It is not very clear whether at any time the establishment of this type of society was considered as a viable program, to be implemented immediately. It was never suggested that, alike with political socialism, collectivism could be enforced by way of legislation. Voluntarism is intrinsic to the Israeli version of collectivist socialism. It is expected that membership in a communal unit is the outcome of mature, individual decision. Thus, young people born in a collectivity are not automatically members. At the age of 18 they have to request the status of membership if they so desire, and the community votes on their acceptance. In some places it is customary to send the young people to live for a year in one of the cities, so that they should be able to deliberate on the basis of a real experience. Collectivist socialism in Israel did not develop a full-fledged model of society, like the Yugoslav self-managing model (Adizes 1971; Kolaja 1965), presumably because there was no serious political movement that intended to establish a collectivistic society. Nevertheless, the collectivistic ideology is not a utopian ideal to be achieved in the future. For a large part of the labor movement it represents the essence of socialism—which is, however, practiced only by a small group of pioneers. Because of this ideological centrality, the influence of the communal settlements and the importance accorded to them exceed by far their objective position. They are entitled to economic privileges and social prestige as the representatives of major societal values. It was expected that the communes would extend their moral influence over the entire social climate (Buber 1967), and it is still expected that members should prove themselves as morally superior. The kibbutz is the prototype of a collectivist community, but it is not the sole carrier of the collectivist orientation. Since the emergence of the first communal groups in the early twentieth century is has been apparent that the strictness and the total commitment of kibbutz life does not appeal to the masses. At the same time the core idea of collectivist socialism, namely the establishment of socialist enclaves, remained an integral part of the labor ideology. The quest for additional types of organization, less orthodox in their collectivist orientation but more accessible to a variety of people, resulted in the establishment of a number of cooperative organizational forms connected with the Histadrut. The level of equality in these organizations depends on their totality or partiality and on the system of allocation adopted.

Cooperatives Connected with the Histadrut

The least egalitarian are the urban housing cooperatives and the neighborhood representative participation. The neighborhood organizations have only one function: to represent the interests of the neighborhood versus those of the municipal organization. Although this places it in the domain of the political power system, the neighborhood va'ad (committee) deals mostly with the allocation of services for the neighborhood. The va'ad is elected or self-elected and approved by the public and the Histadrut local. Until recently its activities did not have a legal basis and it enjoyed only de facto recognition by the municipality. In the near future the neighborhood committees will be granted legal standing as representatives of the specific nonpolitical interests of the neighborhoods. Va'adim are not a universal phenomenon; they usually arise in cohesive, well-organized suburbs, in new housing projects, and in poverty-stricken areas. The initiative for the representation comes equally often from the local inhabitants or from the part of various organizations, mostly the Histadrut and the public housing authorities.

It has been mentioned already that the large majority of dwellings in Israel are condominiums of apartment owners. This form of housing is rooted in the housing cooperatives established before statehood by the Histadrut, which hoped to establish urban cooperative neighborhoods of workers. The plan as originally conceived did not succeed entirely, but the idea of cooperative housing remained, albeit in a much diluted form. The condominiums are managed on a voluntary basis by a committee elected by the tenant owners. The maintenance and the social standard of the house depends very much on the cooperation of the tenants and the activity of the committee (va'ad bayit). The va'ad has the legally recognized right to levy a house tax for maintenance. There are some difficulties in this type of organization. The apartments are bought individually and there is no prior connection between the owners. Such a group does not always have that minimum of common basis for communication that is necessary for self-management. The public housing authorities have shown some awareness of these problems and sometimes are providing consulting services. Recently, there have also been experiments in planning the desirable population mix of new housing projects. Paradoxically, this is one instance in which participation and egalitarianism are inversely correlated. It was found that in order to ensure the success of neighborhood democracy and self-management of the cooperative housing it is necessary that the population should not be exclusively drawn from the lower-income groups or new immigrants. This can be achieved only if housing at below-market prices is offered to people not "properly" entitled to it. The presence of these people in the neighborhood ensures better functioning of local democracy, it lends higher prestige to the area and ensures better maintenance of services, but it also spreads thinner the amount of resources invested in slum clearing. The question to be answered is one of interchangeability among such values as physical equality of housing, compared to residential prestige equality and the opportunity structure of neighborhood democracy.*

The transport cooperatives are the success examples of egalitarian and participatory work organizations (Bar-Yosef and Ramot 1973). Public transportation is, in Israel, responsible for a large slice of the total passenger load carried. The preferred means of public transportation are buses, both in the cities and outside them. The public bus companies are cooperatives and they have the monopoly of the regular inter- and intraurban public transport by road. They also own a touring company which competes in the nonmonopolized tourist market.

These monopolistic rights are granted partly due to the backing of the Histadrut, but also because the charismatic attitude of the governing labor parties toward business organizations that are not private enterprises.

This public transport service is highly subsidized by the government so as to secure relatively low fares for the consumers, who are coming mainly from the lower-income groups:

> The bus cooperatives are associations of member drivers. The Hebrew
> word for membership is Haver, but this also means associate or a

---

*It was found in many sociological studies on housing, in Israel (Bar-Yosef 1974) and elsewhere (Rossi 1955), that residential prestige is a much coveted status dimension.

peer—even a friend. The first transport cooperatives were indeed friendly associations of worker-entrepreneurs having the same skills who brought to the association their own "means of production," viz. their vehicle. The very same principles, although in a more abstract and sophisticated form, are the basis of membership until the present. The cooperatives are no more "friendly associations" as there are too many members for face to face relationships. But on the local level, in the daily routine, much informality is maintained and until the present the original principles are embodied in the formal requirements for membership. The common basis is occupational and all members have to have bus drivers' licences notwithstanding whether their actual job is driving. Membership means part ownership, managerial rights and job duties in the cooperative. . . . The modern driver-member does not "bring with him" his own means of production. He buys a share which represents the equivalent value of this. Each member has only one share, which gives him full "citizenship" rights. . . . The income of the members is paid in the form of wages composed from the usual items of the Israeli wage structure. Dividends as such are not paid, but the wage level is higher than that of the labor market taking into account the investment made by the members. The peculiar feature of the wage-dividend system is the lack of differentiation between the two. The cooperative being a price-controlled public service it works very often with deficit. But it is not expected that this should be carried by the members (Bar-Yosef 1973).

The organization is a direct-participatory democracy, where the supreme authority is vested in the general assembly of the members. A system of elected bureaucrats provides the body of managers, who return to their driving jobs after the end of their office term.

The cooperative organization seems to provide fairly good solutions to problems of the individual worker, such as alienation, feelings of exploitation, insecurity, and so on. Incomes are in the range of the middle class. The payments start on an egalitarian basis but some differentiation occurs due to seniority and overtime additions. The size of the organization and the need for specialization in the field of managerial function cause some difficulties and raise some doubts about the expedience of such a large size, when it is desired to maintain the principles of cooperative organization. Nevertheless, as a form of production organization the transport cooperatives ensure a much higher standard of equality and participation for their members than would be possible to foresee in conventionally organized enterprises where profit sharing, workers' participation in management, or other amendments proposed by the schools of industrial democracy have been implemented (Blumenthal 1956; Tannenbaum 1974; Thorsrud 1970). The contribution of the cooperatives to the egalitarian character of the society is more controversial. The socialism of the cooperative is strictly for its members. But about 40 percent of the manpower needed in running the cooperative are hired nonmembers. Although the employment of hired labor is contrary to the tenets of the cooperative, there are strong economic interests in it. The hired labor is the fluid manpower toward which the company does not have the same binding commitments as toward the members. The compromise solution is the provision of membership opportunities for a certain number of tenured workers. In this situation the Histadrut functions as the representative of the workers and bargains for increases in the membership openings and comfortable conditions of payment for the obligatory share.

There is more acute conflict between the cooperatives and the government. As part of its welfare policy the government decides how much the public will pay for transportation. This means that the government indirectly controls the income of the members of the cooperatives. The amount of subsidies paid by the government, the acceptable price of the tickets, and the legitimate income of the members of the cooperative are issues of periodic contention. Some economists argue that nationalization of the public transportation would cost less in government subsidies, while others propose to revoke the monopolistic rights of the cooperatives and open the market for competition. Both suggestions probe essentially into the intrinsic social value of an egalitarian organization. The welfare policy of political socialism and the class egalitarianism of the Histadrut do not necessarily harmonize with the particularistic interests of the units of collectivistically oriented subculture.

Rural Communities

In the cities the collectivistic orientation did not lead further than the cooperative organization of certain selected areas of activity. Experiments in establishing egalitarian urban communities encompassing all the aspects of life failed. Only in the relative segregation of the rural areas was this ideal achieved in the form of the cooperative smallholders' village (moshav) and the communal settlements (kibbutz or kvutzah), known in Israel also under the cover title of "workers' settlements" (Ben-David 1964). These two forms, in spite of the difference in the basic principles along which the communities are organized, are integrated in the institutional structure of the surrounding society in similar ways:

1. Each village community is settled on publicly owned land and is entitled to a certain amount of budgetary allocation for initial investment.
2. Nearly all are affiliated with the Histadrut.
3. There are national federations of moshavim and kibbutzim, with marketing, purchasing, and other service branches.
4. The national federations function as control agents in safeguarding the cooperative and the communal principles.

5. The national federations function also as power groups, ensuring the representation of the kibbutz and the moshav on the governing bodies of the Histadrut, in the elite circles of the labor parties, and in the government. It is customary that the minister for agriculture should be a member of either a moshav or a kibbutz. Thus, the former minister was a kibbutz member, while the present one is from a moshav.*
6. Each village community has a certain autonomy and sovereignty; while remaining committed to the general principles of its federation, each community tends to create its own lifestyle.

Beyond these very general traits of similarity the moshav and the kibbutz represent different patterns of egalitarian social organization and aim at different levels of equality. It must be emphasized that neither type is homogeneous. There are several variations, resulting from subtle ideological differences from the original culture of the local population, from the age and the site of the settlement, and probably from many other variables. Practically each community has its individual character. The distributive system however is distinctive and prototypical.

The moshav is a cooperative agricultural village where the basic membership unit is the family. The family maintains its own household; the house and the household goods are its own property. The family is allocated a standard-sized (somewhat small) lot of land, which is considered an individual enterprise. If the family leaves, the land reverts to the village, to be allocated to new members or to the new households of young villagers. Large-scale farming projects take place in collectively owned land worked cooperatively; profits are shared in proportion to the labor invested. Hired labor is forbidden, and all the families are requested to take part in the common project. Purchasing and marketing are done exclusively through the cooperative. The political organization of the moshav is a direct democracy: Managerial roles are filled by election; the incumbent manager is accountable to the general assembly and to the national federation. The allocative principle of the moshav is essentially one of equal opportunity, by ensuring equal start. The equality of opportunity is further enhanced by specialized services of planning, information and professional guidance provided by a very efficient network of extension: services run by the Ministry of Agriculture. (The service is not exclusively for the moshav; the individual farmers, who are mostly Arab villagers, benefit from it as well. However, these services function better in a cooperative organization.) The moshav ideology

---

*While this position is offered to the "workers' settlements" as an interest group, other elite positions are often attained by politically active settlement members. In the present government, for example, two ministers are moshav members, and three are kibbutz members.

does not advocate equality of outcome. Variations in standard of living are acceptable and expected, assuming that they are equitable—the result of effort and skill—and contained within the constraints imposed by the cooperative principle. The combination of these two allocative principles produces a limited range of inequalities within each village. The differences among the villages are much larger due to noncontrollable variables of the environment, such as land, water, climate, type of crops, and to a certain extent the age, education, and skill composition of the local population (Weintraub 1964). While it is expected that well-established Moshavim should be ready to contribute advice and guidance to further the success of less endowed villages, there is no attempt to share profits or equalize in other ways the wealth and earnings of all the federated settlements.

The kibbutz is the most radical implementation of the collectivistic ideology in Israel.* Because of the strictness and discipline of the organization, it was and presumably will continue to be a relatively small, elitist form of life, tried out by many people, but permanently chosen by few. At present, there are 95,000 (about 3.2 percent of Israel's Jewish population) living in 140 kibbutzim. The number of people who have lived at some period of their lives as members in a kibbutz is estimated to be about twice that figure. Groups of young people and immigrants spent these shorter periods as participants in various projects hosted by kibbutzim. Though lacking reliable statistics, I would guess that about 15 to 20 percent of Israel's population has had some active experience in kibbutz life.

The overrepresentation of kibbutz members in elite positions of the political establishment and the army, the economic success of the settlements, and the large number of people who have come in contact with the kibbutz are factors that guarantee the kibbutz's special status in the Israeli society.

Although the kibbutz does not live up to the expectations of Martin Buber and of those of the kibbutz movement itself, its impact greatly exceeds its relative numerical strength as a continuous source of ideological and moral influence on the nonkibbutz society. Unlike many other communes that outlasted the generation of the founders, the kibbutz is a secular movement (Kanter 1973). Neither is it a closed society, segregated from and guarded against the intrusion of the individualistic social environment. An intrinsic component of the kibbutz ideology is the identification with the national goals and the interests of the working class. This combination of being unlike the "other" society while being part of it is expressed in the formal official definition heading the charter which specifies the legal position of kibbutz:

---

*In the past two decades much material has been published on the kibbutz: source books (Viteles 1967) bibliographies (Cohen 1964; Shur 1972), digests (Rabin 1970); extensive descriptions and analyses of the kibbutz life (Arian 1968:58-116; Spiro 1956; Garber-Talmon 1970), and many more.

> The kibbutz is a free association of people for purposes of settle-
> ment, establishment of a communal society organized along the
> principles of common ownership of property, work, equality and
> collectivism in the spheres of production, consumption, and edu-
> cation.
>
>   [. . .]
>
> The kibbutz considers itself an inseparable part of the Israeli Labor
> movement which aspires to build the nation as an egalitarian working
> society.
>
>   [. . .]
>
> The aims of the kibbutz are— . . . to promote and to persevere in
> the fulfillment of tasks which strenghen the status, the economy and
> the security of the State of Israel, and the tasks which support the
> working class and the kibbutz movement . . . (Kibbutz Meuchad
> 1966: 22, 23).

The interrelationship between the kibbutz and the politicosocial levels of
policy making provides important status rewards as well as political and economic privileges for the kibbutz. But at the same time it weakens the defenses
of the commune, exposes it to outside influences, opens channels of communication, and imposes on the kibbutz reference norms that are alien to the
principles of the collective.

The kibbutz is not an ascetic society. It recognizes the legitimacy of
aspirations to a higher standard of living, but these have to be limited by the
priority given to the collectivistic goals:

> . . . the kibbutz will provide for the economic, social, cultural, edu-
> cational and personal needs of the members and of their depend-
> ents [;] . . . it will ensure a fair standard of living . . . within the
> limits of the economic potential of the kibbutz while taking into
> account the needs of its economic development and those of its
> other goals (Kibbutz Meuchad 1966:23).

The essential characteristic of the kibbutz is the complete disjunction of
the position of a member in the institutional role structure and his rights of
consumption:

> Superficially, the common household appears to be the chief differ-
> ence between the kibbutz and other types of collective farming.
> Actually, the real differences are the underlying principles of organi-
> zation and living. Most important of them are the complete inte-
> gration of all spheres of life in the community, the principle of
> separation between individual effort and satisfaction of wants, vol-
> untary membership as well as day-to-day behavior, and democratic
> organization on all levels of activity. Many other values of kibbutz
> life, such as satisfaction of wants according to individual needs, the

equal value of physical and intellectual work, the principle of
rotation of managerial functions are but derivations of these values
(Shatil 1968, p. 80).

The distributive system in the kibbutz emerges as an autonomous institution in which all the norms and methods of allocation have to be identified and
decided upon by the political mechanism of the direct democracy. The constraints of the economic potential trace only the outer limits of the possible
manipulation. The exact definition of the principles guiding the distribution is
thus a practical necessity. At the most abstract ideological level the kibbutz is
committed to the idea, "From each according to his ability, to each according
to his need." By necessity, the implementation of this slogan involves additional
constraints and limitations:

> The first principle of the commune is common ownership—the
> absence of private property. We say: "From each according to his
> ability, to each according to his needs." But the extent of our realiz-
> ing this principle is limited to the realistic level of our membership's
> development. When we say: "From each according to his ability,"
> that ability is dependent upon how well we developed it when we
> said: "To each according to his needs". The whole matter depends
> on the extent of our actual ability to furnish those needs. These
> two elements—the development of the member's ability and the
> possibility of furnishing all his needs limit us. We do not provide to
> each according to his needs, for our communal possessions are insuf-
> ficient for that. We strive for equality, not formal equality, but
> actual equality. Formal equality is nothing but inequality (Tabenkin
> 1948:103-04).

The actual principles of distribution range from the exact formal equality,
to the free supply according to personal needs. The application of any such
principle depends on the nature of the commodity, the elasticity of demand and
the ideological leanings of the community toward more or less control over the
individual. Whatever combination of distributive principles is chosen, it always
results in the accomplishment of one type of equality and some decrement in
the other type. Obviously, "free supply according to needs" means free within
limits for those needs which are normatively defined as legitimate needs. Even
within these limits there is the likelihood that such freedom of individual
decision gives rise to feelings of relative deprivation. Mutual trust and strong
normative self-discipline seem to be necessary preconditions for this type of
allocation. Formal equality is more visibly equal. It is easy to manage and it
serves the maintenance of uniform standard of living.

Lately there is a tendency of freeing the community from problems of
controlling and distributing each item of personal consumption. Each member

is provided with a personal budget "which should be used to satisfy his needs in personal apparel, vacation, hobbies, gifts, etc."

Whatever the principle of allocation it is always assumed that there will be no accumulation, no trading and consumption will conform to the "acceptable style of life." The steadily rising wealth of the kibbutz and the involvement of many of its members in activities outside the kibbutz are factors that upset the established egalitarian arrangements. Both necessitate continuous reassessment of the situation, redefinition of the legitimate needs, and reinforcement of the normative constraints. Unlike the closed communities with more or less fixed standards of living, the equality-inequality balance in the kibbutz is an unstable situation that is endangered by routine and inertia and can be maintained only by a dynamic approach.

The question of equality is even more complex when it comes to the more subtle issue of rights and rewards of the occupational and power roles. The technological sophistication of the kibbutz agriculture and the branching out into industrial entrepreneurship require heterogeneous skills based on specialized training. This leads to more complex problems of division of labor, more variety in the intrinsic rewards of work, and probably more differentiation in prestige and attractiveness of the available jobs (Yuchtman 1972). Industrial entrepreneurship introduced the disharmonic element of hierarchical production organization into the communal relationship (Vallier 1962). The traditional equalizing mechanisms of the kibbutz—rotation of executive positions, overtraining, and creation of a reserve of skilled people for rotation in interesting occupations, and universal service duties in unrewarding routine jobs—are not yet well adapted to the complexities of the newly emerging standards of production and services. Although in their traditional form these cannot fully redress the imbalance caused by modernization and development, they undoubtedly reduce their effect (Rosner 1965; 1973).

The kibbutz is a rapidly changing form of organization. Today's 65-year-old Deganya, the first kibbutz, resembles neither the Deganya of 1910 nor that of the 1920s or the 1940s. However, as long as the essential principles are maintained, communal character remains unchanged. The challenge of adapting the collectivistic mode of organization to the changing demands of modernization and industrialization constitutes a testing ground of the viability and applicability of egalitarian distribution.

The study of egalitarian communities and policies reveals new aspects of the structure of society. It does not merely add one more type to the map of known societies; it also deals with dimensions that were neglected by research focused on the functionality of inequalities.

A PARADIGM OF DISTRIBUTIVE SYSTEMS

> "No way has been found of equating a man's value in the market, his value as a citizen and his value for himself"
>
> —T. H. Marshall (1973)

The instances of egalitarian issues described in this chapter disclose the manifold definitions of equality when translated to policy. It has been suggested that the choice of one specific definition of equality is dictated by ideology in some cases, or is determined by circumstances in others. Often, both forces in combination shape the resultant method of distribution. For a systematic analysis of egalitarianism on the macro- or the microsocial level the concept needs to be related to a social model or paradigm of the distributive process. Such paradigms can be found in many treatises that discuss social welfare and egalitarianism.

The paradigm I shall discuss was influenced by many, but specifically by John Kenneth Galbraith (1973), Herbert Gans (1974), T. H. Marshall (1973), S. M. Miller (1974), John Rawls (1973), and J. Tobin (1970). The inferences draw mostly from the Israeli experience. It is postulated that there are three and only three basic distributive mechanisms: distribution as exchange, by right, and positional. As ideal types these are exclusive, but in an operating system of allocation two or all three will be combined.

Market or Exchange Mechanisms

The schematic characterization of a market situation consists of three elements: (a) an exchange type of interaction, (b) scarce resources, and (c) conditions determined by the universalist rules of the market. The normative model of the free market prescribes such policy as will safeguard the autonomous functioning of these elements unhampered by discriminatory practices or extraneous influences. The market model assumes that the individual is the best judge of his own needs and interests. The motivation for exchange interactions is the desire to maximize satisfaction, and with this aim in mind the persons will manage optimally the allocation of the available resources. The ideal type of market situation presupposes two principles of equality: (a) equality of treatment (that is, the same rules of the market apply to all participants) and (b) equal opportunity for maximization of satisfaction, which depends, by definition, on equal access to the desired exchange situations. When these two types of equalities ensure the opportunity for exchange and adherence to the nondiscriminatory market rules, the possession of resources emerges as the crucial problem of equality. Resources are unequally distributed whether by chance, by socialization, inheritance or life history. In order to achieve valid equality of opportunities, it is necessary to reduce the inequality of resources.

Although the market ideology of democratic capitalism answers equalities (as mentioned above), the exchange model when applied to the institutional structure of Israel can ensure either the development of a more egalitarian distribution or the maintenance of a stable balance of equality and inequality.

Equality of Exchange Conditions

The equal conditions of exchange cannot be maintained, even assuming that all discriminatory practices can be eliminated. First, the market value of labor, which is the major source of income, does not correspond to the consumption needs of the earner's family, which is dependent on the ratio of earners to nonearners. Large families with small children thus have lower per capita income than small families.

Second, not all wages and salaries are equally affected by their market value. Organizations that are removed from direct-market activities are less constrained when bargaining with labor. Government employees, the public transportation, cooperative organizations, and so on offer more secure incomes than the market-bound business enterprises.* The white-collar public employee enjoys at present conditions of work and income more favorable than the blue-collar worker, in spite of the avowed intentions of the policy makers to bolster production.

Third, in an inflationary economy, like Israel's, prices are rising continuously. In spite of a cost-of-living correction, the adjustment of wages and salaries lags behind. While this affects all employed people (about 75 percent of the labor force), the burden is unequally distributed. The less elastic the consumer needs of the family (because of its size) and the larger the portion of income spent on basic necessities, the lower the ability to postpone purchases until the adjustment between prices and incomes is attained.

Finally, such a basic necessity as housing is so expensive at regular market prices that a large part of the population does not appear as potential buyer.

These four points were intended to serve as examples from which to conclude that equal conditions of exchange are not feasible and that the resulting

---

*Galbraith (1973:51) says about the salaries paid by big corporations: ". . . a relatively secure and favorable income for participants in the planning system, a less secure, less favorable return for those in the market system."

inequalities can be legitimized neither by such market norms as equity and rationality of distribution nor by the social goals of the society.

Equal Opportunity

The analysis of the concept of equal opportunity leads to a similar conclusion: There is no way to assure equal opportunity by way of the market system. First, opportunities of access for acquiring such relevant resources as incomes information, skills, or certain consumer items are not uniformly available in all sectors of a society. They depend on the geographical areas, rate of urbanization, the composition of the population, and so forth (Roby 1974). Frontier areas (the so-called development towns), poor neighborhoods, and small villages have fewer opportunities than other, better-endowed areas.

Second, there is no necessary correlation between the availability of all the desired resources. Thus, housing is cheaper in remote areas, where other opportunities are scarce. The availability of work does not indicate opportunities for mobility or for choice of interesting occupations.

Third, opportunities are limited, so however equal the opportunity to compete for resources, some will succeed while others will fail. Success in this case is not a function of merit, worth, or investment, but of the structure of opportunities. Time in this case becomes a very important factor. The "late-comers" may find a situation of extreme limitation of opportunities—those opportunities having already been occupied by others. New immigrants and young adults—the new aspirants to mobility—have to compete for the unoccupied situations or depend on the expansion of the opportunity structure. These groups are thus more prone to failure, and some of them may be denied access to all those opportunities that offer the sought-after resources.

Finally, opportunities tend to cluster into patterns, in which one situation leads to another. There are chains of success and chains of failure. At any given time, most people are already at a certain point of these chains, and their actual position will influence their future opportunities.

A policy of equal opportunity is required to neutralize all these constraints of the opportunity structure and to open the access to them. Such policy should ensure the uniform distribution of opportunities, their multiplication according to demand, and the correction of the specific chains of success or failure. Evidently, such corrections, if at all feasible, cannot be made without interference in the autonomous functioning of the market system.

The market mechanism is not adequate for the mediation of a policy of resource enrichment, which by definition has to be based on nonsymmetrical unilateral transfers. Such policies are part of a different system of distribution, which is often labelled the welfare system.

Let us define as welfare allocation a system based on the institutionalized rights of a category of people to receive certain benefits, regardless of their social position or their market activities. The welfare situation is asymmetrical and it can be maintained with a minimum of mutuality between the providing institutions and the recipients. Hence, unlike the market, there is no built-in automatic control, and the major elements of the system need to be defined by policy decision. The minimal dimensions of a welfare system are (a) the scope of the welfare rights, (b) eligibility, and (c) content.

Welfare allocation is essentially contradictory to the market distribution, but in a social system they need not be mutually exclusive. Welfare distribution may serve as a corrective method for inequalities in the market situation, but according to the definition proposed welfare is not necessarily egalitarian, and it may be used as well for the provision of privileges and the enhancing of inequality. In conformity with the topic of this chapter welfare will be considered from the perspective of egalitarianism.

Welfare Distribution

There are two channels of welfare distribution, one intended as a correction of the market allocation and the other as its replacement. The latter is the characteristic distributive method of the family and the kibbutz. Intervention in the market is intended to improve the exchange potential of the participants or to make the exchange situation more manageable. A very large part of the welfare expenses are investments in resource enrichment of certain categories of people. In principle, the more generalized the resources, the more profitable the investment (always assuming that generality corresponds with adaptability to varied and changing market situations). This general principle is not easily applied to programs that have to consider the lead time, the cost, and situational constraints. Such choices as general education versus vocational training, or money payments versus the provision of specific resources do not seem to have one optimal answer. The improvement of general human resources might be considered as the most desirable because of its multifunctionality, but it is a long-range investment with a high uncertainty of outcome. Money is the short-range improvement of the recipients' resource balance, but usually it is directed to consumer needs of the recipients and does not radically change their position.

Situational changes are those reducing the prices of commodities, through price control or subsidies raising minimum wages or creating occupational opportunities. These situational changes indirectly affect the resource balance of the participants. An analysis of various programs reveals that each of these types produces a different balance of equality and inequality. Thus subsidies for consumption items raise the consumption potential and thus the welfare of all groups but do not reduce relative inequality. When there are two price systems, as in the housing market, material equality of the underprivileged is increased but their freedom of choice is reduced. In some cases these specific patterns of resource enrichment or situational interference are highly visible and become symbols of low prestige. If we assume that the reduction of relative deprivation comes also within the scope of welfare policy, then the technique of progressive taxation and progressive prices for services and commodities should be mentioned. The "resource impoverishment" of the privileged seems to be a logical counterpart of the resource enrichment of the underprivileged, but there is no simple inverse correlation between the two, and the discussion of the dynamic relationship between them exceeds the scope of this chapter. A large number of welfare policies, especially on the macrosocial level, are combined patterns in which market and welfare principles are interwoven. Marshall (1973) states that all social insurance represent combined patterns. So are relief work, sheltered workshops, and subsidized housing. Some programs of resource enrichment are outside the market distribution but their results are intended for it. Some services and commodities (for example, free school lunches) are allocated without being related to the market.

Norms of Eligibility

Eligibility in the welfare system is parallel to the rules of exchange in the market system. The concepts of universal or selective service designate the most general alternatives of eligibility. Universal welfare allocation defines the welfare rights of a population category on the basis of one of its attributes (often an ascriptive one), which is not affected by the content of the rights to be allocated. Thus, the attributes of age, family size, physical handicaps, or being insured are not directly involved in the change process. The selective approach restricts the welfare rights to the population needing the welfare allocation, and this need has to be proved. These two approaches indicate different scales of equality. The universal norms ensure that the allocated quantities are equal; the selective norms are intended to achieve equal outcomes or equal satisfaction of need. There is a tendency to confound the equal outcome with the slogan of "to each according to his need."

Although the essence of the need-satisfaction norm is the assumption that needs are different and satisfied differently. The only equal outcome in this case is the equally felt subjective satisfaction. The functioning of each of these norms of eligibility is easily discernible in the distributive system of the kibbutz.

The welfare system is well suited for the manipulation of the equality to inequality ratio, but the assymmetrical relationships, the dependence on determined value or arbitrary decisions concerning the quantity and the quality of the welfare rights, and the mode of distribution create new imbalances. In the welfare situation the recipient has a passive, powerless role. The reasons for the decisions on the quality and quantity of the benefits is not evident, but contrary to the case in the impersonal market, welfare decisions on the governmental level are made by politicians. Hence there is the tendency of the recipients to question the legitimacy of welfare decisions and the heightened sensitivity toward relative deprivation. The typical interaction at the operative level is often turned into a power contest between the recipient and the representative of the institution. Evidently, participation in such a situation is highly relevant both as a compensation for the passive role of the client and as a process of legitimization of the allocation decisions. The participatory collectivities are good examples of such processess, which however occur in a very special social context.

The positional mechanism of distribution involves the system of roles and individual status. The allocation of resources, rewards, and activities is attached to these positions.

Since the concept of roles is an integral part of stratification theories, it would be redundant to summarize here the role theories. Suffice it to note some aspects of the relationship of the role-system models to the paradigm of distributive mechanisms.

A role system is by definition differentiated at least on the dimension of tasks and consequently on the resources needed for the performance of the tasks. While task differentiation does not have to be a task hierarchy also, such a trend is highly probable. The kibbutz intended to eliminate task hierarchy by adopting a value system in which task activity per se was valued. Nevertheless the increasing differentiation of functions strengthened the tendency toward hierarchization of preferences. Role inequalities in the kibbutz are however less relevant to the total balance of inequalities, because the standard of living does not depend on role rewards, and, owing to high interrole mobility, the social position of a person does not become identified with a specific role position.

In a market society, even when the welfare system provides a non-role-attached method of distribution, roles do determine the total reward balance. The most frequent operational definition of the concept of opportunity is access to preferred roles. The discussion of inequality of opportunities is fully transposable to the topic of access to roles. Vacancies, bridging roles, and the advantages accruing from clustering of roles are limiting or multiplying opportunities (Sieber 1974).

The accumulation of roles provides gains that exceed the simple addition of role resources; those who can effectively perform multiple roles earn new resources and develop techniques of manipulating them. The accumulation of roles can be seen as one of the strongest factors of inequality with multiple effects. It reduces the number of vacancies, and creates oligarchies that are able to amass benefits and use them in the market or for further extension of their role access opportunities. A policy that succeeds in reducing role accumulation is therefore equalitarian.

Techniques of reducing role inequality as practiced in the equalitarian communities are to a limited extent used in other social constellations. Role inequalities are reduced (a) by flattening the hierarchy of rewards, (b) by weakening the correlation between types of role rewards, (c) by redesigning the task patterns (job enlargement and job enrichment), (d) by limiting the transferability of specific instrumental role resources to nonrelevant roles, (e) by curtailing role accumulation, and (f) by introducing rotation in privileged roles. The feasibility and the effect of these techniques are among the many topics needing serious exploration by an egalitarian organizational theory.

The paradigm of distributive systems as sketched here is merely an elaboration of the central ideas of this chapter. These ideas can be summarized as follows. Social systems, even the most equalitarian, are characterized by a balance of equality and inequality. The ratio of these two tendencies represents the level of equality. Complete equality is an exceptional state, seldom attained. The various definitions of equality refer to different processes that are not simultaneously attainable. The equality-inequality balance is highly unstable, and inequality tends to gain; hence the level of equality depends on active egalitarian policy.

Given the variety of definitions and patterns of equality, egalitarian policy, more than the non-egalitarian, is guided by ideological considerations.

REFERENCES

Adizes, Ishak. 1971. *Industrial Democracy: Yugoslav Style.* Glencoe, Ill.: The Free Press.

Arian, Alan. 1968. *Ideological Change in Israel.* Cleveland: Case Western Reserve University Press.

Bar-Yosef, Rivka. 1974. "A Case Study Of Urban Cooperation: The Transport Cooperatives in Israel." *International Conference on Cooperatives, Collectives and Nationalized Industries,* Oshkosh.

—— and Tamar Ramot. 1973. *Immigrants in Jerusalem Residential Status.* Jerusalem: Hebrew University.

Ben David, Joseph. 1964. *Agricultural Planning and Village Community in Israel.* Paris: UNESCO.

Beveridge, W. H. 1942. "Social Insurance and Allied Services." London: Interdepartmental Committee in Social Insurance and Allied Services.

——. 1936. *Planning under Socialism.* New York: Longmans, Green.

Borochov, Ber. 1937. *Nationalism and the Class Struggle: Selected Writings.* Westport, Conn.: Greenwood Press.

Blumenthal, W. M. 1956. *Co-determination in German Steel Industry.* Princeton, N.J.: Princeton University Press.

Buber, Martin. 1967. *Der utopische Sozialismus.* Koln: Hegner Bucherei, pp. 217-33.

Cohen, Eric. 1964. *Bibliography of the Kibbutz.* Giv'at Haviva.

Cole, G.D.H. 1957. *The Case for Industrial Partnership.* New York: Macmillan.

———. 1943. *Fabian Socialism.* London: Allen & Unwin.

Crosland, C.A.R. 1956. *The Future of Socialism.* London: J. Cape.

Dahl, Robert, and Charles E. Lindblom. 1953. *Politics, Economics and Welfare.* New York: Harper & Row.

Davis, Kingsley. 1953. "Reply and Comment." *American Sociological Review* 18, no. 4 (August).

——— and Wilbert Moore. 1945. "Some Principles of Stratification." *American Sociological Review* 10, no. 2 (April):242-49.

Derber, Milton. 1970. "Israel's Wage Differential: A Persisting Problem." In *Integration and Development*, edited by S. N. Eisenstadt, R. Bar-Yosef, and C. Adler. Jerusalem: Israel Universities Press, pp. 185-201.

Doron, Abraham. 1975. *The Struggle for Social Insurance in Israel 1948-1953.* Jerusalem: Hebrew University School of Social Work (in Hebrew).

Eisenstadt, S. N. 1967. *Israeli Society.* London: Weidenfeld and Nicolson.

Frankena, William K. 1962. "The Concept of Social Justice." In *Social Justice*, edited by Richard Brandt. Englewood Cliffs, N.J.: Prentice-Hall.

Galbraith, John Kenneth. 1973. *Economics and the Public Purpose.* Boston: Houghton Mifflin.

Gans, Herbert J. 1974. *More Equality.* New York: Random House (Vintage Books).

Garber-Talmon, Yonina. 1970. *The Individual and the Group in the Kibbutz.* Jerusalem: Magnes Press (in Hebrew).

Gewirth, Alan. 1962. "Political Justice." In *Social Justice*, edited by Richard Brandt. Englewood Cliffs, N.J.: Prentice-Hall, pp. 119-69.

Habib, Jack. 1974. *Poverty in Israel before and after Receipt of Public Transfers.* Jerusalem: National Insurance Institute.

Horowitz, Irving Louis. 1970. "Social Science and Public Policy: An Examination of the Political Foundations of Modern Research." In *Transactions of the Sixth World Congress of Sociology.* International Sociological Association, pp. 37-68.

Israel, Central Bureau of Statistics. 1971. *Survey of Housing Conditions, 1971.* Jerusalem: the Bureau.

Israel, Committee on Income Distribution and Social Inequality. 1971. *Report.* Tel Aviv: the Committee.

Israel, Ministry of Housing, Programming Department. 1975. *Population and Building in Israel, 1948-1973.* Jerusalem: the Ministry (in Hebrew).

Kanter, Rosabeth M. 1973. *Communes: Creating and Managing the Collective Life.* New York: Harper & Row.

Kibbutz Meuchad. 1966. *The Style of Life of the Kibbutz Society: Principles, Standards, and Guidelines.* Tel Aviv: The Kibbutz.

Kolaja, Jiri. 1965. *Workers' Councils: The Yugoslav Experience.* London: Tavistock.

Kramer, Daniel C. 1972. *Participatory Democracy: Developing Ideals of the Political Left.* Cambridge, Mass.: Schenkman.

Lindsay, A. D. 1951. *The Modern Democratic State.* New York: Oxford University Press.

Lotan, Giora. 1972. "Ways of Implementing Social Policy to Ensure Maximum Public Participation and Social Justice." In *Report on Developing Social Policy in Conditions of Rapid Change—The Role of Social Welfare,* presented at the Sixteenth International Conference on Social Welfare, The Hague.

Marshall, T. H. 1973. "Value Problems of Welfare Capitalism." *Journal of Sociological Policy* 1, no. 1:15-32.

———. 1964. *Class, Citizenship and Social Development.* Garden City, N.J.: Doubleday.

Miller, S. M. 1974. "Types of Equality, Sorting, Rewarding Performing." Paper presented at the Seventh World Congress of Sociology.

Moore, Wilbert. 1963. "Rejoinder." *American Sociological Review* 28, no. 1 (February):26-28.

Nizan, A. 1973. *Social Security in Israel.* Jerusalem: National Insurance Institute.

Parsons, Talcott. 1970. "Equality and Inequality in Modern Society, or Social Stratification Revisited." *Sociological Inquiry* 40 (Spring):13-71.

———. 1951. *The Social System.* Glencoe, Ill.: The Free Press.

Rabin, A. I. 1970. *Kibbutz Studies: A Digest of Books and Articles on the Kibbutz by Social Scientists.* Lansing: Michigan State University Press.

Rawls, John. 1973. "Distributive Justice." In *Economic Justice,* edited by E. S. Phelps. Hammondsworth: Penguin Education, pp. 319-62.

Roby, Pamela. 1974. *The Poverty Establishment.* Englewood Cliffs, N.J.: Prentice-Hall.

Rosner, Menahem. 1973. "Direct Democracy in the Kibbutz." In *Communes: Creating and Managing the Collective Life,* edited by Rosabeth Moss Kanter. New York: Harper & Row, pp. 178-91.

———. 1965. "Direct Democracy in the Kibbutz." *New Outlook* 8, no. 6:29-41.

Rossi, Peter. 1955. *Why Families Move.* Glencoe, Ill.: The Free Press.

Schumpeter, Joseph. 1951. *Imperialism and Social Classes.* New York: A. M. Kelly.

Shatil, Joseph E. 1968. "On the Validity of Kibbutz Experience." In *Public and Cooperative Economy in Israel,* International Centre of Research and Information on Public and Cooperative Economy CIRIEC, pp. 13-85.

Shur, Shimon. 1972. *Kibbutz Bibliography.* Jerusalem: Van Leer.

Sieber, Sam D. 1974. "Toward a Theory of Role Accumulation." *American Sociological Review* 39 (August):567-78.

Sirkin, Nahman. 1970. "The Socialist Jewish State." In *Haraayon Hatziony,* edited by Avraham Hertzberg. Jerusalem: Keter, p. 271. (In Hebrew)

Spiro, Melford E. 1956. *Kibbutz: Venture in Utopia.* Cambridge, Mass.: Harvard University Press.

Tabenkin, Yitzhak. 1968. "Adam Behevrah" *Mibifnim* 13, (1948): cited by Arian, *Ideological Change in Israel* (Cleveland: Case Western Reserve University Press, 1968): pp. 103-104.

Tannenbaum, Arthur S. 1974. *Hierarchy in Organizations.* New York: McGraw-Hill.

Thompson, Dennis F. 1970. *The Democratic Citizen.* Cambridge, Eng.: Cambridge University Press.

Thorsrud, E. 1970. "Collaborative Experiments: *A Norwegian Approach to Industrial Democracy: A Scandinavian Approach to Industrial Democracy.*" (Resumé of an International Seminar in Oslo.)

Thurow, Lester. 1973. "Toward a Definition of Economic Justice." *The Public Interest* 31 (Spring):56-80.

Titmuss, Richard. 1968. *Commitment to Welfare.* London: Allen & Unwin.

———. 1965. *The Welfare State Objectives in Israel; Reflections on Britain,* pamphlet no. 7. Anglo-Israeli Association.

———. 1950. *Problems of Social Policy.* London: HMSO.

Tobin, J. 1970. "On Limiting the Domain of Inequality." In *Economic Justice,* edited by E. S. Phelps. Hammondsworth: Penguin Education, pp. 447-63.

Tumin, Melvin M. 1963. "On Social Inequality." *American Sociological Review* 28, no. 1 (February):19-26.

———. 1953. "Some Principles of Stratification." *American Sociological Review* 18, no. 4 (August):381-93.

Vallier, Ivan. 1962. "Structural Differentiations, Production Imperatives and Communal Norms: The Kibbutz in Crisis." *Social Forces* 40 (March):234-42.

Viteles, Harry. 1967. *A History of the Cooperative Movement in Israel.* Book 2, "The Evolution of the Kibbutz Movement." London: Vallentine-Mitchell.

Warner, W. Lloyd, M. Meeker, and Kenneth Eels. 1949. *Social Class in America.* Chicago: Science Research Associates.

Weber, Max. 1947. *The Theory of Social and Economic Organization.* New York: Oxford University Press.

————. 1946. *Essays in Sociology.* London: Kegan Paul.

Weintraub, Dov. 1964. "A Study of New Farmers in Israel." *Sociologia Ruralis* 4:3-51.

Weller, Leonard. 1974. *Sociology in Israel.* Westport, Conn.: Greenwood Press.

Wesolowski, Wlodzimierz. 1969. "Strata and Strata Interest in Socialist Society: Toward a New Theoretical Approach." In *Structured Social Inequality: A Reader in Comparative Social Stratification,* edited by Celia S. Heller. New York: Macmillan, pp. 465-77.

Wilensky, Harold L. 1975. *The Welfare State and Equality.* Berkeley: University of California Press.

——— and Charles N. Lebeaux. 1958. *Industrial Society and Social Welfare.* Glencoe, Ill.: The Free Press.

Yuchtman, E. 1972. "Reward Distribution and Work Role Attractiveness in the Kibbutz—Reflections on Equity Theory." *American Sociological Review* 37, no. 5:581-95.

CHAPTER

7

SOCIALISM, WORK,
AND EQUALITY
Walter D. Connor

The aims and the eventual outcomes of the policies pursued by governments are often quite distinct; history testifies eloquently to the frequent "unanticipated consequences" of policy implementation, often opposed to the goals initially sought. Nor, indeed, are the announced goals of policy and its real aims always one and the same. Public support and acquiescence may be sought, for example, for an avowedly "egalitarian" incomes policy, when in fact the real governmental agenda seeks instead to produce a nonegalitarian distributive pattern, whose advantaged and disadvantaged groups will simply be different from those of the preexisting distribution—a new, more *equitable* inequality, as such a government might put it.

One does well to keep these points in mind when considering the record of the Soviet-type socialist regimes in the promotion of equal (or equitable) rewards for their populations, for that record reflects two historic confrontations whose mutual relationship is quite complex: first, a confrontation with the "old," presocialist social and distributive order and, second, a parallel confrontation with the tasks of economic development in relatively backward societies. The outcomes, in general and in their specific forms in the different nations, have been interesting, confusing, and paradoxical.

This chapter is adapted from portions of a much larger draft manuscript, also entitled *Socialism, Work, and Equality.* As an adaptation and condensation it will, no doubt, tend at times to make broader assertions and generalizations than seem warranted by the data it presents.

Research support from the American Council of Learned Societies and the International Research and Exchanges Board is gratefully acknowledged.

The assault on the symbolic systems of the old regimes (for these systems, as well as the distribution of material benefits, are important), for example, has been far from an unqualified success. While poster and banner "art" throughout the socialist world exalts the stern, purposeful and "positive" manual worker, every-day modes of address have sometimes proved remarkably resilient in the face of proletarian attacks on the old *politesse.* In the USSR, to be sure, the old terms *gospodin* ("Sir") and *gospozha* ("Madam") have disappeared from normal use, replaced by *grazhdanin* ("citizen") or *tovarishch* ("comrade"), except when employed in an ironic (and sometimes threatening) manner, or in addressing a Russian-speaking guest from a nonsocialist country.

Matters could scarcely be more different in Poland, where 30 years of socialism have not dispatched "Sir" *(pan)* and "Madam" *(pani)* from every-day use. In fact, a larger percentage of the Polish population employs these terms today than before socialism. Those of equal status do so in situations in which the terms were not used previously; superiors use them toward subordinates where in pre-1939 Poland they would never have done so; and the polite terms have even made some headway in the countryside, where they never would have been heard addressed to, or used among, "rustics" in the past. That this expanded use means that "democratization" has indeed been effected. But it is very different from the Soviet experience in that it is the verbal symbols of the old regime—and behavioral rituals, such as hand kissing—that have been universalized under socialism, rather than new "proletarian" manners. In Poland, "comrade" *(towarzyszcz)* is limited in its use to political contexts and occasions.

Hardly, then, have assaults on the old order been successful across the board. Symbols persist, and despite the tremendous power inherent in tightly centralized one-party regimes with control over the major instruments of mass socialization, so may values and attitudes at variance with "socialist" notions of equity and equality. Even in the early post-"revolution" years, when a nonproletarian social origin was something to be hidden for those seeking advancement at the job or admission to higher education, there were intimations that "old" convictions of the superiority of clean-handed mental work over manual labor were still alive, despite denunciation of those convictions by new ideologues. As a prominent Polish sociologist remarked:

> ... [the] passage of the better paid skilled manual workers to the position of the slightly lower paid white-collar workers ... in the majority of cases is looked on as a promotion ... [although] from the point of view of the new criteria of prestige, this should not be considered a promotion (Ossowski 1957:3, quoted in Lipset 1963: 208-9).

That complaints about the persistence and vitality of "old" evaluative orientations are still heard today is hardly surprising, for reasons that should become clear below.

Thus, insofar as the aims of revolutionary socialist regimes have included the wiping out of old symbols, modes of address, and so on, the evidence shows these aims to be far from a universal achievement. But this, perhaps, is to place too much emphasis on announced, global aims—the sort emblazoned on banners at the peak of revolutionary ferment, promising that those "who have been nothing, shall be all"—and not enough on real, concrete aims that become manifest only later, when a new regime gets down to the tasks of governance. For the socialist states such concrete aims have arisen from practical concerns, been justified and legitimized not only in terms of ideology, but also of the perceived "functional necessities" of building modern industrial societies where they had not existed before. Official understanding and implementation of such aims has brought socialist policy makers to the point at which "equality" and "equity" in rewards elude reconciliation. Thus, we begin to grapple with the major focus of this chapter.

EQUITY AND EQUALITY AS SOCIALIST OBJECTIVES

While the early years of the socialist regimes were marked by radical "levelling" rhetoric, and to some degree by matching short-term policies— dismissal of "bourgeois" from their jobs, the barring of their children from higher education, limiting the rewards of newly appointed socialist functionaries, and so on—the early performance provides only a distorted perspective in the long run. Rhetoric in these early stages often runs very egalitarian in tone, holding out promises that no one will be allowed to raise himself to extraordinary standards of reward and comfort or to fall much below an average standard.

Yet it has always been evident that less-heated discussions of socialist reward policy and specific policy statements generally reject "equality of reward" in concept, with both ideological and practical rationales. On the ideological side it is a matter of the two "phases" distinguished in the march forward to communism: the imperfect transitional phase of socialism and the final culmination of communism itself.

Under socialism, which is marred by a lack of abundance, by a disparity between the legitimate needs of people and the availability of resources to satisfy them, the principle, "From each according to his abilities, to each according to his work," applies. There is thus an explicit justification of differentiated and unequal reward, one that, in the words of a contemporary Polish sociologist, "postulates wages as a function of the quality of labor, that is a function of the level of skill and education required for the performance of a given job. There is a marked difference in that level between, e.g., unskilled laborer and the university professor" (Wesolowski 1967:27). The socialist principle of distribution (even though Wesolowski's words do not touch on it) shares a good deal with the basic functionalist position in its assumption that work is differentially valuable in the contribution it makes to society. Both socialist and functionalist principles may be seen as manifestations of a basic position, called here the "performance principle," to which we shall return later.

The socialist reward principle has received elaborate ideological explications over the years, as well as shorter, crisper, but more authoritarian endorsements, as in Stalin's 1931 speech denouncing "equality mongering" *(uravnilovka)* in industrial wages, which set the stage for a wage-differentiation extreme (even by Western standards) that lasted into the 1950s. It is, of course, open to attack on much the same grounds as the functionalist position: How is the differential value of labor contributions to society to be measured? Is it society that is the object of such contributions, or powerful groups within society, which reward those who make valuable contributions to their interests? To different degrees in the different states, politics prohibits the open and critical discussion of such issues, of the major ideological premises and operational dimensions of socialist distribution. Attacks tend to be oblique in most cases, but there are attacks, since the principle of socialist distribution, however "tempered" by egalitarian commitments, *is* an inegalitarian one. It is a principle of equity, not equality, and there will be disagreement over what is equitable.

The communist principle, "From each according to his abilities, to each according to his needs," is, assuming that similar (human) nature produces similar needs, an egalitarian one, but one whose actualization has been deferred until the future provides the necessary abundance. Meanwhile, its logical and empirical status is rather unclear, both in the writings of hack propagandists and in those of ideologically committed socialist philosophers. How much is abundance? Who will judge when it has been attained? Will distribution according to need in its eventual realization really "look" egalitarian? Finally, and perhaps most important, what role should the principle play today, in the socialist phase?

On this last point, opinions diverge. Some revisionist Marxists see the principle as purely utopian and hence irrelevant now and in the future. Others cling to it but, citing present shortfalls from abundance, see no room for its operation now. Still others, such as the Yugoslav Svetozar Stojanovic (1973:215-16), while acknowledging that the "communist principle" is fundamentally utopian, see no way to insure the equity of socialist distribution except by introducing today, as far as resources allow, distribution "according to need" in the spheres of health, education, and so on. It probably does not go too far to say that for those who recall that socialism's early promise, in its self-presentation to the masses, was an egalitarian one, the socialist (functionalist, "performance") principle must be tempered in its operation by elements of "communist" distribution independent of function and performance: differentiation of reward necessary to spur performance, yes; unbounded differentiation, even in the quest of yet more performance, no.

That is the ideological background that legitimates and yet leaves open to criticism a socialist distributive principle that aims directly at equity, while retaining, in some sense, equality as an eventual goal. But there is more involved here than ideology. There are also the matters of economic growth and practical politics.

For all the egalitarian promise of Soviet socialism in the 1920s, and similar promises in Eastern Europe in the late 1940s, the new regimes confronted the problem of underdevelopment everywhere but in Czechoslovakia. Basic resources—administrative ability, technical expertise, manual skill, even literacy and the ability to calculate—were scarce, and their scarcity dictated high rewards, much as it had under the less development-oriented *anciens regimes*. High rewards, in a distinctly functionalist sense, were also seen as necessary to motivate persons to acquire the training and skills to swell the ranks of the "qualified" and thus relieve the scarcity. Thus, the eras of the five-year plans in the USSR and in Eastern Europe were marked by an inegalitarianism, dictated by practical concerns and additionally justified through (as well as contributing to the elaboration of) the socialist principle of distribution. Though much of the socialist world has now moved into industrial maturity, though the early scarcities have been moderated, the legacy of socialist industrialization is still evident.

The decades of socialism have given rise to groups, categories, and socio-occupational strata that benefit from this "equitable" distribution and to groups whose shares of still-scarce resources are much more modest. Whether or not their functions in fact justify their rewards, party and government bureaucrats, technical intelligentsia, and skilled workers in heavy industry have a stake in maintaining the current equities and see threats to their position in the possibility of any different set of equities. The "new class" and its servitors perceive that they have a good deal to lose through change, and they might be expected to resist it, much as privileged groups do in nonsocialist systems.

What, then, can we expect of the distribution of material resources (essentially income) in the socialist states that are the objects of inquiry here? We might, logically, expect that three claims would be made for the socialist states. First, socialist distribution, though not egalitarian, is roughly "just" in the rewards it attaches to various types of work and is therefore equitable. Second, it is more equitable, given the elimination of large concentrations of private property, than is capitalist distribution, and also more egalitarian due to the modification of differentiation by the communist principle of distribution. Third, it is also both more equitable and egalitarian than the patterns of distribution that prevailed under the presocialist regimes in Russia and Eastern Europe. As it turns out, none of these claims is, perhaps, really testable in a manner technically precise, neither are they general enough to convince all who are interested in answers. But our data are not so scarce as to prohibit attacking the questions at all.

BASIC DIMENSIONS OF
SOCIALIST INCOME DISTRIBUTION

By the most general sorts of measurements that make up the ordnance of economists—Gini coefficients, Lorenz curves, various quartile ratios—the income distribution in socialist countries in somewhat more egalitarian than that found in Western states. Quintile distribution figures for 1962 show, for example, that the "top" 20 percent of the Hungarian population received 34.9 percent of income distributed, and the bottom fifth 9.2 percent, while the comparable figures for Austria and France in the same year were 36.8 percent to 8.5, and 43.1 percent to 7.5. In 1964 Czechoslovakia's top quintile received 30.5 percent of all income; its bottom quintile, 11.9 percent; the comparable figures were 36.2 and 8.1 percent for West Germany (Vecernik 1969:298). The percentage differences are not large, viewed "in the raw," although economists might make much of them. They do, however, show a rather substantial gap between Czechoslovakia (the most egalitarian of the socialist states) and a country like France.

Similarly, quartile ratios on employees' and workers' average earnings—the ratio of the bottom to the third quartile—show differences supporting the notion of a more egalitarian socialist pattern (UN 1967:18, 41):

Bulgaria (1962)	1.60
Czechoslovakia (1964)	1.60
Hungary (1964)	1.61
Poland (1964)	1.81
United Kingdom (1964)	2.04
West Germany (1964)	1.76
Netherlands (1962)	2.62
Sweden (1963)	2.62
France (1962)	1.89

These are, of course, rather broad measures, and they cloak some of the reality that more sensitive measures would catch. But, as "snapshots" taken at points in time, the figures give some basis for talking about a socialist achievement in income egalitarianism.

However, they tell us nothing about progress over time, either with respect to the distributive patterns of the presocialist regimes or within the socialist period itself. Evidence is scanty for the presocialist period,but, given the destruction of private concentrations of income-producing wealth, the full-employment strategies of the socialist regimes, and the extremely inegalitarian patterns prevalent in Tsarist Russia and interwar Eastern Europe, there is little reason to doubt that the socialist regimes have bettered their predecessors in this regard. To have failed to do so would have been remarkable.

More interesting (and less clear at the outset) are trends in the socialist period. As we observed above, any ideological-political commitments to egalitarianism, however sincere, faced the simultaneous commitment to rapid industrial growth in a context of scarcity of talent, education, and skills. Unequal reward was used as an instrument to mobilize those scarce resources: Had inequality diminished as resources grew less scarce, and if so, by how much? Recent calculations by the British economist Peter Wiles give us some general answers (see Table 7.1).

These decile ratios show a rather marked stability across the ten years for all countries, save the USSR. Over the 1960-70 period its ratio grows markedly more egalitarian, while still remaining least so in comparison with the other countries. What we see are the marks of a transition in the USSR, termed more than ten years ago the "Soviet income revolution" by one specialist (Yanowitch 1963). No socialist country, probably, ever reached the inegalitarian peaks the USSR attained. Decile-ratio estimates for 1934 (4.15) and 1956 (4.4) (Wiles 1975:33) show a degree of inequality hardly inferior to the capitalist economies of the time—and even these figures miss the peak of inequality that probably came around 1940. But with the mid-1950s, equalizing forces came into play, and they continue to operate. Education, manual skill, literacy—the scarce resources of the 1920s—are no longer so scarce. Moderately "devalued," they command less of a premium. While there are more manual workers who are skilled, the unskilled worker is far from disappearing, and in a situation

TABLE 7.1

Decile Ratios, Workers' and Employees' Earnings, Socialist Sector

	1960	1970
Bulgaria	2.4 (1967)	–
Czechoslovakia	2.4 (1959)	2.4
Hungary	2.5	2.6
Poland	3.1	3.2
Romania	–	2.3
USSR	3.7 (1964)	3.2

Source: Peter J. D. Wiles, "Recent Data on Soviet Income Distribution," *Survey* 21, no. 3 (Summer 1975):33.

where increasing general educational levels make unskilled work ever less attractive, prudence has dictated governmental action to close the income gap between
skilled and unskilled work, in order to insure continued occupation of the onerous (but necessary) slots. The same reasoning explains moves in the 1960s and
1970s toward a long-overdue upgrading of the reward structure for the collective-
farm peasants—the perpetually depressed bottom of the Soviet labor force. The
peasantry no longer represents a manpower surplus, and there are still strong
desires to leave agriculture. Income policy has been called upon to counter
them.

Economic reasons, then, have played a major role in the increasing income
egalitarianism in the USSR. The role to be assigned to ideology is less clear.
Moves away from the peak of inegalitarianism preceded Khrushchev's rise, but
his own populist style and his desire to shake up the upper bureaucracy through
reduction of its privileges (and the emphasizing of their "contingency") accelerated the process. It is one the Brezhnev-Kosygin leadership has done a good
deal to advance, especially in economic "uplift" for the peasants, but has also
moderated, in assuring the bureaucrats that their privileged economic positions
and ability to pass advantages, through education, on to their children, will not
be seriously challenged. All in all, the USSR continues to moderate its income
inequality, although its earlier history leaves it still less egalitarian than its East
European neighbors.

If the USSR sits at one pole, Czechoslovakia occupies the other; it is a
socialist state whose striking egalitarianism has been and remains controversial.
The sources of Czech "exceptionalism" are manifold. First, and hardest to
define, there is a cultural tradition of egalitarianism, predating socialism, that
dictates satisfaction with little, as long as one's neighbor has no more (see Ulc
1974); this tradition is happily manipulable by a regime committed to reinvest-
ing a great deal of the national income.

Second, and probably more important, alone among the states that entered
the Soviet orbit after World War II, Czechoslovakia was already an industrial
society. The republic of Masaryk and Benes inherited the main industrial center
of the Austro-Hungarian empire, developed further in the interwar years, and
suffered relatively little devastation during World War II. Its human resources—
technical and managerial talent, education, and manual skill—were in much
greater supply than in the USSR of the 1920s (or the Poland, Bulgaria, Romania,
and so on of the 1940s). Hence, the functionalist rationale of a premium on
scarcity need not have operated—and it did not do so.

Third, Czech history almost demanded that a Soviet-type socialist regime
pursue an extremely egalitarian income policy, as compensation for what such a
regime would "cost." Czechoslovakia had been unique also in interwar Central
and Eastern Europe in that it remained a functioning democracy with a Western
pattern of civil liberties. After 1948 it became and remained under Novotny's
rule the most "Stalinist," unreformed polity among the Soviet client states.

Attempts to keep the political lid on after 1953 and after de-Stalinization took hold elsewhere in 1956 reflected a fear of a populace, a large proportion of which had been "socialized" earlier in a liberal-democratic vein. Hence, the tradeoff: for the lost freedom and political democracy, a sort of egalitarian economic democracy, a levelling down and up, made possible by the existence of a well-developed economy. As one commentator on the Czech scene put it, viewing earlier years from the perspective of the events of 1968 when political forces were no longer to be contained by economic manipulation, "just because the country was *already* industrial, it could use egalitarianism to compensate for the *other* deformations and buy off popular discontent in some measure ..." (Gellner 1972:34).

The Czech egalitarian recipe has been no panacea: Whatever mass content it generated was insufficient to stem the forces of the Prague Spring of 1968 that rose against political "deformations," and its economic consequences were, in the view of many economists, near-disastrous over the long run. However, post-"normalization" Czechoslovakia remains the most egalitarian socialist state, and the USSR probably the least. Between them are ranged the other nations: Poland and Hungary, with long and persisting inegalitarian traditions rooted in an aristocratic-gentry heritage, and the states of the Balkans, whose more egalitarian traditions (though hardly like those of Czechoslovakia) flow from the long absence of native ruling classes and the consequent "peasant" national characters they preserve, in some measure, even today.

Thus, the socialist "experience," measured by data such as those cited in this section, has been diverse. Full equality remains elusive (and no doubt impossible), but different regimes have done better or worse in their approximations of it. The data show that, by and large, income distribution is somewhat more egalitarian in the socialist states than elsewhere, but the differences are far from massive. Large private concentrations of wealth have been abolished, of course, and this makes a difference (the same can hardly be said of large concentrations of power, but these can scarcely be called "public" in systems so narrowly centralized). As an earlier, meticulous study of selected cases of capitalist-communist income distribution concluded, the main difference appears to be that capitalism does produce *some* very rich people with very great wealth while socialism does not; for those located along the rest of the distribution, whether in a socialist or in a capitalist economy, the difference is only quite moderate (see Wiles and Markowski 1971).

Such statistics, however, seem rather bloodless to the present author. What sort of people, holding what sorts of occupations, receive the high and the low incomes? How do farmers fare compared to workers, workers compared to professionals, and the lower white-collar functionaries compared to the skilled manuals? Is the group structure of economic stratification familiar to the view of a Western observer? These are real groups, not the "quartiles" of the data thus far presented, and it is such groups that demand our attention if we are to appreciate how considerations of equity and equality are reflected in the lives and welfare of the component parts of socialist populations.

THE INCOMES OF DIFFERENT PEOPLE

To read both the programmatic words and slogans of the early years of socialist regimes and the claims of accomplishments since is to get some feeling for the groups with which socialist policy concerned itself: those that were seen as overrewarded and those that were seen as underrewarded. Paramount among the latter were the workers (the class toward which socialists aimed their appeals, the "revolutionary class") and the peasants (a more difficult category, comprising not only the landless laborers felt to be "natural" allies of the workers, but also the small peasant proprietors who, as owners, were in a sense "capitalists," but whose poverty placed them among the "toilers"). "Overrewarded" groups included those marked for abolition (powerful capitalists, landowners, and so on), as well as the stratum of lower or routine white-collar functionaries who made up the bloated government offices of Tsarist Russia and the interwar East European states, who served as bookkeepers and accountants in industry and commerce, and so forth. They could scarcely be done away with, but their rewards—higher, according to socialist sources, than the pay of even the most skilled manual workers—would be lessened. The Marxist position, that only material production really created value, combined with the frequent denunciations of the petty bourgeois paper pushers, clinging to white collars and clean hands and lording it over proletarians, made of this stratum a "target population," with the promise that its rewards would be reduced to a point below those of more "valuable" workers.

More ambiguous was the position of the qualified professionals—in the terminology of the region, the intelligentsia. Sometimes seen as lackeys of the capitalists, their overpaid servitors, they nonetheless possessed skills that the new regimes needed and had contributed some of their number to the leadership of the revolutionary movements. The objectives of the new regimes naturally implied the development of a new, "socialist" intelligentsia, which would, as we have seen, be "paid for" while "populist" impulses and the desire to maintain the image of a "workers' state" would be left to moderate the degree of differentiation allowable.

Thus, it is these four groups which interest us. We do not, of course, anticipate that their incomes will be equal, but whatever pattern has emerged can be taken as some indication of what is put forward as equitable. Furthermore, in concentrating on these four groupings (and later on, on more detailed

TABLE 7.2

Average Pay, by Occupational Category
(industrial worker = 100)

	1960	1965	1970	1973
Bulgaria				
Intelligentsia	142.1	145.0	140.3	132.1
Routine white-collar	93.8	100.3	102.5	95.5
Worker	100.0	100.0	100.0	100.0
Peasant	92.1	84.7	86.2	91.5
Czechoslovakia				
Intelligentsia	116.8	120.2	121.6	120.4
Routine white-collar	77.0	77.1	81.8	81.3
Worker	100.0	100.0	100.0	100.0
Peasant	79.2	85.5	95.0	98.1
Hungary				
Intelligentsia	157.2	155.1	150.7	142.4
Routine white-collar	94.8	96.0	96.5	92.4
Worker	100.0	100.0	100.0	100.0
Peasant	—	88.1	100.0	94.1
Poland				
Intelligentsia	156.7	161.0	150.0	144.3
Routine white-collar	105.1	108.0	102.8	100.1
Worker	100.0	100.0	100.0	100.0
Peasant	—	72.0	75.0	7.7.5
USSR				
Intelligentsia	150.9	145.9	136.3	134.1
Routine white-collar	82.1	84.4	85.5	84.5
Worker	100.0	100.0	100.0	100.0
Peasant	57.7	71.2	75.4	76.5

Note: Intelligentsia, routine nonmanuals, and workers are all in state industry; "peasants" and workers are in state/socialist agriculture, including private farming and cooperative-collective sector.

Sources: Adapted from *Statisticheski Godishnik NR Bulgaria 1974*, pp. 68-69, 155; *Statisticka Rocenka CSSR 1974*, pp. 135, 253; *Hungarian Statistical Yearbook 1973*, pp. 151, 242-43; *Rocznik Statystyecny 1974*, pp. 234, 321; *Narodnoe Khoziaistvo SSSR 1922-1972*, pp. 350-51.

breakdowns), we do not exhaust the sources of inequality, which involve other elements that space constraints force us to leave unexamined.*

Table 7.2 provides the best approximation to the broad data we require. Limited unfortunately to industry in the first three occupation categories (intelligentsia means engineering-technical employees, generally; routine white-collar means administrative or clerical personnel), it indexes average pay to that of industrial workers. Our "peasants," too, are not quite the "real thing," but instead the best available alternative: manual workers in state agriculture (except for Czechoslovakia, where all state-agriculture workers are included), rather than the independent peasants of Poland and Yugoslavia or the collective-farm peasants of the other countries. The latter categories, with extremely variable incomes, are not nearly so well reported in official statistics.

The basic import of the table can be readily summarized. First, measuring equality by the distance between extreme groups, on the whole it seems that all the countries have become more egalitarian over the period reflected here; the USSR has been particularly notable in this respect. Second, the relative welfare of farmers has improved for the most part, and especially in Czechoslovakia and the USSR. Finally, the intelligentsia's rewards are far from symbolic; they are decisively the best-paid group, and most so in the two countries with presocialist traditions.

Sexual stratification is a major source in determining the reward structure in East Europe. As Table 7.2 indicated, "workers" do earn more than routine white-collar employees (except in Poland) when males and females are lumped together. The figures in Table 7.3 for males alone in Poland and Hungary change this picture but little. However, additional data, this time from Czechoslovakia, throws further light on the issue. Table 7.4, based on 1967 data, indexes the base pay of male and female intelligentsia and routine white-collars to the average earnings of all workers, male and female. Its implications seem clear: First, the routine white-collar category is overwhelmingly female in composition (true of the other socialist countries as well); second, it is the low pay of these females that plays the major role in lowering "clerical" pay to the point where it is overlapped by that of workers. The male minority among "routine

---

*Two seem most important. First, there are differences in compensation levels by sector of the economy and by branch within industry. A manager and a skilled worker in heavy industry will be separated by a substantial income gap, but each will make more than his counterpart in a "light" industry such as clothing or food processing. Our figures tend to average out these differences and hence produce a truncated range of incomes. Second, the hidden and quasi-hidden material privileges of political and managerial elites do not figure in our "intelligentsia" figures, since they are not reported as income. If counted, they would considerably broaden the range between income extremes.

TABLE 7.3

Average Income, Male Household Heads, Hungary and Poland
(unskilled worker = 100)

| | Poland | | | | | Hungary |
	Koszalin 1964	Szczecin 1964	Lodz 1964	Lodz 1967	(National, 1963)
Intelligentsia	190.4	163.3	195.6	206.4	201.0
Professional nonmanual	–	–	–	–	152.1
Technician	153.7	137.3	145.2	156.2	–
Clerical	141.0	123.3	129.2	129.0	123.3
Foreman, etc.	141.3	125.6	144.7	137.0	–
Artisan	148.5	134.0	144.9	143.7	–
Physical/mental worker	110.7	106.5	106.7	111.1	–
Skilled manual	118.3	119.7	111.3	116.2	145.4
Semiskilled manual	102.6	100.4	104.0	105.0	119.5
Unskilled manual	100.0	100.0	100.0	100.0	100.0

Sources: Polish data: K. M. Slomczynski and K. Szafnicki, "Zroznicowanie dochodow z pracy," in *Zroznicowanie spoleczne,* W. Wesolowski, ed. (Wroclaw-Warsaw-Krakow: Ossolineum, 1970), Table 4 following p. 164; Hungarian data: Central Statistical Office, *Social Stratification in Hungary* (Budapest, 1967), pp. 38, 43.

158

TABLE 7.4

Base Pay of Male and Female Nonmanuals as Multiple of
Industrial Workers' Average Total Earnings, and Sexual Composition
of Nonmanual Categories, Czechoslovakia, State Industry, 1967
(worker's earnings = 100.0)

Group	Base Pay, Index	Percent of Category
Intelligentsia		
Male	119.3	85.2
Female	89.1	14.8
Routine white-collar		
Male	105.2	14.6
Female	75.8	85.4

Source: Adapted from Augustin Kudrna, "Diferenciace v odmenovani," *Planovane hospodarstvi* 9 (1968):2,5.

white-collars" has a base pay higher than that of the worker category.* Indeed, women's pay is so low that even female intelligentsia earn less than the workers' average.

It may seem that we make much of little here, and, to be sure, the partial nature of these national data is distressing. Still, the "compression" of the female income range is a reality, and a broad range of data confirms that women tend generally to be excluded from top income categories in social economies (as elsewhere), "compressing" the whole income range when males and females are viewed in the aggregate (see GUS 1975:167; HCSO 1973:112; Kudrna 1968; Vecernik 1969:300-301). In essence, the outcome is a marked negative correlation between the percentage of women in an occupational group (or sector of the economy or branch of industry) and the level of salary/wages in that category. Some examples from national statistical data by economic sector for 1973

---

*There is, of course, a tradeoff in our data. Male workers' average earnings, taken alone, must be higher than the average for the sexes combined; hence, ours is in some sense an underestimate of worker compensation. But on the other hand, the average earnings of the two nonmanual groups would be higher than their base pay, too. This complication we cannot, unfortunately, resolve.

may serve to make the point: In Bulgaria, the correlation (r) between average pay and percentage of women across 11 sectors was -0.802; in Hungary (4 sectors), -0.984; in the USSR (12 sectors), -0.723.

Thus, (a) much of the overlap between the wages of skilled workers (especially) and routine clericals reflects not revolutionary egalitarianism so much as feminization of the latter category, in contrast to the very predominantly masculine composition of the skilled worker category; (b) some of the moderation of intelligentsia incomes is also a function of the "underrewarding" of the intelligentsia's female minority. Such "levelling" is not uncharacteristic of the advanced Western capitalist countries, where feminization of certain sectors and occupations has depressed the relative rewards of work in them. Regarding female earners as "auxiliaries" seems to have similar effects, East and West. In neither case does the "equalizing" effect of a truncated range of female compensation really bespeak a pursuit of egalitarian policies.

There may be in the minds of socialist planners a sort of crude equity in the manner in which women are paid; indeed, to the degree that the feminization of the routine white-collar stratum is seen as downgrading the status of that stratum, it *has* been levelled in relation to the predominantly male skilled manual labor force. Yet, whatever we think of this, comparing the average pay of lower white-collars with that of skilled workers is to compare females with males, secondary earners with household heads for the most part, and hence to muddy the waters through which we hope to see the patterns of income inequality by occupational stratum.

Let us take another step: one that gets us a bit beyond policy and its direct outcomes and into the indirect results of policy in addition to the decisions made in household contexts, which together determine the final material situations of the individuals in those households. Table 7.5 returns us to the results of the Hungarian and Polish surveys of Table 7.3, this time indexing the per capita income in households headed by those of differing occupational strata. As we see and might expect, adding the income generated by secondary earners (predominantly working wives) and spreading total income across the numbers in households moderates the total range—the extremes draw closer together.

But closer attention to the "middle ranges" reveals an interesting phenomenon in the relationship of clerical and skilled-worker households. In Hungary the earlier relationship is reversed: though male clericals earned less individually than male skilled workers, the per capita income in the latters' households is lower than in those of the former. In Poland the advantage of clericals over skilled increases: In the three-city data for 1964-65, clerical per capita incomes outspace even those of foremen and artisans (the latter a heavily "private-enterprise" group in Poland, whose generally high incomes are subject to heavy taxation) and gain on the intelligentsia. At the per capita level, then, the "old"

TABLE 7.5

Base Pay, by Occupational Category
(unskilled manual = 100.0)

| | Poland | | |
| | Three Cities | Lodz | Hungary |
Household Head	1964-65	1967	(National, 1963)
Intelligentsia	168.6	175.9	186.6
Professional nonmanual	–	–	154.9
Technician	143.5	144.3	–
Clerical	132.2	124.8	145.0
Foreman, etc.	129.2	126.4	–
Artisan	–	122.0	–
Physical/mental worker	112.4	104.4	–
Skilled manual	107.9	110.0	132.6
Semiskilled manual	107.6	102.5	114.7
Unskilled manual	100.0	100.0	100.0

Sources: Lodz 1967 from K. M. Slomczynski and K. Szafnicki, "Zroznicowanie dochodow z pracy," in *Zroznicowanie spoleczne*, W. Wesolowski, ed. (Wroclaw-Warsaw-Krakow: Ossolineum, 1970), Table 3, pp. 174-75; three-city data from K. M. Slomczynski and W. Wesolowski, "Zroznicowanie spoleczne: podstawowne wyniki," in *Zroznicowanie spoleczne*, Table 3; Hungarian data as in Table 7.3.

ordinal relationship of lower nonmanuals and "upper" manuals has been restored despite a socialist policy that seems to militate against it.

Again, space constraints preclude a lengthy exposition of the sources of this change. Suffice it here to say that a great deal of evidence on the marriage "choices" of male clericals (Srb 1967; HCSO 1967; Warzywoda-Kruszynska 1973) indicates that their marriages are more economically "advantageous" than those of skilled workers: Predominantly, they lean towards *female* clericals whose incomes, while low, are higher than the incomes of the female semi-skilled and unskilled manuals whom male skilled workers tend to marry. This factor and the somewhat lower fertility in "clerical" or routine white-collar households, and consequently more advantageous earner-dependent ratios, seem to account for the greater part of the white-collar per capita advantage.

This, then, in brutally short summary, is the basic pattern of socialist income distribution among occupational strata. While the absence of full national data on all dimensions renders the picture unavoidably incomplete, some basic points seem supportable at present:

1. The range of stratum-specific average incomes is a relatively egalitarian one;
2. Incomes of specific strata have, on the whole, moved closer together over the long run;
3. "Progress," from an egalitarian-socialist viewpoint, has been less marked in changing the ordering of strata; by and large, the "overlap" in basic incomes between routine nonmanuals and the upper portion of the working class seems a product not only of egalitarian mores, but also of
4. The extreme feminization of the routine nonmanual stratum (and consequent low pay) versus the predominantly male composition of the skilled manual stratum, which has commanded higher rewards;
5. Even where the overlap is "real," where comparable earners (male household heads) are compared, it disappears when household per capita income is considered—evidence that "levelling" has not resulted in the "proletarianization" of the routine nonmanual stratum.

A reasonably clear hierarchy, then, is still evident: On the average, households (the basic unit of stratification, economic and cultural, wherefrom "new generations" take off on their own careers) headed by intelligentsia are most favorably placed; those headed by routine nonmanuals, next (since the males in this predominantly female category are, on the whole, less "routinely" employed than the females): the working class is next, and peasants trail. The hierarchical order, of itself less inegalitarian than in the past, is not new, nor is it greatly altered by the value of family allowances, "free" education, or medical care.*

Is this an equitable hierarchy? As with so many such questions, the answer will depend on one's perspective. For some "old proletarians," the advantages of the intelligentsia today may not seem so much less than those they enjoyed in the past: socialist "promise" only partially fulfilled. For the intelligentsia, the conclusion is likely to be quite different: more comfortable now that they are a valued stratum, no longer the target of the populist rhetoric of the 1940s and earlier 1950s, they nonetheless no doubt feel underpaid for their training and services. Peasants and workers, if on the whole better off than in the bad old

---

*Family allowances, while welcome no doubt, do not recompense for high fertility—even several children (in countries where the norm is one or two), will not produce "allowances" equal in toto to one average annual wage. Education is "free," but not wholly. In higher education stipends are not always adequate for all living expenses; better-off families can supplement them, and it is their children who, for economic and "cultural" reasons, "overutilize" universities. Much as in the West's state universities, education involves transfer payments from the poor and "middling" to the relatively well-off. "Basic" medical care is free to all, but the better-off, those occupationally well placed, either have free access to medical personnel and facilities far beyond those allocated to the general public, or have them available on a fee-for-service basis—and it is these they use.

days, still struggle to make ends meet and are quite aware of their place in the hierarchy. Socialist income distribution is the product of a compromise between the "performance principle" and the necessity of some commitment to egalitarianism—and no compromise satisfies everyone.

THE EQUITY-EQUALITY DEBATE

For some the data thus far, in what they indicate or suggest about socialist-capitalist differences, will be quite readily verbalized in terms of "hardly," "as little as," and so on; for others, no doubt, the terms coming most readily to mind will be "markedly," "as much as," "a substantial ___ percent." Readers can and will judge for themselves; the author's main argument, deferred until the final section of this chapter, is one that explicitly deals in values and depends on these as much as on the figures presented herein. What should be well understood here is that these same figures are received differently by socialist economists, sociologists, and philosophers as well—that there is a debate, or at least clear differences of opinion, about how much equality is proper and good in a socialist system, among those who inhabit it, and articulate its values.

In the West, the debate over equality—its meaning (of opportunity, or of results?), the means of achieving it, its desirability and the costs to be borne in any more vigorous pursuit of it—has been one of the most deeply cutting, attention getting, and fundamental of contemporary controversies. The United States especially has seen in recent times expressions of proequality convictions going well beyond the equality of opportunity generally accepted, if imperfectly realized, as an operative element of the U.S. creed. These have included a major philosophical statement liking the widest possible egalitarianism with "justice" (Rawls 1971), and both essayistic (Gans 1973) and research-based (Jencks et al. 1972) sociological works arguing for the conscious pursuit of equality of results as desirable public policy.

The summarization of the thrust of these and other statements in few lines is an awesome task, but one might at least assert that for these, equity and equality are quasi-identical. Fundamentally, it is only equality that guarantees equity; though absolute equality be unattainable, and even if so have its own costs, residual inequality is only preserved/tolerated at the price of parallel inequity. For the new egalitarians, equality of opportunity is either illusory, in that "success" depends more on luck and personality characteristics than on education, which can be "equalized" (Jencks et al. 1972), or simply insufficient as a moral goal, in that it randomizes or "democratizes" the struggle for success without reducing the profits of winning or the costs of losing, when the gap these represent is seen as wrong (inequitable) itself. While the new egalitarians realize that the equality they desire as end result is yet far off and demands a sobering amount of governmental intervention for its achievement, they still hold it desirable as a concrete goal.

In essence, we see here a denial of the "performance principle," of a loosely functionalist view of stratification as, roughly, "just," in favor of a more radical egalitarianism than seems "native" to the American (or, a fortiori, West European) tradition—certainly different from the equality that Lipset has seen, linked with achievement, as a critical element of the U.S. value system (Lipset 1963). It is not surprising, then, that the assault has generated a defense, mounted by intellectuals who, despite broad variations in ideological provenance, have frequently been called "neoconservatives." Seymor M. Lipset, Nathan Glazer, Robert Nisbet, Irving Kristol, Daniel Bell, and others are frequently grouped under that rubric. For the "neoconservatives" (again to summarize brutally) the performance principle—reward according to the kind of work one does, and how well one does it—retains a logic, and "success" need be seen as a result, at least in part, of effort, which is invested and which "entitles" one to reward, rather than simply of luck and personality factors, which are nonentitling. More importantly, while many neoconservatives could accept more equality, they assess at much higher cost the consequences of the necessarily more interventionist governmental policies necessary to promote it. At stake (for them) is individual liberty—not always, or often, readily reconcilable with equality.

This excursion into the equality debate in the West has a definite point in the present context. The point is that, allowing for all the differences in "official" ideology, for the restrictions on open debate in the socialist countries, and for the fact that all the socialist regimes are quite interventionist, the equality debate in the East is about many of the same issues as its Western counterpart, and it may be better understood by reference to the Western debate with which many readers of this book will be more familiar.

First, it should be understood that socialist revolutions, in their very success, have set up a tension between equality and achievement values not altogether unlike the tension Lipset sees as characteristic of the United States. Equality has been part of socialism's long-term promise. Achievement, on the other hand, is a value implied and immediately promoted by socialism in the concrete historical circumstances in which it came to power. Marxist socialism, with its emphasis on man's capacity to transform his existence, to change the world through the calculated application of human effort, found ready applicability in the tasks of economic development in previously traditional, underdeveloped societies whose religious heritage (predominantly Roman Catholic and Eastern Orthodox, with an admixture of Islam) and political histories (Ottoman domination in the Balkans; rule by landowning aristocracies in Poland, Hungary, and the eastern portions of what would become Czechoslovakia) militated against development. Marxism brought a secular equivalent of the Protestant Ethic to these societies—one that provided a mobilizing force for both societal and individual energies, the latter through expanded educational opportunities, the recruitment of peasants from the overpopulated countryside to the new industrialized complexes, and the combined political-educational "merit" system of promotion and placement. Achievement has coexisted tensely with equality. It has emphasized—however much ideologists have stressed "social" orientations and nonmaterial means of stimulating effort—individual striving, individual effort to qualify for, achieve, and execute "better" jobs and enjoy the elevated rewards that, according to the socialist principle of distribution, are connected to them.

The tension between equality and achievement sets the lines of debate between two lines of socialist thought: *ideological egalitarianism* and *pragmatic reformism.*

Ideological egalitarianism expresses a discontent with the persistent results of adherence to the socialist "according-to-work" reward principle: discontent with the sort of income stratification that has left intelligentsia, routine nonmanuals, workers, and peasants in the truncated but "traditional" hierarchy sketched in the previous section; discontent with the continued cultural differences that see "overuse" of higher education by nonmanual offspring and underelection by those of workers and peasants; discontent, essentially, with the "performance principle" as it operates under socialism.

Of such a persuasion are some of the Yugoslav philosophers and sociologists grouped around the journal *Praxis,* and intellectuals both "established" and dissident in other East European states. One of the most concise and pointed in her positions is the Budapest sociologist Susan Ferge, who argues for "the reduction of differences of social origin and of *social consequences,* that stem from the actual character of the social structure, where socially significant differences are interrelated, forming a hierarchical system" (Ferge 1972:217; emphasis added). While Ferge cautions against striving to eliminate "all differences" and says that society "should not aim at rigid conformity or 'egalitarianism,'" it seems clear that "more equality" of results in Hungary is her target. Like Jencks, Gans, and other U.S. egalitarians, Ferge is not impressed by opportunity per se, or even by high rates of intergenerational mobility. Individual vertical mobility may be instrumental "not in changing but in conserving the structure" (Ferge 1972:219) she wishes to see changed. It is not bad that a peasant or worker child may succeed in becoming a professional, an academician, a responsible official, but the gap between the worlds of elite and mass, in economic and cultural terms, which makes such a transition remarkable (though more common today than in presocialist Hungary), is objectionable. The strata must be drawn closer together, by governmental action to abolish the "dirty" job, to uplift the lower strata, until the distance is not so great, and "collective mobility" becomes a natural and unremarkable phenomenon.

Svetozar Stojanovic, while not a fully committed egalitarian, draws on egalitarian logic in his critique of "anarcho-liberals," as he calls those Yugoslavs who, in the context of the decisive moves toward "market socialism" over the past 10 to 15 years, have come to "*identify* distribution according to the products of labor with distribution according to successes on the market" (Stojanovic

1973:216). He is unwilling to see identity between market distribution and "socialist" distribution, and he argues for curbing the market's operations when its results, effective as they may be in stimulating productivity, threaten excessive departures from the egalitarian side of socialism. The unhampered market might make Yugoslavia a society of "abundance," but it could not make it what Stojanovic wishes: a communist society. For those who argue that productivity is still hampered in Yugoslavia by too little income differentiation, and who support their arguments by referring to the differentials in advanced capitalist countries, he has a ready answer: "the very nature of their standard reveals the true color of their communism!" (Stojanovic 1973:220).

Both Ferge and Stojanovic (especially the latter) live in societies where incomes are, by socialist standards, rather differentiated: Yugoslavia's by virtue of its "marketization" and Hungary's through its reform program, the New Economic Mechanism, which has operated controversially since 1968 to increase general consumption levels, but also to produce new affluence among groups whose "quasi-market" situation has been favorable. Certainly, such trends are disquieting to those who see egalitarianism as a "concrete" ideal. Whether, given broader circulation, they would strike responsive chords among the masses is another question. Equality may be less a matter of concern to the man in the street than the absolute level of his own rewards, his own comfort, and the prospect of seeing things get "better" if not more equal. Jencks et al. (1972: 232,264) found little evidence that the current pattern of inequality bothers Americans: A higher level of concrete payoffs, a larger absolute slice made possible by a larger "pie" divided in the same relative pattern—these concern them more. Unsystematic evidence seems to point to similar convictions among socialist publics. Disturbances arise over threats to absolute living standards, to expectations of improvement—more than ever over inequality of reward per se, as is indicated by the series of disturbances in Poland and East Germany in 1953, in the USSR in 1962, and most recently the sharp response to threatened price rises in Poland in 1970 and 1976.

What then of the other side of the controversy—the critics of the egalitarianism that socialist states have produced? These were called the "pragmatic reformers" for two reasons. First, their arguments have been couched in pragmatic terms. Presumably, beneficial yields in productivity, in stimulus to work harder and better, have been advanced as justifications for proposals for greater income differentiation, greater wage-salary inequality between professionals and rank-and-file workers, between industrious and "lazy" workers, and so on. Second, such proposals have come in the context of reform programs (general economic reform) advocated, and adopted at various times wholesale or piecemeal in most socialist countries, with support coming most vocally from economists, but also from a broader spectrum of intellectuals and professionals.

Pragmatic reformism arises from an aspect of the equality-achievement tension that the United States and the socialist states do *not* share. An extremely high level of productivity and affluence characterized the United States, moderating that tension. Even those whose relative share of the total was small enjoyed a standard of living elevated, in absolute terms, over their European working-class counterparts. But the countries where socialism triumphed were on the whole neither rich nor productive. To those who pressed the claims of equal distribution, there were those who replied that equality meant little when there was so little to distribute; the promise of socialism was better served by a (temporary?) expansion of inequality in pursuit of greater productivity, an increase in the stock of goods and services sufficient so that egalitarian distribution, when readopted, would lead to comfortable circumstances, rather than ascetisicm.

Yugoslavia, rather decisively, has gone the way of pragmatic reformism, and consequently swallowed the pill, bitter to some, of contrast between new affluence for the qualified, energetic, and "lucky" and markedly less improvement for others; of unemployment handled by the export of *gastarbeiter*. In Hungary the New Economic Mechanism, operating with much of the same logic but with the "trimming" necessitated by the greater degree of Soviet tutelage, has also brought "dislocations" as it has modified the economic status of various groups (see Connor 1975).

Perhaps the most explicit presentation of the pragmatic reformist critique of egalitarianism, however, was that of the Czech economic reformers of the 1960s, whose long dissatisfaction with the performance of the economy in that most egalitarian socialist state grew into major and articulate participation in the events leading to the Prague Spring.

Ota Sik, the renowned economist, pointed to the "increasingly damaging levelling of wages, which in turn had a harmful effect on progress in science and technology" (Sik 1965:22)—a harmful effect economists saw measured, among other things, in the disastrous "negative growth" achieved by the Czech economy in the early 1960s. His sentiments were echoed by the sociologist Pavel Machonin, leader of a research team that produced a massive and meticulous study of Czechoslovak stratification patterns (Machonin et al 1969), who found the degree of wage differentiation "absolutely insufficient from the viewpoint of the postulates of a mature socialist society and especially from the viewpoint of the immediate needs of further development of science, technology and culture" (Machonin 1968:50). The Czech reformers thus saw danger in the egalitarianism at low levels consumption that supported the "Schwiekism" of the Czech masses at work and is verbalized throughout the socialist countries in go-slow, restrict-output slogans, such as "He who does not steal from the state steals from his family" and "We pretend to work, and they pretend to pay us."

The reformist acts of 1968 amounted to a complex package, of course: Economic delevelling was combined with a program for political liberalization whose unpalatability to the USSR brought the tanks of August. For the workers grown used to egalitarianism, the economic program probably detracted from their support of the political package, and, as Frank Parkin (1971:177) observes, there were probably elements of self-interest involved on the reformers' side, since the vociferous supporters of reform were "the white-collar specialists who seemed most likely to gain from the erosion of egalitarianism."

For all the qualifying factors of differing economic situations and differing national traditions, the lines between "ideological egalitarians" and "pragmatic reformers" seem clearly drawn. For the first, like Jencks, Gans, and others in the United States, the most impressive fact is persistent inequality, a phenomenon defined as moral problem, and one that is not assuaged by general affluence. Egalitarians are distrustful of arguments that present a logic of unequal endowments, effort, or energy as justification for unequal results, and find the promotion of "equality of opportunity" irrelevant to the results they desire.

On the other hand, those we have called "pragmatic reformers," without generally endorsing an unlimited inequality, a free-for-all operation of the performance principle, do accept the logic of Wesolowski's words that "the scale of skills seems to be greater than the scale of income" in socialism, underrewarding those of extraordinary skill and training while overrewarding those at the other end of the spectrum (Wesolowski 1967:33). For them, as for U.S. opponents of the new egalitarians, education, effort, and scarcity of skills are "entitling," deserve extra reward. Ignoring this is seen to lead not only to injustice but to inefficiency that hampers the whole economy and thus the welfare of all. The conflict, between the writers, professionals, and intellectuals who articulate the two views remains unresolved, and there is no reason to expect any final resolution on this level. The real solution occurs at the "top." It is a matter for the party-government leaders and their executives in the national economic ministries who, consulting or not with those who express one or another set of values, have created and re-created in the wage targets of national plans the reward distributions we saw earlier in this chapter. Power and prerogative are jealously guarded, and, except *in extremis,* nothing compels the Brezhnevs, Giereks, or Ceaucescus to attend to the advice of ideological egalitarians or pragmatic reformers over the short or medium term. Schooled in the art of compromise, like politicians in more familiar systems they have seemingly listened somewhat to both sides, pleasing neither completely in the final balance.

FREEDOM, SOCIALISM, AND EQUALITY

World War II left human and economic devastation in many parts of Europe, East and West. The interest and inclinations of the two great powers— the United States and the Soviet Union—called forth "restorative" processes of differing types. In the West, under the U.S. umbrella, the Marshall Plan and other programs produced a striking recovery, bringing much of Western Europe to a takeoff point, from which it moved into affluence and high mass consumption on its own. Multiparty systems and market economies were preserved.

In the East, the "recipe" was quite different. Under Soviet pressure, Czechoslovakia was forced to reject Marshall Plan aid, and like the other nations it assumed the characteristically Soviet one-party system and planned economy. Affluence on the Western scale was neither the object nor the outcome of socialist restoration—living standards in the East lag well behind those of the West today. The success, rather, was registered in economic developments of a more basic sort: industrialization, the lessening of rural overpopulation, and the development of educational and public health systems to mobilize and conserve populations for economic tasks more grandiose than those ever dreamed of by the interwar regimes. High reinvestment rates meant current necessity (weak consumer sectors, shortages of everyday goods and services), the "gray" world of Eastern Europe, so striking in the 1950s and the earlier 1960s when one entered it from the West. Only in recent times has a very modest "affluence," so long deferred, been noticeable on the streets of Warsaw, Budapest, and other capitals.

The socialist East is, according to the sorts of measures and data we have seen, more egalitarian than the West in its distribution of the wealth that exists (although here we do not take into account the material "privileges of office" enjoyed by the top strata in the USSR and the other socialist states, not generally registered in income data, but socially quite relevant nonetheless). For egalitarians, who see equality as "equitable" and "just," this is a plus for socialist systems. Some might assess the degree of egalitarianism as impressive, others find it, on balance, not much of an advance over patterns characteristic of the capitalist West.

Whatever the judgment, it seems appropriate now to take up the question of the costs (costs of a sort that concern egalitarians and libertarians alike) that may have been incurred in achieving this level of equality. In assessing costs, clearly, values play a role, and thus the author's should be made explicit here.

First, I should scarcely rank myself with those I have described as "new egalitarians" in their emphasis on equality of result. While cognizant of many contemporary inequalities of condition too glaring, too extreme not to be morally repugnant, I am far from convinced that directly seeking equality of result, bypassing equality of opportunity, is a reasonable course. To be sure, absolute equality of opportunity, like other absolutes, is unattainable in the concrete, but opportunity can be made more equal than it is now, and it is in the pursuit of this goal, and of the relief of contemporary misery of the really oppressed, that I see the appropriate rationale for moves toward more equality of condition: *not* in pursuit of a general equality of result. I cannot rid myself of the conviction, unfashionable though it be, that effort and achievement are real, that talent, though a gift, deserves reward when its possessor develops and uses it. That luck and personality play a role in success and failure, I am not inclined to doubt; that their operation sometimes produces inequity, injustice also seems clear. But that they and their results are anything but a part of the human condition which cannot be "designed out," I doubt—and I fear the potential results of concentrated attempts to do so.

This fear stems from a concern with liberty, with freedom, with individual autonomy in a civil society. That these values, and the play they necessarily give to achievement, are in tension with equality is not a matter for doubt. All civil societies have limited them in the attempt to ensure a necessary order, and most in the attempt to ensure a certain minimum standard of welfare below which a person will not be allowed to descend. This is appropriate, indeed necessary. But I question whether the quasi-program of "new egalitarianism" does not threaten these values (values realized imperfectly in the West, but incomparably more there than in the Communist states) a great deal more gravely than its proponents realize—even given their concerns about increased governmental intervention. One may well raise the standard objection: Liberty and freedom are meaningless on an empty stomach; they require for their realization a decent supply of the things that make life livable. From this I do not really dissent, except in emphasis—but emphases here are quite important. This objection does not demonstrate that the civic, legal equality that is the base of liberty requires a radical material-economic equality, and one should not draw such conclusions from it. Freedom can and does coexist with economic inequality, though, as the case of India (most recently and among others) shows, it is imperiled by grinding poverty. Whether individual liberty can coexist with the sort of measures necessary to bring about equalized material results is the major question, and here prudence seems to dictate assuming that the answer is negative, until and if proven otherwise. This prudence, of course, has its base in a conviction that liberty and freedom are indeed paramount values, not inferior to equality, not means to equality and therefore to be disregarded and abandoned if they seem to stand in its way, but ends in themselves, desirable and defensible as such.

Realizing that not all will share this particular set of value emphases in assessing the socialist experience, I shall try in my assessment to reflect not only these, but also the concerns of those closer in conviction to the new egalitarians. My posing of the question of the "costs" of egalitarianism under socialism resolves itself, then, into a few major components. First, is the equality achieved a product of the type of political-economic regime existing in the socialist states, or could it have been achieved in alternative ways? Has there, in other words, been a necessary loss of political freedom in the promotion of greater economic equality? Second, how great is socialism's egalitarian advantage over the developed capitalist economies of the West? Is it large enough that, if we conclude in answer to the first question that a tradeoff is necessary, a new egalitarian might nonetheless think it worth the loss in political freedom? Finally, to what degree is the generally lower socialist living standard a product of political choice, and thus to what degree need it be weighed, in the balance, against the measure of egalitarian distribution achieved?

To one who values freedom and liberty as much as equality (and who sees them as distinct), the first question is the crucial one. Here, though answers to such questions must come in the form of judgments rendered with less than scientific precision, I think the answer must be affirmative. The West European economies, restored to health and producing affluent societies under liberal-democratic, multiparty systems, have not managed to promote so much economic equality as have the socialist states, and their greater degree of personal autonomy, of free play given to divergent political and economic interests, has limited the equality that could be achieved. In this judgment, I find myself much in agreement with Frank Parkin's diagnosis of the reasons why Western social democratic parties, operating in multiparty systems, have been less successful in promoting egalitarian distribution of material goods than the socialist regimes in the East. As Parkin observes (1971:181), in the Western capitalist societies "the combination of a market economy and political pluralism is one which makes the redistribution of advantage between social classes difficult to bring about." A one-party, nonpluralist system with a planned or "command" economy can do more, since privileged groups are not accorded the political rights and facilities for challenging or negating redistributive measures (Parkin 1971:182). Finally, he suggests that socialist egalitarianism is "not readily compatible" with the pluralist Western political order:

> ... perhaps ... socialist egalitarianism is not readily compatible with a pluralist political order of the classic western type. Egalitarianism seems to require a political system in which the state is able continually to hold in check those social and occupational groups which, by virtue of their skills or education or personal attributes, might otherwise attempt to stake claims to a disproportionate share of society's rewards. The most effective way of holding such groups in check is by denying them the right to organize politically, or in other ways, to undermine social equality (Parkin 1971:183).

One might question the scope of Parkin's remark on privileged groups; those of the old order were certainly not accorded "rights and facilities" of self-defense, but in socialism its own privileged groups are guaranteed a good deal of their status by the political order itself. But on the whole, his argument is convincing: The current distributive structure of socialism is a product of the political-economic regime of socialism, and another system, more democratic in its political processes, would not have produced it.

Some may object to registering the restricted political freedoms as a "cost," citing the undemocratic, authoritarian systems of Tsarist Russia and interwar Eastern Europe that preceded socialism. Here, one can only recommend a reading of political history: While Czechoslovakia was, indeed, the only Western-style "democracy," the other predecessor regimes, undemocratic and often corrupt as they were, simply lacked the focused and efficient mechanisms for repression of thought, expression, and organization possessed by Soviet-type socialism. They did not seek to "mobilize" and discipline the populaces to the same degree, nor did they find it necessary to imprison so many—the latter not a bad measure of the (always imperfect) degree of freedom and liberty available in a given political system. Finally, one must here assert that, even allowing for the undemocratic natures of the regimes that socialism displaced, the organizational weapons at the disposal of the new regimes, and the "guarantee" of their power by Soviet hegemony, have effectively prevented the possible development of Western-type liberties to accompany the equality. This, certainly, must count as a cost.

If curtailment of liberty has then been a necessary element in the socialist achievement of greater equality, how much more equality has been achieved? Let us assume here that we are agreed on the essential "goodness" of equality, that we have no qualms about it, as objective. Then, from all the evidence, I think even the most convinced egalitarians would conclude that the gains have not been sufficient. The "equality-of-opportunity" consequences aside, socialism's approximation to equality of result is still a very distant one. The old capitalists and landowners are gone, but material privileges remain for the elite: both visible in their salary rates and less visible in the material prerequisites they enjoy (hidden salary supplements, "special" stores, medical care, access to scarce goods and housing, and so on). If income distributions have been compressed, so that the average incomes of the top 10 percent of earners are no longer as many multiples of the bottom 10 percent as they once were, workers still are— and know they are—significantly less rewarded than educated professionals, with peasants generally still at the bottom of the whole reward structure. Groups may have drawn closer together, but they have not changed relative places. As we have seen, some socialist thinkers see too little equality achieved here; others, already too much. We need not take either side; it seems to me that to say that the measure of equality achieved (the benefits that equality itself has conferred) on the whole are scarcely sufficient to balance the losses in the area of freedom and liberty—of personal security—that socialist citizens must bear.

Here, it might again be objected that the loss of freedom is not experienced as loss, that it was a rare commodity in any case, and that people are more interested in full stomachs than in free thought. All this may be true in some measure—the last true of the "democratic" West as well—but seems rather beside the point. Democratic institutions, on balance, protect people even against their lack of concern with freedom and with "politics." Lacking such protections, socialist citizens have been subject to death, arrest, and to reasoned or random political repression more than they might otherwise have been. This might be accounted a loss, however imperfectly the mass of socialist citizens understand it, if we are to judge the political characteristics of socialist regimes and not simply presuppose them.

Then, we confront the stark fact that, compared to the capitalist West, the egalitarian socialist East remains poor. A skilled French or German worker's wages may represent a smaller proportion of, say, a corporate vice president's or chief engineer's than the pay packet of his Polish or Czech counterpart, but his absolute living standard is one they cannot hope to attain. Is this particular gap the result of socialist policy? Is it thus a cost to be assessed against the benefits of socialist egalitarianism?

The answer here is a partial "yes." Partial, because there has always been an East-West gap. In the nineteenth and early twentieth centuries, Russia was a "poor" great power, a underdeveloped giant. The interwar years, for the most part, saw Eastern Europe the poorer and backward half of the continent. Thus, the socialist regimes began with an economic disadvantage; however, they did rather little to deal with the human side of it. For all the long-term calculations that growth of the industrial base—heavy industry—is necessarily antecedent to a strong, diverse economy, this is not necessarily everywhere the case. The emphasis on heavy industry, to the extent that the consumer and service sectors were "orphaned," was a phenomenon, born of Soviet political decisions initially and the imposition of the Soviet experience later on the East European states. Neither in the Soviet Union, nor elsewhere, was it absolutely necessary to proceed this way: other paths, more balanced in their attention to investment versus consumption, producer goods versus consumer goods, might have been chosen but were not. The moderately greater material equality of contemporary socialist nations has been achieved not only at considerable cost in the realm of liberty, but also at the probable cost of lower-than-necessary living standards. Though things continue, on the whole, to get better in the East, it is hard indeed to say that the recent improvements amount to adequate recompense for the earlier deprivations.

These are, to be sure, broad judgments, imprecise and open to various objections on matters of detail. They depend, moreover, on values, on particular relative emphases of values that not all will share. But they are made on the basis of real-world data, from which I can draw no other conclusion. For one who sees equality as *the* supreme, almost exclusive value, the increments of equality achieved under socialism may be clear gain, the costs illusory. For one who would balance equality against the possibility of abundance, the good material life for all, though with differences in the level of that good life, a different conclusion suggests itself. And, for one to whom personal liberty is as important as (or even more important than) either equality or affluence, the socialist "achievement," in the unchosen paths, the unexplored alternatives it represents, has been costly indeed. The sheet does not balance: The egalitarian gains are dwarfed by the political losses, to the general detriment of socialist citizens.

REFERENCES

Connor, Walter. 1975. "De l'utopie à la société 'pragmatique': les consequences sociales des réformes économiques en Europe de l'Est." *Revue de l'Est* 6 no. 1 (March):107-41.

Ferge, Susan. 1972. "Some Relations between Social Structure and the School System." In *Hungarian Sociological Studies (The Sociological Review Monograph* no. 17), edited by Paul Holmes. Keele, United Kingdom: 1972, pp. 217-46.

Gans, Herbert. 1973. *More Equality.* New York: Pantheon.

Gellner, Ernest. 1972. "The Populist Anti-Levellers of Prague." *Government and Opposition* 7, no. 1 (Winter).

Glowny Urzad Statystyczny (GUS). 1975. *Rocznik Statystyczny 1974.* Warsaw.

Hungarian Central Statistical Office (HCSO). 1973. *Statistical Yearbook 1973.* Budapest.

———. 1967. *Social Stratification in Hungary.* Budapest.

Jencks, Christopher, Marshall Smith, Henry Acland, and Mary Jo Bane. 1972. *Inequality: A Reassessment of the Effect of Family and Schooling in America.* New York: Basic Books.

Kudrna, Augustin. 1968. "Diferenciace v odmenovani." *Planovane hospodarstvi* 9.

Lipset, Seymour Martin. 1963. *The First New Nation: The United States in Historical and Comparative Perspective.* New York: Basic Books (Doubleday Anchor ed., 1967).

Machonin, Pavel. 1968. "Socialni rozvrstveni nasi spolecnosti." *Nova mysl* (April):466-74. (*JPRS Political Translations on Eastern Europe,* no. 351 [May 31, 1968].)

——— et al. 1969. *Ceskoslovenska spolecnost: Sociologicka analyza socialni stratifikace.* Bratislava: Epocha.

Ossowski, Stanislaw. 1957. "Social Mobility Brought about by Social Revolutions." *Fourth Working Conference on Social Stratification and Social Mobility.* International Sociological Association.

Parkin, Frank. 1971. *Class Inequality and Political Order.* New York: Praeger.

Rawls, John. 1971. *A Theory of Justice.* Cambridge, Mass.: Harvard University Press.

Sik, Ota. 1965. "Czechoslovakia's New System of Economic Planning and Management." *Eastern European Economics* (Fall).

Slomczynski, K. M., and K. Szafnicki. 1970. "Zroznicowanie dochodow z pracy." In *Zroznicowanie spoleczne,* edited by W. Wesolowski. Wroclaw-Warsaw-Krakow: Wydawnictwo Polskiej Akademii Nauk, pp. 147-85.

Srb, Vladimir. 1967. "K dynamice socio-profesionalni heterogamie v CSSR." *Sociologicky casopis* 3, no. 1:33-37.

Stojanovic, Svetozar. 1973. *Between Myths and Reality*. New York: Oxford University Press.

Ulc, Otto. 1974. *Politics in Czechoslovakia*. San Francisco: W. H. Freeman.

United Nations. 1967. *Incomes in Post-War Europe: A Study of Policies, Growth and Distribution (Economic Survey of Europe in 1965, Part 2)*. Secretariat of the Economic Commission for Europe, Geneva.

Vecernik, Jiri. 1969. "Problemy prijmu a zivotni urovne v socialni diferenciaci." In Pavel Machonin et al. *Ceskoslovenska spolecnost: Sociologicka analyza socialni stratifikace*. Bratislava: Europa, 1969, pp. 295-321.

Warzywoda-Kruszynska, W. 1973. "Zbieznosc cech spolecznych wspolmalzonkow." In *Struktura i ruchliwosc spoleczna*, edited by K. M. Slomczynski and W. Wesolowski. Wroclaw-Warsaw-Krakow-Gdansk: Wydawnictow Polskiej Akademii Nauk, 1973, pp. 125-66.

Wesolowski, Wlodzimierz. 1967. "Social Stratification in Socialist Society (Some Theoretical Problems)." *Polish Sociological Bulletin* No. 1.

Wiles, Peter J. D. 1975. "Recent Data on Soviet Income Distribution." *Survey* 21, no. 3 (Summer).

—— and Stefan Markowski. 1971. "Income Distribution under Communism and Capitalism: Some Facts about Poland, the UK, the USA and the USSR." *Soviet Studies* 22, no. 3:344-69; no. 4:487-511.

Yanowitch, Murray. 1963. "The Soviet Income Revolution." *Slavic Review* 22, no. 4.

8

**INCOME MAINTENANCE
IN THE SOVIET UNION
IN EASTERN AND WESTERN
PERSPECTIVE**
Jack Minkoff
Lynn Turgeon

Public interest in income maintenance programs rises and falls with the unemployment rate. In prosperous years the inadequacies of our nation's programs do not seem to provoke any major social concern. The plight of the lower crust—the urban ghetto dwellers, the migrant farm workers, the trapped residents of economically declining communities, the illegal immigrants, to name only the most easily identifiable groups experiencing income insecurity in good times as well as bad—seems to be beyond the powers of recognition of either the public at large or government officials. But when the rot penetrates deeper into the fabric of society and members of powerful unions, the middle classes, and even college professors find themselves among the unemployed or feel threatened by that fate, then the decibel level of the public clamor for improvement of our income maintenance measures is audible even to least responsive public officials.

Thus, it was not a coincidence that the basic portion of our current income maintenance program was created in the Depression years of the 1930s. With the benefit of hindsight we now understand that the New Deal was too cautious, that the tide in favor of social reform was running so strongly then that the Congress would have adopted an even broader program of income security had it been seriously proposed. Roosevelt's hesitancy cost the United States dearly, for with the change in political climate, the real possibilities of the 1930s became the impossible dreams of the 1940s, 1950s, and 1960s. Now, with the economic hardship again spreading in the 1970s, the state of public opinion makes fundamental improvement in our economic security arrangements once again a more realistic goal. While the opportunity exists, the question still remains as to whether those who can provide leadership will persevere in the effort.

This is a particularly timely moment to examine the income-maintenance programs of the Soviet Union and the other East European socialist states. It is not that these programs can serve as an ideal model for us to emulate—far from it, for as we shall see, they too have shortcomings. It is that when the programs of the Soviet Union and the other Eastern European states are contrasted with that of the United States, the weaknesses and strengths of the various programs emerge in bold relief. The competing advanced capitalist and noncapitalist systems each seem to have developed income-maintenance programs that are strongest or most advanced in those areas where the opposing system shows itself to be weakest. Thus, an examination of income-maintenance programs also exposes the underlying social structures of the respective societies.

This article focuses on a comparison of the current income maintenance program of the Soviet Union with those of Bulgaria, Czechoslovakia, the German Democratic Republic (GDR), Hungary, Poland, and Romania. We first examine the principles that give shape to the complex and extensive measures constituting the Soviet income-maintenance program and, in this connection, consider how these principles differ from those of the United States. The main section will be devoted to a description of the major components of the Soviet program to determine the degree of income protection offered the Soviet population and to illustrate how the Soviet program is designed to further the government's socio-economic goals. The comparable aspects of the income-maintenance programs of the six other Eastern European countries will also be reviewed, to determine how closely the various countries adhere to the Soviet model and to ascertain, if possible, which members of the Soviet bloc provide the most equitable arrangements for their nonworking citizens. In the course of this exposition, there will also be some comparisons with the programs in effect in the United States and in other major advanced capitalist states.

Before proceeding, it is necessary to delineate the scope of the term *income maintenance,* as used here. At times, income maintenance is given a very broad meaning encompassing measures designed to protect against all risks to continuity of adequacy of income. In this all-inclusive definition, income maintenance measures not only include sick, maternity, and unemployment benefits and pensions, but also family allowances, rent subsidies, real and monetary supplements to low wage earners, medical insurance or services, and so forth. But an investigation of such breadth would require much more space than can be devoted here, and would present many difficulties. If, for example, the reimbursement of medical costs or the provision of medical services is included among income-maintenance measures, then a comparative study must evaluate the quality of the medical care provided. A nation may claim that it has entirely socialized the costs of medical care, but unless it actually provides the required services, such a claim is hollow. Furthermore, a comparative evaluation of measures designed to combat inadequate income presents possibly even thornier problems. If supplements to low-wage earners, welfare grants, negative income tax schemes, food stamps, and family-allowance plans are designed to insure the adequacy of a family's income, how do we assess the success of these measures without a firm standard of income adequacy for each of the countries studied? The prevailing minimum wage in each nation might be used as a guide, but that would be at best a very rough measure. For all the above reasons, this chapter employs a more restrictive meaning of income maintenance, embracing only those measures that are designed to substitute for the interrupted or discontinued customary earnings of employees.

The chapter focuses on the circumstances in which benefits are furnished and the level of benefits awarded. In comparing nations, we evaluate the relative degree of protection afforded by examining the ease with which persons may qualify for benefits and the portion of earnings represented by the benefits awarded. Thus, the study sheds light on the degree to which each society protects the customary living standards of its labor-force participants when such persons are cut off from their ordinary earnings.

PRINCIPLES OF SOVIET INCOME MAINTENANCE

Several principles have governed the Soviet income-maintenance program virtually since its inception. Broadly speaking, the following underlying principles can be distinguished:

1. Nonuniversality, particularly the historic discrimination against the agricultural population;
2. Variations in the level of income maintenance by occupation within the nonagricultural sector;
3. Tying of benefits to earnings;
4. Guaranteeing of employment rather than unemployment compensation;
5. Exclusive state responsibility for income maintenance and its funding for the nonagricultural labor force.

Since the dominant theme of Soviet state policy has been the maximization of economic growth and development, it has sought to prevent the income maintenance program from weakening work incentives. In the capitalist world, on the other hand, with its different aims and institutional arrangements, we find fundamental differences with the Soviet principles of income maintenance.

Nonuniversality

An enduring principle of Soviet income maintenance has been to restrict the coverage of the nation's basic scheme—the social insurance program—to those defined as "employed persons." This has meant that throughout most of Soviet history the government accepted no responsibility for furnishing alternative income to the vast majority of the Soviet agricultural labor force. Prior to collectivization, the peasants could properly be classified as self-employed and thus ineligible for coverage under a program deemed necessary only for employed persons. But the later contention that collective farmers are not employees but rather independent entrepreneurs can only be treated as chimerical. Yet this is precisely the position Khrushchev took as late as 1956 when, in response to some peasant expression of discontent over their exclusion from the program, he admonished them to look to their own efforts for security in their old age rather than to expect government support. Up to 1964, the peasants' source of aid when they could not work was their own collective farm rather than the state. As the assistance granted was usually in the form of food and other aid-in-kind, this practice no doubt limited the peasants' unplanned mobility, which is precisely what the state planners preferred.

The farmers' situation was in all respects inferior to that of the workers. Even in 1964, when the government finally accepted responsibility for furnishing alternative income to collective farmers who could not work and/or who were aged, it chose to restrict older farm workers' mobility by creating a separate nationwide scheme for them rather than absorb them into the original social insurance system. And although the collective farm scheme has been liberalized in the intervening years (and is now in fact almost identical to the noncollective farm social insurance program), it does not provide benefits that are in all cases as generous as those furnished under the social insurance system.* The second-class status of collective farmers with respect to income security has thus not yet been fully erased.[1]

The other noncapitalist states of Eastern Europe also exclude collective farmer and independent peasants from the coverage of their basic state income-maintenance programs and, like the Soviets, have established a separate system for persons working in agriculture who are not state employees. (State farmers, of course, receive all the benefits of industrial workers, including all income-maintenance provisions.) Collective farmers in the GDR, Bulgaria (since July 1, 1975), and Poland—and in Czechoslovakia those working on farms classified as "highly efficient"—enjoy virtually the same rights as do other state employees.

---

*For example, the sick benefit rate is still somewhat lower for collective farmers with long continuous records of employment. There is also no partial disability pension for collective farmers while the minimum pension is 20 rubles per month compared to 45 rubles per month elsewhere. While in part these differences in benefits between collective farmers and those covered by social insurance may reflect the income (monetary and in-kind) that collective farmers can be expected to earn from their private plots, collective farmers who are physically incapacitated do not have this option.

(Bulgaria, which has a high percentage of collective farmers, has recently provided income-maintenance parity with industrial workers. They also introduced pensions to their farmers in advance of the Soviets.[2]) But in Poland the private sector predominates in the agricultural sphere, and the independent peasants, who constitute about 40 percent of the labor force, are left to their own devices. They can claim a small pension from the state only if they have turned over all their land holdings to the government sector. In this manner, the exclusion of the private agricultural labor force from the Polish state income-maintenance program serves as a lever inducing the gradual transfer of agricultural land to the collectivized sector.

In Hungary and Romania, the range of benefits, the qualifying conditions, and/or the benefit rates are not conceived as liberally for collective farmers as they are for state employees. This discrimination appears to be particularly serious in the latter country where the agricultural labor force constitutes a large proportion of the total labor force.

The Soviet and Eastern European policy of discriminatory exclusion from the coverage of the basic state income maintenance programs is in sharp contrast to the arrangements usually found in the advanced capitalist world. Here we find that coverage of the basic scheme tends, particularly in recent years, toward universality. Coverage may extend to all citizens or, as in the case of the United States, to all gainfully employed or self-employed persons. Clearly, universality is the more desirable arrangement since it is the most likely route toward the elimination of invidious distinctions. Though, as we shall see, a nation may have universal coverage of its basic scheme and yet provide advantages to powerful or favored groups by other, less obvious means.

Variations by Occupation

Another principle embodied in the Soviet income-maintenance program—one that is also geared to furthering the planners' economic objectives—is that of differentiating among those covered by the basic program according to the type of work performed. Thus, the Soviet differential approach is taken one step further. This too is in contrast to our own Social Security Act, which provides for uniform qualifying conditions, benefit rates, and retirement tests for all persons coming under the act. The Soviet social insurance system, on the other hand, increases the pension rates and lowers the retirement age and the years of employment required for an old-age pension for persons employed in especially arduous occupations and surroundings. But beyond that, an extensive list of work categories having no necessary connection with the strenuousness of the job but deemed to be especially important today entitle a working pensioner to keep his or her full pension without regard to the level of earnings, while in most cases very moderate earnings lead to the suspension of the pension.* Again we see the dominant influence of the state planners' economic goals in shaping the social insurance regulations.

Similar occupational distinctions are found in the income-maintenance programs of the six other East European countries. Bulgaria, Czechoslovakia, and Romania follow the Soviet system most closely and divide their labor force into three classes, although Czechoslovakia, interestingly enough, requires the same years of employment for the old-age pension from all three classes. Five of the six countries have established a more lenient income retirement test for various favored occupations. The sixth, the GDR, more simply pays out full pensions to all working pensioners and thus avoids discriminating directly among occupations.

The Tying of Benefits to Earnings

The third major structural feature of the Soviet income-maintenance program, the tying of benefits to earnings, is designed to foster the state planners' aim of strengthening work incentives. The method used in the computations of earnings for pension purposes can seriously erode the principle of furnishing differential benefits in accordance with work productivity. If the approach taken is to have pensions based on average lifetime earnings, as it is under the U.S. Social Security system, then in times of rapidly rising wages, the level of an individual's pension will be determined more by how recently he or she retired rather than by the importance of the jobs held. And with long-term inflation, pensions may be turned into a flat-rate scheme for a large body of beneficiaries. For if over time the minimum pension is related to some standard of adequacy, then an increasing number of older pensioners will find the minimum rate higher than their wage-related pension.

The Soviets partially avoid this trap by basing pensions on recent earnings, either the average of earnings over the past 12 months of work or the best five consecutive years among the past ten, whichever is higher. Bulgaria, Czechoslovakia, Hungary, Poland, and Romania utilize some form of recent-earnings computation. Only the socialist Germans, with their historic Bismarckian tradition of a social insurance-earnings tax on workers, relate pensions to lifetime earnings, and, as we shall see, the gap between pensions and current average wages is widest in the GDR.

---

*Not only production workers and foremen are permitted to keep their full pension while working; so are postmen, persons engaged in retail trade and public catering, lottery-ticket salespersons, rural schoolteachers, and so on.

Although the tying of benefits to recent earnings rather than to lifetime earnings assures that benefit differentials will more clearly reflect wage differentials, even this arrangement is not without weaknesses over the long haul. With increasing longevity, persons may live a score of years beyond retirement. Over this time span, average wages may roughly double and the problems associated with the lifetime earnings concept will also emerge in systems based on recent earnings concepts. The pension of the well-paid worker of an earlier generation may be smaller than that of a recently retired unskilled worker.

The Federal Republic of Germany (FRG) has adopted a technique that facilitates the maintenance of relative living standards during the period of retirement. In effect, the West Germans adjust pensions annually to take into account wage trends in the pensioners' former occupation. Thus pensioners in the FRG can expect during their retirement years to enjoy the same relative status among pensioners that they had achieved as wage earners.

This imaginative strategy of the West Germans finds no parallel in the Soviet Union or the six other Eastern European countries. The only hesitant step taken in this direction has been the institution in Hungary as of 1970 of an automatic annual 2-percent increase in payments that, although not tied to the cost-of-living index, is similar in concept to the United States' recently adopted Social Security escalator clause. (It is perhaps significant that Hungary has the greatest overall price increases in its cost-of-living indexes, and its statistical handbooks include separate indexes for pensioners.) Neither the five other Eastern European countries nor the Soviet Union makes provision for regular periodic increases in benefits. Instead, pensions, particularly minimum pensions, are raised sporadically whenever the nations' leaders are moved to act.[3] Thus, in these countries, the income of pensioners tends over extended periods to lag behind the constantly rising standard of living.

Guaranteed Employment Rather Than Unemployment Compensation

The fourth principle governing the Soviet income-maintenance program most sharply sets that program apart from the income-maintenance schemes of advanced capitalist societies. While the Soviets acknowledge state responsibility for protecting employed persons against all forms of risks to continuity of income, the management of unemployment comes under the state's economic-planning policies rather than within the framework of the income-maintenance program. To the Soviets, income security for those capable of working is answered through the guarantee of work opportunities rather than through the availability of unemployment benefits. According to Soviet law, the right to a job is a constitutionally guaranteed right. Thus, unemployment benefits, which play a prominent role in the income-maintenance program of capitalist countries, are absent from the Soviet program.

The lack of unemployment compensation in the Soviet Union unquestionably creates hardships for some small number of people since there is some evidence of frictional unemployment, the time elapsing between jobs averaging about a month. In situations involving staff reductions or retraining, the workers' plight is eased by allowing them to draw their former salary for a stipulated period—at times for as long as three months. But all such arrangements only add up to a very uncertain system of security for those who are (if only briefly) unemployed.

Again we find that in bringing the social-insurance regulations into conformity with the state's economic aims, the end result is an extreme posture. The availability of unemployment benefits to the involuntarily unemployed could hardly create a serious problem of malingering or a reduction in output. Yet the needs of the frictionally unemployed have apparently been sacrificed to that specter. For with the absence of unemployment benefits, the Soviets place maximum pressure on the unemployed not to procrastinate in choosing one of the many available jobs.

For some years after World War II there was a refreshing diversity in the historic treatment of unemployment in the six other East European countries. In this instance, it would appear that the influence of the Soviet model was not quite so overpowering. The Soviets abolished unemployment benefits in 1930 as soon as the First Five-Year Plan had eroded the 7 percent of the labor force that was officially unemployed by the end of the period of the New Economic Policy. Not too surprisingly, the East Germans adopted an unemployment scheme in 1947, at a time when their economy faced severe dislocation problems. But more surprising was the adoption of unemployment-benefit systems in Hungary in 1957 and in Bulgaria in 1958. The latest issue (1975) of the U.S. Social Security Administration's publication, *Social Security Programs throughout the World,* lists these programs as having current status. However, we have found no evidence showing that these laws are still in effect. It is our belief that currently all other Eastern European countries, like the Soviet Union, make no special provision for former unemployment benefits but instead provide ample job opportunities for those seeking work.

When one considers the treatment of the unemployed in the capitalist countries, any criticism made of the Soviet arrangement pales into insignificance. Jobs are preferable to monetary benefits in all respects, as many Westerners are sadly learning: preferable in terms of human dignity, feeling of self-worth, and psychological well-being. Furthermore, since employment customarily confers access to an extensive array of fringe benefits, joblessness can result in comprehensive insecurity. The short-term unemployed may lose their medical insurance and their company life insurance along with their job; the long-term unemployed may never qualify for the company pension, and they also receive a smaller social security pension than if they had worked continuously. In short, for the individual, joblessness is the most threatening form of insecurity.

From society's point of view, unemployment represents institutional failure. Modern society cannot refuse to accept some responsibility for alleviating the plight of the unemployed so that people capable of working, instead of contributing to the wealth of society, become unwilling burdens on those who do work. This absurd situation prevails most strikingly today in many of our urban centers. Despite the pressing need to put people to work and to make our cities more decent places in which to live, the city fathers find themselves forced to fire essential civil servants. The support of the unemployed has another undesirable consequence: Not only is society impoverished by the loss of potential increases in goods and services, but the level of aid society finds possible to extend to those who physically cannot work or who have reached retirement is reduced because of the larger body of persons requiring support.

We have noted that the unavailability of unemployment benefits in the Soviet Union today testifies to their steadfast pursuit of maximum production. The existence of large-scale unemployment and subemployment in the major capitalist centers of the world testifies to the institutional irrationality of these societies. Which of these social ills reflects the more serious state of social pathology is not debatable in our view.

Exclusive State Responsibility

The fifth principle governing the Soviet income-maintenance program is that the sole responsibility in this field for those covered by the primary program—the social insurance program—rests with the state. Although personal savings have greatly increased in recent years and personal insurance may be purchased, workers must look in the main to the state for alternative income when they lose their customary earnings.[4] Enterprises may seek to attract workers by providing superior housing facilities or other amenities, but they may not establish their own schemes for income maintenance. Thus, an examination of the state social insurance system sets forth the full extent of the income protection enjoyed by those coming under its umbrella. And as a logical extension of the principle of sole responsibility, the state bears the full monetary costs of the social insurance system through earmarked taxes on the employing agencies and allocations from general revenue.

The discriminatory features of the Soviet income-maintenance arrangements emerge now even more clearly. Until 1964 workers received benefits financed by the state, while collective farmers were left to depend on the resources of their collective. And today, although there is a separate income-maintenance system for collective farmers (underwritten in part by government allocations), government finances still provide somewhat more liberal benefits for workers outside the collective farms. Incidentally, one of the goals of the current Plan X is to bring the benefits of the two pension programs nearer together.

Bulgaria, Czechoslovakia, and Poland follow the Soviet precept without variation. In the GDR and Hungary, however, an earnings tax is levied on employees to defray, at least partially, the monetary costs of the program. In addition, both the GDR and Romania have established additional voluntary pension schemes requiring worker contributions to supplement the basic state benefits.

The precept of the state having sole responsibility for income maintenance is foreign to the philosophy prevailing in most capitalist societies. The public acceptance of state responsibility in this sphere was achieved in the United States only after a long struggle on the part of our labor movement. While today few would argue for complete reliance on individual initiative, the preferred arrangement is seen more as a mix of individual, employer, and state programs. In our own country, for example, some employees will enjoy a much greater degree of security than that furnished by the social security program. Unequal treatment, then, is endemic to our own income-maintenance arrangements as well as to the Soviet system. It is only that the discriminatory aspects of the Soviet system are more readily apparent; they are found in the differences between the systems for collective farmers and for state workers and in the special treatment accorded to various classes of workers within the social insurance program.

To appreciate the inequality in the income protection extended to our own labor force, one would have to investigate all labor-management contracts. But one point is not in question: fringe benefit arrangements concluded between unions and management compound the extent of inequality among segments of United States labor. For it is the strongest unions, whose members already enjoy higher pay scales, that have been most successful in winning protection provisions in their contracts. Thus, the least secure workers—the workers in nonunion plants in the lower level of the dual economy, and those who have little savings to fall back on—are the ones who are most likely to be dependent solely upon the limited provisions of the social security program.

One may say that one effect of the philosophy of divided responsibility for income-maintenance programs has been to enable our government to ward off criticism against the weaknesses in the social security program by claiming that other institutions bear the responsibility for improvement. The philosophy of divided responsibility has been a force for conservatism to the extent that the demands of the most powerful elements of the labor force for greater security have been satisfied through collective bargaining, and the political pressures for any extensive reform of the social security system have consequently been blunted.

We have noted that a universal income-maintenance program would be a step forward for the Soviet Union and certain other East European countries. In our own country, there is an even more distinct need for greater government responsibility in the field of income maintenance in order to extend the breadth of protection available to the less favored segments of the labor force and to foster greater equity in the treatment of all persons.

CURRENT INCOME-MAINTENANCE REGULATIONS

The remainder of this chapter is devoted to an examination of various components of the social insurance program. As we have noted, the Soviet social insurance system embraces, for all practical purposes, the entire labor force, with the exception of collective farmers. Thus, the Soviet regulations described apply to about 80 percent of the total population of the USSR.

The Soviet social insurance program, as well as the programs of the six other East European socialist states, makes provisions for all of the commonly identified risks to continuity of income with the exception, as noted above, of unemployment. We will first examine the sick-benefit regulations, and then consider the old-age, disability, and survivors' pensions. The material presented in these sections will be applicable either to both sexes or to men alone, as indicated in the discussion, and the last section will describe special provisions with respect to women.

The Sick Benefit

The Soviet sick-benefit provisions are liberally cast. All employed persons are eligible for this benefit, which is payable from the first day of incapacity up to the date of recovery or until the person is classified as permanently disabled. (Excepted are those who had been discharged for a violation of labor discipline and who must complete six months of continuous service at their new job before qualifying for the benefit. This restriction does not apply to persons disabled in the course of work.) The benefit rate is tied to the years of continuous employment, and the rate structure allows for generous payments. Union members (including practically the entire nonagricultural labor force) employed in the state sector get the following amounts: Individuals with less than three years of continuous employment, 50 percent of earnings; those with three to five years, 60 percent; those with five to eight years, 80 percent; and those with eight years and more, 100 percent. Fragmentary evidence suggests that most beneficiaries receive about 80 percent of earnings.[5] In work-related cases, the sick benefit is uniformly 100 percent of earnings. Where there are three or more children under the age of 16 (18 if a student) in a family, the benefit is also a flat 100 percent of earnings.

The sick benefit regulations of the six other Eastern European countries for the most part closely parallel those of the USSR. Bulgaria, Czechoslovakia, Hungary, and Romania also use the benefit to combat labor turnover and base

TABLE 8.1

Current Sick-Benefit Rates of Selected Socialist Countries, by Length of Continuous Employment
(percent)

Country	Less than One Year	Beginning the Fourth Year	Beginning the Sixth Year	Beginning the Eleventh Year
Bulgaria	60	60	70	80
Czechoslovakia	60	70	80	90
Hungary	65	75	75	75
Romania	50	65	75	85
Soviet Union	50	60	80	100

Sources: I.L.O., *Legislative Series; International Social Security Review* (See bibliographical note at end of chapter).

the rate structure on the years of continuous employment. On the other hand, the GDR and Poland do not vary their benefit rates. The workers of socialist Germany get 50 percent of their wages from the social insurance fund plus another 40 percent from their employer for the first six weeks of incapacity; for periods beyond six weeks, the benefit amounts to 50 percent of wages in addition to a dependency allowance of up to 40 percent. The East Germans alone make provisions for a dependency allowance; this is understandable, since the basic rate is the lowest for the longer-term illnesses. The Poles are the most generous: Their uniform benefit rate is 100 percent of earnings, regardless of continuity of employment.[6] The other four countries have maximum rates that are below 100 percent of earnings: Hungary, 75 percent; Romania, 85 percent; Bulgaria and Czechoslovakia, 90 percent.

Table 8.1 compares the relative liberality of the benefit rates in the Soviet Union and the four countries that also vary their rate with the years of employment. For persons with fewer than five years of continuous employment, the least generous rates are paid in Bulgaria, Romania, and the Soviet Union, while Bulgaria and Hungary pay out the lowest rates to employees having 11 or more years of continuous employment.

These rate structures, however, do not appear illiberal when compared with the sick-benefit arrangements in the advanced capitalist nations. The United States appears the most unenlightened of societies in this area since the Social Security Act does not even mention the sick benefit, and only five of the 50 states make any provision for guaranteed sick benefits, with the maximum benefit rate being no more than two-thirds of earnings. The United Kingdom allows up to 85 percent of earnings in sick benefits. The West Germans, who have one of the most generous schemes, require the employer to pay out full earnings in benefits for the first six weeks of sickness. Thereafter, the insurance fund pays out 75 percent of earnings in addition to a variable dependency allowance—a system like the GDR's.

Thus, the sick-benefit schemes of the Soviet Union and the other East European countries (with the exception of the GDR) compare favorably with the arrangements found in the advanced capitalist societies. The distinctive feature of the sick-benefit provisions in the Soviet Union and in East European countries (except for the GDR and Poland) is the tying of benefits to the length of continuous employment. The capitalist societies, with unemployment disciplining the labor force (as well as an extensive array of nonvested fringe benefits), are less concerned with labor turnover, and thus a uniform benefit is the rule.

Old-Age Pensions

The essential considerations with respect to the old-age pension are the age of retirement, the years of employment required, and the benefit rates. Table 8.2 presents the qualifying age and the necessary years of employment for men in ordinary employment in the Soviet Union and the other six Eastern European countries.

The common age of retirement for men in the Soviet Union is 60 years of age; only the GDR and Poland stipulate the more advanced age of 65. Furthermore, as we have already noted, certain job classifications carry an earlier retirement age. Thus, in the Soviet Union males employed underground or in unhealthy

TABLE 8.2

Current Retirement Age and Years of Employment Required of Men in Ordinary Employment for the Old-Age Pension

Country	Qualifying Age	Years of Work Required
Bulgaria	60	25
Czechoslovakia	60	25
GDR	65	15
Hungary	60	25
Poland	65	25
Romania	60	25

Sources: I.L.O., *Legislative Series; International Social Security Review* (See bibliographical note at end of chapter).

conditions ("dangerous conditions") may retire at 50, while those employed under conditions deemed arduous may retire at 55. The East European countries, with the exception of the GDR, also stipulate lower retirement ages for similar occupations; the Bulgarians most closely follow the Soviet pattern. To qualify for the earlier retirement age and the shorter work period, the Soviets require that an individual must have completed at least half of the needed period of time in the stipulated employment. The other nations impose variations of this requirement.

There can be no objection to the younger retirement age if it is intended to counterbalance the shorter lifespan or earlier onset of debility for persons in these occupations. However, this is probably only a partial explanation. The primary intent is to reward individuals for stability of employment. With increasing longevity, the effect of both the relatively young general retirement age and the even lower preferential requirement has been the swelling of the pension rolls. For example, pensioners constitute about 16 percent of the Hungarian population, 17 percent of the Soviet population, and 20 percent in the GDR. This situation explains the progressive easing of limits on pensioners' earnings that has taken place over the years in all these countries, and in particular why the East Germans impose no limit whatsoever on earnings. Thus, as we have seen above, for many of the youngest old-age pension recipients the pension actually has become a supplement to their wages. There is little logic to an arrangement that presents a bonus to a person who is fully capable of working and continues to work simply because he or she has attained the age of 60.

The Soviets' quandary is that they established 60 as the general retirement age in an earlier period when, because of poor economic and health conditions, the work capability of the elderly was, as a general rule, adversely affected by that time in life. In the context of a worldwide trend toward earlier retirement, the Soviet leadership would now experience some embarrassment if it proposed raising the nation's retirement age. In this matter, then, political face saving seems to have taken precedence over advantageous reform. For in contrast to the West, the Soviet bloc has no reason to use the old-age pension as a lever to achieve "painless" work sharing. In removing the younger, able-bodied individuals from the pension rolls, the state would have greater resources to support those of still more advanced age who are more likely to have a reduced working capacity.

The liberality of the retirement age in the Soviet Union, Bulgaria, Czechoslovakia, Hungary, and Romania is apparent when compared to the qualifying age adopted by most of the advanced capitalist nations. Sixty-five is the most common requirement, although Sweden has recently reversed the trend and increased the retirement age to 67. Of the major Western European powers, only France has a retirement age of 60.

Table 8.2 also shows the years of employment required of men in ordinary work for a full old-age pension. Only the socialist Germans diverge from the norm of 25 years, and this divergence is more formal than substantive. For under the GDR system, the basic pension rate is dependent upon the years of employment, and persons who just meet the minimum requirement receive a very small pension. This is comparable to the partial pensions offered in the other East European countries, with the exception of Poland. These nations allow for partial payments, proportional to the years of employment completed, upon attainment of the retirement age, to those who cannot satisfy the ordinary employment requirement, subject to the most minimal eligibility conditions. The Soviets require a minimum of five years of work for a partial pension, while the other countries generally stipulate a minimum of ten years. Thus, we do not stray very far from the truth if we view the GDR, too, as requiring 25 years of employment for a full pension.

The Western nations require approximately the same length of employment for the old-age pension. Those nations, like the United States, that relate the pension paid to the length of employment, may have a lesser qualifying condition, but as in the case of the GDR, this may be seen as conferring eligibility for only a partial pension.

The employment requirement of the Soviet Union and the other East European countries is hardly a serious obstacle to pension entitlement, particularly since in most instances military service and, if the individual had previously been employed, the years spent in technical and higher educational institutions are counted as part of the employment record. The only persons likely to have difficulty satisfying the requirement are former collective farmers who transferred to the state sector at an advanced age (since ordinary collective farm work has no bearing on social insurance eligibility) and women who entered employment in their middle years. The partial pensions will thus have significance for such persons.

The Soviet old-age benefit formula varies the benefit rate inversely with the level of earnings. The benefit rate for both sexes whose employment conditions were other than dangerous ranges from more than 100 percent of earnings for those with earnings of less than the minimum pension to 50 percent of earnings for those whose wages were more than 100 rubles monthly. Persons employed in dangerous conditions enjoy a 5-percent higher payout rate. The minimum pension is 45 rubles per month, while the maximum is 120 rubles per month. Since the current average Soviet wage is 135 rubles per month, and since pensions are based on recent earnings, the typical benefit rate for recent retirees must be about 50 percent of earnings.

The Bulgarians, Poles, and Romanians follow the Soviet model closely. They too have a formula that pays out a greater degree of earnings at the lower end of the income scale, an arrangement that provides some assurance of adequacy of payments. On the other hand, the Czechs, East Germans, and Hungarians do not weight the lower range of earnings, so their benefit formulas provide less assurance of adequate payments to lowest-income workers. The

Czechs have a fixed rate for each work classification. Most workers get 50 percent of their earnings in pension, and the rate of persons in dangerous occupations is 60 percent. The Hungarians have a 50-percent rate for all persons, and 0.5 percent of earnings is added for each year of covered employment. The socialist Germans have a basic award of 110 Marks monthly, to which is added 1 percent of the pensioners' average lifetime earnings times the number of years worked.

The essential difference between the benefit formulas of both Hungary and the GDR and the other countries is not that the former have a fixed rather than a variable benefit rate but that they incorporate into their basic formula the length of the work record. The other nations achieve the same end by providing for supplements to the basic rate for long periods of employment. For example, both Romania and Hungary require 25 years of employment for an old-age pension, and in both countries individuals who have worked longer periods get for each such year 0.5 percent more of their earnings in pension than is paid to those who meet only the minimal eligibility requirement. Thus, all the countries concerned shape their old-age benefit provisions to promote steady work habits.

A description of all of the benefit formulas would overwhelm this chapter with unnecessary detail. To illustrate the relative liberality of the several formulas, we have compared the percentage of earnings that would be paid in pensions to persons earning the prevailing average wage. It should be recalled that, with the exception of the GDR, the earnings base used for pensions is recent earnings, and so in all the other countries recent pension awards would commonly be derived from sums close to the current average wage. To strengthen the comparability of our figures, we have assumed that in each case the worker has had 35 years of covered employment under ordinary working conditions. Finally, we have examined separately the pension rate that would be paid (a) to a single old-age pensioner and (b) to a pensioner with one dependent, since more than one dependent would be extremely rare for an old-age pensioner.

Table 8.3 presents the comparative data. A certain symmetry appears, with the wealthiest countries—the GDR, Czechoslovakia, and the USSR—paying out the smallest percentage of earnings in pension. Furthermore, it should be noted that the very low rate calculated for the GDR may actually be overstated. For we have assumed in our computation that the pension was based on average lifetime earnings of 600 Marks per month—the maximum sum considered under the GDR compulsory pension scheme. As wages in the GDR now average 843 Marks per month, the majority of recent retirees may well have had average lifetime earnings below 600 Marks per month. Even when we include the possible payments of the voluntary pensions, the GDR remains the most niggardly society. In such cases, the payout rate rises to only 43 percent for a single individual (and to 50 percent for pensioner with a dependent) who retired in 1975 and had elected to participate in the voluntary scheme since its inception in 1968, and whose earnings averaged 843 Marks per month over that

TABLE 8.3

Percentage of Current Average Wage Paid in Old-Age Pension, Based on Current Average Earnings and 35 Years of Ordinary Working Conditions, 1973

Country	Single Pensioner	Pensioner with 1 Dependent
Bulgaria	72	72
Czechoslovakia	57	62[a]
GDR	38[b]	50[b]
Hungary	68	68
Poland	72	73
Romania	75	75
Soviet Union	55	61

[a]Based on minimum dependency allowance.
[b]Based on average lifetime earnings of 600 Marks per month.
Source: Sotsial'noe Obespechenie No. 10 (1973):62-3.

period. Under similar assumptions, the Romanian compulsory and voluntary plans combined result in pension awards equal to 86 percent of earnings in both cases.

Table 8.3 also demonstrates that, at best, the dependency allowance is only a very modest supplement to the pension. Bulgaria and Romania make no provision for dependency allowances. In Hungary, quite small pension awards result in ineligibility for the allowance. The GDR dependency allowance is the most generous, result in a 31-percent increase in pension, but even with this the GDR still has the lowest payout rate.

The treatment of dependents in the Soviet Union and the six other Eastern European countries contrasts sharply with the approach taken in the United States and other advanced capitalist societies. For example, in the United States a 50-percent increase in pensions is given for a dependent spouse. Benefit payments are thus more closely tied to earnings levels in the socialist world. It is the socialist countries that most consistently shape their pension provisions to strengthen work incentives, with the Bulgarians and the Romanians most single-mindedly pursuing this objective.

To compare the level of support afforded old-age pensioners in the Soviet Union and Eastern Europe with that provided pensioners in other advanced capitalist societies, we again examine the relationship between pensions recently awarded and the current average wage. A recent study of pension adequacy concluded that for the United States, the maintenance of the living standards of retiring persons requires that pensions should replace two-thirds of recent earnings, with subsequent adjustments for rises in the price level and/or the general level of real wages over the remaining life span of the pensioner.[7]

If we use the two-thirds replacement rate as our benchmark for an acceptable level of support, we find that, for a single worker, Bulgaria, Hungary, Poland, and Romania meet this test, but the Soviet Union, Czechoslovakia, and the GDR fall short. Taking into account the dependency allowance, all socialist countries with the exception of the GDR come close to or exceed this standard.

The state retirement systems of other advanced industrial societies prove to be much less generous as a rule. U.S. Social Security retirement pensions for a single person awarded in January 1975 represent on the average only 29 percent of the average wage, and the pension for a husband and wife, 43 percent.[8] An international comparison of the replacement levels of the old-age-pension systems of 13 countries in 1968 showed that the replacement rate for a single worker varied from 21 percent in Switzerland to 54 percent in Italy, with a median figure of 33 percent, which is lower than the lowest rate found among socialist countries.[9] For a couple, the study showed a replacement rate ranging from 34 to 68 percent, with a median figure of 44 percent, which again is lower than the replacement rate for the GDR, the least generous of the socialist countries.

This study of the 13 Western nations disregarded the private pension plans existing in these countries. Of course, when combined with the compulsory state pension system, private plans would raise the various replacement rates. However, as we noted above, reliance on supplementary private pension plans widens the disparity in the living conditions of the former members of the labor force since the weakest elements are least likely to acquire this additional protection.

Thus, we may tentatively conclude that, with the exception of the GDR, retirees in the socialist countries are less likely to experience a sharp drop in the living standards they enjoyed just before retirement than are those in the capitalist, industrialized nations. If we accept as the desirable standard a two-thirds replacement of recent earnings through pensions, then we may also say—again excepting the GDR—that the socialist countries furnish a very respectable level of support for newly retiring persons. The major weakness of the Soviet and Eastern European systems in this connection is that, with the exception of Hungary with its very minor adjustment mechanism, none of the countries has adopted an automatic adjustment provision so that pensions previously awarded will regularly keep pace with rising wage levels.

Disability Pensions

The salient features of disability pension arrangements are the extent of disability that entitles a person to a pension, the qualifying period of employment, and the benefit rates.

TABLE 8.4

Years of Employment Currently Required for the Disability Pension
According to the Age at which Disability Occurred,
East European Socialist Countries

Country	25 Years Old	35 Years Old	45 Years Old	55 Years Old
Bulgaria	3	5	5	5
Czechoslovakia	3	(5 years in last 10)		
GDR	(Two-thirds of years elapsed since entered employment with 5 years minimum)			
Hungary	6	11	17	23
Poland	4	(5 years in last 10)		
Romania	6	12	16	20
Soviet Union	3	7	12	16

Source: I. L. O., *Legislative Series; International Social Security Review* (See biblio-graphical note at end of chapter).

The Soviet program distinguishes among and provides for payments to three grades of disability. Grade I includes total invalids requiring constant attendance; grade II, other totally disabled persons; grade III, the partially disabled. All the other six Eastern European countries allow for payments to both the totally and partially disabled. The Bulgarians, Poles, and Romanians duplicate the Soviet model exactly; the others more simply recognize persons as being either partially or totally disabled. Though regulations differ, the general interpretation of partial disability is the loss of at least two-thirds of earning capacity. In the later discussion of benefit rates, we will focus on the regulations pertaining to the more common form of total disability: the grade II class of the Soviet definition.

The qualifying period of employment varies considerably among the seven countries (for all seven, no period of employment is required if the disability is work connected). The Soviets, Romanians, and Hungarians impose an employment requirement that rises with advancing years, ranging upward to 23 years for persons disabled late in life. The other countries commonly require of all but the youngest workers five years of employment over a recent period. For workers under 20 the Soviets, Bulgarians, and Czechs require no stipulated period of employment, only attachment to the covered labor force (this applies for workers under 18 in Poland). The Romanians and Hungarians, less generously, require at least one year and two years employment, respectively, from even the youngest workers. The GDR again presents the strictest case, stipulating five years of covered employment from all persons, a qualifying condition that must be an almost insurmountable obstacle to most young workers.

Table 8.4 presents the years of employment required of males in ordinary employment who have been disabled at ages 25, 35, 45, and 55. Bulgaria proves to be the most generous country, while Hungary, Romania and the GDR are the most restrictive. The Soviet regulation appears to be comparatively lenient, demanding about one year of work for every two that elapses after one turns 20—not an unreasonable time to fix as the date of entrance into the labor force. The Hungarians, Romanians, and socialist Germans require about two years of work out of three over a similar period. While the Soviet regulation is not likely to prevent a significant number of people from qualifying for the disability pension, the Bulgarian, Czech, and Polish regulations give greater assurance that collective farmers who transfer to state employment in middle life will qualify for this pension.

The benefit-rate formulas for the disability pension closely parallel the old-age pension formulas. The nations with old-age pension formulas that pay out smaller proportions of earnings at high earnings levels—the USSR, Bulgaria, Poland, and Romania—apply the same principle to the disability pension. The other nations either simply pay out a uniform proportion to all (Czechoslovakia) or a fixed sum or percentage in addition to a further amount dependent upon the length of employment (GDR and Hungary).

TABLE 8.5

Disability Pension Based on Current Average Wage, as Percentage of Current Average Wage, Assuming Ten Years of Employment in Ordinary Working Conditions, Socialist Countries, 1973

Country	Single Pensioner	Pensioner with Dependent Wife and Two Young Children
Bulgaria	53	53
Czechoslovakia	57	62[a]
GDR	38[b]	60[b]
Hungary	61	61
Poland	54	54
Romania	48	48
Soviet Union	45	60

[a]Based on minimum dependency allowance.
[b]Based on average lifetime earnings of 600 Marks per month.

Table 8.5 compares the percentage of earnings that would be paid in disability pensions to persons who earned the current average wage. Again, it should be noted that, with the exception of the GDR, since pensions are based on recent earnings, the table illustrates the relationship of recent awards to the current average wage. We have assumed for sake of comparison that the individual was employed in ordinary working conditions, that the disability occurred after 10 years of work, that the individual is totally disabled (Soviet grade II), and that the disability was not work-related. In work-related cases, higher benefit rates are paid. We provide comparisons of the pensions payable to single disabled workers and to a disabled worker with a dependent wife and two young children.

Examining the payout rate to single disabled pensioners, we again find that the GDR provides the least support. Comparing the disability and old-age pension rates, we find that three of the countries (the GDR, Poland, and the USSR) keep their relative positions; two (Czechoslovakia and Hungary) rise in rank; and two (Bulgaria and Romania) fall. Romania experiences the most dramatic drop in rank, falling from first place in the relative liberality of its old-age pension to fifth place in its disability pension. (If consideration is given to the voluntary pension schemes of Romania and the GDR, under the assumptions cited in our discussion of the old-age pension, then the payout rate for Romania rises to 60 percent and in the GDR to 51 percent.)

But the most startling fact emerging from a comparison of the disability and old-age pension formulas is the sharply lower percentage of earnings paid to disability pensioners. None of the countries pays a higher proportion of earnings to disability pensioners; the two most developed—the GDR and Czechoslovakia—pay the same proportion to old-age and disability pensioners, but five pay less—and in some cases substantially less—to the single disabled pensioner than to the single old-age pensioner.

This discriminatory behavior against the disability pensioner is obviously a product of rigid adherence to the Soviet precept of rewarding most generously those who have given the longest service to society. But one can only question the justice of an arrangement which penalizes persons who are cut off from normal productive work at an early age through no fault of their own. If we set a two-thirds replacement rate as the desirable goal for maintaining the living standards of pensioners, we further highlight the impoverished lot of the disability pensioners.

Pensioners of the Soviet Union and the six other East European countries might take some small comfort from the knowledge that disability pensions in the United States are relatively even more inadequate. Recent average Social Security disability awards have constituted only 32 percent of the current average wage.[10] But, interestingly enough, this low percentage of current average earnings paid to U.S. disability pensioners is still higher than the payout rate to old-age pensioners.

When considering the disability pension paid to disabled workers with three dependents, we again see that most of the socialist countries pay little attention to the extra burdens that dependents place on a pensioner. (We have excluded family allowances from our calculations, since they are an addition to wages as well as to pensions. Our aim is to determine the percentage of earnings retained in pension.) Bulgaria, Poland, and Romania make no provision for dependency grants. In Hungary a pension based on the average wage leads to ineligibility for the spouse-dependency supplement. Only the Soviet Union and the GDR provide substantial increments to the basic pension for dependents. In the GDR the allowance for three dependents increases the basic pension by almost 60 percent; in the Soviet Union it increases by one-third. And it must be noted that when we take into account the German voluntary pension scheme, the GDR replacement rate for a disability pensioner with three dependents rises to 73 percent, a figure exceeding that of any other country.

The U.S. Social Security system also provides for substantial dependency allowances. Recent average awards to disabled workers with three dependents come to about 51 percent of our current average wage, which represents an increase of more than 50 percent over the awards received by single pensioners.

The niggardliness of the Soviet and East European disability pension provisions appears in sharpest perspective when one compares the pension payable to an old-age pensioner and spouse and to a disabled worker with dependent spouse and two children. Only the GDR—one of the most pronatalist societies—grants the larger family group a greater sum. Czechoslovakia and, as a practical matter, the Soviet Union issue identical amounts in both situations. But the other countries all provide the larger family group substantially smaller sums, the discount running as high as 36 percent for Romania. Thus, when one considers the fact that the replacement rate for both single disability pensions and for family groups falls below the two-thirds standard and that, in addition, a large family unit supported by a disabled pensioner gets smaller sums than a retiree and spouse, one must conclude that the Soviet and East European leadership demonstrate precious little consideration for the needs of disabled pensioners and their dependents.

Survivor Pensions

The crucial elements of the survivor pension provisions are the circle of dependents entitled to a pension, the employment qualifying conditions, and the benefit rate.

The Soviets narrowly circumscribe the right of adults to receive a survivor pension with the obvious intent of forcing the able-bodied individual into joining the labor force. The spouse or parent of a deceaased breadwinner can obtain a pension only if he or she is caring for a child under eight years of age, attains the retirement age, or becomes disabled within five years after the death of the breadwinner. Children or dependent siblings of the deceased receive pensions until their sixteenth birthday (or eighteenth if the recipient is a student) or indefinitely if they become disabled before that age. The crucial element here is that a young or a middle-aged widow is not likely to qualify for a pension in her old age since she is not likely to turn 60 within five years after the youngest child she is caring for has reached the eighth year. (An exception to this rule permits the awarding of a survivors pension to otherwise qualified spouses, without regard to time restrictions, providing they have no children capable of furnishing support.)

Clearly, the Soviet regulations bear the unambiguous message that women had best be looking to their own work experience for assurance of income in old age or in the event of disability. Only the GDR imposes such narrow limits on the right of a spouse to obtain a survivors' pension. In the GDR, the spouse of a deceased worker with a single child is entitled to a pension only so long as the child is less than three years of age; the spouse can continue receiving a pension until a child's eighth year only if there are at least two children being cared for. However, the Germans—in contrast to the Soviets—at least allow for the payments to all widows of 230 Marks per month (the minimum survivors' pension) for a two-year period after the breadwinner's death. This transitional grant to widows is found in all the other East European countries with the exception of Bulgaria.

The Czechs and the Hungarians both pay a pension for a year to all widows. The Polish time limit is also a year, but only dependent widows qualify. And the Romanians provide for payments to tide the widow over until a job is found, subject to a maximum of six months.

The Bulgarians, Czechs, Hungarians, Poles, and Romanians place much less pressure on women to undertake work than do the Soviets and socialist Germans, since in the former countries women can more easily qualify for a survivors' pension. The most important element here is the fact that these countries permit a woman to receive a survivors' pension until her child reaches the age of 16, and in some cases if the child is in an advanced educational institution, the widow retains her eligibility until the offspring's twenty-sixth year. It would seem that these countries believe that mothers are the most desirable for bringing up children and are therefore willing to sacrifice the potential output these women would contribute to the economy if they put their children in child-care facilities and worked. Alternatively, it is conceivable that the more liberal attitude is a consequence of the comparative underinvestment in child-care facilities in these countries.

The other provisions respecting widows in the East European countries are essentially the same as those found in the Soviet Union. As a rule, to obtain a survivors' pension, the widow must be disabled or have reached retirement age, although in most of the countries, widows with several children may qualify at an earlier age. And, as in the case of the Soviet Union, some of the countries

TABLE 8.6

Survivors' Pension Based on Current Average Wage as Percentage of Current Average Wage, Socialist Countries, 1973

Country	Single, Aged Widow	Surviving Family of Widow and Two Young Children
Bulgaria	36	53
Czechoslovakia	34	68
GDR	27	51*
Hungary	34	61
Poland	43	45
Romania	37	55
Soviet Union	20	50

*Based on average lifetime earnings of 600 Marks per month.

Source: Statisticheski ezhgodnik stran-chlenov soveta ekonomicheskoi vsaimopo-moshchi 73 (1974): 413-15.

require that such entitlement be established within a fixed period after the death of the breadwinner.

As regards children, they generally maintain their pension rights until the age of 16, although the period is extended if they continue their schooling. The Poles, Romanians, and Czechs are most liberal in this regard, allowing students to keep their pensions until the ages of 24, 25, and 26, respectively. Furthermore, children of deceased breadwinners who are disabled before they lose entitlement to a pension keep their pension for life.

The employment requirement for the survivors' pension in all seven countries merely duplicates the condition stipulated for the old-age pension or for the disability pension. That is, a family is eligible for a survivors' pension if, at the time of death, the breadwinner had been eligible for an old-age or disability pension or had been receiving a pension. Thus, the earlier discussion on the relative severity of the employment qualifying condition for the old-age and disability pensions applies here as well.

The survivors' pension rates are also tied to either the old-age or the disability pension rates. In Table 8.6 we present our usual comparisons. This table shows what proportion of the current average wage a survivors' pension would represent if the breadwinner's recent earnings were equal to the current average wage. The table assumes that the breadwinner has been employed under ordinary working conditions, and we consider two common beneficiary categories: (a) the single, aged widow whose deceased husband had qualified for an old-age pension after 35 years of employment, and (b) the surviving family consisting of a widow and two young children whose breadwinner died after ten years of employment.

This table demonstrates that the lot of survivors is the saddest of all. Every one of the countries pays smaller sums to a single survivor than to an old-age pensioner or disabled worker. Several of the countries pay a single survivor 50 percent of the old-age pension the breadwinner would have been awarded. The Soviets are the most miserly, paying the single survivor only about one-third of the old-age pension award. As a result, the Soviets earn the dubious honor of having the lowest relative survivors' pension payment, even nosing out the socialist Germans in this area.

Table 8.6 also shows that the plight of the larger surviving family unit is not much improved. Only the socialist Germans and the Czechs grant a larger sum to a surviving family of three than to a retired couple. Five of the countries, including the Soviet Union, provide a smaller amount to the former. Thus, whether one sets the survivors'-benefit formula against the standard of the two-thirds replacement rate or the benefits payable to old-age pensioners, the inescapable conclusion is that destitution stalks the lives of survivorship pensioners.

The U.S. Social Security benefit formulas also do not provide a munificent level of support for survivors. Recent average awards for single survivors constitute only 27 percent of the current average wage, for a family of three, 42 percent. But the U.S. system at least adopts the more logical arrangement of furnishing virtually identical benefit levels to all types of pensioners. Under the U.S. scheme, the level of the pension is determined primarily by the past earnings of the worker and the number of persons dependent upon the pension, the type of pension being relatively inconsequential. Thus, recent awards to a single widow are almost identical to those of a retiree.

The explanation for the low status of survivorship pensioners can be traced to the economic aims of the Soviets and the East European states. It does not seem farfetched to argue that the Soviets and their friends are so single-mindedly concerned with providing the greatest awards to those who have served the economy well that nonwork participants are allowed only the barest claim on state resources. Again, the message is loud and clear: The wife should not withdraw from work and rely on the earnings of the husband; if she seeks assurance of relatively adequate support in her old age or in the event of a disability, she had better establish an independent work record. It must be charged against the Soviets and the East Europeans that their pursuit of increased production has made a mockery out of society's pledge to provide income security to all in need.[11]

Special Provisions for Women

The biological role of women in childbearing and the greater responsibility that societies customarily place on women in rearing children require special provisions in income-maintenance programs if women and men are to be treated equitably. We refer not only to the obvious need for benefits during maternity, but also for modifying the number of years of employment required for other benefits since women generally encounter more interruptions in their work experience than do men. The Soviets and East Europeans furnish maternity benefits and also have liberalized the pension eligibility conditions for women.

In all respects the maternity benefit is cast in a most liberal manner. In the Soviet Union, Poland, and Romania all currently employed females are eligible to receive the benefit, while the other countries impose relatively minimal employment periods as a qualifying condition. Again, the GDR is the most restrictive, but it still requires only six months of employment in the past 12 months, or 10 months within the past two years. Benefits in place of wages are paid for 16 weeks in the Soviet Union, Poland, and Romania, 17 weeks in Bulgaria, 20 weeks in Hungary, and 26 weeks in the GDR and Czechoslovakia. (This is the length of the maternity leave period for normal deliveries and single births, and where applicable for the first child. In some instances, longer periods are granted in cases of unnatural deliveries, multiple births, and for the second and subsequent deliveries. In the case of Bulgaria, 120 days are allowed for the first child, but 150 and 180 days for the second and third, respectively.) The leave period is ordinarily intended to cover an equal number of weeks before and after delivery.

In addition to the pregnancy and confinement leave benefit, which is tied to the mother's earnings, the GDR, Czechoslovakia, and Hungary allow for the payment of a fixed monthly sum for a more extended period for those mothers who wish to care for their offspring at home. (The current Soviet Plan X proposes the introduction of similar partially paid leaves for Soviet mothers during the first year after childbirth.) The Germans pay an extended maternity-leave allowance for one year after the birth of a second child. The Czech allowance is paid upon the birth of the second or later child, up to the younger child's second birthday, as long as the older child is of less than school age. In Hungary the extended leave allowance lasts until a single child's third birthday.[12] The Hungarian allowance amounts to 600 forints per month for each child under the mother's care. Although these special allowances are not so generous as the ordinary maternity leave benefits, the Germans, Czechs, and Hungarians have all reduced pressures on women to return to work soon after the birth of their children.

These economically more advanced socialist countries show themselves to be more willing than the other countries to waive potential increases in output in order to give the young mother a freer choice in deciding whether she wishes to work or to care for her own child. The liberality of the Czechs and Hungarians in this regard coincides with the prevailing expert opinion in these countries—in contrast to the view in the GDR—that a child's emotional development is best served when it is cared for by its mother. From the standpoint of the planners in Hungary at least, this program was also expected to put a halt to the declining birth rates.

The benefit during the ordinary maternity leave in all seven countries is tied to the mother's wages, and the maternity benefit, in all instances, provides the highest payments found in the income-security programs. The Soviet Union, Bulgaria, the GDR, Hungary, and Poland all grant full wages during the maternity-leave period; the Czechs allow 90 percent, and the Romanians from 65 to 85 percent of earnings, depending upon the length of continuous employment. And in the latter country 94 percent of earnings are paid to all mothers upon the birth of the third or later child. It is not an exaggeration to say that women workers are assured their customary earnings when they cease work because of childbirth. Childbirth has ceased, then, to be a cause of income insecurity for women workers in the Soviet Union and the other Eastern European countries. This benefit shines as the brightest star among the elements of the income maintenance programs in the socialist countries.

Women qualify for an old-age pension at an earlier retirement age than men in the Soviet Union and the six other Eastern European countries. The common rule is an earlier retirement age of five years so that most women in the seven countries can retire at the age of 55. (This is the regulation for women employed in ordinary conditions of employment; the retirement age may be five to ten years lower for those working in arduous or dangerous conditions.) As the retirement age for men in the GDR and Poland is higher than that found in the other countries, women here may retire at the age of 60. The Czechs are unique in their general retirement age for women of 57.

The Soviet Union, Bulgaria, Czechoslovakia, and Romania drop the retirement age further for women who give birth to and care for a stipulated number of children. The Soviets set age 50, and the Bulgarians age 45, as the retirement age for women who have given birth to five children and have cared for them until the eighth year. The Czechs and Romanians lower the retirement age in successive steps depending upon the number of children the mother has borne, with 53 being the earliest retirement age in Czechoslovakia and 52 in Romania.

Accompanying the earlier retirement ages for women are lower employ-ment eligibility requirements. The general rule is that the lower employment requirement parallels the earlier retirement arrangements, so it is common that women need only 20 years of employment to qualify for an old-age pension, while men need 25 years. The exceptions here are the GDR, Czechoslovakia, and Hungary. It will be recalled that the socialist Germans allow males to qualify for the old-age pension with only 15 years' employment, and this pro-vision is not changed for women. The Hungarians and Czechs also apply the same employment standards to both sexes. (In Hungary women who have been employed in dangerous conditions are allowed to qualify for the old-age pension with five years fewer than men working in similar conditions; in Czechoslovakia the employment requirement is the same for all conditions of employment.) In these countries women as well as men must establish work records of 25 years to qualify for the old-age pension.

While at first glance it would seem that the Czechs and Hungarians pay no heed to the special circumstances of a woman's life, they in fact provide the most equitable arrangement. For these countries count as part of the employment record those periods when the mother is not working but devoting herself to the care of a child under the age of three, providing she had been previously employed for at least a year. (The Bulgarians include in the employment record a stipulated period for the care of an infant depending upon the birth order of the child, ranging from 12 months for the third child to three months for the fourth and subsequent children.) Since it is childbearing and child rearing that interrupt a woman's work experience and not the mere fact of being female, the Czech and Hungarian arrangement has the advantage of not favoring women over men and yet taking into account the special responsibilities of motherhood. It must be noted that here again we find, as in the case of the extended maternity-leave provision, the Czechs and Hungarians have acted so as to reduce the compulsion on mothers with infants to return to work. Clearly, the Czech and Hungarian social insurance systems treat mothers with the greatest degree of consideration and are the least sexist in their orientation. The programs of the other countries are sexist to the extent that they contain unwarranted favors for women simply because they are women. There is no reason why women who bear no children should not have to meet the same employment requirement for benefits as do men. And the only consideration that supports an earlier retirement age for women than men is that since a wife is still usually younger than her husband, it may be a desirable social policy to enable the couple to retire at the same time. But this thought does not justify a substantially earlier retirement age for women whether or not they have given birth to many children.

Thus, the desirability of the very young retirement ages cited for mothers of large families must be questioned. This feature of course is explained by the pronatalist policy of all seven countries. Once again it must be observed that the income-maintenance programs have been tailored to serve a more fundamental socioeconomic objective. Yet the government could seemingly achieve the same end through a more equitable approach. Instead of allowing mothers of large families to retire at a very early age, the government could promote a higher birth rate by giving larger monetary awards to such mothers, by establishing more generous family allowances for large families, or by lengthening the paid period of maternity leave. If, in addition, the Czech and Hungarian scheme, which counts as employment the number of years mothers have infants in their care, was universally applied, women in the other socialist countries would not longer fear that a large family would jeopardize an adequate old-age pension.

The disability pension requires little comment since only the Soviet Union and Romania modify for women the years of employment necessary to qualify for that pension. In those countries women may qualify for the disability pension with up to five fewer years of employment as compared to men, depending upon the age at which they become disabled. Here too we see the advantages of the Czech and Hungarian arrangement. They need adopt no special provision for women in respect to the disability or old-age pension since their general rule gives due allowance to the years of work a mother may lose because of her child-rearing responsibilities.

To sum up, one may say that the special circumstances of a woman's existence receive proper and in some cases excessive consideration in the income-maintenance programs of all seven socialist countries.

Paid maternity leaves are also the rule in Western Europe. Both the United Kingdom and Sweden provide flat rates, the former for 18 weeks and the latter for 26 weeks. On the other hand, France and the FRG relate these payments to the individual's wage. France pays 90 percent of the wage for 14 weeks, and the FRG pays 100 percent of the wage for that amount of time.

CONCLUSIONS

We have examined the Soviet income maintenance program in the perspective of the programs of the other socialist countries of Eastern Europe and, to a lesser extent, the programs of the capitalist West. We have found that, with the exception of the GDR, all the East European countries adhere closely to the principles that determine the contours of the Soviet program. This rough correspondence is no mere coincidence, since the Soviets and the East European nations have similar socioeconomic goals. The attainment of a maximum rate of economic growth and development is the priority goal. Thus, it was to be expected that the East European states and the USSR would shape their programs to enhance work incentives and to promote a high rate of labor participation. The substitution of a policy of full or "overfull" employment rather than offering unemployment benefits is the clearest expression of the socioeconomic goals of these societies—stable full employment with maximum output. The principle of tying benefits to recent earnings is also intended to increase production. And in strict adherence to this principle, very little weight is given to the number of dependents in fixing the benefit level.

The provision of privileged conditions for workers in selected sectors raises some troublesome questions. No one would doubt the equity of lowering both the necessary years of employment for the old-age pension and the retirement age for those who have worked under trying conditions (such as mining) that may shorten the life span. But allowing selected classes of workers to retain their full pension while working transforms pensions from a means of support to those whose earnings have ceased into a tool or lever for raising the income of a favored class of older wage earners: those whose services the planners require. It can be argued that the lowest-paid pensioners—those who retired long ago and are now incapable of working—have a more legitimate claim on any funds used in this manner.

One may even question whether some of the occupational distinctions have actually served some broader state purpose, rather than merely presenting unwarranted advantages to some favored group. The Soviets have allowed for more generous pension rates to certain groups of workers on the assumption that these more liberal conditions will attract workers to the jobs. But this reasoning is not very persuasive. The most potent influence on the sector of employment chosen by a worker would seem to be wage differentials, as well as working and housing conditions. And since benefits are related to wages, workers in favored sectors would obtain higher benefits as a matter of course. Thus, it would be foolhardy to assert that differential pension rates have had any significant influence on job selection. All one can say is that the income-maintenance programs of the Soviet Union and the other Eastern European countries have been consistent with the aim of promoting employment in the key economic sectors and the extension of the active working life.

Most of the East European countries have not strayed too far from the Soviet model, although there is certainly no monolithic conformity. This has had especially unhappy consequences for a large portion of the labor force in Poland and Romania, for in these countries the peasants weigh heavily in the total labor force and yet have only minimal rights to state protection against income loss. We have found that the GDR diverges furthest from the Soviet principles of income maintenance. The socialist Germans have benefits based on lifetime earnings, tax workers directly for social insurance, and prescribe essentially uniform conditions for all persons covered. The GDR's exceptionality is a consequence of its unique historic tradition among the East European countries (particularly their long-established presocialist income-maintenance program), rather than of differing socioeconomic goals.

The only other deviation of substance is the lesser emphasis the Germans, Czechs, and Hungarians now place on persuading mothers to enter the labor force. Granting women benefits while they care for an infant and counting the time so spent as part of the work record obviously allows a woman greater freedom of choice in deciding whether she wishes to be a full-time mother or a worker. This innovation—which is about to be emulated by the USSR—may signify that at least some of the socialist countries have reached a stage of affluence in which they are willing to downgrade the role of income maintenance in advancing production and to stress other, more humanistic, social concerns, such as children's healthy emotional development.

One must credit the Soviets and the other East European countries for taking into account the special circumstances encountered by women. They all

TABLE 8.7

Ranking of Seven East European Socialist Countries with Respect to Various Aspects of Income-Maintenance Programs

Country	Sick Benefit	Old-Age Pension	Disability Pension Employment Required	Payout Rate Single Person	Payout Rate Dependent Plus Two Children	Survivors' Pension Single, Aged Widow	Survivors' Pension Widow Plus Two Children	Number of Weeks Maternity Leave
Bulgaria	4	2	1	4	6	3	4	4
Czechoslovakia	2	5	2	2	1	4	1	1
GDR	7	7	5	7	3 (1)*	6	5	1
Hungary	5	4	7	1	2	4	2	3
Poland	1	2	4	3	5	1	7	6
Romania	6	1	6	5	7	2	3	6
Soviet Union	2	6	3	6	3	7	6	6

Note: 1 = best.
*Includes voluntary contributions.
Sources: I.L.O., Legislative Series; International Social Security Review (See bibliographical note at end of chapter).

grant very high benefit payments for a maternity period of generous length. And all lower the retirement age and some of the qualifying employment conditions for all women. It may even be said that the treatment of women in this regard extends unwarranted advantages to some women. For it is dubious at best to reduce the years of employment women need complete for a pension if they have had no children. The Czech and Hungarian design—which, instead of lowering the requirement for women generally, counts as employment the years a woman devotes to caring for children under three years of age—is the most equitable arrangement and carries the least sexist or paternalistic connotation.

As to the benefit levels furnished by the Soviet Union and the six other East European socialist countries, they all set the maternity and sick benefits at a very high level in relationship to earnings. If we consider a two-thirds benefit to earnings replacement rate as the standard of adequacy in protecting the former living standard of pensioners, we can conclude that in all these societies except the GDR the old-age pensions meets the test of adequacy.

An examination of the comparative liberality of benefit awards in the seven countries shows that with respect to pensions—the generally viewed heart of an income maintenance program—the least developed countries economically pay out the highest benefits in relationship to earnings, and vice versa. Thus, the Bulgarians and Romanians have the most generous relative awards to retirees, while the socialist Germans and the Soviets are the most niggardly. It is perhaps not coincidental that the latter two countries have the tightest labor markets and the highest labor-participation rates. (Since the absolute standards of living are higher in both the GDR and the USSR, particularly in the former, the absolute standard of living for those receiving income maintenance payments may be roughly similar throughout the Soviet bloc.) Our summary results are included in Table 8.7, where we rank the East European countries according to major aspects of their income maintenance programs.

A consideration of the principles of the Soviet bloc's income-maintenance programs brings into sharp focus the essential differences in income-maintenance policy between the capitalist and the socialist nations. The most fundamental distinction is the treatment of unemployment. In all capitalist countries the unemployment benefit is an integral part of their income-maintenance programs. While capitalist countries differ somewhat in this respect, none of the major capitalist powers has been able to achieve genuine full employment—a job for every person wishing to work—except during a war or as an immediate result of one. Since advanced capitalist economies suffer from a generally excessive labor supply, their unemployment benefit can alleviate suffering without carrying the risk of lowering economic output. In fact, conventional post-Keynesian wisdom has it that income-maintenance programs are important built-in stabilizers softening the periodic declines in economic activity, as well as cooling off the reverse situation. On the other hand, the Soviets maximize economic growth by abjuring the unemployment benefit and accepting as a state responsibility the provision of ample job opportunities for all who wish to work.

The contrast in the scope of state responsibility for income maintenance under socialism and capitalism underlies other key differences in the programs of the competing systems. The Soviet government currently has essentially sole responsibility for furnishing alternative income to those who have been cut off from their earnings, yet the government still rejects the adoption of a single, universal income-maintenance system for the entire labor force. In the capitalist world, except for the United States, the state's income-maintenance programs border on universality. Here, the existence of privately negotiated income-security clauses in labor-management contracts results in greater inequality in the income security enjoyed by different segments of the labor force than is the case in the socialist countries.

The philosophy of shared responsibility in income-maintenance affairs has had the most unhappy consequences for the United States. In other capitalist countries, private institutional arrangements have primarily served to supplement the benefit levels furnished by the state, but the state still provides basic comprehensive protection against the various forms of income loss. In the United States, however, the philosophy of shared responsibility has served to justify the state's committing itself to only a truncated program of income security, since such short-term risks as sickness and maternity are deemed to be the responsibility of local governments and private institutions. This lack of comprehensiveness in our national program of income security is another major difference in the principles governing the Soviet system and ours. Indeed, since the absence of state action in income maintenance hits the weakest elements of the labor force hardest, the U.S. income-maintenance program embodies features that make for even less equitable treatment of the labor force than that found in other advanced capitalist countries.

One final question remains to be considered: What substantial changes may prove necessary in the long run in the Soviet income-maintenance program? The Soviets claim they are building a communist society; one of the fundamental precepts of communism is that the income distribution will be based on need rather than on work: on the practical application of egalitarian principles. Although Marx was contemptuous of bourgeois egalitarianism, the thrust of his remarks on income distribution under communism suggested that differences in income arising out of differing needs would primarily reflect conditions necessary for the performance of a given job and the number of dependents supported by a worker. While exact equality was rejected as bourgeois, the impression given was that communist distribution based on need would be closer to that arrangement than to the extremes of inequality found under capitalism or to the lesser inequality found under socialism. If the Soviets are seriously entertaining the idea of constructing a communist future, it would seem sensible to take the first step in this direction with pensioners, since their needs, however defined, are likely not to be dissimilar, and since they cannot work or are not expected to work. Introducing flat-rate benefits with dependency allowances or equal per capita income for this segment of society would have the least adverse effect on work incentives.

But communism also assumes virtually equal income for all, not only among those who do not work. Thus, the Soviets in the future, if they are to be true to their ideal, will not only have to introduce rough equality of income for the entire labor force but also raise the common benefit payment for those not working to the level of the income paid to the working population. At that time, Soviet income-maintenance history will have come full circle, for the Soviets will finally have put into effect the philosophy articulated in the preplanning period. In those more romantic times, the goal officials had in mind was to provide income protection in "a manner that there would be no material difference between workers laboring at the bench and workers unable to work."[13] But to conclude on a more realistic note, there would seem to be little evidence supporting the belief that these flights of fancy fall within the intellectual framework of a rather unimaginative and conservative leadership currently controlling the Soviet Union. In the tradeoff between equity and growth, there is little evidence that the former is receiving the higher priority.

A SHORT BIBLIOGRAPHICAL NOTE

Textual Sources

International Labour Office, *Legislative Series*

International Labour Review

International Social Security Review

Sotsial'noe Obespechenie (Social Maintenance)

Okhrana Truda i Sotsial'noe Strakhovanie (Labor Protection and Social Insurance)

U.S. Social Security Administration, *Social Security Programs throughout the World, 1975*

Tabular Sources

Pogorelov, Ia. "Sotsial'noe obespechenie rabochikh i sluzhashchikh v nekotorykh evropeiskikh sotsialisticheskikh stranakh" (Social Maintenance of Workers and Employees in Several European Socialist Countries). *Sotsial'noe Obespechenie* 2 (1973). This article describes the social insurance programs of most of the East European socialist countries.

Bulgaria

I.L.O. *Legislative Series*, 1951–Bul. 2; 1957–Bul. 1; 1957–Bul. 2; 1968–Bul. 1.

International Social Security Association Bulletin, nos. 11-12 (1966):493-94.

Czechoslovakia

I.L.O. *Legislative Series*, 1956–Cz. 3; 1964–Cz. 2; 1968–Cz. 3.

International Social Security Review, no. 5 (1971):560-62.

German Democratic Republic

I.L.O. *Legislative Series*, 1961–GDR 6.

International Social Security Review, no. 4 (1967):414-28.

Sotsial'noe Obespechenie, no. 10 (1973):62-63.

Hungary

I.L.O. *Legislative Series*, 1955–Hun. 1; 1967–Hun. 2B.

International Social Security Association Bulletin, nos. 3-4 (1966):91-109.

International Social Security Review, no. 3 (1968):449-50.

Official statement by Hungarian social insurance office interpreting legal aspects of Hungarian social insurance regulation presented to the U.S. Social Security Administration, located in files of the Social Security Administration, Washington, D.C.

Poland

Legislative Series, 1968–Pol. 1; 1972–Pol. 1.

International Social Security Review, no. 4 (1972):444-46.

Romania

Legislative Series, 1965–Rum. 1; 1966–Rum. 2.

T. Siionenko. "Sotsial'noe strakhovanie v Rumynuu." *Okhrana Truda i Sotsial'noe Strakhovanie*, no. 7 (1974):32-33.

The latest (October 11, 1972) revision of the 1966 pension law was translated for us from a compendium of laws by the staff of the Romania Library, 866 Second Avenue, New York, New York.

Soviet Union

Sotsial'noe Obespechenie i Strakhovanie v SSSR. Moscow, 1964. This is a collection of social security and social insurance regulations in force as of January 1964. Subsequent revisions have been published in the Soviet journals cited above and in *Pravda* and *Izvestiia.*

Vedomosti Verkhovnogo Soveta SSSR, no. 48 (1973):678. The latest amendment (November 21, 1973) to the pension law may be found in this source.

Sovet ekonomicheskoi vsaimopomoshchi sekretariat. *Statisticheskii ezhgodnik stran-chlenov soveta ekonomicheskoi vsaimopomoshchi* (1974):73, 413-15. The average wage figures for 1973 were obtained from this source.

REFERENCES

1. For a refreshingly frank Soviet appraisal, see L. P. Yakushev, "Old People's Rights in the USSR and Other European Socialist Countries," *International Labour Review* (March-April 1976):243-56.

2. For the details of the new decree effective July 1, 1975, see *International Social Security Review*, no. 3 (1975):293.

3. In this connection, see "East Berlin Acts on Social Reform," New York *Times*, June 6, 1976. According to this article, the new decree increasing various income-maintenance payments followed "unrest" among the population.

4. Between 1960 and 1973 total personal savings increased more than sixfold. For information on private insurance, see Robert J. Myers, "Voluntary Insurance in USSR," *Eastern Underwriter*, May 22, 1959.

5. See, for example, *Narodnoe Khoziaistvo,* 1963, p. 484.

6. For evidence that these generous Polish benefits are being misused, see New York *Times,* October 9, 1975.

7. James Schulz et al., *Providing Adequate Retirement Income* (Hanover, N.H.: University Press of New England, 1974), pp. 21, 57.

8. Based on data in *Social Security Bulletin* (May 1975):50. Average wage is for private nonfarm workers given in *Survey of Current Business,* S-16, March 1975.

9. Max Horlick, "The Earnings Replacement Rate of Old-Age Benefits: An International Comparison," *Social Security Bulletin* (March 1970):3-16. Wherever possible we have used the figures shown for workers with 35 years of employment, for greater comparability with the socialist countries.

10. Based on data in *Social Security Bulletin* (May 1975).

11. It is interesting to note that when the Poles liberalized their social security scheme in January 1975, they made no change in the previously existing survivorship pension regulations. See *International Social Security Review* 1 (1975).

12. In the first two years of its operation, about two-thirds of the young Hungarian mothers took advantage of this benefit, including three-fourths of those manually employed and almost three-fifths of the intellectually employed ones. See *The New York Times Magazine,* May 21, 1972, p. 96.

13. *Voprosy Strakhovaniia* (Problems of Insurance) 44 (1928):1-2.

CHAPTER

9

INCOME DISTRIBUTION AND THE ERADICATION OF POVERTY IN TANZANIA

Reginald H. Green

Eradication of absolute poverty and a radically more equal distribution of income, including access to public services, lie at the heart of Tanzania's commitment to attain a transition to socialism. This is so true, that it is difficult to identify and analyze them separately without embarking on a total review of 1961-76 social, political, and economic goals, strategies, policies, programs, institutions, and results. Commitment to egalitarianism and absolute poverty eradication is not a program designed by a few technocrats to please foreign donors nor an ad hoc package of platitudes and poultices for use as a political first aid kit. On the contrary it would be almost literally true to say that TANU's (Tanzania Africa National Union)* definition of development really is attainment of relatively equal personal consumption capacity and access to public services combined with elimination of severe deprivation and exploitation.

There is a weakness flowing from and paralleling the strength. Income distribution and poverty eradication planning is usually treated as an element in and a constraint on actions directed to narrower and more concrete ends. A formal income distribution or poverty eradication plan does not exist, despite a large number of institutions and measures clearly directed to these ends and implicitly forming components of such plans. As a result the technical awareness of the

---

*TANU was originally the initials of the English name of the major, subsequently sole, mainland Tanzania party—the Tanganyika Africa National Union. However, TANU has increasingly become a Swahili word rather than an English acronym.

goals is generally lower and narrower than the political, with the somewhat surprising exception of the Ministry of Finance. Further, the implicit approach to planning is neither easy to operate, likely to avoid unnecessary contradictions, nor consistent with Tanzania's steady move to use multiple, overlapping planning frames as a means to generalizing, internalizing, and implementing the planning (*not* just the Plan production) process (Chenery 1974).

This pattern leads to cases of imprecision, apparent conflict, and genuine disagreement. The working definition of a relatively egalitarian income distribution has changed (narrowing acceptable ranges) over time. In terms of personal consumption power (including fringe benefits) 8 to 1 maximum differentials might now be seen as acceptable. For citizen, public sector, urban employees this has, in fact, virtually been attained; for the urban sector as a whole and especially for the urban and rural sector taken together it is still a medium-term goal. Some confusion arises because the degree of progressiveness of both direct and indirect taxes is not fully grasped; comparisons of pretax income are used as substitutes for consumption power. Equality of access to public services is seen as making an increasing array free of all fees—for example, education at all levels—and physically available to all Tanzanians within given target periods—for example, adult literacy by 1976; universal primary education by 1979; universal rural water by 1982. The interaction of these aims with fringe benefits by employers gives rise to distinct second-order disagreements—for example, over subsidized housing and free transport for workers, both of which cut across general public-sector service programs and (in present practice) tend to increase inequality.

Poverty eradication is not defined in terms of achieving "Western" consumption standards any more than development is defined in terms of maximum growth of GDP. Education, water, preventive and curative medicine, adequate diet, decent housing, clothing, at least some household furnishings (furniture, cooking utensils, and dishes), certain basic consumer durables (particularly radios and bicycles), and a margin for some discretionary spending are seen as constituting an escape from the oppression of absolute poverty. However, they are seen as necessary, not as sufficient conditions. Opportunity to participate in the making, implementation, and revision of decisions affecting their own lives is taken as a priority goal in eliminating the absolute social and human poverty that comes from viewing people as machines with certain physical requirements, rather than as human beings with social needs and human rights (Nyerere 1973; Pratt 1976).

Development is seen as impossible without mass participation, one of whose aims is to end the oppression of absolute poverty, the humiliation of extreme relative poverty, and the exploitation of relative and absolute poverty and its accompanying weakness. To achieve this, it is recognized that sacrifice of material progress to participation may be necessary, but it is also held that, at least for the vast majority of workers and peasants, the two go hand in hand more often than they clash.

To use an alternative formulation, TANU's leadership is committed (and increasingly tightly held to that commitment by its worker and peasant base) to giving strategic priority to meeting basic human needs, which can be grouped in five clusters:

1. Personal consumer goods: food, clothing, housing, basic furnishing
2. Universal access to services: primary and adult education, pure water, preventive and simple curative medicine, habitat (environmental sanitation, urban and rural community infrastructure), communications;
3. The physical, human, and technological infrastructure and the capacity to produce the capital and intermediate goods necessary to provide the consumer goods and services;
4. Productive employment yielding both sufficiently high output and equitable remuneration so that individuals, families, and communal units earn (and produce for their own use) enough to have effective access to consumer goods; and
5. Mass participation in decision making and review, in strategy formulation and control of leaders, and in implementing projects and carrying out decisions.

Tanzania's political and economic planning process, as seen by TANU (although not entirely as it operates to date), begins with determination of mass needs by collecting data on the experiences and expressed preferences of workers and peasants. Then follows the analysis of that data to create a basis for formulating precise long- and short-term aims and operating strategies and policies to achieve them. After that, policies are put into effect, following their approval by representatives of the workers and peasants. During the implementation phase, data are gathered on the objective results of and subjective response to that phase; these form a basis for revision and reemphasis (Brown 1974).

In practice the degree of participation varies. Strong political, economic, and sociopolitical components are introduced by politicians, but the width of the base of data and opinion from which the political initiatives or correctives are taken varies with the particular case. The political imperatives and goals— while clearly developing over time—have in basic direction and content been consistent and rational. Criticism that the planning process is marginal or ignored usually confuses the process with plan documents and/or the identified views of a handful of (often expatriate) technocrats or isolated intellectuals. This is a confusion to which Tanzanian technocratic managers in the public sector and the parastatal sector (as well as their critics) are prone. However, it is true—not least in the case of income-distribution and poverty-eradication planning—that initiatives often come from a very limited group of committed socialist politicians, are formulated into strategy-policy-institution program packages by a handful of technically competent public-sector civil and parastatal servants, and, following political-level amendment and approval, are presented as accomplished facts to those who will need to implement them and to the general public. This is planning *for* the people (at least given the politicians and public servants involved), but only intuitively is it planning *by* them. Openness to criticism and amendment after the event is not so satisfactory as a broader forum of discussion at an earlier stage.

MAJOR GOALS

Tanzanian goals as defined by its decision makers include transition to socialism; attainment of economic independence; rapid growth in the level of productive forces; structural change in production and use patterns; structural change in respect of international trade; decentralization and participation; effective central planning; an egalitarian income distribution, including elimination of exploitation; and overcoming absolute poverty, linked with attention to organizing production (and public services) to meet mass requirements (TANU 1971, Nyerere 1973). Certain of these might be classified as intermediate ends, since they are necessary but not sufficient for attaining other goals, rather than ends in themselves. For presenting the goal framework within which planning takes place, this distinction is not relevant. These are operational goals, not paper statements of intent: Policies, programs, and projects are instituted because of the goals, evaluated in terms of them, and modified or dropped if in conflict with them. Inconsistencies and delays do exist in reconciling projects and programs with strategies and goals, but these are specific weaknesses, not evidence that stated goals are not seriously meant or not related to key planning and management decisions.

Transition to a Socialist Mode of Production and Sociopolitical Organization. This is Tanzania's dominant goal. In a rather vague way TANU has been committed to this goal since 1961 and "Ujamaa" (then a less rigorous, more communal philosophy) by President Nyerere dates to 1962 (Nyerere 1966). However, systematic articulation and forceful implementation date to the Arusha Declaration of 1967 and the *Mwongozo* (guidelines) of 1971. The mode of investment is already dominantly socialist, as is the mode of large-scale production, except for construction. Well over 80 percent of monetized production is either by public-sector units or by small private units effectively controlled by public-sector marketing channels. Small-scale enterprise is largely private because of the slower growth of decentralized public-sector capacity to create and operate businesses. Ujamaa and development villages now number about 7500 with more than 13 million members, or about 90 percent of the peasant population (Mwansasu 1972), but genuinely communal or collective output is probably well under 10 percent of the total for nonplantation agriculture.

Tanzania's definition of socialism is wider than ownership of the means of production. Elimination of human exploitation is seen as requiring participatory, mass-oriented decision-making processes, particularly respecting surplus appropriation and allocation. A managerial-bureaucratic-political elite structure (of the type that social democratic critics like Djilas term "the new class" and the Chinese describe as "social imperialism" or "capitalist road") clearly can operate a socialist mode of production for its own benefit and in an exploitative manner. This is seen by TANU as a real danger in Tanzania (Nyerere 1966, 1968, 1973).

Egalitarian income distribution, decentralization, and participation are seen as integral elements of socialist transformation by TANU. They are treated separately, partly for convenience and partly because, while Yugoslavia and the PRC would agree with this formulation, the USSR (which practices none of the three and does not even endorse them with much enthusiasm) certainly would not, and it is logically difficult to attempt a general definition of socialism that excludes the USSR.

Attainment of National Economic Independence. This is linked with the transition to socialism because, to quote President Nyerere (1968):

> The pragmatist in Africa . . . will find that the choice is between foreign private ownership on the one hand and collective ownership on the other. . . .[A] capitalistic economy means a foreign controlled economy. . . . The only way in which national control of the economy can be achieved is through the economic institutions of socialism.

Capitalism in Tanzania could neither be nor become Tanzanian capitalism.

Economic independence—together with structural change—is usually expressed as "self-reliance" (TANU 1967). This requires national ownership of the means of production, citizen dominance in top management positions, and the development of substantial domestic knowledge creation and adaptation capacity in applied research and consultancy, as well as in technical and higher education. The first condition is largely fulfilled; the second will be met by 1980; the third poses very considerable difficulties.

Ownership of the productive sector is seen as analogous to sovereignty in the political sphere; it is a starting point establishing certain formal rights on the basis of which to develop actual capacity and power to make political or economic independence meaningful. Ownership transfers—by both de jure and de facto nationalization and occasionally by collecting the bona vacante of departed foreign owners—have been a widely emphasized element in Tanzanian policy since 1967. The way to develop national managerial capacity (and the steps to take in the interim) has been hotly debated. From an income-distribution point of view (even taking compensation into account), the effect has been to increase the national and public-sector share in GDP and to make possible the introduction of a much less unequal pattern of direct productive-sector wages and salaries than would be possible were expatriates the rule instead of (increasingly) the exception.

Rapid Growth. Rapid growth (say, 5 to 7 percent a year) in the level of productive forces is seen as a necessary and important (but not a sufficient and overriding) condition for development (Tanzania [Plan] 1969, [Budget Speech] 1967-75). Without such sustained increases in available real resources, adequate surpluses to appropriate and allocate and incomes to redistribute will not be available. In that event development, however defined, would grand to a halt, and mass faith in TANU's leadership and policy would be gravely shaken.

Structural Change in Production and Use Patterns. Change to end a nationally disintegrated economy in which a high share of monetized output is not usable locally, and a high proportion of domestic needs not producible in Tanzania—this is a key component of self-reliance. Given relative income elasticities of different products and the need to maximize forward and backward linkages to spread the impact of development, it is also critical to the attainment of more rapid growth in the level of productive forces and of effective decentralization of production (J. F. Rweyemamu 1974).

Structural Change in Respect of International Trade. This is a third goal linked with self-reliance. Tanzania is not committed to zero export growth; the "achievement" of that result in physical terms over 1966-76 relates to implementation failures and the absence of strategy.

Tanzania is committed to regional economic integration, Pan-African economic cooperation, a "trade union of the poor" countries and "co-operation against poverty" (Tanzania 1971). In each of these instances one goal is to build up interdependent trade relationships including exports containing significant value added beyond the raw-material stage. That target exists in respect to broader trade relations as well; TANU has stressed that preexport processing should be expanded rapidly, particularly in sisal (twine), cashew nuts (kernels), and hides and skins (leather), while President Nyerere has endorsed Dom Helder Camara's view that "no more unprocessed exports" should be a rallying cry in the battle for economic development through economic independence. Tanzania views the quest for a New International Economic Order as an international extension of and critical to the continued success of its domestic policy.

Decentralization and Participation. These are seen as integrally related by TANU and the Tanzanian government, if not necessarily by all of its civil servants and public-sector managers, and certainly not by some of its foreign consultants

(Rweyemamu and Mwansasu 1974; Rweyemamu et al. 1972; Tanzania [Decentralization] 1972). Over 1961-69, independent Tanzania steadily centralized the government sector (Pratt 1976). The results included serious inefficiencies in responding to local needs and small-scale projects or policies, and a growing gulf between workers and peasants and effective public-policy decision-making points.

The tools of decentralization and participation include "independent," public-sector, directly productive enterprises with (in principle and increasingly, though still not generally in practice) strong workers councils and worker directors, powerful regional and district government units with district and regional development committees with noncivil service majorities as policy and planning formulation and review bodies, and the Ujamaa villages with their member-elected management committees. Since these initiatives began in 1969 and were not fully formulated until mid-1972 it is hardly surprising that results have been uneven to date. Enough cases of success exist to suggest that the real problems are of implementation and of practice, and in particular of worker and peasant consciousness and initiative adequate to utilize their potential power, not of strategy and of principle.

Effective Central Planning. Linking political and technical processes and all levels of productive and public service operating units, central planning is seen as essential to efficiency in allocating resources to achieve the best possible progress toward national targets. The process is intended to provide opportunity for coordinating and technically checking proposals to ensure a consistent, flexible, and efficient production, surplus-attainment, appropriation, and allocation process.

The greatest problem has been the weakness of many of the decentralized planning operations and the tendency to concentrate too many resources and too much detailed work in the Ministry of Planning. This reduced the ministry's ability to devote adequate attention to defining key targets and strategies and to coordinating these with the programs, policies, and projects that must embody them. It also reduced operating-unit understanding of and commitment to the planning exercise. The difficulty in securing genuine local level plans over 1972-75 is not a new one: Both the 1964-69 and 1969-74 plans were intended to have grass-roots regional-plan components, but they failed to achieve them.

Egalitarian Income Distribution. This is linked with the elimination of exploitation for the benefit of private individuals or firms. In its pure form this includes objections to the use of seasonal hired labor (premature implementation of this objective has on occasion caused significant disruption in rural harvesting and secondary-income generation patterns). Presumably, a labor and surplus-exchange scheme between two Ujamaa villages could overcome the objections to private use of seasonal labor. A similar problem exists with the old-line cooperatives (abolished in mid-1976), especially their manufacturing and plantation activities. Clearly, they were capitalist in nature: The hired workers were not eligible to be cooperative members and the surpluses went either to lower charges to members or to expanding the productive units owned by the cooperative on behalf of its members.

Large-scale private property holding in Tanzania, especially by citizens, grows increasingly rare. With high death duties and income taxes plus limited opportunities for private entrepreneurship (as opposed to entrepreneurship in the public service, the benefits from which are collectively owned), even these family fortunes are likely to have disappeared by the late 1980s, and no more will emerge. In that sense nationalizations and fiscal policy have already done the bulk of the task of reducing the unearned (property) income of the private sector to relatively low and highly fragmented levels.

The chief remaining pockets of exploitation include retail trade and small-scale landlordism. (Large-scale private landlords and wholesale trade have been largely eliminated by nationalization.) The first is dominated by citizens and expatriates of Asian ancestry, the latter by citizens of African ancestry. Few of the first group and almost none of the second are very wealthy, but the degree of exploitation is often quite high (despite fairly effective price- and quite ineffective rent-control systems), and the victims tend to be lower-income group members. The problem of achieving change is compounded by the need to develop cooperative and District Development Corporation retailing gradually and soundly (avoiding repetition of the 1964-65 co-op debate and the 1970-73 near collapse of several District Development Corporations). Identifying any effective vehicle for public-sector rental of improved traditional houses seems unlikely; the Workers and Peasants Housing Development Fund (1974) should continue to assist by making more low- and middle-income workers owner-occupiers and by increasing total housing, thus reducing the scarcity premium on rooms.

Perhaps the most potentially expansive form of exploitation by Tanzanians of African ancestry was by rural elites. At least through the 1960s they dominated many local TANU units, received preferential treatment in allocation of good land, formed symbiotic relations with rural government officials, and controlled cooperative unions in several districts. However, they probably numbered little more than 10,000 families, were by no means unchallenged at grass-roots level, and (with few exceptions) were proto-kulaks rather than an emerged rural capitalist class. Ujamaa villages have in most cases cut their power as have local level TANU unit takeovers from below and purges from above. The old line cooperatives in most regions, were weakened significantly over 1969-74, and their apex organization, the Co-operative Union of Tanzania, was stripped of much of its prestige and power. Their rural official alliances were weakened—in most regions—by the shift of local-level agricultural officers to regional government and also by the creation of a strong Ministry of Rural Development (headed by the prime minister), much less sympathetic to them than the old-line officials in the Ministry of Agriculture had been up to the early 1970s. In 1976 the rural cooperatives were dissolved, and their functions were transferred to village councils, DDCs, and parastatals.

Elimination of Absolute Poverty. This is linked with concentration on production of services (rural water, adult education) and goods (textiles, sugar, farm implements) oriented to meeting mass needs. The linkage is critical because 1969-74 experience showed that effective income redistribution had a dramatic upward impact on demand for these products. For example, from gross overcapacity as late as early 1971, the textile industry moved to four-shift production in 1974, while textile and garment imports have skyrocketed from Shs 80 million in 1971 to Shs 260 million in 1973.

This highlights a major planning problem in Tanzania. All 1969 estimates for the growth in demand for mass market consumer goods proved too low, despite being above historic Tanzanian growth rates and above those characteristic of very poor economies with 5 percent real annual growth rates. Since luxury-goods consumption has fallen in real terms by at least 50 percent, it would appear that the explanation lies in income-distribution policy. Because underestimation leads to severe shortages and heavy foreign exchange bills (as well as loss of potential employment and investible surpluses), 1976-81 plan estimates will need to be checked carefully with the 1969-74 record in mind.

Participation, decentralization, and a coherent national goal and policy framework do involve potential contradictions. This is perhaps especially true in respect to income distribution and poverty elimination. While it is clearly not valid to assume that workers' councils with complete wage and salary determination powers would opt for uniform pay (nor even that they would necessarily cut present top and upper-middle citizen salaries in the public sector very much), it can be assumed that they would raise wages and lower-level salaries and make bonus distributions out of investible surplus in a way quite inconsistent with preventing wider urban/rural income disparities, regaining relative price stability, and providing for adequate investment out of direct public enterprise surpluses.

Villages with radically different ecological, infrastructural, and educational levels are likely to generate very different income and investment flows, leading (in the absence of corrective taxation or finance-injection mechanisms) to a new form of income stratification. This was precisely the situation in respect of the pre-1972 district councils. Their finances were substantially collected from their districts augmented by central government grants that were, in effect, some multiple of the funds the district council could raise itself. Thus, the transfers operated to increase, not decrease, local inequality.

These are basic conflicts of interest, not examples of seeking to revert to a capitalist path as normally defined. On the other hand they are precisely what

Chairman Mao termed problems of "economism" and the "capitalist road." Within the village or the firm, egalitarianism and the eradication of poverty may well be progressing, but intervillage, interfirm, and town/country trends require further control. This is not the same as successful attempts by a handful of senior public servants to raise their own salaries or fringe benefits, or by authoritarian bureaucrats or traders to infiltrate local-level party posts. It represents not a rejection of national objectives as such but an inadequate level of data and of consciousness to fit the microdecisions into the national context.

If national aims and strategies are genuinely based on mass needs and tested against worker and peasant opinion, guidelines and coordination based on them will leave wide areas for effective, decentralized, participatory decision making and action. A region is no more prevented from formulating policies and programs and allocating resources by the need to agree its budget with the Treasury and the Economic Committee of the Cabinet than is a central ministry. Workers in general endorsed the 1967-74 wages and salaries policy, with its limits on absolute wage and salary increases and its deliberate pushing up of the bottom (and to a lesser extent the middle) pay levels. If the guidelines are so detailed as to become physical directives or so contradictory to mass desires as to be deeply resented, the contradiction between coherent national-goal pursuit and decentralization and participation is likely to become overt and antagonistic. That has rarely been the case in Tanzania.

PROGRESS TO DATE: AN OVERVIEW

A quick sketch of the basic income distribution and absolute poverty position in Tanzania in 1974-76 and of certain difficulties faced in achieving effective planning in these areas can serve as a background to more detailed historical examination of policy and planning.

Measured in terms of personal purchasing power, income distribution in Tanzania is rather more inequitable than that in Scandinavia or in socialist Europe and distinctly more unequal than that in the PRC or in Cuba. However, it is significantly less inequitable than in neighboring countries or nonsocialist developing countries as a group and has very rapidly become less inequitable within the urban sector. Since 1967, and excluding severe drought years, it is at best about static on urban/rural division, but this is an improvement over *radical* worsening over 1961-65.

Personal-consumption power distribution to 1974 was probably not changing much in terms of overall equality within the rural sector as a whole, but there were diverse micro swings. Ujamaa villages could make it less unequal once they number, say, 40 to 60 percent of the rural population and have higher growth rates for personal and communal consumption per capita than the 1 to 3 percent proto-kulak larger farmers. However, the present tea and tobacco smallholder schemes and the tea and tobacco specialized "Ujamaa" villages are clearly forces for increasing rural inequality as they are now structured. As in the PRC communal production in very varied resource contexts does not lead unambiguously toward sectoral equality. It is shifting strongly in favor of citizens of African ancestry. For individuals the change is away from property incomes to wages and salaries. The salary share in the total of wages plus salaries is probably rising slightly because salary employment is growing more rapidly than wage employment, even though the differentials between average salary and average wage are being systematically eroded.

For the economy distribution is shifting marginally toward production-unit surpluses because the parastatal sector has been more profitable than its private predecessors. Certainly, there is a major swing in favor of the public sector as opposed to the private sector. In Tanzania this means a more equitable division of consumption power on income group and urban/rural bases.

Changes have included a rapid erosion of effective purchasing power of any salary earner in a fixed salary post (and a slower erosion on an incremental scale) decreasingly masked for any one individual by rapid promotion. Even more rapid erosion of real purchasing-power prospects has applied to new entrants into salaried groups. Tanzania's employment pattern is characterized by a relatively small unorganized urban sector (perhaps 20 to 25 percent of urban populations, including domestic employees), of whom about half probably have incomes at or near the minimum wage and a quarter more perhaps three-quarters of that. This pattern links with fairly low and stable levels of urban unemployment in most towns with a 1966-74 urban population-growth rate about the same as or marginally less than recorded urban-employment growth. This somewhat unusual phenomenon is associated with a relatively high out-migration of unemployed, and very high job stability among the employed, suggesting a relatively marginal core urban poverty problem and fairly good access to rural (self-) employment for the discouraged urban job seekers.

In the public-sector wage and salary group the maximum gross income differential for citizens is about 13 to 1 (Shs 60,000 to Shs 4560) in cash terms and perhaps 15 to 1 including fringe benefits. In post-tax private purchasing power the difference is on the order of 8 to 1 and 9 to 1. Using late colonial period scales (directly substituting for expatriates with citizens on the same terms) and 1961 tax structures, the difference was in 1960 about 70/80 to 1 cash and 100 to 1 including fringes gross, and 50/60 to 1 cash and 80/85 to 1 including fringes in post-tax purchasing power. The purchasing power estimate takes into account the progressive nature of the 1976 indirect tax package for incomes up to about Shs 30,000.

This does not mean there has been this great a reduction in individual purchasing power because top posts were not held by citizens in 1960. It does show how policies have both achieved an actual reduction and have altered the system to prevent the increases that would have resulted from unchanged wage/salary/fringe-benefit and tax structures.

The urban/peasant gap—for what the figures are worth and excluding the plantation sector—was over 1971-73 and 1975-76 probably about 6 to 1 on average pre-tax (and perhaps 5 to 1 in post-tax) purchasing power, but the divergences within the rural sector and the problems of evaluating nonmarketed (or locally marketed) production mean that caution must be used in evaluating specific policies affecting rural or urban subgroups against this average inequality test. As indirect taxes bear only on money income that is much more inequitably distributed than nonmarketed income, they are less prone to ambiguous results than other instruments. In real private material-goods-consumption power, a rural family raising most of its own food, building its own house, and achieving a net cash income of Shs 1250 to Shs 1500 a year is comparable to a minimum wage earner at Shs 4560 cash income and limited (if any) income in kind if he has the same sized family. However, in this case the range of services and goods available, the chance of advancing to a higher income level, and the greater availability of public consumption (primary education, health, pure water) in urban areas has an inverse effect in favor of urban dwellers, albeit a falling one with the shifts in health, water, and education emphasis.

On these estimates (which parallel those achieved by another set of calculations adjusting from the 1969 Household Budget Survey) about 30 percent of the self-employed rural population has consumption power equal to or above urban minimum wage; another 30 percent has more than two-thirds the consuming power of a minimum wage earner, and 40 percent (about 4 million people) has under two-thirds the consumption power of the urban minimum-wage earner (Awiti 1973). The data on rural (as compared with low-income urban) housing and on the share of mass market manufactured goods sold to rural consumers appears broadly consistent with this conclusion.

Public consumption directly affecting individuals is less unevenly distributed than private and is growing more rapidly. The urban/rural differential may still be 6 to 1, but it is falling. The income-group differential is probably not higher than 3 or 4 to 1. This is largely true because piped water is profit making and kiosk and rural water free, and similar divisions exist in certain other services: for example, public-sector house rents or servants. Certainly, upper-income groups use more education, health, and so on at public expense per capita than do lower-income groups. This is especially true at secondary and university-education levels.

Policy formulation, implementation, and evaluation labors under several handicaps. While these are common to most aspects of planning in Tanzania, they are particularly troublesome in direct, basic human-needs fulfillment.

Precise, usable data are almost nonexistent. The only real exception is wage and salary income of those working for employers with more than ten employees. Rural data are "available" only by heroic estimation from a quite inadequate number of particular microobservations. No useful budget studies for precise estimation of indirect tax incidence exist; product-by-product best guesses have been used in the belief that individual errors should largely cancel out. The official split of the initial sales tax estimates in 1969 (Shs 50 million rural to Shs 150 million urban) was for example, built up in this way. The household-budget survey does provide data on rural consumption. However, the values applied to self-produced food and owner-occupied (and usually owner-constructed) houses are very much lower than the cost of a comparable consumption standard to an urban minimum-wage earner. Given official and professional national accounting standards (as backed by the UN and OECD) this result is inevitable; consuming power is not at all what the accounts set out to measure.

Complex divisions exist within broad groups. Rural/urban is a useful division, but (even if estate labor is classed as urban) it overlaps significantly with a total income (cash-and-kind) classification; that is, not all peasants are poor by Tanzanian standards. This can lead to great complexity in handling policies. An increase in coffee-grower prices by a coffee export-tax reduction and an increase in, say, cigarette tax would narrow the urban/rural division (pro-rural); it would worsen the inequality of aftertax incomes overall and within the rural sector, as most coffee is grown by an above average income group. Further it would make proto-kulak/Ujamaa village differentials worse, given the actual and probable near-future patterns of coffee output and Ujamaa village membership.

The number of income-distribution policy instruments (and the division into those affecting pre-tax income, after direct-tax income, purchasing power of after-tax income, and levels of communal consumption) makes a coordinated approach difficult and raises the danger of different institutions' using similar instruments at cross purposes. Before 1972 there was a tendency for the former local authorities to vary local produce inversely with export taxes.

The limited (even if large) number of instruments in relation to that of problems and subgroups leads to situations where solutions are hard to achieve. Rural meat producers form a lower income group than do urban meat eaters. The very low pre-1972 urban meat prices therefore had a negative income-distribution effect on urban/rural and individual income-level grounds. Further, they created strains by being below export prices (including those on nonlegal as well as legal exports) and thus tending to cause diversion of meat away from the organized urban market. However, because meat is not an insignificant item in urban worker budgets (Shs 380 to Shs 500 per month), the price was kept low. This was seen to limit pressure on the wages policy whose collapse would—on 1955-66 record—have led to drastic income swings to urban and against rural areas. Meat prices were raised sharply in mid-1972 at the same time that the minimum wage was raised, thus utilizing two instruments in an attempt to make simultaneous progress toward two targets.

FROM INDEPENDENCE TO ARUSHA

From the perspective of poverty eradication and income redistribution, the 1961-66 record was markedly unsuccessful. In fact, if the trends that began to emerge then had been allowed to entrench themselves, permanent barriers would have been created within the system to any transition to socialism or any serious emphasis on radical redistribution and major priority to poverty elimination in resource allocation. Tanzania would have become more and more like Kenya in its operational goals and commitment to nationalizing the colonial structure, refurbishing it modestly, and operating it (rather more efficiently than the colonial power) for the primary benefit of the elite and its foreign allies. Since the opportunities for elite entry were much narrower in Tanzania, pressures for radical change would have built up faster but been equally unresolvable within the system. This is not to assert that TANU or the government was seeking greater inequality. On balance, the reverse was true for the majority of the leadership and certainly for the stated (if vague) policy declarations (Pratt 1976; Green 1970). The reality was summarized on the urban/rural income distribution side in the 1967/68 *Background to the Budget* (Budget Survey 1967-68).

Wages have risen absolutely and relative to salaries. But a parallel rate of rural income expansion has not taken place. Even with 1966's successful crop results it appears that rural *per capita* purchasing power is not more than five per cent above 1961 while average urban employed purchasing power has risen at least 50 per cent over the same period. The widening gap between an employed tenth of the labour force and a rural self-employed eight tenths is a matter of primary concern to the government.

Salary scales had not risen rapidly. In the government sector the Adu Report on salaries implemented just before independence had de facto reduced them by ensuring that the colonial overseas allowance and certain fringe benefits were not consolidated into the citizen salary scales. However, any competent citizen could expect virtually meteoric promotion, so that for him effective salary earned was rising by an average of at least 10 percent a year. Within the wage group, despite government planning efforts, the low-wage subgroup did not receive more rapid increases than the top. Changes basically pushed upward the old colonial structure with its anomalies—for example, very low wages for primary school teachers, paratechnical personnel, and artisans relative to clerical and minor administrative posts. Only in the case of plantations (particularly sisal) was a real breakthrough to upgrading a previously low-income subgroup made, and in that case at the expense of a 50 percent or greater fall in employment.

Even more serious was the rapid initial progress of stratification evident in a significant number of rural districts. A rural elite of improving landlords ("progressive farmers") was emerging, allying itself with the rural bureaucracy and much of the Ministry of Agriculture senior staff, dominating rural institutions (notably many cooperatives, and probably the central Co-operative Union of Tanzania), especially in respect of their salaried posts. They used this economic base to gain control of a high and increasing share of TANU, local government, and other political leadership positions with a feedback effect of manipulating land allocation (Cliffe and Saul 1972).

These trends were most evident in areas such as Ismani, Mbulu, and Rungwe, with relatively scarce land (or, more exactly, scarce land of good quality), potential for significant cash-crop production increases, and the possibility of hiring seasonal or permanent labor to work on large farms. They have been demonstrated fairly conclusively in a number of micro studies (Finacune 1976, Cliffe and Saul 1972). On the other hand, the situation in 1967 could not reasonably have been described as one of an established rural class structure with an interlocked kulak-government, bureaucrat-cooperative, salariat-political leader elite in firm control. The number of proto-kulak farm families can hardly have exceeded 20,000 (10,000 may be a better estimate), and very significant opposition to the trend existed. It manifested itself, for example, in Lake Victoria Cooperative Federation and West Lake TANU factional and leadership battles. The real danger from the point of view of egalitarianism was the trend.

This danger was heightened by the amazing warping of the village settlement program between its conception and its implementation. The initial premises set out in the president's inaugural speech (Nyerere 1966) read very like those of "Socialism and Rural Development" (Nyerere 1968) and the early Ujamaa village program (Tanzania [Plan] 1969). Villagization to increase the possibility of providing infrastructure and services, as well as to give opportunities for communal production using improved farm management and physical inputs, hard-work overtime to reap rewards with basic village self-reliance, and a broad front approach are the main themes.

These concepts were not adequately articulated at political level; the agricultural bureaucracy was largely oriented to "progressive farmer" emphasis and distrusted both broad front and communal efforts, and the "implementation" package proposal of the World Bank experts was simply not checked to see whether it was "as ordered." It certainly was not. Villages remained, as did greatly enhanced levels of infrastructure and service provision. Communal management had given way to a neo-Gaullist or neo-McKinsey type of "participation," in which an outside expert manager to all intents and purposes ran the village as if it were a plantation. The broad-front approach was dropped because the capital cost per family of the "revised" approach was dauntingly high, while the need to work hard and to be self-reliant to prosper was virtually removed from members. The whole episode became an object lesson in the dangers of using foreign expertise to formulate a program without laying down clear guidelines and providing for built-in checks by local expertise committed to and comprehending the basic political-economic goals. As a result the successful villages—a not-inconsiderable proportion, if output and member incomes are taken as tests—contributed to the breakdown of the previously quasi-communal, relatively egalitarian social and production systems, *not* to their transformation toward more modern variants at higher levels of technology and of productive forces.

The dangers of these trends were perceived. A succinct summary by Nyerere warned:

If this kind of capitalist development takes place widely over the country we may get a good statistical increase in the national wealth of Tanzania, but the masses of the people will not necessarily be better off. On the contrary, as land becomes more scarce we shall find ourselves with a farmers' class and a labourers' class, with the latter being unable to work for themselves or to receive a full return for the contribution they are making to output. They will become a 'rural proletariat' depending on the decisions of other men for their existence, and subject in consequence to all the subservience, social and economic inequality, and insecurity, which such a position involves. If you abandon the idea and the goal of equality, and allow the clever and fortunate to exploit the others, then the glittering prizes of material success will be attractive to all and the temptations of individualism will be further increased. No one likes to be exploited, but all of us are tempted by opportunities to exploit others (Nyerere 1968).

Access to public services was also becoming more unequally available. This was particularly true of English medium primary schools, which, given the low caliber of English instruction in many Swahili medium schools, had broader effects on subsequent effective access to secondary and tertiary education. The rapid build-up of medical services was concentrated on a handful of hospitals in major cities (particularly Dar es Salaam) and on a sincere but misguided view that the first priority was to make these exemplary models of European or North American hospitals. The effect was increased access to quite good curative facilities for the emergent elite, increased access to badly staffed and stocked dispensaries and clinics for urban and some rural workers, downgrading of the old mission-hospital theme of a less-sophisticated, lower-cost, broader-thrust hospital system, and a near absence of preventive medicine or environmental sanitation emphasis, apart from mosquito spraying in upper income urban areas (Rweyemamu et al. 1972).

Reinforcing and integrating these trends was the emergence of an inter-locked elite group that within a few years might well have been able to consoli-date its power position. Nationalist it was and oriented toward modernization and development; egalitarian or socialist many of its spokesmen were not, as was to become clear after the Arusha Declaration. The Kambona family is a good example of this section of the elite, but this family was not alone.

The protokulak, civil servant, political post, cooperative management alliance in rural areas has been cited. Similar coalitions were emerging in urban areas covering political office, senior civil service posts, private business, and well-paid board and/or (rather decorative) senior management posts in foreign or domestic minority community firms. The trend and the pattern were there to see, and the end result could be predicted by comparison with West Africa or Uganda. The late growth of the protoelite coalition in Tanzania (which made radical redirection in 1966-67 more readily possible within the system) probably related to the extreme poverty of Tanzania and the low levels of colonial educa-tion. These made the elite group very small indeed at the time of independence.

By 1967 individuals—and more especially extended families—were already playing several elite roles apiece. It was widely believed close knit family groups combined significant national and local political office, cooperative salariat posts, senior civil-service positions, private businesses, and "representative" posts with foreign or minority community firms. From such a base flowed national and local political and economic power, and the potential to consoli-date the families and individuals holding it into a cohesive ruling class playing the standard compradore role vis-a-vis foreign interests, and a quasi-independent capitalist ownership and salariat one vis-a-vis other domestic strata.

In all probability 1965-66 was the period during which broad worker and peasant discontent was greatest, and morale was lowest. Understandably, this point of view was not shared by the emergent elite for whom the system seemed to be operating well, and who with few exceptions were unaware of or uncon-cerned with underlying rural and low-income urban-worker complaints and problems.

What is unusual in the Tanzanian case is not the trends just outlined: Rather it is the response to them. The growing popular sense of increasing discontent and loss of confidence in the course their party and state appeared to be steering were well known to at least some political leaders. They appar-ently were brought home especially forcefully to President Nyerere on his long rural safari in 1966. At this point the decision to take radical steps to reverse existing trends was taken, and its crystallization into action via government and party discussion (within a fairly narrow circle) was begun on a very intensive basis.

The preliminary actions fell into three groups.

1. National service was made compulsory for graduates of tertiary education to provide an occasion for their receiving political and social education both formally and through being involved in manual activities in a rural setting. A side issue (until it became a point of confrontation) was the deduction of a nominal 60 percent (in practice usually nearer to one-third) of salary during national-service period to help defray the costs of the program. The university student segment of the emergent elite promptly rioted—purportedly against senior official salaries and national service, in practice almost totally over the latter. The program was enforced unchanged (Pratt 1976).

2. Salary cuts ranging from 5 percent (lower senior civil service) to 20 percent (president) were imposed to demonstrate in a clear and meaningful manner that all Tanzanians had to share in the belt tightening needed for development. While the students had verbally demanded this, it appears likely it was the last thing they actually wanted, as it injured their future earnings.

3. A wages policy limiting increases to a maximum of 5 percent a year was introduced as a holding operation until the government's ongoing study on wages and incomes policy could be completed and approved. This study is usually seen as based on the Turner Report, but that view is an oversimplification. Proponents of wages policy (divided between conservatives concerned with government budget costs and incentives to investment, and radicals concerned with intraurban and urban/rural income distribution) had been pushing for such a policy since 1965. They believed, correctly, that an ILO report would carry the day for their case, and that Turner would recommend a restrictive incomes policy. In fact the basic target was achieved by presidential directive long before the appearance of the government paper, which differs notably from Turner's study in stressing greater intraurban equality (pay boosts concentrated at the bottom end)—the precise opposite to the report's thrust. Given the clear presidential directive and the subsequent Arusha Declaration, it was the radical income-redistribution advocates who had become dominant at official technical preparation level (Tanzania [Wages] 1967).

These steps—which in most other African countries would have been viewed as so radical as to require at least a two-year rest period to consolidate—were in Tanzania holding operations or preludes before the February 1967 Arusha Declaration (TANU 1967).

The declaration banned party, government, and public sector (including parastatal) leaders from any form of involvement with private business, thus moving to prevent (and in existing cases eliminate) a political, bureaucratic, public, manager, private-domestic, private-foreign sector interlocking elite of the type that has so often become the "neocolonial settlement's" most ardent and effective defender and spokesman. It placed far greater stress on rural development and the narrowing (or at least halting of the widening) of the urban-rural gulf. Equity was stressed and defined in terms of effective personal consumption capacity in relation that that of all Tanzanians, not in relation to that of those holding similar posts in rich countries (or citizens of rich countries holding posts in Tanzania). Emphasis was placed on self-reliance and a lower concern with what external technocrats and financiers thought the proper strategies for Tanzania should be. Massive expansion (initially by nationalization but, over time, dominantly by creation) of the directly productive public sector to allow it to dominate the economy by its size and control of strategic institutions (such as banks) was made central on the production-institution side. At this point the term "strategic heights" strategy was applicable in its genuine sense (as opposed to the actual British Labour policy of nationalizing "sinking sands"); the rapid tidying-up by acquisition on a broader front was a later revision based largely on the success of the initial program. By February 15, 1967, the stage had been set for a very different pattern of development over 1967-74—how different very few Tanzanians realized in the immediate post-Arusha days.

POLICY INSTRUMENTS

Policy-instrument examination is in danger of becoming a checklist rather than an analysis in the Tanzanian case. At least 14 clusters of instruments have had an income-distribution and basic-need fulfillment content and have been used partly with those goals in mind. However, few if any do not have other purposes to serve and the reasons for uses of particular instruments at different times are not easy to disentangle, even for those employing them.

Taxation and similar charges taken together are highly progressive, running from about 12.5 percent on rural (excluding plantation-sector) cash and kind incomes through 17.5 percent on minimum-wage earners through 40 percent at around Shs 20,000-a-year income and as high as 80 percent on a few top citizens' incomes. This includes indirect taxes as well as fees and charges as being deductions from personal purchasing power. It necessarily makes rather arbitrary assessments of final tax incidence. These are basically that all indirect taxes on local market goods are passed on to the final user; all export taxes are borne by local producers; and all direct taxes borne by the immediate taxpayer, not passed forward. Sales-tax experience suggests that not all indirect taxes are passed on, while common sense suggests that if some direct-tax burden can be shifted, the two effects may cancel out. Taxation as defined in 1975 was of the order of 35 percent of monetary GDP at market prices. It is doubtful that much further redistribution through raising overall levels of taxation is practicable on political or political-economic grounds in the next few years, except in the case of incomes benefiting by some windfall gain. In 1973/75 certain export and production taxes were raised on this basis, but in the face of rapid inflation the coffee-tax boost was partially reversed in 1975/76. In the absence of severe inflation the tax system is income-elastic; that is, it more or less automatically collects a rising share of GDP per capita as average GDP per capita rises. This is less true in the context of sharp price increases because a number of major indirect taxes are specific rather than ad valorem, necessitating some rate changes to maintain moderate buoyancy and more when (as in 1974/75) redistributionist measures on the wages front and cost inflation combine to present a particularly large increase in recurrent expenditure demands (cf. Huang 1976).

Wages Policy. This has been less than homogeneous. The Industrial Tribunal has held to its guidelines granting 4 to 5 percent annual wage bill increases skewed to be 5 to 7 percent at the lower and 2 to 3 percent at the higher end of the wages spectrum. It has been quite strict in rejecting bogus productivity and bonus agreements but has sanctioned several genuine physical productivity increase or bonus schemes (for example, in sugar and grain milling) that appear to be working reasonably well. Two loopholes have been exploited. "Voluntary" and "informal" wage-increase arrangements violating the guidelines have been agreed by NUTA officials and some employers operating as nonbinding "gifts" avoiding the present wording of the law. The Standing Committee on Parastatals has produced wage-increment guidelines for parastatals that concentrate increases at the top, not at the bottom, of the wage scale. Several parastatals have (with very little semblance of legality) bypassed the Tribunal.

Minimum-wage increases in 1969, 1972, 1974, and 1975 and the 1974 wage-price-tax package as a whole are probably complementary. In 1969 and 1972 were minimum-wage-only exercises that sharply reduced differentials for up to 50 percent of all employed persons. In 1974 there was quite openly a very special package to deal with what was hoped to be a temporary inflation with balance-of-payments crisis situation (Green 1976c).

Salaries Policy. This has been less complete and consistent (basically, Shs 1000 a month and above constitute salaries). From 1961 to 1974 the citizen civil-service salaries were spoken of as frozen; actually, there were cuts in 1961 and 1966 and a few fairly minor, upward revisions to remove anomalies. Over 1967-68, the citizen parastatal scales were brought into line with the civil service (taking into account the latter's noncontributory pension scheme) and (with some doubts in certain institutional cases, such as Tanzania Investment Bank) with each other and the Standing Committee on Parastatals (SCOPO) created as a watchdog. "Standing still" at the top while the bottom could "catch up" was the summary policy statement. However, with tax and price changes and a fortiori a slowdown in promotion as Tanzanianization of high-level posts swept past the 50 percent mark in the public sector in 1972 and reached nearly 90 percent in purely administrative posts in government and parastatals taken together, "standing still" became "sinking swiftly," forcing the partial lifebelt increases in 1974.

Other 1974 changes included anomaly correction (for example, regarding primary school teachers and medical aides, who actually fall in the upper wage category) and a premium for science (including agriculture), technology, medicine, accounting, and economics graduates to offset this longer training (Tanzania [Budget Speech] 1974).

Private-sector salaries have not been controlled; however, with its limited prospects, the sector is probably no longer so energetically seeking to bid away public-sector managers. The East African Community and Corporations occupies an intermediate position: the slowness of its reviews has more than totally eroded its former premium wages and left the lower salary levels equal to Tanzania's but the higher levels still far above.

Foreign high-level manpower has always been handled as a special case. A 10 percent training levy on their gross emoluments (paid by the employer), high personal income tax rates (up to 95 percent marginal and 80 percent average), and formal checking procedures before hiring is approved are designed to hold expatriates to the minimum necessary level. Salaries (within somewhat unrealistic limits in the case of parastatals and government direct-hire) are then negotiable at rates well above those for citizens. Salaries of technical assistance officers are not seen as directly concerning Tanzanian income-distribution policy.

Fringe-Benefits Policy. This has proved difficult to coordinate in the public sector, and impossible in the private. However, a series of not-insignificant steps has been taken in respect of the former. Certain benefits—for example, a personal car, free housing—have been banned for direct-hire employees, citizen or non-citizen. Rentals for public-sector housing have been set at 7.5, 10, and 12.5 percent of wages, low salaries, and high salaries to make them progressive. The employer actually pays normal rent on outside buildings and thus makes a collection of profits and losses while the National Housing Corporation and Registrar of Buildings have a simplified collection system. Transferability and continuity of pension rights have been provided in the public sector, and plans to consolidate all parastatal pensions into a single, contributory, funded scheme (and presumably later to convert the government scheme to the same basis for new entrants) are nearing completion.

Promotion Procedure. Promotion-procedure (and post-regrading) control by establishments, the Civil Service Commission, and SCOPO has been intended to prevent evasion of salary control. On the whole, while perhaps somewhat leaky, especially in the case of specialized posts in parastatals, it has worked moderately effectively, with one major group of exceptions: the various McKinsey reorganization proposals, all of which create radical increases in upper salary posts and, in this respect at least, seem to have been by the salariat, for the salariat, and of the salariat. In practice, these delayed the acute pressure on salary scales resulting from the slowing down of promotion from 1972 to 1974 by causing a once-and-for-all surge of promotions to new regional, district, and ministry posts.

Prices. Prices are now regulated for a wide range of commodities by the National Price Commission. Agricultural prices to the grower and a few others remain with other bodies. The commission is a counterpart to the Permanent Labour Tribunal, with detailed guidelines on objectives (including distribution of purchasing power, promoting of producer-seller efficiency, and protection of investible surpluses), and with a technical secretariat to allow informed action. Some evasion takes place, and some delays and mistakes arise, but the overall record seems to be fairly good, given the pressures on prices over 1973-76 and the record of comparable bodies elsewhere. To the extent possible, the commission has sought by selective coverage and differential mark-up ceilings to influence the relative price structure in favor of the low-income consumer.

Before the creation of the price commission, price controls were a mixed bag. Requiring fixed, posted prices for all goods to avoid discrimination between customers and to allow consumers to know where best to shop when a choice existed was repeatedly approved but not implemented until the new commission came into existence. Selective key-item price controls on a national (or more often regional) basis existed for about two-dozen items, but was very unevenly operational. Panterritorial pricing existed for cigarettes, sugar, and iron sheets and was extended sharply by the price commission. These price controls do tend to protect lower-income groups. The chief gainers are probably town dwellers in low- and middle-income groups and upper-income farmers.

Two other price-control forms exist: one to prevent price increases on untaxed stocks after tax changes, and one to utilize sales tax and price control as an excess-profits tax. The former probably has a positive income-distribution effect against traders and for consumers in general; the latter has a positive effect in that any alternative revenue source would tend to bear more heavily on lower-income groups.

Grower-Price Policy. This has not been used systematically and positively to act on income distribution. It has been used negatively to prevent declines by cutting grain prices less than would otherwise have been deemed desirable, or raising them to counter inflation. For some export produce price changes would benefit upper-income (even if rural) groups—for example, flue-cured tobacco. Adequate data to understand some results do not exist; for example, marketed output of oilseeds fell steadily over 1966-73, while the cross-ratio of maize to oilseeds prices shifted by at least 25 percent and perhaps by more than one-third to oilseeds, and maize output in some areas rose. Clear conflicts of interest arise; for example, meat and grain prices operate in diametrically opposed directions in respect to rural and urban target groups. Over 1973-75 rather more attention was devoted to increasing both domestic and export agricultural-product prices paid to the grower to sustain rural purchasing power, but the dominant motivation was clearly to provide production incentives, and the income-distribution and poverty-eradication implications were not examined in any detail.

The shift to a dominantly socialist mode of investment and of large-scale production has basically shifted property income from foreign (and to a lesser extent domestic) private to public ownership and has had some tendency to reduce average salaries, with a resultant shift of income from upper-income segments of the wage/salary class to the government. To the extent that these funds substitute for taxes, they clearly tend to have a redistributive effect in favor of lower-income groups in the short run. To the extent that they augment public-sector investment, their redistributive impact will also be positive, but its timing and degree (and the impact, if any, on absolute poverty) will depend on the particular investment pattern.

Buildings Acquisition. This concerns all rented properties worth $12,500 or more. Whatever else it did, building acquisition has sharply reduced rental incomes. This reduction should, even after tax losses and deferred compensation, marginally improve short-term income distribution. However, a rent reduction for the particular tenants involved would have had a negative income-distribution effect, because the registrar's buildings are almost all occupied by persons with incomes very much above the Tanzanian average. Since the net effect was really, as one not-unsympathetic commentator put it, "to stop the exploitation of one group of rich exploiters by another group who were perhaps marginally richer," the basic effects are probably psychological or consciousness raising: Landlordism has been wiped out as an urban business, and with it, property speculation.

Credit and Investment Allocation. These can prevent luxury investment and fringe-benefit provision and cause concentration on projects having high-income rural (raw material, initial processing, food) and lower-income worker (component manufacture, service establishment, direct plant employee) incomes. The preventive role has begun to be played, but the positive remains patchy, partly because to date small-industry projects seem to have a higher capital/output ratio and a not much lower capital/labor ratio than large plants, suggesting an urgent need to replan the small-industry program on more grounds than its income-distribution effect. A side consequence of controls in this field as in the immediately preceding one is to hit the earnings of low- as well as high-income construction workers.

On the positive side, the annual credit plan does tend to be more flexible in relation to firms producing mass consumer goods. Agriculture inputs presumably help to limit shortages (and the costs associated with illicit "parallel markets") in the first case and assist in raising agricultural production with a positive rural/urban impact in the second. The moves to control over-surpluses and to annual parastatal operating-budget planning coordination by the Treasury flowing from the 1972 Regulation of Dividends and Surpluses Act is likely to improve parastatal operating efficiency and trim unnecessary expenditure. Given the strong Treasury commitment to redistribution and mass-needs-oriented production, it is probable that this will yield net benefits in lower tax increases, greater availability of goods, additional wage employment, and perhaps occasionally lower prices to lower-income groups, especially in urban areas.

Decentralization. Regional policy both in terms of decentralization and of the nine towns' urban growth-pole approach is intended to improve the geographic balance-of-income distribution by providing incentives, finance, and pressures for greater activity in the poorer regions and in the nine towns. The urban growth-pole policy is designed to create a series of industrial and institutional economic complexes capable of generating enough agricultural and small-scale secondary and tertiary production to have a significant regional economic impact. Over 1969-74 the policy certainly did influence project siting away from Dar es Salaam—but basically to five of the nine towns: Tanga, Arusha-Moshi, and Mwanza, and to a lesser degree Morogoro and Tabora (Coulson 1975). How much secondary impact the new units will have is unclear to date. The policy is continuing with, for example, the new textile facilities, all to be sited in up-country towns. Major productive-sector project distribution remains highly unequal geographically and rather harder to change rapidly than many other patterns.

Changing the Capital. The capital shift to Dodoma over 1974-84 is not seen as related to income distribution and poverty eradication in a material sense, although it should provide opportunity for raising agricultural income in what is now a very poor region. Dar has had very few spread effects; the Coast Region is clearly among the poorest fifth of all regions in Tanzania, but this is partly because it is in a most ecologically unfavored zone.

The psychological impact of having a capital in a productive rural area and the greater distance between government offices and large-scale urban-oriented business units (whose head offices are intended to remain in Dar) could be significant in raising the degree of priority in time allocation given to rural and small-scale sectoral problems. Finally, by braking the trend to "Dar es Salaam centrism" presently based on its capital (transport and commercial), light industrial leadership, the Dodoma shift should make the regional growth-pole approach easier by reducing the "obvious" advantages of a Dar es Salaam location. This will be complemented in the 1980s by the heavy industrial focus in the South around coal, iron, steel, and probably engineering and chemicals.

Regionalization (decentralization) in 1972 certainly shifted expenditure (including salary income) to regional, and to a lesser degree district, centers. How much of this affected low-level-income recipients or the absolutely poor is more questionable. However, as also seen in the earlier Regional Development Fund program, decentralization of investment control leads to more and smaller projects, to more voluntary communal labor input, and to fewer delays in locally oriented project implementation. Over time the accumulation of these decisions and shifts should raise the earning capacity of regions and the ability of at least some rural groups to escape from absolute poverty rather faster than a more centralized system would have done. The development of village councils was formalized and backed by significant power transfers in 1975. Taken together with the shift from scattered homesteads to villages, the Act reinforces the alteration of peasant/official power balance toward the peasants.

Ujamaa Villages. These are the central policy instrument for medium-term rural poverty elimination and short-term distribution of access to public services on a more egalitarian basis. To date they have fulfilled the second role (clearly perceived for them from 1962 onward) rather better than they have the first.

By the end of 1974 at least 7500 Ujamaa villages grouping about 3 million people (30 percent of the agricultural self-employed) were in existence, compared to a handful as late as 1970. There is clear evidence that in normal cases (as opposed to the upper-income IBRD-designed settlement-scheme projects for tea and tobacco rather imperfectly "converted" to Ujamaa villages during implementation) the poorer districts in the poorer regions show the highest response to the concepts of living and working together in units large enough to receive (and to provide for themselves) basic public services, of adopting modifications in production and marketing patterns and (much less uniformly) of conducting an increasing proportion of production and distribution on a communal basis. This suggests that the villages group a very high proportion of the rural absolutely poor population, and also that this population, to the extent that it moves to villages, is not conservative in the sense of being unwilling to accept change as the cost of progress.

By 1973-74 at least Shs 300 million a year of recurrent funds (for example, those for education, road and water maintenance, extension services, and health) and capital funds (for example, Regional Development Fund, increases in Rural Development Bank credits, roads, health and education buildings, and water development) were being deployed in support of Ujamaa villages. On the access-to-public-services front progress was rapid. On the production-development front problems arise. Certainly, at least since 1972, there has been emphasis on utilizing the potential of larger joint labor forces (for example, for off-season, small-scale investment or for industrial production), larger farm units (for example, through different farm-management and production techniques), and easier communication channels (for example, for agricultural-extension demonstrations and advice to groups, as well as for providing resident paraprofessionals in health, construction, and other fields). However, the illusion that the basic need is either finance or finance in addition to exhortation of peasants* dies hard. However, over 1973-76 Ujamaa village committees began in some cases to become much more assertive in respect of civil servants and to insist (successfully) that those whose competence, energy or attitudes were incompatible with the village's welfare be transferred.

Development Villages. On the order of 10 million residents by the end of 1976 will not be Ujamaa villagers. Villagization as a compulsory TANU policy was adoped in 1973 because development of social consciousness, access to basic services, and rising productivity could not be achieved if scattered homesteads (85 percent of the peasants in 1967, perhaps 65 to 70 percent in 1973) remained dominant. By mid-1976 90 percent of nonurban Tanzanians were village residents (Tanzania [Vijiji] 1976). Ujamaaization remained voluntary.

By 1977 the population pattern will be about 4 to 4.5 million wage earners, urban self-employed and dependents; 3 to 3.5 million Ujamaa villagers; 7 to 8 million development- (including rechristened older settlements) village residents primarily engaged in nonplantation agriculture; 1 to 1.5 million homestead and seasonally migratory. The 1974 villagization was marred by many incidents of bad planning and coercion, largely by regional or lower-level political figures and against central directions. These were never dominant (Tanzania does not possess the force to coerce several million peasants in that way) and were sharply reduced after October 1974 intervention by the TANU executive.

The villages do improve access to basic services. Until they are more firmly established, they have minimal (positive or negative) production effect despite their evident potential. Social consciousness and the opportunity to mobilize to control local officials create the control mechanisms with which to strengthen the supporters of egalitarianism.

Participation. Participation and broadening of decision making is, like a number of other areas cited, neither solely nor primarily seen as an income-distribution device. Indeed, one problem with workers' control is that it can increase urban/ rural and intraurban inequality if potential investible surpluses are used for personal or limited group communal consumption, as in some rejected or reversed Tanzanian "bonus" scheme proposals.

In the case of Ujamaa vijijini and the Regional Development Corporation the income-distribution effect is likely to be unambiguously favorable on urban/rural grounds. The intrarural impact depends on how often protokulak

---

*Exhortation of the more traditional and elitist elements of the rural and rural-oriented agricultural and educational and health bureaucracy is a different matter.

and self-oriented "leader" individuals succeed in getting investment and service allocations benefiting primarily themselves. This is an endemic complaint with respect to co-ops, and ujamaa vijijini that is at least sometimes valid (Cliffe and Saul 1972; Finacune 1976), but on its generality of impact and trend no usable studies exist. The number and background of local level TANU candidates vetoed in 1974 suggests a major past problem in some regions as well as a serious effort to tackle it as do two or three of the defeats of incumbent MPs in the 1975 election. Workers' councils will probably be a force to lessen income inequality within their units primarily, perhaps, by seeing that salaries remain frozen until wages are much higher, and by forcing increases in wage earners' fringe benefits, especially in respect of travel to work, hot midwork meals, job-linked medical attention. So long as the national prices and wages frame holds this should not be at the expense of peasants, although the history of the urban meat price does give cause for some concern in that direction.

Participation as a means of raising the level of productive forces through more total use of human capacity will take time to produce results. Both managers and workers need to be educated to understand it, including educated through successful (and unsuccessful) initial steps. In some cases, for example, Ubungo Farm Implements (Mapolo 1972), National Bank of Commerce productivity results and more attention to meeting particular rural and lower-income needs are already evident. In others, management's refusal to give any real substance to the form of participation and workers' belief that it is a grievance- or benefit-provision forum, not a self-planning and management approach based on internalized self-discipline and commitment (by managers at least as much as by other workers), have given rise to operational problems.

In the area of altering income distribution through controlling the pattern of consumption a good deal of confusion exists, though the one major measure is in itself sound. Specific taxes or subsidies (which are considered in the light of their final probable incidence of costs or benefits) do influence income distribution and (probably rather peripherally) total supplies of goods available. If the rates of tax are prohibitive, there is sumptuary legislation that influences consumption by de facto and de jure (for example, ban on imported beer), preventing the use of one or more goods, but there is quite an unpredicable effect both on income distribution and foreign exchange.

Unless one follows a ban on certain consumer goods with progressive taxes, one merely causes a shift in consumption. As goods likely to be banned have high tax rates and (therefore) low foreign-exchange/retain-price ratios, the foreign-exchange, tax, and income-distribution effects of sumptuary legislation alone are likely to be negative and to offset its potentially positive psychological and demonstration effects.

Unequal commercial margins on consumer goods could be used to influence income distribution. The public-sector trading companies seek to do this in principle, and margins in milling/baking are controlled. However, this is—in a socialist context—analogous to a tax (since it affects public-sector investible surplus) rather than to a scheme for setting consumption patterns per se, unless the lower margins are balanced by increases on amenity or luxury goods, in which case the margin differentials constitute a progressive tax in themselves. It should be noted that the case for controlling consumption patterns in Tanzanian terms is not really one for static income redistribution.

The most important element, especially over 1974-76, has been the limiting of recognized radical inequalities in conspicuous consumption and the demonstration that all belts are being tightened. In the medium term this is linked to pushing demand into a structure more consistent with self-reliance and less dependent on imports, and with creating a psychological/demonstration effect toward equal or greater individual satisfaction with a less elaborate "package" of consumer goods. It also includes the promoting of certain goods seen as socially desirable (such as books) and, probably more ciritical, the limiting of the growth-of-expenditure patterns, which require very high incomes to sustain them (A. H. Rweyemamu 1974). The most evident case is automobiles: Counting depreciation, the lowest likely annual cost of a four-year-old car that will last another six years is Shs 7500, or 50 percent of the starting (net) salary of a university graduate in the public service.

The right to buy new or less than three-year-old used cars has been subject to restrictive licensing since 1971. Individuals must prove a social or national need as well as a personal to secure a permit. Government and parastatal bodies are also subject to restrictions and cars may not be provided to managers and officials as fringe benefits. The debate leading to the formulation and imposition of these restrictions turned largely on demands for the reduction of conspicuous inequality. The other stated reason—saving foreign exchange—was not actually politically critical to this particular decision. In any event, because saloon cars were heavily taxed it is doubtful whether forcing would-be car owners to refrain from automobile buying and shift their consumption to other consumer luxury goods would actually have a net positive effect on foreign exchange use.

In Tanzania, to claim that a major share of domestic output is now in narrow-market luxury goods is inaccurate. Beer, cigarettes, and sugar—the main examples of major "nonnecessity" consumer goods—are each consumed by at least 2 million persons. Therefore, they are mass-market goods, and as they are also of low-import content and high-revenue producing, the case for cutting back has to be either an ascetic antiamenity one or a belief that they have particular harmful effects in themselves. The recent bans on local brew are related to poverty eradication (if at all) through reducing damage to health and energy from excessive drinking, thus allowing more attention to production.

Income redistribution and poverty eradication so far as major payoff goes, must in a country as poor as Tanzania be overwhelmingly incremental and heavily weighted toward raising the income-generation capacity of the poor. Actual cutting at the top—especially once affluence based on domestic private ownership of means of production is reduced to a few pockets—has little to offer in direct gains. Austerity for the top is critical both economically, to ensure that the incremental allocations are to the right target groups, and psychologically, to maintain mass support. The latter is critical because, on the most optimistic assumptions, to raise the minimum normal level of personal-consumption capacity and access to services for all Tanzanians to that now provided for urban minimum-wage earners will take 10 years. The fact that Tanzania has never sought to operate short-term, fine-tuning demand-management policies and that it has treated credit planning dominantly as a means to effect planned physical decisions (not to cause and only secondarily to influence them) has probably helped allow major, if not always well coordinated, attention to be paid to the medium- and long-term income distribution and absolute-poverty-eradication aspects of policy. It may also explain why the Treasury has tended to be the most concerned and most active ministry in this field over the 1965-74 period.

What is less clear is the extent to which raising the productive forces under the control of the rural poor, and especially of providing them with the means to expand these productive forces, has received adequate and adequately articulated emphasis. The Treasury is not at all equipped to pay the leading role in this field because of the technical data needed: Its efforts at support will not work without measures for back-up and financing.

Agriculture, on the other hand, has not faced income distribution and poverty eradication as a distinct planning target (or even as a separate policy issue). The rural-development and Ujamaa-village sections of the prime minister's office have done so, but to date they have had limited technical knowledge and capacity for ensuring that effective capacity to increase output and to direct surpluses (including surplus labor time) to that end were within the reach of the rural poor. They have had a distinct tendency to yearn for uniformity and order at the expense of local participation.

The dynamic pattern of strategic, institutional, and policy development over 1967-75 can usefully be surveyed chronologically. Major initiatives and their follow-up developments can be ordered from their time of initiation with some gain in comprehensibility, if also with some loss in chronological logic.

1967   Arusha Declaration (nationalization, SCOPO) and formal wages/ incomes policy; Regional Development Fund

1968   Ujamaa-village commitment

1969   Sales tax (and related price-control devices); minimum-wage increase; Second Five-Year Plan

1971   Twenty-year Rural Water Plan; acquisition of buildings; motor-vehicle ownership control; workers councils

1972   Agricultural-development priority by TANU; cooperative organization; government decentralization; adult-education commitment; regulation of dividends- and surpluses-control framework

1973   Price commission; income tax; mass adult-education breakthrough

1974   Wage, price, production, and finance package; villagization

1975   Worker-board members; unification Treasury and Devplan; accelerated universal primary education and water targets

The 1967 policy and institutional developments flowed directly from the first stages of implementation of the Arusha Declaration and proved to be the first re-evaluation of ongoing programs. Nationalization measures had several effects in respect of income distribution beyond the immediate ones of a significant shift of income from foreign investors (and a few domestic) to the state even after netting out compensation payments and speeding up Tanzanianization of senior posts that, while creating more relatively well-paid Tanzanians, on balance substantially reduced salaries in comparison to wages. Most basic was the creation of a public, directly productive sector that tended to dominate by its sheer size and therefore could be used as a tool of egalitarianism on both the production and allocation sides. On the allocation side, the creation of the Standing Committee on Parastatals (SCOPO)* to harmonize all public-sector wage, salary, and fringe-benefit levels was at least intended to be egalitarian, even if its old-line establishment-office personnel sometimes acted otherwise in details. Over 1967-76 a reorientation of investment decisions toward mass-market consumer goods and backward integration into intermediate-good production shifted production toward self-reliance in production. Dominance of financial institutions and therefore of micro as well as of macro credit allocation, laid the basis for detailed national credit planning (tentatively begun in the 1969-74 plan and fully articulated in 1970/71). Nationalization set in train a dynamic that has left construction the only major area of economic activity in which large-scale enterprise remains dominantly private and, equally critically, has established a base for sharply expanded productive-sector surpluses available for reinvestment in Tanzania—surpluses that by 1973-74 were running about 6 percent of GDP.

---

*Parastatal is the Tanzanian (and United Nations) term for a semi-autonomous, self-accounting public sector (or majority public sector) entity. The formal legal basis for parastatals varies—some have been created by act of parliament, some by subsidiary legislation, and others are incorporated under the Companies' Act.

The formal wages and incomes policy provided an institutional mechanism for implementing the 1966 presidential directive and for relating wage increases to productivity gains while graduating them in such a way as to reduce income inequality within the wage-earning group. Its effect was fairly dramatic since wage increases had been running at 12 to 15 percent a year and were cut back to 5 percent. Since in the 1967-71 period price increases were perhaps 3 to 4 percent a year, the 5 percent in addition to increments for length of service or promotion gave a typical worker a good chance of 2 to 5 percent a year growth in real income. This was still above the possible rate of growth of real farm income per family but less widely divergent than the 10 percent versus 0.5 percent of 1961-66.

While the government paper (Tanzania 1967) covered wages, incomes, rural development, investment, and price policy, it was in fact a wages-and-salaries-policy paper with somewhat anodyne restatement of policies existing in the other areas. The last 1967 initiative was the Rural Development Fund, the first step toward decentralization. The fund provided for regional decisions on local productive or economic infrastructure projects proposed by district development committees. This was seen as a way of promoting the small project directly benefiting the rural poor, which otherwise became entombed in central ministerial files. In practice, the results were uneven and often limited by concentration of power in the technical (ministerial officials') subcommittees of the DDCs, by a rather overly cautious selection of projects, and by failure of several regions to use their entire allocations. However, it was successful enough to demonstrate that for small projects decentralized decision making close to the people affected was at least as technically competent and much faster than the former totally centralized system.

While foreshadowed by the Arusha Declaration (TANU 1967) and the 1967 presidential paper, "Socialism and Rural Development" (Nyerere 1968), the Ujamaa-village program as such began in 1968. At least through 1969 its organizational and production-oriented aspects remained in a state of considerable flux and imprecision, as evidenced by the relevant section in the Second Five-Year Plan (Tanzania 1969). The growing movement of peasants (in the main, poor peasants) to villages demonstrated both a willingness to try a new approach and a response to the concentration of additional rural public services (and RDF finance) on Ujamaa villages.

Reorganization of knowledge transfers by professional staff (for example, extension officers) and by training village paraprofessional staff via rural training centers continued to move relatively slowly and with an apparent lack of creative imagination until 1973-74. The 1974 allocation of Shs 18 million to the Co-operative College to set up five zonal centers for Ujamaa-village bookkeeping/accounting/financial-management personnel selected by the villages was the first breakthrough to large projects aimed at providing each village with the human resources needed for them to practice effective self-management and to improve all aspects of their living standards through contributions of skills from their own members (Tanzania [Budget Speech] 1974]. Parallel programs in para-building skill workers (linked to Ardhi's building research and regional construction units using improved traditional methods and materials) and paramedical ("barefoot doctor," advanced first-aid) cadres have been discussed but do not yet exist on an adequate scale or with equally clear targets, though the health one is more advanced in actual numbers trained to date.

The greatest gap remains in farm-management skills. No large-scale training program for village-selected candidates exists, and, despite research at the agricultural faculty, it is unclear how far appropriate methods for medium-sized, labor-intensive, communal units have been decided on and tested. The gap is serious because it leaves a dichotomy of communal operations conducted like large-scale individual shambas and a few highly mechanized units, most making less than effective use of import-intensive machinery. The necessary knowledge inputs to make Ujamaa a clear success in productivity have too rarely been transferred to the village members.

The association of protokulaks and middle-strata peasants in Ujamaa villages has posed problems. To the extent that they dominated village committees they stultified both the income equalization and growth of communal-production goals. To the extent that they were unwilling members they represented a drag. To the extent they were dispossessed they often became "professional" informants to researchers or journalists on the evils of Ujamaa.

With the acceleration of the program (dating to Operation Dodoma in 1970), the importance of facing the technical and financial input needs to achieve greater productivity has become more urgent, if the aim of advancing the earning capacity of the poorer peasants rapidly is to be met. Despite some administrative and supply problems the financial-resource provision appears reasonably well in hand, but the knowledge one less so.

The Second Five-Year Plan launched in 1969 was characterized by much greater concern with strategies, policies, and sociopolitical aims and much less with particular project details and relatively heuristic macro models than the first plan. It clearly was a political economic document seeking to further national aims within tight resource constraints. Poverty elimination and income-distribution alteration were cited as goals and implicitly underlay several sections, including those on Ujamaa villages and low-cost urban-site and service-housing schemes (the latter not implemented as intended until 1973).

While apparently including a complex of regional plans, the second plan was actually centrally formulated with the regional volume and then abstracted from the national program so that the local-level initiative is more apparent than real. However, the primary education and rural health programs were deliberately drawn up to provide for higher growth in particularly poorly served regions and districts, and the nine-development-town approach to influencing major industrial and institutional location was introduced.

Major fiscal changes in 1969 abolished the flat-rate development levy, merged it into the progressive personal tax system, and abolished local poll taxes and produce cesses with a sales tax (which also yielded additional revenue). Both measures shifted taxation from rural to urban incomes (probably of the order of Shs 50 to 60 million a year), and both made the tax system more progressive. In the case of sales tax this was achieved by differential rates—zero on unprocessed foods and maize meal, 10 percent on most consumer goods, 20 percent on luxuries. Over time, sales-tax rates have risen, and the differentiation against upper-income purchased goods (and two mass-consumed amenities: beer and cigarettes) has increased in terms of relative tax rates. Specific note of the income-redistribution effects was taken in the 1969 Budget Speech and in several later ones (Tanzania [Budget Speech] 1970-75).

The 1969 budget exercise also included a minimum-wage increase of Shs 20 per month, explicitly designed to offset the impact of the sales tax at that income level and to make partial restoration of inflationary erosion since the previous minimum-wage fixing. While it was not entirely explicit at that point, this was to become a precedent for regular review of the minimum wage to allow its adjustment to maintain real purchasing capacity in the face of price changes.

The TANU Guidelines of 1971 marked a reaffirmation of the Arusha Declaration, a reiteration of the need to achieve greater incomes for peasants and output from agriculture, and a much clearer assertion of the importance of mass participation in decision making—the last at least in part to guard against bureaucratic or managerial attempts to stall or reverse policies designed to reduce salariat privileges and narrow effective-income differentials (Mwansasu 1972).

Related to this last strand in Mwongozo (Guidelines) was the launching of the Workers Council program as the first step towards full worker participation in firm management. In fact the step was a rather cautious one as the council's full powers were largely advisory; the Executive Committee, which had powers also, had a managerial majority, and the worker-directors were appointed on a significant scale (two per board in general) only in 1975 with a decision to raise the total to 40 percent of board members taken in 1976. The effects varied, as discussed earlier. Further related to Mwongozo was a 20-year rural water-development plan designed to ensure pure water within a reasonable distance of all rural Tanzanians by the early 1990s. Given actual rural attitudes (as shown by interviews and by the priorities given by TANU local-level leadership), this responded to a felt mass need. This plan represented a move toward defining a cut-off date for the elimination of one of the components of absolute rural poverty. While implementation initially lagged somewhat, rural water held its place as a top-priority field and one in which physical implementation capacity steadily increased, probably to more than 500,000 additional persons supplied in 1973-74. In 1976 the success of the plan's first five years led to a decision to accelerate it and set 1981 as a target date, while also increasing the emphasis on local participation through spring protection and pipeline and well building to complement the centrally provided borehole program.

The most dramatic of 1971's measures was the Buildings Acquisitions Act. The underlying intent was to end landlordism, or at least large-scale landlordism based on ownership of rental properties with a value of over Shs 100,000. The reasoning appears to have been twofold: to reduce the economic base of the private sector and, more important, to eliminate a subsector in which blatant exploitation was common. Rent control existed, but quite apart from statutorily allowing exploitative rents for older buildings, was widely and successfully flouted. A gradual, "tax-the-profit-out-of-it" approach beginning with a special 5-percent tax on rental income (intended to be raised gradually) had been begun in 1970 (Tanzania [Budget Speech]1970) but was seen as too slow and probably added to rather than subtracted from the pressures for buildings acquisition.

As a direct means of housing the poor the act—predictably, given the value of the buildings involved—had no effect. As a tool of income distribution it transferred from a private, upper-income group to the state, especially since the compensation formula was a special, truncated one to take into account the high legal past rents and the widespread abuses. In practice, the short-run effect of the act on the poor strata of the population was probably negative for a special reason: It was seized upon by store owners (many of whom had lost rental properties) as an occasion to boost margins either to recoup their losses or to make surpluses while they were still to be made.

The motor-vehicle registration regulations designed to limit purchases of new (and up to five-year-old) saloon cars to those needed for development and social purposes was based on a mass demand to curb elite conspicuous consumption. It reduced seen disparities in consumption based purely on wealth, in the same sense that buildings acquisition did. On the whole, the automobile restrictions have worked; permits have been issued in cases of need, but the fall in new saloon car registrations indicated that the regulation had teeth.

Government and parastatal car purchases have also been limited and since mid-1974 virtually halted both to husband investible surpluses and to block off a possible substitution of a de facto private car paid for by the public sector for a self-owned one. This effort may have been successful insofar as numbers are concerned, but not in limiting, much less ending, abuse. Misuse of public vehicles for private purposes by senior government and parastatal servants is not uncommon, is believed to be more common that it is, and is a source of major public resentment. It is therefore a far higher candidate for control to end its corrosion of public servant morality and erosion of mass faith in public-sector integrity and devotion to egalitarianism than its purely economic cost might suggest.

In 1972 decentralization measures based largely on the report of a study team headed by A. J. Nsekela and Cranford Pratt, with substantial political contributions by the party and technical ones by a handful of prodecentralization senior civil servants, were brought into operation (Tanzania 1972). The linking of this operation with the McKinsey consultants is accurate in administrative and organizational detail but not in basic content: Indeed, McKinsey favored a very different and totally nonparticipatory concept of decentralization.

The change, like the earlier RDF, was designed to bring government closer to the people in the literal sense in order to bring decisions to a level at which local data would be available, and local needs evident, to political, technical, and managerial decision makers. In addition, it sought to create a pattern of organization and control in which district and regional government activity was integrated and coordinated at that level, rather than depending on coordination in Dar es Salaam at the top of a number of separate hierarchies whose regional and district representatives had escaped from effective regional and area commissioner control. Emphasis was placed on providing structures (the DDCs and RDCs in which representatives of the people and of mass organizations could take part in decision making to increase the scope for, and reality of, broadly-based participation, especially in rural areas). The 1972-75 results indicated clear progress on the first four targets, with one glaring exception. Serious regional proposals for the 1975-80 plan were to have reached the prime minister's office for review and coordination work to commence early in mid-1974. By late 1974 many regions and districts (by no means all) seemed not to have started, let alone completed, a serious planning exercise.

The early evidence on expenditure levels and patterns strongly suggests that decentralization has raised the share of spending going to rural areas, to mass-need-oriented services, and to some (not all) of the poorer districts. Its basic thrust, therefore, is conducive to poverty eradication, especially if its potential for greater efficiency in identifying and meeting local needs in terms of local conditions and opportunities come to be less unevenly and more fully exploited. One major side effect has been to raise the number of senior public-sector posts with relatively high salaries, affording another burst of rapid promotions for able, young middle-level civil servants. This evidently is not particularly consistent with greater egalitarianism, but by reopening promotion channels and thus allowing a substantial number of the salariat to achieve real income gains, it did reduce pressure for government salary revisions significantly over the 1972-73 period.

Adult education—aimed at universal literacy by 1976—was launched on a broad-front basis in 1972. Built around work units in cities and primary schools in the rural areas, it is seen as providing a basis for participation, communication, and subsequent transfer of applied knowledge.

By 1974-75 adult education enrollment at more than 3 million exceeded one-fifth the total population, and adult and pupil combined totalled about one-third. By 1976 adult education enrollment alone exceeded one-third and first-year primary school intake had reached at least three-quarters of the relevant age group. More important, about two-thirds of the students were not in basic literacy but in other courses, ranging from political education to bookkeeping, from French to child and mother care, from agriculture to literature, from nutrition to mechanical skills. Parallel to this major breakthrough—if lagging it— was a rapid growth of paraprofessional programs in accounting, agriculture, mechanical work, construction, environmental sanitation, and simple curative medicine, designed to create skills in and for villages and by villagers. Inadequate in size, articulation, and coordination though they clearly were in 1976, the change from 1972 was exceedingly rapid.

TANU's third major declaration (following Arusha and Mwongozo) of the period came in 1972 and related directly to agricultural-productivity enhancement and, therefore, to absolute poverty eradication. The stress was heavily on seed, fertilizer, farm management, improved hand tools, small-scale irrigation, animal-drawn cultivation, better techniques, and selective mechanization, and therefore on what the rural population, given adequate knowledge transfers and supplementary resource inputs, could do to tackle the problem of rural development through their own efforts.

The technical follow-up through 1975 has been inadequate in quality and conception as well as in quantity. Mass needs and experiences have been articulated well from a fairly broad base; the analysis leading to policies to meet mass needs continues to lag broadly behind. The 1973-75 drought crisis, it can be hoped, served as a stimulus for truly concentrated and sustained attention to the overall rural organization, knowledge, and inputs strategy needed to secure sharp increases in production on a broad front and to create a self-sustaining dynamic toward elimination of rural absolute poverty, blending mass effort and public sector complementary service and resource provision. But the psychological and technical obstacles to such an outcome still appear very great, though not more so than obstacles in other areas, which have been surmounted.

Because absolute shortages and gaps in supply of basic consumer goods, building materials, and agricultural inputs certainly do not meet mass needs, create incentives to greater production needed to escape from poverty, or generate confidence in the system, the reform of the state Trading Corporation begun by a Tanzanian ad hoc consultancy group in 1972 (following a disastrous reorganization based on a foreign consultancy study) ranks as a major initiative toward the eradication of absolute poverty and fairer allocation of effective purchasing power. It is interesting to note that the reorganization has laid great stress on decentralization, to regional level, of wholesale activity (since reinforced by merging textile wholesaling into the regional trading companies), while grouping specialized technical activities (import/export and goods, such as pharmaceuticals and complex machinery with major sales knowledge or follow-up maintenance requirements) into single-purpose national companies and creating a coordinating, advisory, technical assistance, and last-resort control body (not a holding company) in the Board of Internal Trade.

The regional companies are seen as working closely with and having boards composed of representatives of functional and political groups of regional government. Stress is laid on the absolute necessity of determining and meeting mass needs adequately and promptly and of avoiding waste and inefficiency that would raise prices to peasants and workers. The implementation phase over late 1972-74 proceeded rapidly and relatively smoothly. Certainly, efficiency, as judged by the declining number of complaints, has risen rapidly, as have financial surpluses achieved without raising percentage mark-ups.

A somewhat similar exercise was initiated by the National Bank of Commerce over 1973-74, unlike the old STC, a highly successful institution partly because it has always sought to identify and correct weaknesses and to seek out and build on potential areas of strength. Regionalization, savings promotion, and foreign banking activity concentration in a specialized branch are among the areas of ongoing change.

The 1972 budget session saw major minimum-wage increases—both to offset inflation and to raise real purchasing power—and the consolidation of the scattered minimum wages into two: urban and rural (more accurately agricultural, small-scale mining, rural construction, rural domestic, and rural voluntary nonprofit employment). The lower rural minimum relates to a belief that the rural employee can usually grow some of his own food and also builds his own house or has rooms provided by his employer as a fringe benefit, reducing his effective cash cost of living. The 1972 announcement clearly implied that regular reviews of this type were envisioned. The 1969-1972-1975 sequence was, in fact, broken because of the emergency situation in 1974, with the revisions brought forward by one year (Tanzania [Budget Speech] 1969, 1972, 1974). A Sh 40 (10 percent) minimum-wage increase was made in 1975, but none in 1976.

The Regulation of Dividends and Surpluses Act (and subsequent amendments) placed very substantial powers to secure complete information, regulate dividends, and influence investments of all large companies (public and private) in the hands of the Treasury Register (now commissioner of public investments of the Ministry of Finance and Planning). It further empowers him to conduct annual parastatal operating-plans, physical and financial reviews in terms of corporations reaching their national objectives, and to report on these to the appropriate ministry. Taken together with the Audit Corporation Act, it also gives him automatic access to detailed audit criticisms and queries as a means of identifying areas of weakness, inefficiency, and impropriety (Tanzania [Budget Speech] 1971, 1973, 1974). Given the in-built Treasury concern with greater egalitarianism, more directly productive investment, and support for local small-scale poverty overcoming initiatives, these powers, once fully exercised, seem likely to underpin the resources available for such ends and to provide a check on parastatals drifting off course.

The 1974 creation of designated revenue productivity funds for mass consumer-goods production, export processing, and rural-development knowledge inputs can be seen in the same way as can the Workers and Peasants Housing Fund, financed by a 2-percent payroll tax on employers (including government) with worker-controlled savings and credit or housing cooperatives and Ujamaa-village or other peasant-controlled housing societies the main designated channels for utilization of funds (Tanzania [Budget Speech] 1974). While not adequate to cover the full cost of the skeletal ten-year Decent Housing Plan, taken in conjunction with Arhi's building research and regional improved traditional construction units, the National Housing Corporation's low-cost housing schemes, it should provide a real dynamic toward overcoming the inadequate housing component of urban and rural deprivation, and in encouraging greater production to meet the one-sixth initial-savings requirement for loans. By the end of the 1970s the total number of absolutely ill-housed Tanzanians is likely to begin to decline, as did the total number without access to pure water by the middle of the decade. The fully articulated Price Commission created in late 1973 (but in interim operation some months earlier) was occasioned by a felt need to avoid profiteering and to limit cost-of-living increases following the early 1973 devaluation. It was prepared by a Tanzanian ad hoc consultancy group presenting both basic principles and detailed data to allow price control at importer/manufacturer, wholesaler, and retailer level on almost all basic (and some not so basic) commodities. The basic targets were excessive margins, discriminatory pricing between individuals, and open or overt oligopolistic practices. These had been accentuated over 1971-73 because two devaluations had made it easy to blame any price increase on import costs; the steady advance of socialism and egalitarianism had led many retailers to leave and the others to feel they should raise margins to make money while they could; the 1971 Buildings Acquisition Act had both exacerbated the second factor and led to a desire to recover building losses from trade profits; and the reality of physical shortages (even if brief and scattered—and in 1972 up-country shortages were more often long and numerous) gave occasion to claim shortages and charge "under-the-counter" prices even for goods that were not scarce.

The Act set out detailed goals and bases for price decisions. Of the eight goals, three specifically relate to income distribution, two to preserving government and productive-sector ability to finance expansion, and one to avoiding shortages, especially in rural areas. Mid-1973 through early 1976 has hardly been an easy time for such a program to begin. However, it certainly has calculated, analyzed, and set prices regularly and—with a handful of exceptions—rationally. Further, detailed comparisons of Tanzanian and Kenyan (let alone Ugandan) price movements over the period suggest it has had a very considerable impact. Kenyan food prices rose much less because the country did not suffer a 30 percent drought loss on grain plugged by higher cost imports. This is easier to see on the Tanzanian side because prices must be marked on goods or shelves and on official price lists displayed in shops.

The income-tax legislation of 1973 reestablished the principle that the minimum wage should not be subject to direct tax. With consequential adjustments to other lower income rates, this probably eliminated tax obligations for 75,000 workers (and a few thousand peasants) and reduced them for another 100,000. The revenue loss was balanced by a new tax on parnership income as such (analogous to, but at half the rate of company tax), as well as in its final form as partners' personal income and by raising upper-income marginal rates.

At the same time family and married allowances (which had applied only to upper-income taxpayers) were abolished and a married woman's income disaggregated from her husband's for tax purposes. While these changes were needed on administrative grounds, they tended to benefit lower-income taxpayers relative to upper-income taxpayers and to encourage women to take up jobs. As a result, some upper-income families had much higher but some (for example, husband and wife in senior positions, with no children) marginally lower rates of tax.

The bill led to the most formidable attack on Tanzania's income-redistribution strategy to date. The opposition in the National Assembly quite clearly indicated that members felt that both they and their fellow elite members had been squeezed too much and deserved redress, not new taxes. The final passage of the act, after a direct party-parliament confrontation, represented a reaffirmation of the strategy considerably more critical than the rather minor income-redistribution benefits the act itself provided. A major elite challenge had been turned back because the National Assembly believed that TANU, spearheaded by a deeply committed and outraged president, had the power to mobolize mass support—for example, if a national election were to have been called on the issue.

In 1973-74 there was a revival of the twin drives to eliminate corruption and the mixture of leadership and business roles, which in the Tanzanian context is perceived as a variant of corruption. These efforts have more relevance to income distribution and poverty elimination than may be evident at first glance. The cost of bribes weighs particularly heavily on the poor: They cannot afford to pay a second time for the services that the budget should have provided them. At best, private business interests draw off the public servant's time and create a strong possibility of conflict between public and private interests, and of growing obligations to and dependence on the capitalist business community (including the local representatives of foreign capital). Acceptance of bribes or favors (houses, automobile repairs, provisions at far below market cost) from businesses (including public-sector businesses) is clearly likely to lead to favoritism in decision making, higher costs (to recover the monies paid as well as a profit) to the public sector, and at worst a warping of the pattern of individual decisions or priorities. Those abuses that do exist (even though at a level probably much lower than rumored and certain low by world standards) corrode mass faith not simply in suspect individuals but in the leadership. More particularly, the grievances of the middle-level leaders—whose expectations of legitimate high salaries and rapid promotion have been part of the price of income-redistribution and mass-needs-oriented development against a system that (as they see it) tolerates hidden corruption and near-corruption by some of its top leaders—are expressed (at least in private) in very harsh, bitter and specific terms.

There is no doubt of the senior leadership's and especially the president's commitment to these efforts. However, as after Arusha when initial progress to compliance was rapid but lagged as attention turned to other areas, the real question is whether the process can be institutionalized. Periodic major campaigns may well be needed, but so is a regular day-to-day institutional procedure for collecting and sifting complaints and evidence, acting on proven cases and letting that action be widely known. The substantial number of internal disciplinary cases and firings where evidence is adequate to prove incompetence but not fraud or corruption may deter imitators, but it is inadequate to reassure the public. The last is critical both to reassure the honest and to strengthen the belief among the potentially dishonest that corruption and private-interest cases are found out, acted upon, and publicized.

EXTERNAL CRISIS AND INTERNAL RESPONSE IN 1974-76

External events in late 1973 and 1974 combined to create a major crisis for Tanzania. The fact that the overt signs of the crisis relate primarily to foreign exchange and prices in no way contradicts the proposition that the way in which it is being faced and its success or failure will determine whether the strategy for more egalitarian income distribution and absolute poverty elimination is given a strengthened dynamic, emerges shaken but still largely intact, or is sent into reverse.

Tanzania cannot singlehandedly change the world economic order, break the global grain cartel, or halt industrial economy inflation but can only respond to reorder its own allocations and priorities in a defensive manner alone or in conjunction with other peripheral economies. In that sense the global economic crisis resembles the 1972-74 weather conditions. It also resembles them in that Tanzanian decisions have had to take some view of probable future developments. The question, "Will 1975 bring a rerun of 1930 in the world economic system?" was as critical to strategy and policy formulation as, "Will the 1974/75 short and long rains fall?"

Tanzania's particular problems were a drought leading to a 1972/73 and 1972/74 loss of 30 percent of grain output with a resultant 1973/75 grain deficit of over 500,000 tons. World grain, sugar, and milk prices more or less tripled since the early 1970s, and this tripled the serious impact of a fivefold increase in petroleum cost. By 1975/76 the grain-import bill was receding but replaced by general importation of global inflation especially in respect to capital goods.

Massive subsidies to hold down prices (whether by decision or by simple inertia on selling prices) would have eroded either productive-sector investible surplus and ability to invest or government revenue available to programs critical to poverty eradication. On the other hand, rising prices threatened to erode the purchasing power of lower-income groups, most through their disproportionate effects on staple foodstuffs, rural transport, and agricultural inputs.

Last and perhaps worst, the failure to resolve the external-balance crisis would deliver Tanzanian political economic strategy as a hostage to whoever could provide finance to buy food imports, a situation not likely to be conducive to maintaining a radical socialist poverty-eradication and income-redistribution policy if, say, the IMF, the EEC, or the United States were the dominant financier, and only slightly less unlikely if the IBRD bureaucracy were centrally involved.

The result of inflation on the fixed salary scales in the public sector had reduced the purchasing power of an officer in the same post as in 1961 to about 40 percent of its original level and of one last promoted in 1970 (a much more common situation) to 75 percent. This degree and pace of reducing salariat purchasing power was likely to give rise to major commitment and morale problems (indeed was already doing so) quite separable from the general strategy of egalitarianism. "Standing still" with rapid inflation and slow promotion in 1973/74 did not mean the same thing as in 1961-70 with slow inflation and rapid promotion.

The strategy chosen in the first half of 1974 was in one sense a crisis response (or impending crisis response, as strategic planning and decisions preceded the objective external reserve and price crises by four to six months) but in a special sense. The decisions taken sought to maintain progress toward objectives, use the short-term crisis to lay a foundation for later advance and to take short-term decisions with a clear look at their long-term consequences (Tanzania [Budget Speech] 1974). This pattern, while more overt in 1974, has characterized enough earlier strategic decisions to be seen as a basic element in the Tanzanian decision-making process, albeit less uniformly in the technical preparation, analysis, and briefing for it.

The strategy turned on raising minimum wages sharply (40 percent), salaries moderately (15 percent), grower prices for basic foods sharply (up to 100 percent), importing (and in drought-stricken areas distributing free) enough grain to ensure no starvation and only minor shortages, and then seeking external refinancing, since to do that first would have meant starvation for many as in Ethiopia under both the past and present governments in the face of lower national relative food-output shortfalls. The economic interaction of the changes was projected for at least two to three years and partly published in the budget speech and UN submissions.

Price and tax changes to remove interim parastatal deficits and restore public-sector surpluses for basic service expansion and investment were worked out beginning with May-June 1974 price and tax boosts and continuing through the end of the year. Subsidies were perceived, except for drought relief and as incentives to adopt fertilizers, as counterproductive in terms of income distribution because of their opportunity cost in basic service and production expansion.

The longer-term elements in the strategy can be summarized as follows: Produce out of trouble; accelerate the rate of advance in mass service provision; decentralize production units as well as government; increase participation. This strategy was perceived as having a high risk of failure; in December 1974 President Nyerere sadly broadcast that another main rain failure would mean starvation. However, the alternative to jettisoning the transition to egalitarianism while retrenching on mass services and other development inputs was perceived to be suicidal. At best, the basic goals would recede, and with luck Tanzania might regain its 1973-74 position and dynamic in 1984. At worst, the state would sink into internal chaos and total external dependency because its leaders would be perceived as having both failed and betrayed the masses.

Through 1975 the strategy formed the working skeleton of most major Tanzanian policy and program decisions. Despite rather worse 1974 harvests and markedly worse terms of trade than anticipated, the party, the state, and in large measure the development dynamic have survived. The years 1976 through 1978 are certain to be difficult years but not as grim as 1975 and faced with more assurance because of the hard-won partial successes of 1974-75 and the sharply better crop results of 1975 and 1976. The external-balance position must be corrected by more exports (Tanzania is in its own terms far too dependent on aid and has cut its imports to the bone) but the programs to achieve that over 1976-81 and to restore a 4- to 6-percent growth rate to provide resources for a sustained advance toward basic need fulfilment are partly under implementation and partly under fairly advanced designing. They may not succeed, but they are on the face of it more realistic even in ascetic output and "value-free" technical-plausibility terms than any previous Tanzanian production-planning exercises, as well as being more clearly informed by the aims of advancing transitions toward socialism, self-reliance, egalitarianism, and basic-need fulfilment.

A special problem arose in the nature of institutional strategic and technical responses to the crisis.

Judging from its published statements and ministerial speeches beginning in February, the Treasury clearly saw the crisis as a major one and saw its long-term solution in production boosting in selected areas. It also placed emphasis on avoiding damage to income distribution and saw rural production increases and poverty eradication as complementary. The policy positions on wages, prices, taxes, and investment flowed from this strategic approach, as did the determination to secure bridging foreign-exchange cover. The financial parastatals have responded similarly.

Mincom (now two ministries) equally stressed production enhancement to meet short-term real-income losses without recession and has worked closely with several of its parastatals in this direction. The Price Commission and Board of Internal Trade have also sought to protect supplies and prices of basic necessities subject to the constraint of not destroying the investible surpluses needed to provide long- and medium-term domestic-capacity expansion.

The Ministry of Agriculture has faced greater problems. The totally spineless response to the production aspects of rural poverty (Green 1976; Coulson 1975), and the failure to devise effective means to realign research and extension (centrally or regionally) to implement the Iringa Declaration or the Ujamaa-village program, greatly limited its ability to contribute to meeting the strategic challenge posed by grain. In the cases of sugar and dairy products, more articulated programs existed and could be pushed ahead; unfortunately, unlike grain, these are unlikely to provide frontal assaults on rural poverty in more than a limited number of areas.

Devplan's historic pattern of primary attention to micro-project analysis and budgeting for short-term bricks and mortar investment on the one hand and long-term plan preparation on the other (often with the two hands operating independently of each other) left it in a poor position to tackle the challenge strategically. Coupled with its historic lack of sustained attention to income distribution or poverty eradication as goals in their own right and its basically conservative approach (seeking to create more technical salariat posts and more expensive pieces of bricks and mortar is a very conservative approach to development, however fiscally imprudent its consequences may be), this led to its technical-level proposals adding up to recipes for reducing current real output (by draconian credit restraint) and reducing the future growth of production (by stringent control on directly productive parastatal investment to the benefit of ministerial bricks and mortar).

This is clearly not a response consistent with maintaining any development dynamic, let alone an egalitarian one. The cure does not lie in changing individuals or formal structures but in reorienting priorities to emphasize strategy and policy, to decentralize most project and program articulation to ministries and parastatals and to define basic objectives first and move from them to programs and projects, instead of treating the last as separable from the first. The 1975 merger of the Treasury and planning is rational in that context partly because the Treasury has developed greater strategic planning and policy competence and partly because central economic-policy coordination is not usefully divided. Perhaps more basic, the combined ministry is likely to pursue a decentralizing and spinning-off course to allow it to concentrate on key areas.

One apparently rather inconsistent element in the 1974 salary-increase package illustrates both the careful balancing of basic objectives and interim policies that goes into Tanzanian political economic policy and the consensual nature of decisions. This element is the special increases given to technically qualified professional-level salaried officers (doctors, engineers, research workers, especially in agriculture, accountants, and economists), who have had their entry points placed above the normal bottom-of-scale position so that for most of their careers they will be one increment ahead of other graduates of tertiary educational institutions. The reasoning as stated by the minister of education was as follows:

> . . . we need more scientists than artists now to run and develop our industries. We'll get these scientists from our schools. By paying more to science teachers we will encourage them and will attract more children to take science subjects (Mwambene 1973:4).

This clearly endorses a market-value, material-incentive approach to coping with the major problems of keeping a scientific/technical high-level manpower-training scheme on or near target. It is interesting to contrast two 1974 statements by the president. First:

> Personally I am very emphatically against material incentives. If I have a doctor and he talks to me about his market value I ridicule him; I say "We are a poor country, we cannot afford you." We will not bribe a Tanzanian to work for Tanzania (Nyerere 1974-b).

The second:

> . . . no human being has a market value except a slave. . . . The value of a human being cannot depend on his salary, his house or his car; not on the uniform of his chauffeur. . . . When such things are said the individuals saying them believe they are arguing for their "rights" [,] . . . that they are asserting the value of their education— and of themselves. In reality they are doing the opposite. For in effect they are saying "This education I have been given has turned me into a marketable commodity, like cotton or sisal or coffee." . . . [The] education they have received has degraded their humanity. . . . It is as objects or commodites that they have been taught to regard themselves, and others (Nyerere 1974a).

One can rationalize the higher entry point: The technical courses tend to be a year longer than the arts in many cases, so the salaried worker starts a year later. However, the compromise is a real one: providing a nominal incentive on a market-scarcity rationale for new workers educated at state expense in schools at least in principle committed to instilling belief in egalitarian, participatory, democratic socialism in their faculty/student/staff communities.

STRUGGLE, CRITICISM, AND COMMENT

The single most serious problem in respect to the maintenance of the present income-distribution/poverty-elimination dynamic in Tanzania was summed up succinctly by Nyerere in 1969:

> Tanzania is attempting to achieve change by deliberate policy, and to maintain stability by involving all the people in both the direction and the process of change. We are under no illusions about the difficulty of the task we have undertaken. With few socialists we are trying to build socialism; with few people conscious of the basic requirements of democracy we are trying to achieve change by democratic means; with few technicians we are trying to effect a fundamental transformation of our economy. And with an educated elite whose whole teaching encouraged motives of individualistic advancement we are trying to create an egalitarian society (Nyerere 1973).

The Tanzanian political, managerial, technical, and educational leadership is quite clearly an elite. Its income levels and resultant consumption patterns are distinctly different from those of the main body of workers and peasants. In that sense the term "petty bourgeois" is applicable. Whether the Tanzanian elite is consistent with Cabral's definition will ultimately be a question of fact, not of speculation. To date, with some exceptions, it is consistent. The Tanzanian public-sector elite have accepted material rewards very substantially below those of neighboring states and below those that pertained in Tanzania itself in the late 1960s. Neither morale nor, a fortiori, loyalty has faltered generally, not can it realistically be said that broad elite efforts to sabotage the implementation of the Arusha Declaration and Mwongozo have been the order of the day. Creative and energetic attempts at implementation have been at least as common, with an intermediate stance in which a genuine puzzlement as to how to proceed and a tendency to be quite cautious in making change is more common than either of the extreme positions.

This is not to deny the number of elite members who believe that the strategy and policies of Arusha and Mwongozo—to the extent they reduce elite welfare—have been carried too far. The most dramatic confrontation was the 1973 clash in the national assembly on the bill for a national income tax to replace the East African tax described earlier. A lesser clash had occurred on income tax and coffee export tax in 1968 and contributed to subsequent expulsion of some of its leaders from TANU.

Once the issue had been posed in these terms of a confrontation on principle, no compromise was possible. The president, supported by the TANU Executive Committee, stated, prior to its immediate resubmission with no changes in rates: "If you reject the bill you are not Socialists." It was perfectly clear that a second defeat would mean a general election on the issue of redistributive taxation and income distribution. The bill passed. Perhaps equally important, no widespread sympathy was expressed for the parliamentary criticism by other members of the elite, even before it was clear that a collision course had been set, and what support there was melted very rapidly. By late 1974, while the subsequent Income Tax Act revisions had helped low-income Tanzanians and certainly high-income expatriates (by raising the exempt income and setting a ceiling of 75 percent on average tax), the complaint that it was unfair to upper-income Tanzanians was no longer canvassed. The salary increases made in May were welcomed, even though the limits to the amount they compensated for the past 1970 cost-of-living increases were evident; indeed, the increase after tax at Shs 100 per month was the same for minimum-wage earners and principle secretaries, albeit higher at intermediate levels. Morale, on the whole, seemed distinctly improved, probably as much because the scale increases (the first in independent Tanzania) demonstrated party and government concern with the personal welfare of the leadership as because of the absolute level of the gains.

However, significant discontent by upper, middle, and lower top-cadre public servants continues to exist and to manifest itself partly in rather passive approaches to duties, partly in private grumbling, and partly in pseudoradical attacks on the income-distribution policy as insufficient, because the "big potatoes" of the senior leadership are better off than these individuals. "Small potatoes," as these discontented junior elite members misdescribe themselves (typically they are in the top five-thousandth of the national income distribution and hardly poor or deprived by any other group of Tanzanians' standards), are not atypical of recently graduated senior public servants who face loss of pre-1967 expectations of a typical comfortable African elite role and reward pattern, and have joined the service too late to benefit from the abnormally rapid promotion of the earlier years. But they are common enough to give cause for concern. The president's July 1974 statement, "We have been raising the base and lowering salaries of the better paid . . . and we will continue being harder with the top, with the leadership," is not one they can or will commit themselves to implementing, and some are exceedingly bitter in criticizing senior leaders who are willing to accept it and commit themselves to its implementation.

This problem is linked to that of the university. Alone among major Tanzanian institutions, it has become more elitist, isolated, and averse to participation. For the conservative faculty and students this is understandable, as is the attempt to reverse elitist separation of a more national-consciousness-attuned body of students and faculty, including the vice chancellor. The surprising factor is that the conservatives are paralleled by the self-titled Left critics. This phenomenon appears to relate to their own limited influence, especially after 1969-71. However, that in itself resulted from their unfounded belief that the government and TANU's acceptance of their services (until then increasingly on offer) as technical advisors gave them a right to make political decisions and convert TANU to a very authoritarian (even if leftist authoritarian) posture. TANU and the government do not knowingly (nor often even by accident) allow technocrats to take major decisions. To demand the right to decide while refusing to secure validation through participation in politics from the local level on was perceived by the party as elitist deviationism even more serious than that of those individuals the university left criticized.

In respect of poverty eradication, problems have arisen from the psychological and material gap between managerial and technical personnel (both citizen and expatriate) and the urban and rural poor. In one extreme example the manager of a meat-packing plant asserted that traditional cattle production was no work and therefore cattle should be collected compulsorily at perhaps Shs 50 per head (about one-third of the then-current price). In another, the statement, "The chief obstacle to rural development is the peasant himself," was proposed as the lead sentence for a government paper. Both examples were put by expatriates, but the second was initially defended by several citizen officers and turned back only when two expatriate officers led a vehement attack on its underlying philosophy.

In a different form the gap causes criticism of low-cost housing, especially the improved traditional-style house built by a small team and supervised by the owner to be. This cost in 1973-74 about Shs 4000 for a house of several rooms with a metal roof, windows, and doors, and a thin cement floor in one or two rooms, and is viewed by at least a large number of Dar es Salaam workers with great approval. (In contrast, the cheapest modern-style cottage—rather smaller than the previously cited house—cost at least Shs 12,500 to Shs 15,000.) The apparent problem is that the senior officials are really judging a house by whether they would like to live in it, a worse than irrelevant criteria if it prevents assisting programs to allow poor workers to build houses that they themselves find both better than their present accommodation and reasonably acceptable. The 1974 Workers and Peasants Housing Development Fund with its use of savings and credit or housing cooperative societies as credit retailers should be able to channel funds in support of the genuinely low-cost houses (in 1975-76 it made a start with 8000 such loans); a centralized Housing Bank could not, because of administration and supervision costs.

The contradiction between structural change and equality must be faced if it is to be overcome. Because average urban wage-earner consumption is more than twice the average peasant consumption, the present structural shift with urban employment growing 6 percent a year and peasant self-employment about

2 percent has tended to cause a 1.5- to 2-percent increase in average consumption and a 3.75 percent growth in personal consumption demand, even assuming no worker and no peasant had a higher real income than in the previous year.

This contradiction will persist until the rural growth rate averages at least 4 to 5 percent a year. At that point structural change and elimination of rural poverty become complementary, not alternative, goals. The realization of this, and the existence of a basic food deficit, presumably underlay the Chinese planning to give absolute priority to rural (and especially food) development during the first decade of the People's Republic. Tanzania's objective position in this respect was almost identical in 1974 to China's in the early 1950s.

A related contradiction turns on the relationship between income redistribution and import capacity until mass-market consumer-goods industries are radically expanded. The 1969-74 record amply demonstrates this, most notably in the rise of textile and garment imports from Shs 80 million in 1971 to Shs 260 million in 1973, despite a rise of more than one-third in domestic production. Egalitarianism cannot be meaningful unless mass-consumed products, including food, manufactured necessities, and simple manufactured amenities (such as low-cost radios, cigarettes, bicycles, beer, sewing machines, and metal sheet for roofs), are readily available.

Again, the Chinese case is most instructive: Second priority went to mass market consumer-goods manufacture (including some amenities ranging from plastic combs through beer and cigarettes to pens and carved figures), not to "heavy" industry. The contrary Soviet example was not in fact intended to maximize either growth of GDP nor of "heavy" industry in any general sense but of national armaments capacity, an aim quite possibly necessary and attainable for the USSR in the 1930s but less so for Tanzania in the 1960s through the 1980s.

The incentives problem in Tanzania has received inadequate attention, especially in respect to nonmaterial incentives. The most important of these are the individual's contribution to the nation (or a smaller community) and a sense of a job well done. Both are strengthened by formal public recognition— a point taken (sometimes to extremes) by most socialist states, as well as by France and the United Kingdom (for example). Only sporadic use has been made of official and quasi-official public acknowledgment of achievement, except at quite senior levels. Criticism (and action including removal from post at all levels) is more systematically used, but logically it should be a complement to recognition.

Material incentives, especially at lower- and middle-income levels, cannot be ignored. Wanting to be able to afford a radio, a metal roof, or even a refrigerator is not at all the same as lusting after an electric toothbrush and a nightly outing at the Kilimanjaro Hotel Simba Room nightclub! Only the supremely dedicated, the ascetic, and the moderately well-off can totally disregard material gain, and these are unlikely ever to be the majority.

This does not, in the Tanzanian context, imply the need for great inequality. If competent work leads to promotion, and promotion (in itself a formal and officially endorsed nonmaterial incentive) carries some increase in consumption power, then an incentive system exists, even if the differentiation is relatively small. Similarly, as TANU decided after considerable debate, bonuses for exceptional achievement are consistent with a transition to socialism. (For Ujamaa village members, of course, they are even more integral and, indeed, inevitable, unless output above targets is confiscated, which would be a patent absurdity.) The problem is articulating a system. It is already clear that monetary profit and turnover are bad yardsticks, especially given rapid inflation. The National Milling Corporation's scheme suggests physical output is a better base and one more widely applicable than usually assumed, if both ingenuity and a willingness to accept approximate accuracy, not formal precision, are combined in tackling the task.

The problem of efficiency is central to the meeting of basic needs, because resources are scarce. It is first necessary to define efficiency case by case in terms of relevant goals (not simply profit maximization) so that an objective evaluation is possible. For example, if Dar Municipal Transport's availability ratio of vehicles had declined, as it said, from more than 90 percent in 1970 to about 70 percent in 1974, that was inefficiency, no matter how many more passengers were carried or how much investible surplus was achieved. Conversely, if The National Milling Corporation's 200-odd rural agencies provide a basis for rural savings mobilization and services for rural development, then (assuming unnecessary costs are held down) they are efficient, even if they marginally reduce NBC's investible surplus.

It is equally critical to build a base for separating external events and costs of learning from inefficiency to avoid penalizing those hampered by the former or absolving those guilty of the latter. For example, in 1973/74 National Milling did not cause the drought and was only marginally responsible for cooperative inefficiency in buying the surpluses that were available. Soon after the middle of 1973, it projected import needs through June 1974 with a considerable degree of accuracy. Its failure by February 1974 to have moved its local grain stocks or to have placed (let alone taken delivery of) adequate import orders is quite different; it was gross inefficiency fully justifying the president's summary dismissal of the general manager.

In a society that is engaged in a transition to socialism it is vital to recognize that surpluses must be secured from the directly productive sector. With the main means of production owned through the state by workers and peasants, the main flow of resources for development services and development investment must come from them, as stressed by A. H. Jamal in the 1971 Budget Speech:

[They] will be expected to carry out their functions while keeping their operating costs as low as possible; administrative and head-quarters expense—whether capital or recurrent—beyond that essential for efficient operations is both a denial of our socialist principles and a luxury Tanzania can ill afford.

... the efficiency of the parastatal institutions will have to be given the highest priority attention. Every shilling of potential invest-ible surplus needlessly lost by a parastatal is a shilling less of possible investment or a shilling more of taxes and price increases. Where the substance of economic management is vested in the state's and the people's institutions our future sources of investible surpluses are those institutions and activities.

Two points require reiteration: waste is not a socialist objective, and efficiency is not a capitalist mystification. Real resources are as vital to the achieving of egalitarian income distribution and eradication of absolute poverty as they are to any other objectives; investible surpluses are a vital tool for implementing radical reform rapidly and thoroughly. However, efficiency is always relative to goals; Tanzania's income policy is relatively efficient as seen by TANU's leadership and Kenya's very different one is perceived as efficient by President Kenyatta and his closest decision, taking associates in terms of their goals.

A special problem arises in respect to intrastate regional institutions. Kenya is committed to a strategy of maximizing gains for its elite; in other words it gives no serious operational priority (as opposed to verbal obeisance) to poverty elimination and actively promotes the increase of inequality to build up its salariat and middle-class businessmen and to develop an alliance of politicians, business men, the civil service, the press, and intellectuals in support of the status quo. It is no accident that senior public-sector salaries in Kenya have a purchasing power 50 to 75 percent above Tanzanian, and minimum wages one-third to 50 percent less. Zambia's formal political and social commitments are similar to Tanzania's, but it is a much softer state, with much more effective elite resistance and distortion of President Kaunda's and the party's aims. Taken together with higher living costs, this means that its salaries and upper-level wages are much above Tanzania's or even Kenya's. Quite apart from demonstration-effect difficulties, these patterns create severe strains in agreeing joint institution salary and wage scales for joint Tanzania-Zambia enterprises.

The underlying problem confronting strategy and policy flowing from the combination of very low levels of productive forces and very distorted institutional and resource-use structures is fairly simple to state but complex to tackle. With very low levels of resources available, it is essential both to select the correct priorities and to avoid needless waste; the margin of error for inefficiency is very narrow. The pattern of distortion means that marginal consolidating changes (to improve efficiency) must follow major structural changes to create more adequate frames for progress. Unfortunately, the latter have inevitable short-term costs of dislocation and learning that are, in a sense, investment in change, *not* inefficiency. In practice, "investment in change" of this kind can all too easily be confused with inefficiency by hostile critics and, more dangerously, by those wishing to explain away their own mistakes and inefficiencies. The lack of adequate and prompt data flows, arising out of the low level of productive forces and distortions, probably has a more limited effect than normally supposed in obscuring what basic priorities and strategic change decisions should be. It does make the costs of such change very hard to estimate, even approximately, and also to obscure the margin between necessary costs and inefficiencies.

The Tanzanian pattern of selected structural changes with high-potential gains (medium term) and significant dislocation costs (short term) followed by consolidation of efficiency within the new framework is a rational way of tackling the two types of change, even if it appears to produce a zigzag pattern. (After all, it is mathematics, not even economics, and much less the real world, that moves smoothly, slowly, marginally on precisely forecastable paths). A clearer separation of the two phases might lead to greater efficiency in deciding the one to use at a given time. In particular the failure to distinguish allows sectors where no radical structural change has occurred (for example, the Tanzania Tourist Corporation) to hide failure to identify and take consolidating steps under the pretense of "cost of change" and to cause a feeling of unease if all of the benefits expected of structural changes are not realized at once (for example, the frenetic search for new savings-bank-type outlets when the NBC consolidation program has generated rapid increases and by 1975 will cover virtually all subdistricts). To let a weed grow under the illusion that it is a food plant is wasteful, but equally wasteful is pulling a food plant up every month to see why it is not yet ready for harvesting.

This problem is seen, at least as far as priority selection and resource allocation goes, as one of choice. The 1969 Introduction of the Second Development Plan (Second Five Year Plan 1969) to the TANU congress, "To Plan Is to Choose," and the way the plan is constructed and presented make that clear, as do the 1974 responses to the world economic-system crises and the May and August 1974 presidential speeches on the wage and price increases and the food crisis. Whether the same can be said for choice between structural and consolidating policy measures and for following through and evaluating each according to its own logic is less clear.

With respect to critics, it is useful to start with President Nyerere's endorsement of honest criticism:

> Mistakes are mistakes. Exploitation is exploitation regardless of whether those indulging in it are big people or the majority. A party

that adheres to truth and justice must give its members freedom to correct mistakes and remove exploitation. Party members who do not use that freedom for fear of being hated, unpopular or losing their positions are harbouring a great enemy of justice and truth (Nyerere 1968).

While practice doubtless often falls short of prescription, that statement is official Tanzanian policy. The liveliness and even misplaced sweep of some of the criticism published in Tanzania is evidence of that fact and in that sense one of the more important pieces of evidence that the dynamic outline in this study will confront its own shortcomings.

In some ways the most effective critics have been those who argued that a particular strategy or policy or institution was inconsistent with the national goal frame and therefore needed significant or even radical transformation. Two areas in which this is notable are health and management/planning efficiency. In two additional areas—the lag in rural strategy articulation and implementation and the slow growth of participation—the critics are as common but the results much less striking, partly because the critics themselves are often less certain what to propose as alternatives.

For special reasons probably centering on the inherently conservative nature of medical training and practice and that profession's unique ability to treat all unwelcome proposals as though they were a delirious patient's misdiagnosis of his own illness (an ability economists have fortunately never managed to acquire), health strategy in Tanzania through 1971 remained in the pre-Arusha mold and became more and more inconsistent with national goals and the strategies of other sectors. Urban-oriented, dominated by three high-quality consultancy hospitals for the few, starving rural facilities of low-cost drugs to use high-cost drugs lavishly at the center, unwilling to accept the validity of any cadre analogous to "barefoot doctors," systematically downgrading preventive medicine—it was very near the paradigm model of the neocolonial public service (Rweyemamu et al. 1972).

This was already recognized by some medical and political leaders, but the struggle for change was crystallized by a university-based critic whose detailed presentation of reality and illusion radically strengthened the hands of proponents of change. Rural health by 1974 genuinely did have top priority for new funds; preventive medicine had begun to move to parity with curative; rural medical-personnel training at paramedical level was proceeding at a rapid pace. In the late 1970s perhaps 15 percent of health expenditure was on rural services; the 50 percent mark will be passed before 1980. An attempt to reopen the debate by a conservative critic led to sharp letters to the editor including at least one by a doctor. The demand for specialized equipment to serve rare cases was answered:

> If health planning is going to be based on [this] it will under the circumstances mean that people at the same time choose that hundreds of up country children will die for want of just some cheap anti-malarials drinking water or food (Makene 1974).

Criticism of the emphasis on paramedical cadres was answered, too:

> the Ministry of Health is right in having as its priorities a crash training programme for rural medical aids and maternal and child health aids, and health education to serve the rural population who form 94 per cent of the people of Tanzania (Wennen 1974).

To anyone who followed the 1969-71 debate the change, both of emphasis by the ministry and of general tenor of debate, was breathtaking.

More efficient parastatal planning and management is a less compact subject than health. The pressure for change has been publicly spearheaded by several managerial figures, as well as by academic critics (Rweyemamu et al. 1972). Certainly, many inefficiencies remain, but several evident advances have been made. Perhaps the most dramatic is the acceptance by many institutions that ad hoc or local institutions consultancy teams are better for broad policy and institutional studies than are imported groups. The successful STC, price commission, and textile-distribution studies and the ongoing NBC one give evidence that this acceptance is not purely verbal, as does the provision of posts and finance to the Institute of Finance Management and National Institute of Productivity for consultancy wings. The relevance of this to income distribution is that the external studies uniformly proposed more high-salaried posts, greater income differentials by post, and a highly hierarchical nonparticipatory management-worker structure. The rural-development critics (Cliffe and Saul 1972; Awiti 1973) have made many valid points; indeed, at times they were evidently pushing on an open door. Some, however, clearly wanted a far more centrally directed and less locally initiated, member-controlled approach to Ujamaa villages than did the party or the president. The basic problem, however, is that the nature of the criticisms in this case did little to define a concrete alternative. The same applies to the well-founded criticisms of the very slow development of workers-council participation in form decision making and the apparent failure of both NUTA and the Ministry of Labour to devise effective pressures and sanctions to accelerate it (Mapolo 1972).

The growth versus the redistribution line of criticism has been fairly rare in Tanzania *by Tanzanians* (excluding those immediately suffering from redistribution) but not by resident or visiting expatriates. Often, the question is put in a genuine desire for information, though sometimes it is evidently seen as rhetorical.

A Marxist variant of the productionist criticism exists—that is, that Tanzania is inadequately modernizing and production-maximization oriented. The strength of this critique in detail is great, but its weaknesses (rather like those of the IBRD and McKinsey) as to strategy are greater, in that it tends to want to cut back on mass education, health, water, and housing to achieve participatory development of production (Coulson 1975). The politicians' judgment that in Tanzania this is a contradiction in terms is probably better economics than the analysis of either the conservative or radical productionists.

In the Tanzanian context there is little evidence of a general decline in growth rates over 1967-72 (especially if the utterly aberrational 1966 is excluded) until the drought and terms of trade crisis, and 1975 again saw a respectable result. Sector-by-sector growth is comparable to Kenya. Kenya's is higher because its secondary sector is larger than its primary. It is hard to see how more private saving (or luxury consumption?), less rural development spending, more capital-intensive capitalist farming, and less industrialization would contribute to medium-term growth, much less development in any broader sense.

In any event, the question is posed incorrectly. Why assume that growth of GDP is the overriding factor in development or that development, so defined, is always the sole proper national objective? Japan and the USSR are about the only pure examples of such a strategy on record; the PRC choice is very different and, interestingly (because there is no direct connection), rather similar to the emergent Tanzanian strategy.

The real issue may lie in terms of Myrdal's "hard" and "soft" states. However, this distinction does not turn on regard or disregard for human welfare, and it turns still less on GDP maximization versus a more balanced set of goals. It is defined in terms of clear national-power objectives, articulated into a coherent strategy with resources allocated appropriately and adequate discipline and sanctions to limit deviations from appropriate goals, allocations, and conduct. In these terms Ghana under President Nkrumah was an exceedingly soft state, while President Boigny's Ivory Coast was (and is) a relatively hard one (Green 1971a).

In these terms, too, Tanzania becomes increasingly a harder state. The drives continue against capitalist-roaders in the party; more and more avenues of exploitation are taken over or walled off; corruption and inefficiency are often punished; campaigns to enforce bans on excessive drinking or failure to join mass-supported communal projects or sloppy cultivation are, while far less than totally effective, seriously undertaken. There is a sense of direction and of a control frame, deviations from which will not be tolerated. Criticism and participation are encouraged to keep this sense of direction responsive to mass opinion. Certainly, Tanzania is very far from a monolithic police state. It has neither the resources nor the inclination to become one. But its having held for nearly a decade to the course it set in 1967 shows sufficiently that it is not a soft state either.

Wage-earner criticism of selling prices and farmer criticism of buying prices is widespread, but this has been the case internationally, especially over 1974-76, so evaluation of this criticism is difficult. The use of joint packages of price increases offset (at the bottom) by wage increases appears to be understood and accepted as necessary and is not seen as a cynical gimmick. Prices to farmers arouse more basic criticism, but that criticism appears to have been directed in particular at the marketing cooperative hierarchy. Since much of this sector was still in the hands of the 1961-66 emergent elite and was run with little more participation than at the earlier time, and since it was also often rather better at creating salaried posts than at lowering costs and raising farmer payout, this strand of criticism was directed more against failure to carry through radical changes than against egalitarianism per se. More than this is difficult to tell; the readily available cross-section of complaints do not seem to be basically opposed to the strategy as much as to inefficiencies or gaps in carrying it forward and do not seem to suffer from such a degree of mildness of wording as to suggest self-censorship.

The adequacy of Tanzania's ideological development and its relationship to particular weaknesses (not so much the weaknesses themselves) has concerned a group of basically sympathetic critics (Rodney 1972; Saul 1972, 1973). The tentative conclusion often reached, that ideology also develops in an historic context and in the course of overcoming contradictions, would appear at one level to be the correct answer. However, the question as to how broadly informed internalized commitment and especially the ability to develop ideological changes has become rooted in Tanzania is a valid one.

Three factors have caused this type of criticism to be perhaps unduly harshly received. First, there has been confusion between comments on Tanzania and on other African situations. Second, there are often rather tortured attempts to treat scientific socialism as a theological subject and to use exegesis of texts as a key technique. Third, being ostentatiously more royalist than the king (or more Tanzanian than the Tanzanians) is never a very popular stance, and perhaps not a very effective one either.

Root-and-branch criticism contending that nothing has really changed since 1961 or 1967 is not uncommon. It comes in three variants: unsophisticated to the point of caricature (Msuya 1971, 1972), well articulated but so selective as to distort by historic and contextual omission (Shivje 1973), and carefully modeled and argued in detail on a broad front (Tschannerl 1974). Of the first there is little useful to be said: If one accepts that freedom of speech is needed because what is said may be valuable, freedom to criticize rather inaccurately is as necessary as freedom to praise uncritically (indeed, probably more so).

The second school of critics centered initially on a particular set of interim relationships with foreign interests largely negotiated by one institution (and indeed a handful of individuals within it) and widely criticized by many senior public servants. There is little doubt that many of the specific points are valid, but the lack of historical context or general breadth makes the sweeping conclusion that the Tanzanian managerial, public-services, and (by implication at least) political elite are part of the international corporate structure's global middle class and pursue that class' interests, not Tanzania's, exceedingly hard to sustain. Indeed, other critics (Cliffe and Saul 1972), none of whom can be accused of "Right deviationism" or of being apologists for Tanzania, made precisely these points in a public forum. The real problem in cases like this is that the valuable issues raised and specific errors cited are likely to be lost in the countercriticism of the ill-constructed analytical framework and tenuous broadbrush generalizations.

The third type of general critique has at least one impressive example (Tschannerl 1974). It certainly marshalls all the weaknesses and documents them carefully. However, it is selective, does not really consider the evidence on which the contrary conclusions of this chapter are based. Further, the period used is 1961-71, which creates a difficulty if 1961-66 and 1967-74 are viewed as distinctly different in terms of operational commitments and priorities and in terms of results. This does not detract from its value in demonstrating how far from complete the transition is. Another example (Shivje 1976) is less useful or successful because it almost totally ignores the rural sector and substitutes assertions for either argument or serious analysis of inconvenient data.

It is a mistake either to perceive Tanzanian development as primarily a "bottom-up" class struggle or to ignore that 1967-76 has been a decade of very real class struggle. The salariat, the ex-landlords, many ex-capitalist farmers, and, perhaps most critically, many ex-managers and government officials who sacked, demoted, or transferred as a result of worker and peasant direct action against them can testify to that struggle. The future course of the struggle may be less deceptively placid: Worker and peasant direct action is likely to become more important, and there will be top-down action more often in support of bottom-up initiatives. Further, Tanzania is now less fragile than in 1961 or 1967, and the need to mute clashes, even at the price of slowing transition, is less constraining.

Equally, while worker and peasant consciousness is certainly uneven and certainly far below that of the leaders, it is neither negligible nor static. Many Tanzanians have come to see the state and its institutions as theirs in a way that implies it the duty of the state and parastatals to serve them and of citizens to exercise self-discipline and initiative. This is very different from the colonial or 1961-67 pattern. Rural elites are facing far more serious challenges than in 1970, an evolution relating partly to decentralization, Ujamaa, and villagization, but perhaps even more to mass adult education and the associated rise in the rural literacy rate to perhaps 50 percent. However, a barrier that President Nyerere warned against in 1966 does remain a major obstacle to the growth and expression of and action on consciousness:

> This is your country.... Any country must be looked after by people. ... If we do not remove fear from our country and if you do not abolish the two classes of master and servants from our society, clever people will emerge from us to take the place of the Europeans, Indians and Arabs ... will continue to exploit our fear for their own benefit. And we leaders can become clever people. ... This is going to happen if you do not remove fear from your minds (Pratt 1976).

The fear is being eroded but it would be inaccurate to assert that as of 1976 the limits on the clever people are set or policed by (as opposed to approved by and appealed to) the majority of workers and peasants as much as by the socialist members of the elite and in particular Mwalimu Nyerere.

Excessive secrecy is one of the causes for too much ill-informed and too little incisive criticism, for the failure to marry experience and analysis and to apply the experience of one part of the economy in another, and for weaknesses in participation structures. In practice the nondisclosure of information on analysis, experience, problems, and reviews has several damaging effects. It very greatly limits meaningful participation, because without information one can hardly participate usefully, and at the same time it ensures uninformed criticism and general feelings of unease that are often quite wide of the mark. Further, it inevitably leads to partial and self-serving leakages of data that worsen both of the defects mentioned at the same time that it greatly hampers the serious critic actually wishing to understand what has happened, why it has happened, and how it might usefully be changed. Finally, it prevents the application of experience gained (often at very considerable cost) in one operation to others to which it may be relevant.

To take an example, there is a perfectly respectable case for compulsory publication of all government and other public-sector contracts (including management, sale construction, technical services, and other agreements) with a potential financial turnover over the whole contract period of Shs 1 million or more with parallel regulations specifying much lower sums for district-development corporations, cooperatives, and regional and district government. Evidently certain national-security limitations (in the literal defense and security sense) would be needed. However, in the bulk of the cases secrecy is in fact an illusion because the outside parties who really want to know the details can find them out whether by illicit means from Tanzanian sources or by licit or illicit ones from the other parties to the agreement. In general, Tanzania injures itself (in all the ways cited) more than any other party by withholding much of the data.

At the same time, secrecy also does sweep some very unfortunate contracts and decisions out of sight (doubtless to the relief of those who made them) when they should be criticized and used as examples of what to avoid, and creates a quite false impression that most contracts and decisions that would stand detailed scrutiny have something wrong about them and therefore "need" to be kept hidden. Few things can be more damaging to the mutual trust, free dialogue, and effective interaction needed to make a decentralized, participatory democratic system meaningful. Few are more corrosive to the sense of acting within and with the support of national actions as well as statements vital to tackling the challenge of entrenched rural poverty by peasant-initiated and peasant-designed efforts backed by complementary knowledge and input support. Few are less conducive to raising levels of consciousness.

This criticism is relative to Tanzania's own goals. By many standards, Tanzania does have fairly wide and deep access to government data and analysis (for example, in the president's major addresses in the budget speeches), a relatively inquisitive press, and some public-sector enterprises that make a great deal of information available. Discussion by officials as well as by politicians at open meetings is often frank, and detailed data and/or reasons for action are often cited (documents are seen as secret much more often than are their contents). However, in terms of TANU's goals (not excluding reduction of inspired, hostile rumors) the standard achieved by 1974-76 is inadequate.

Speaking to the Sixth Pan-African Congress, Nyerere (March 30, 1974) posed a challenge: "We must look at ourselves, at our governments and our progress; we must ask ourselves whether there is evidence that black people . . . are everywhere trying really hard to establish just societies." For Tanzania the answer to that challenge on the basis of the record adduced above can be affirmative. But it is a transitional "yes" because Tanzania is, by its own claim, in transition to a democratic, egalitarian, participatory, socialist system; it has not arrived at that stage. Basic human needs are not yet fully met for all Tanzanians, nor, on present targets, will they be before about 1986. The progress of transition has been seen by Tanzania's leadership as involving the successive identification of the most urgent and immediate problems and contradictions and their resolution to reach a temporary synthesis (containing its own contradictions) to serve as a basis for a new advance. In that sense 1961-66 was a temporary synthesis following independence, during which the immediate problem became the rise of the basis for an antiegalitarian elite—a contradiction with the stated aims of TANU met in the Arusha Declaration and its implementation.

If that is a correct view to take of the Tanzanian trend and dynamic to date, it also follows that the only stability in the transition is a dynamic of advance: To attempt to stand still is to slide back. The only context for consolidating the gains of one set of structural advances is a context containing new structural advances. In 1968 Nyerere posed this issue starkly:

For although political and social stability are necessary to any real national or personal freedom, so too is change. . . . A very great change in our economic well-being is necessary before we can meet [the] responsibilities of national freedom. . . . What freedom has our subsistence farmer? He scratches a bare living from the soil provided the rains do not fail; his children work at his side without schooling, medical care, or even good feeding. Certainly he has freedom to speak and to vote as he wishes. But these freedoms are much less real to him than his freedom to be exploited. Only as his poverty is reduced will his existing political freedom become properly meaningful and his right to human dignity become a fact of human dignity. This essential economic change will not, and cannot take place in isolation. It depends upon, and it brings social and political change (Nyerere 1973).

To date Tanzania's income-distribution and poverty-eradication effort has concentrated on the following categories:

. . . clearly construing the development problem and generating comprehensive strategies (which is, in effect, an *ideological* challenge), of confronting vested interests and establishing the effective popular base necessary to undertake more meaningful policies (a political challenge), and of giving sustained and progressive institutional expression to such advances as can be made in these two areas (this being an *organisational* challenge . . .) (Saul 1973).

It has attained some definite and substantial results: The Arusha Declaration and Mwongozo, the nationalizations and the passage of the income tax bill, the participatory bodies and the Ujamaa villages—these are far from negligible.

Rather surprisingly, as this is precisely the opposite of normal political economic planning strengths and weaknesses, the "technical" and "mechanical" aspects of implementing the ideological, political, and organizational transitions have remained too implicit and too little coordinated. Often, projects accumulate until they obscure or warp aims, and techniques advance until they supplant the ends (this occurs more often elsewhere, perhaps, but Tanzania is not free of these technocratic and academic weaknesses in other fields). However, in respect to egalitarianism and poverty eradication the ideological framework, the political commitment, and the institutional means are far better developed than the technical and mechanical tools at their service.

To say this is to take a first step toward answering the question, "What next?" It is not a denial of the record but an affirmation, because in many states the answer would have to be at the ideological and political level (as in Ethiopia in 1974), not at the technical or coordinating level. A series of planning reforms and reformulations appear to be urgently needed to safeguard the dynamic now existing and to carry out certain consolidating gains. These include formal recognition that more equitable income distribution and poverty eradication constitute a major planning focus that requires formal specific attention at least as much as foreign exchange or credit planning, leading to setting explicit quantitative targets within this planning area and engaging in regular evaluation of what has (or has not) been achieved and why (or why not). To do this requires development of a data base more adequate for policy formulation, action evaluation, and new problem identification in respect to income redistribution and absolute poverty eradication.

The first cluster requires the inauguration of a formal annual income-distribution (or incomes-and-prices) plan to fit into the package now led by the annual plan as a policy and priority framework and including the recurrent budget plan, government investment- (ludicrously titled "development") budget plan, the credit plan, the foreign-exchange plan, the manpower plan, the parastatal fixed-investment plan (prepared, even if neither fully consolidated nor published), and the parastatal operating plan. The tenth should be the incomes and prices plan. This is not a frivolous point. Creation of a new plan of this type would force explicit, combined consideration of income distribution and absolute poverty eradication goals as a central-priority area, with other policies and projects then reviewed in the light of their positive or negative contributions to the attainment of more equal access to public services, greater capability of the absolutely poor to raise their productivity, and lessened inequality of personal consumption power. The rather vague sketch plan prepared annually by the Treasury—usually only for fiscal purposes, albeit in April 1974 for rather broader use—is not an adequate substitute, especially as it does not provide for effective involvement of the secretariats of the Price Commission and Labour Tribunal.

The need for explicit quantitative targets is as great in this field as in, say, high-level manpower. The 1981 self-sufficiency target for high-level manpower *has* had very real operational significance and will—on present trends—be 90 percent attained. Without a clear target date backed by detailed quantitative demand and training studies in 1964, it is exceedingly doubtful whether that would have been the case. Some of the targets that might be considered for 1981 (the twentieth anniversary of formal independence) include:

1. An urban minimum wage (in 1974 price terms) of Shs 375 per month (a 10 percent real improvement from mid-1974 and 15 to 20 percent from mid-1976 levels)
2. Rural purchasing-power (including self-consumed food and housing valued at comparable urban cost) distribution of 40 percent at or above the urban minimum wage (30 percent today), 40 percent between 80 and 100 percent (15 percent today), and 20 percent between two-thirds and 80 percent (15 percent today). None to be below two-thirds (40 percent today)

3. A maximum inequality of effective purchasing power of urban-sector citizens after taking account of direct and indirect taxes of six to one (versus about eight to one for the public sector today)
4. Detailed plans for universal access to a basic preventive/curative medical center and access to minimally acceptable housing by 1986
5. Provision of trained cadres in paramedical, nutrition, mother and child care, farm management, agricultural techniques, mechanical repairs, construction (both works like minor dams and simple buildings), adult education, dance and drama, small-scale crafts or industries, financial recording and management to *each* Ujamaa village (by 1981), with the cadres for training selected by and from the village
6. Attainment of production of at least 95 percent of all mass consumer goods (first and foremost including all basic foods), basic building materials, agricultural recurrent inputs, and simple agricultural and craft tools and implements based dominantly on sectoral development from local raw materials through finished products
7. Development of a viable, largely small-town and rural small-industry subsector contributing at least 20 percent of the output needed to meet the manufacturing targets
8. Building of a coherent, articulated natural- and social-science and hard- and soft-technology research, adaptation, design, and development-planning process with significant domestic capacity in applied research and adaptation, design and construction, consultancy and supervision, and some areas of capital-goods production
9. A decentralized communication system based on district newspapers and regional radio programs and fed by more and more detailed information, elaboration, comment and criticism on all aspects of development.

These proposals are neither modest nor impossible. Continued spending of Shs 500 million a year in support of village development should raise the income earned by the poorest rural strata by perhaps Shs 1.5 to 2 billion annually by 1981, if efficiently used in terms of a poverty eradication strategy. That would be an increase of the order of magnitude to meet the second target. Urban wage-increase proposals are also feasible: A rate of increase in real terms of 4 percent at the bottom tailing off to zero at the top of the public sector and running from about 5 percent to -5 percent for the private sector should not average more than 2 percent, especially given the savings resulting from the continuing absolute decline in expatriates required.

This emphasis on the need for more specific goals and more formal planning machinery is not in any way a statement that Tanzania should adopt any globally agreed "antipoverty plan" or any "modern standard" of appropriate consumption patterns. That would be to turn its back on the strengths of the 1961-74 record and, as it happens, on the actual specific goals that flow from that record and its dynamic.

There is a sense in which this prescription is inevitably wrong. Tanzania's strategic advances have never turned on predominantly technical consideration. The weather, the international economic order, and internal struggle have created opportunities to face and major challenges to surmount. To have waited because detailed data were unavailable (or turned to less key or less ripe areas where it was) would have been fatal. The technical package proposed will be meaningful if and only if it is based on a current estimation of the actual struggles, challenges, and strategic interim synthesis TANU will cause and face over 1976-81. Otherwise, it is irrelevant.

This study has been Tanzaniacentric. It has not sought to place Tanzania in the international political economic order because to do so would have been far too lengthy and run the risk of a Eurocentric treatment of Tanzanian strategy as an intriguing byproduct of the evolution of imperialism. Tanzanian leaders since 1964 have evolved a steadily bleaker and sharper view of the world economic order as characterized by inequality and inequity, classes of states as well as classes within states, penetration and exploitation. They have sought "Co-operation Against Poverty" (Tanzania 1971) and "A Trade Union of the Poor" (Nyerere November 22, 1975) to organize the proletarian states for bargaining or confrontation. Tanzanian leaders view collective self-reliance as an international extension of the national.

> The truth is that however much we reorganise our economic system
> to serve the interests of the mass of the people, and however much
> our government tries to weight income distribution in favour of the
> poorest people, we are merely redistributing poverty and we remain
> subject to economic decisions and interests beyond our control...
> on economic decisions made by wealthy nations in the interests of
> making the rich even richer (Nyerere November 22, 1975).

Without solidarity (organized if one likes on the lines of a secondary but immediate and antagonistic contradiction), Tanzania cannot do much to alter the hostile external environment that, in the president's words, gives it only two rights: "to sell cheap and to buy dear."

Self-determination, self-reliance, self-analysis, and self-acceptance are the only basis for a sustained dynamic of struggle and transition towards egalitarianism and eradication of absolute poverty. They are not the fruits of economic progress but the preconditions for it to be fruitful, not the harvest of development but the seed from which it must spring.

REFERENCES

Tanzanian Government Publications

Budget Survey (subsequently *Background to the Budget*) *Economic Survey.* 1960/61 through 1975/76.

Second Five-Year Plan. 1969. Four volumes.

Annual Plan. 1970/71 through 1975/76.

Budget Speech. 1964-1975.

Economic and Operations Report and *Economic Bulletin,* Bank of Tanzania 1968 through 1975.

Bureau of Statistics. *National Accounts 1966-1972.*

———. *1969 Household Budget Survey.* Three volumes.

———. *1967 Population Census,* volume 4, "Economic Statistics."

Wages, Incomes, Rural Development, Investment and Price Policy, Government Paper no. 4. 1967.

"The Establishment of Workers Councils, Executive Boards and Boards of Directors." *Presidential Circular no. 1.* 1970.

TANU. 1971. *Mwongoso wa TANU.*

———. 1967. *Arusha Declaration.*

Nyerere, J. K. 1972. *Decentralization.*

Co-operation against Poverty. 1971.

Vijiji.. Prime Minister's Office, 1976.

Other Books

Cliffe, L., and J. S. Saul, editors. 1972. *Socialism in Tanzania.* Volume 1, "Politics;" Volume 2, "Policies." Dar es Salaam: East African Publishing House.

Chenery, H., M. Ahluwalia, C.L.G. Bell, J. H. Duloy, and A. R. Jolly. 1974. *Redistribution with Growth.* Oxford.

Finacune, J. 1976. *Bureaucracy and Development in Tanzania: The Case of Mwanza Region.* Doctoral dissertation, London University. In press.

Nyerere, J. K. 1973. *Freedom and Development.* Dar es Salaam: Oxford University Press.

———. 1968. *Freedom and Socialism.* Dar es Salaam: Oxford University Press.

———. 1966. *Freedom and Unity.* Dar es Salaam: Oxford University Press.

Pratt, C. 1976. *The Critical Phase in Tanzania, 1945-1968: Nyerere and the Emergence of a Socialist Strategy.* Cambridge: Cambridge University Press.

Rweyemamu, A. H. and B. U. Mwansasu, editors. 1974. *Planning in Tanzania: Background to Decentralization.* Dar es Salaam: East African Literature Bureau.

Rweyemamu, J. F. 1974. *Underdevelopment and Industrialization in Tanzania.* Oxford.

———, J. Loxley, J. Wicken, and C. Nyirabu, editors. 1972. *Towards Socialist Planning.* Dar es Salaam: Tanzania Publishing House.

Shivje, I. G. 1976. *Class Struggles in Tanzania.* Heinemann and Tanzania Publishing House.

Tandon, Y. A., editor. 1973. *Technical Assistance Administrations in East Africa.* Uppsala: Dag Hammarskjold Foundation.

Vaitsos, C. V. 1974. *Intercountry Income Distribution and Transnational Enterprises.* Oxford.

Articles and Papers

Awiti, A. 1973. "Economic Differentiation in Ismani, Ismani Region." *African Review* 3, no. 2.

Brown, I. 1974. "Twenty Years of TANU: The Forging of Africa's Premier Grass Roots Political Party." *African Development* (Saba Saba Suppl.) July.

Coulson, A. 1975. "Decentralization and the Government Budget." Economic Research Bureau, University of Dar es Salaam.

Gottlieb, M. 1973. "The Extent and Character of Differentiation in Tanzanian Agricultural and Rural Society 1967-69." *African Review* 3, no. 2.

Green, R. H. 1976a. "Aspects of the World Monetary and Resource Transfer System in 1974: A View From the Extreme Periphery." In *A World Divided: The Less Developed Countries in the International Economy,* edited by G. K. Helleiner. Cambridge.

———. 1976b. "The Skeletal Structure of African Rural Poverty with Special Reference to Tanzania and Ghana: Notes toward a Strategy of Eradication and Liberation." Development Studies Centres, University of Cape Coast, Ghana.

———. 1976c. "Monetary and Credit Policy in a Transition to Socialism: Reflections on Tanzanian Experience." In Bank of Tanzania, Tenth Anniversary Column.

——. 1975. "The Peripheral African Economy and the MNC." In *Multinational Corporations in Africa,* edited by Widstrand. Uppsala: Scandinavian Institute of African Affairs.

——. 1974. "The Role of the State as an Agent of Economic and Social Development in the Least Developed Countries." *Journal of Development Planning,* no. 6.

——. 1972. "The Road from Arusha: Elements Toward a Self Reliant, Socialist Tanzanian Development Strategy." Dakar: African Institute for Economic Development and Planning.

——. 1971b. "Resources, Demands, Investible Surpluses and Efficiency." *Taamuli* 2, no. 1 (December).

——. 1971a. "Reflections on Economic Strategy, Structure, Implementation and Necessity: Ghana and the Ivory Coast, 1957-67." In *Ghana and the Ivory Coast: Perspectives on Modernization,* edited by G. Foster and A. Zolberg. Chicago.

——. 1970. "Political Independence and the National Economy." In *African Perspectives,* edited by Allen and Johnson. Cambridge.

Hall, B. L. 1975. "The Structure of Adult Education and Rural Development in Tanzania." Institute of Development Studies (Sussex), Discussion Paper no. 87.

Helleiner, G. K. 1972. "Beyond Growth Rates and Plan Volumes: Planning for Africa in the 1970s." *Journal of Modern African Studies* 10, no. 3.

Huang, Yukon. 1976. "Distribution of the Tax Burden in Tanzania." *Economic Journal,* March.

Hutchison, A. 1974. "Saba Saba Day: Mwalimu Speaks to African Development." *African Development* (Saba Saba Supplement: July).

Mapolo, H. 1972. "The Organization and Participation of Workers in Tanzania." *African Review* 2, no. 3.

Mwansasu, B. U. 1972. "Commentary on Mwongozo wa TANU, 1971." *African Review* 1, no. 4 (April).

Rodney, W. 1972. "Tanzanian Ujamaa and Scientific Socialism." *African Review* 1, no. 4 (April).

Saul, J. H. 1973. "The Political Aspects of Economic Independence." In *Economic Independence in Africa,* edited by Ghai. Nairobi: East African Literature Bureau.

——. 1972. "African Socialism in One Country—Tanzania." Dakar: African Institute for Economic Development and Planning.

Shivje, I. 1973. "Capitalism Unlimited: Public Corporations in Partnership with Multinational Corporations." *African Review* 3, no. 3.

Tschannerl, G. 1974. "Periphery Development and the Working Population in Tanzania." Dar es Salaam: World University Service.

Wallerstein, I. 1974. "Dependence in an Interdependent World: The Limited Possibilities of Transformation within the Capitalist World Economy." *African Studies Review* 17, no. 1 (April).

Newspaper Stories and Features
(All Tanzania *Daily News* or *Sunday News*)

1973. "Increase of Salaries Will Not End Corruption–PM." July 12, p. 3.

1974. "MPs Accept Anti-Coruption Bill." March 13, p. 1.

Makene, J. 1974. "Medicine and Progress." August 12.

Msuya, S. 1972. "Are We Really Serious about Removing Inequality?" October 24.

———. 1971. "Buy Tanzania but at What Price?" December 29, p. 4.

Nyerere, J. K. 1975. "The Economic Challenge: Dialogue or Confrontation." November 22.

———. 1974a. "Education Must Liberate Man." May 21, pp. 1-4.

———. 1974b. "Africa Can Build Socialism." March 30, p. 1.

Shivje, I. 1976a. "Capital Imports Negligible and the Training Clauses Carefully Evaded." September 7, p. 4.

———. 1976b. "We Become Helpful to Those Who Claim to Help Us." September 6, p. 7.

Wennen, E. 1974. "Would You Like to See Your Child Die?" Letter to Editor, August 22, p. 7.

CHAPTER

10

OBSERVATIONS ON
ECONOMIC EQUALITY
AND SOCIAL CLASS
Seymour Martin Lipset

The stage we have reached in the discussion of equality, equity, and opportunity is somewhat confusing, but to a great extent it is rewarding too. Because of an increased commitment to equality and because of quantitative studies and empirical observations about various countries we have much more information, data, and experience with efforts to increase equality. We have seen in earlier chapters that the experiences of the countries vary enormously; the distinctions between capitalist and socialist, Western and non-Western, free and nonfree societies have become less meaningful than many once thought. These categories are not analytical or even descriptive. Variations within systems have become as great as variations among systems, and one might better consider general cross-systems concepts, experimentation within mixed economic systems, and some of the structural possibilities these imply.

Despite the increase in data we are unable to make reliable judgments as to differences. We can compare wages, but there are many perquisites in Western and Eastern societies alike that are not accounted for by "wages." There are all sorts of income that just are not in the statistics. For example, universities have many policies, such as light teaching loads and three-month or longer vacations, which permit faculty members to earn money from other sources not entered into the salary statistics. I do not know of any study of academe that includes fees over and above salaries. The figures of the American Association of University Professors do not really touch on a great deal of faculty income. This problem is at least as true of communist countries. Western business executives get all sorts of perquisites that are not included as income, but so too do executives, managers, party elite, and generals in Eastern Europe.

Income comparisons are also difficult because most countries do not consider transfer payments as income. The proportion received by the lower groups in the population is often much greater than that recorded in the comparative statistics because a considerable share of their total income is in the form of social benefits: welfare payments, medical coverage, government housing, pensions, maternal benefits, and such. Conversely, some other publicly supported activities are differentially used by the more privileged sectors—free higher education and cultural institutions. These represent, as Henry George and Karl Marx pointed out, subsidies to the well-to-do by the poor. In the Soviet Union, Western Europe, and the United States studies of the social background of university students indicate that they come disproportionately from the more privileged sectors, a tendency that is intensified for those studying in the most prestigious schools or departments.

Alexis de Tocqueville made an observation some time ago that is especially pertinent to our discussion. He said, in effect: Once the idea of equality came into the world it was unbeatable. Once people began to question the idea of inequality of reward, status, or power, the moral basis of hierarchical society, as outlined, for example, in religious teachings, was in jeopardy. Tocqueville said the idea, itself, was the beginning of the end of inequality. There are more poor people than there are rich people, more powerless people than powerful, and inevitably the former would challenge the status quo, thus undermining the system. To de Tocqueville, that was dangerous because the struggle to obtain more equality would challenge the structural bases for liberty. We are seeing, and people will continue to see after our lifetime, the working out of de Tocqueville's prognoses.

Right after the second communist revolution (Bela Kun's revolution in Hungary in 1919), Eugene Varga, a Hungarian who later played an important role in the Soviet Union, made a speech, as the minister of Economics, to the Hungarian soviets. He posed an interesting issue. He said that history has known two methods to get people to work: one, the knot (that is the whip); the other, the carrot (or material incentives). We have rejected both, he said, and are trying a third method, that of moral persuasion. But, he went on to say, the third method is not working. The workers do not work. They do not work as hard as they did when they had the carrot. It is not that they are disloyal to the revolution; whenever the White Guard armies approach Budapest the workers rush out of the factories and are ready to die. But they won't work. The same people who are willing to die for the revolution won't work if we don't pay them enough; if we don't give them economic incentives. He thought the communists might have to return to the method of the knot.

Varga's prediction unfortunately turned out to be correct for the Soviet Union and other communist countries. There was an interesting debate at the Tenth Party Congress in the Soviet Union in 1920 on the role of trade unions in a socialist-communist society that pointed up the potential tension between managers and workers. Ironically, it was, in part, a debate between Lenin and Trotsky, in which Stalin was on Lenin's side. Trotsky said: We have a workers' state, a workers' party, and workers' unions; they all have the same objectives, and therefore there is no basis for real conflict among them. Unions do not need the right to strike. Trotsky's formulation is an abstraction, Lenin replied. We have a workers' state but it is run by bureaucrats, and bureaucrats will try to keep their power. The only protection the workers have against the workers' bureaucrats is the right to strike. Unless workers can resist the party and the state, they have no rights. As we know, workers were never in a position to resist the party and the state in the Soviet Union—not in Lenin's time, and certainly less so in Stalin's time, and they still do not have the right to strike or organize against the policy of the state or party.

In recent years in the Soviet world questions of equality and inequality are discussed in a standard fashion which involves considerable agreement between Soviet scholars and Western functionalist sociologists and economists who adhere to classical economic theory. These intellectuals (who though differently labelled in the West and the Soviet Union, write in much the same language) both argue that inequality is necessary to distribute the variety of jobs and tasks that are required by society. If you have a society in which all wage and reward differences are abolished, people will not want to take on onerous jobs, requiring years of study, long hours, and/or tension-creating responsibility. They will not want to be directors of factories, physicians, or professors. If high status is not assigned to these occupations and if there are no particular economic rewards, why should someone study for ten years to be a doctor or a professor? Or why should someone work eighty hours a week as a director of a factory and suffer the psychological pressures involved? In effect, functionalists, economists, and Soviet scholars argue that to motivate people to seek jobs that take more time and more work, more energy, more psychic strain, and so on, it is necessary to have unequal rewards. They assume that differentiated reward is the only way to place the most competent, best trained, and most industrious people in the socially most necessary positions.

Marx probably would have agreed with this argument. He wrote that as long as there is scarcity in economic resources, inequality must exist. Equality of result is only possible and communism can only emerge under conditions of abundance. But prior to this era of abundance, sharp stratification must continue, as sociological functionalists and non-Marxist economists have argued. Marx, of course, contended that it was impossible to describe a communist society, but he did occasionally. What would characterize the era of communist abundance? It will be a society in which people can hunt in the morning, fish in the afternoon, and criticize poetry in the evening. It is clear that in such a society work would have to be abolished; there would be no division of labor; machines would do all the work. In effect, though Marx never said so explicitly, as long as there is a division of labor, as long as men must work, inequality will exist. All existing societies are clearly far from an era of abundance, but modern technology presumably shows us that the goal is at least technically feasible in the distant future. One can link possibilities of a greater degree of equality to material conditions.

One of the great ironies of contemporary radicalism is that those who argue for the creation of an egalitarian society in Tanzania, the PRC, Cambodia, Cuba, Israel, or any other less-developed country are idealists in the classic sense; that is, they are the opposite of materialists. In Marxist terms, they are utopian socialists. They believe it is possible to create a socialist social structure in the absence of the necessary underlying material conditions because men will it. They emphasize will, motivation, and ideals as tools to overcome underlying inappropriate material conditions. They call themselves Marxists, although they ignore the fact that Marx believed that socialism must emerge first in the most advanced capitalist countries. To use a contemporary phrase, socialism would be a post-industrial society.

Today we find movements calling themselves socialist and communist in power in preindustrial societies. The contemporary communists are utopians at best, that is, unrealistic and impractical. From a Marxist point of view, they have produced sociological monstrosities, social systems that must make things worse, not better. They use Marx's name, but essentially they have totally ignored everything he wrote. Marx has no relevance to the workings, operations or even the politics of contemporary communism. Today's movements are like the peasant revolts of the Middle Ages. Marx characterized these premature efforts at egalitarianism as utopianism. Yet today we have a revival of this pre-Marxian socialism. That this could happen suggests that few on the left really read Marx. Few treat him seriously as an analyst of society and of possible or feasible social change. What remains are gigantic idealist, that is, non-materialist, movements.

Tocqueville's observation that the idea of inequality once advanced must triumph is basic to this discussion. Paul Samuelson once put it in a way that other economists have noted as well: As an economist he believes that it is impossible to have an expanding economic system, or even just a functioning one, without a great deal of inequality of reward, but as a moral person he cannot justify inequality. Why should some people be rewarded and others punished for a difference in intellectual aptitudes or other characteristics? We now take it for granted that sex, race, color, and creed should not be a basis for social reward; but as Samuelson said, neither is there any greater moral justification for someone with lower intelligence to be paid less than someone with a higher I.Q., or for a good looking person to be hired in preference to an ugly one. Discrimination because of intelligence is basically no different from other sorts of discrimination. There is no moral justification for saying that a person who is crippled or feeble-minded should be less rewarded. Morally speaking, all human beings are equals and are owed the same rewards. Samuelson, moreover, believes that there is a necessary link between a free critical society and a free enterprise system even if its system of inequality of reward lacks moral justification. In a communist society, too, the same moral issues are raised.

We can examine the meaning of equality in at least two senses. The first, equality of opportunity, is supposedly the classic American meaning of the term. It subsumes the ideal of a competitive system in which there is great social mobility, in which people are supposed to be able to rise according to ability, regardless of social background. The communist world also emphasizes this form of equality. The second, equality of results, is a new, elaborate way of referring to the old socialist credo from "each according to his ability," to "each according to his needs." These meanings of equality are not really that different. Equality of opportunity can not really exist without equality of result. It is impossible to have equality of opportunity if people start out highly unequal. If you say you are committed to equality of opportunity, then you have to be committed to a high level of equality, if not perfect equality, of result, a relationship which socialists once supported and which some Americans are starting to accept.

To point up the beginning of the acceptance of equality of result, it may be noted that Paul McCracken, who was the head of the Council of Economic Advisors under President Nixon, and a member of the council under President Eisenhower, said a couple years ago in a speech to the Business Council, an association of the country's top businessmen: All of us here know that we are here, in large part, because we are more lucky than others, or come from the right families. But this does not justify the very high incomes we have. Hence, we have to recognize the increased demand for equality of result as a legitimate one, that in terms of future planning and working out of the American economic system, the economic system must move toward greater equality of result.

We have to think increasingly of a tradeoff. We cannot achieve absolute equality, but we can come a lot closer to equality of result, or less inegalitarianism than there is at present. There are a number of books that discuss this tradeoff. It has become a subject for political debate and scholarly analysis in the United States, and the topic has been opened for discussion in the Soviet Union and the PRC. The same language, the same arguments, and the same theses have been advanced in the United States and in the Soviet Union. For example, arguments pro and con for affirmative action, for quotas for people from less-privileged backgrounds in admission to universities or jobs, have been advanced in the East and in the West in exactly the same terms.

The Soviets have rejected the notion of effective affirmative action through quotas proposed by Khrushchev because they say it is economically inefficient. They reiterate the traditional Marxist formula that equality of results can only occur with abundance. If you are committed to equality of results, Soviet writers argue, you must be committed to the most rapid possible growth in production. This implies, according to some, that when university places are scarce that women should not be admitted on an equal basis to men since many women do not fully use their training in later life. Empirically, it is true, as Soviet analysts note, that many women who study engineering, for example, do not become engineers. Some raise children instead, or refuse to consider jobs that require separation from their husband and family. Therefore, it is asserted that in practical terms, to admit women to universities on a completely equal basis with men is to retard the achievement of socialism, because women as a group will not repay the state as fully as men. All other things being roughly equal, one should give preference to men. Soviet writers who argue this thesis go on to say that women should support preferential treatment for men because women can gain full equality only under communism, the more rapid achievement of which is dependent on giving preference to men today. The goal of equality becomes a justification for inequality in the East as it does in the West.

Power is another concept which has been discussed in the context of Tocqueville's concern about the tension between the struggles for liberty and equality. Power must be seen as independent of economic reward. It is the ability to control others, to affect the decision-making structure of the society. Engels has an interesting essay, "On Authority," in which he says that over every factory should be written: "He who enters here gives up his freedom." If you read this essay you will see that he did not limit this generalization to capitalism. Rather, he believed that he who enters any factory, at any time, gives up his freedom. He argued that a factory, like a ship, cannot be run without differentiated power and authority. Factory workers cannot vote on every major decision. This argument is another version of the basic Marxist notion that as long as there is division of labor there must be inequality. Engels emphasized that power differentiation is inherent in a complex society. An interesting Polish Marxist sociologist, Wlodzimierz Wesolowski, has attempted to combine Engels' analysis of power with contemporary sociological functionalism. He writes that contemporary communism may not need sharply differentiated economic rewards, but it requires differentiated power to run a system characterized by the division of labor.

These functionalist arguments for inequality under communism seemingly have as little impact in the East on the opinions of the less privileged and of the less powerful as they do in the West. Survey data from communist and non-communist countries indicate that everywhere the lowest strata want more equality and seek to narrow the gap between themselves and the elite. Opinion polls from Poland, Yugoslavia, and Czechoslovakia before 1968 revealed class-related opinions basically very much like those found in the West. The lower the income and the skill level of respondents, the narrower they felt income differentiation should be; the higher their skill and educational attainment, the wider they thought it ought to be.

To turn from equality to equity, it is interesting to note that the concept of equity has been used both in the East and in the West, in communist and in noncommunist countries, to justify inequality. Equity is considered the appropriate reward for levels of occupation and skill, rewards that are justified by what the person puts into the job, by the level of intelligence, and training and education thought appropriate. In Sweden and Israel, the two most social-democratic Western countries (or have the most socialist, if you will, goal objectives), the upper-strata employees and professionals have been very strongly organized in trade unions. These unions strike often. Seeking to widen the salary gap between upper-level and lower-level jobs, they strike against equality. Professors, doctors, airline pilots, and television personnel go on strike in Israel; they object to a small income gap between the top and bottom. The same is true to a somewhat lesser degree in Sweden. In the communist countries, upper-level people can not go on strike, but they attempt to manipulate the system to accomplish the same objectives.

At the end of the independent Czech regime in 1968, an interesting book by Radovan Richta and others, *Civilization at the Crossroads,* analyzed post-industrial society in terms similar to those used by Western writers. The authors stressed the educational, scientific, and technological changes in post-industrial societies, although the book mainly addressed the problems of the communist world. Greater inequality was openly advocated as facilitating economic growth. Richta argued that those who contribute to society with their intelligence (professors, scientists, factory directors) are always working in the evening, on weekends, on vacation. If their off-the-job efforts are diverted, say, to manual labor, that is wasteful. To make people who are the brain power of the society wash dishes at home is a waste society cannot afford. According to a calculus of efficiency, therefore, a communist society should have servants. In Soviet society there are special stores so that the upper-level intelligentsia do not wait in line; the elite get longer vacations; they may have dachas.

If we compare West and East it appears that the socialist countries are more egalitarian economically, although we cannot make reliable statistical comparisons. The Eastern countries, however, are much less egalitarian than the West in distribution of power. In the Soviet Union or in the PRC, workers do not have the right to strike, they do not have the right to vote people out of office. Clearly power is more concentrated in the communist world than in the noncommunist developed countries. Analyses seeking to evaluate which system is more egalitarian are necessarily confused by ideologies and abstractions. We need to know a great deal more than we now do about the nature of power, income distribution, status differences, and social mobility rates in the East and in the West.

Finally, I would like to touch on the problem of inheritence, an issue that Plato focused on when discussing the conditions for achieving a communist society. In *The Republic* he made the point that the agency most involved in perpetuating inequality is the family. Inherent in the nature of the institution we call the family is the requirement that those who are part of a family unit have strong relations, mutually support each other, and share whatever privileges, status, and advantages any one member has among all. Plato argued, therefore, that to have communism, it would be necessary to take the children away from the family since any family unit will seek to give to the children advantages that have been achieved. Ideally children should be reared by the state and parents would not know their offspring. No society has attempted this, although occasionally there have been proposals of this kind.

If we consider comparatively the question of inheritance, specifically inheritance of position, it appears, insofar as we have data, that there is considerable inheritance, particularly of elite status, in both types of society. On a mass level, however, there is a fairly open system in both communist and noncommunist systems. The most recent American researchers on social mobility, Peter Blau, Otis Dudley Duncan, Robert Hauser, and Christopher Jencks, all report a remarkable amount of opportunity available in American society. Jencks, looking at income data, finds only a $500-a-year income difference between siblings and totally unrelated individuals, selected randomly. The most recent study of the social backgrounds of the American business elite found a considerable increase in the number of people from poor and lower-middle-class backgrounds in top level positions. This increase is because of the bureaucratization of corporate life; a development which makes opportunity in U.S. bureaucratic corporate business resemble that in government-owned business in communist countries. In America, access to the business elite involves going to college, entering a bureaucracy, and rising through the levels. Family background plays much less of a role in where people end up than it did in earlier periods. Jencks suggests that luck, intelligence, and training are the main factors. There is a comparable situation in Eastern Europe. For many in both the East and West, however, privilege still begets privilege.

Both the United States and the Soviet Union are open, competitive societies. Each stresses that everyone, regardless of social origin, should seek to move up. Ironically, therefore, variations in property-relations aside, one of the main effects of the Russian Revolution has been to Americanize the Soviet Union, to make it a much more competitive society than the status-bound Czarist Russia was. In both societies today, one finds the kinds of negative consequences of an open competitive society that Merton outlined analytically in his article "Social Structure and Anomie." He pointed out that in open competitive systems only some people can get ahead by legitimate means. Many must inevitably fail to attain the high positions the value system of an open society encourages them to seek. Failure puts pressure on people to innovate, to seek to get ahead by any means. Innovation for Merton includes not only invention but crime, cheating, corruption, and the like. There is an enormous amount of illegal innovation in both systems, as well as large numbers of people involved in hedonistic withdrawal: alcoholism, use of drugs, refusal to work in approved jobs, and so on. Drunkenness is a major growing problem in Eastern

Europe. Reading Soviet publications gives one the impression that the amount of drunkenness among the poor in Soviet society is much greater than in the West. Such behavior reflects the alienation that is endemic in a highly competitive society in which most people cannot succeed, in which most people must have relatively unrewarding jobs. No matter how equal opportunity is, there are massive numbers who will fail in open societies. This returns us to the Marxist dictum that as long as there is division of labor and economic scarcity, there will be inequality of income, status and power.

Words like *socialism, capitalism,* and *social democracy* only serve to confuse and conceal the real tensions of stratification systems in all societies that are committed to greater equality, but lack the means to support such equality. That is, they lack the material resources and the technological levels that would permit an egalitarian society in which no one had to be inferior to any other because machines, not people, do all the onerous work, in which people can fulfill Marx's dream of spending all their time engaged in what we now consider leisure or creative intellectual and artistic activity. But to move to greater equality, we need more than increased production: we need freedom for the less privileged to impose their claims on the ruling elites. Authoritarian rule is authoritarian, regardless of the ideological or theological myth it uses to legitimate itself. Power can only be constrained, weakened, by counter-power. Those who have privilege seek to institutionalize it. These truisms enunciated by political analysts from Plato to Marx apply equally as well today to Peking and Moscow as to Paris, Tokyo, and New York.

ABOUT THE EDITOR AND CONTRIBUTORS

Editor

IRVING LOUIS HOROWITZ is Professor of Sociology and Political Science at Rutgers University, and Director of Studies in Comparative International Development. He is also editor-in-chief of *Transaction/Society*, the leading multidisciplinary periodical in American social science. Before coming to Rutgers in 1969, Professor Horowitz was Professor of Sociology at Washington University. He has held visiting professorships at the Universities of Stanford, Wisconsin, and California; and overseas at the London School of Economics, the University of Buenos Aires, the National University of Mexico, Queen's University in Canada, and Hebrew University in Jerusalem. *Social Science and Public Policy in the United States,* published by Praeger in 1975, completed a trilogy of volumes on this same theme begun with *The Rise and Fall of Project Camelot: Studies in the Relationship between Social Science and Practical Politics* (1967; rev. ed. 1974); and *The Use and Abuse of Social Science: Behavioral Science and National Policy Making* (1971; rev. ed. 1975). His most recent work is *Ideology and Utopia in the United States.*

Contributors

RIFKA WEISS BAR-YOSEF is presently the Director of the Work and Welfare Research Institute of the Hebrew University and teaching Sociology at the Department of Sociology. Her main interests are in the field of Work Sociology and Social Planning. Besides her academic interests she is involved in public activities as a consultant to various government offices and as a member of national committees dealing with the problem of social planning and the status of women. Her recent research projects are on workers' participation in management and on adult vocational training and retraining.

WALTER D. CONNOR is currently Director of the Foreign Service Institute of the U.S. State Department. He also holds an adjunct professorship in sociology at the University of Pennsylvania. Before that, he was professor of sociology at the University of Michigan, and a member of its Center for the Study of Conflict and Conflict Resolution. He is the author of a major study soon to be published on the subject of socialism, work and equality, a work whose completion was supported by research grants from the American Council of Hemispheric Societies and the International Research and Exchanges Board.

REGINALD HERBOLD GREEN is Professorial Fellow of the Institute of Development Studies at the University of Sussex. He has held academic positions at Yale University, the University of Ghana, Makerere University, and the University of Dar es Salaam, and served as advisor to the Uganda Planning Office and—for nine years, through 1974—the Tanzania Treasury. Among his one hundred odd articles, reviews, chapters, monographs and books are: *Productive Employment in Africa; Unity or Poverty; The Economics of Pan-Africanism* (with A. Seidman); *Stages in Economic Development: Changes in the Structures of Production, Demand and International Trade,* "Adult Education, basic human needs and integrated development planning," "Relevance, Efficiency, Romanticism and Confusion in Tanzania Planning," "Aspects of the World Monetary and Resource Transfer System: A View From the Extreme Periphery," "The MNC and the Peripheral African Economy," and "Political Independence and the national economy." He was also a major contributor to the 1975 Dag Hammarskjold project report, *What Now: Another Development.*

D. FRANCES FERGUSON has recently completed her graduate studies at the University of Texas and is currently a staff member of the U.S. Department of Commerce, in its Office of Personnel. She has contributed articles to *Comparative Studies in Society and History,* and the *Journal of Political and Military Sociology.* Her main areas of interest are in political sociology and comparative government.

SYLVIA ANN HEWLETT is Professor of Economics at Barnard College of Columbia University. Before that, she served as Kennedy Scholar at Harvard University and a Fellow of Girton College at Cambridge University. She is the author of a forthcoming study entitled: *Authoritarian Capitalism: The Political Economy of Contemporary Brazil,* and has published articles in *Latin American Perspectives, Journal of Economic Issues,* and *Journal of Developing Economies.* She has served in overseas posts as a Ford Foundation Scholar in Ghana, Economic Consultant to the Brazilian National Institute of Scientific Research, and to the Brazilian Ministry of Planning, and also—with the aid of a research award by the Nuffield Foundation—as visiting professor at the Fundaçao Getulio Vargas in Rio de Janeiro. Her main area of work is in the economies of Latin America.

ROBERT J. LAMPMAN is William F. Vilas Professor of Economics at the University of Wisconsin. He is also a Fellow of the Institute for Research on Poverty. He has been at Wisconsin since 1958. From 1948 to 1958 he was a faculty member of the University of Washington in Seattle. He has been visiting professor at the American University of Beirut in Lebanon (1951-52), the University of the Philippines (1966-67), and Cornell University (1973-74). He was research associate at the National Bureau of Economic Research in New York, 1957-58. In 1962-63 he was a staff member of the Council of Economic Advisers. His principal publications include: *The Low Income Population and Economic Growth; Top Wealth-Holders' Share of National Wealth; Washington Medical Service Corporations* (co-author); and *Ends and Means of Reducing Income Poverty.*

SEYMOUR MARTIN LIPSET is Professor of Political Science and Sociology and Senior Fellow at the Hoover Institution on War, Revolution, And Peace at Stanford University. He was formerly a Professor at Harvard University and at the University of California, Berkeley. His recent interests are in the study of intellectual and academic life. He is the author of such major works as *Political Man; The First New Nation; The Politics of Unreason; Revolution and Counterrevolution;* and co-author of *Rebellion in the University and Union Democracy.* His most recent book is *Socialism: Its Conspicuous Absence in American Politics.*

JACK MINKOFF is Professor of Economics at Pratt Institute in New York and is the author of a dissertation on *The Soviet Social Insurance System.* In the past he was a Fellow of the Social Science Research Council and the Ford Foundation and directed studies in medical economics and comparative welfare systems at Columbia University in its School of Public Health. His articles have appeared in *Slavic Review, Journal of Economic History,* and *Social Policy.*

ALEJANDRO PORTES is Professor of Sociology at Duke University, and prior to that, Professor of Sociology at the University of Texas. He is currently engaged in developmental research in Brazil in connection with a Ford Foundation grant on development. He has served as visiting professor in Brasilia and was a member of the National Research Council of the National Academy of Sciences. Among his major writings are: *Urban Latin America: The Political Condition From Above And Below,* co-authored with John Walton, and he is the author of some thirty-five articles in major professional publications including the *American Journal of Sociology, Studies in Comparative International Development, Sociological Quarterly, Rural Sociology,* and the *American Sociological Review.*

GEORGE RITZER is currently a Professor of Sociology at the University of Maryland, College Park, Md. He is the author of a number of books and anthologies, including *Sociology: A Multiple Paradigm Science; Man and His Work: Conflict and Change*; and *An Occupation in Conflict.* Articles have appeared in *Social Forces, The American Sociologist,* and many other journals. Professor Ritzer is editor of a series on controversies in sociology for Allyn and Bacon and an advisory editor to *Sociological Quarterly.* He is the holder of a number of fellowships including a Fulbright-Hays Fellowship in 1975. While on the Fulbright Professor Ritzer did research on the democratization of work in Sweden. He is currently working on a book seeking, on a theoretical level, to integrate sociology's multiple paradigms.

LYNN TURGEON is Professor of Economics at Hofstra University and has previously taught at the State University of California at San Jose, and was formerly economic consultant between 1950 and 1957 at The Rand Corporation. He is the author of such leading texts as *The Contrasting Economies; Cost-Price Relationships in Basic Industries During the Soviet Planning Era,* and has contributed to such periodicals as the *American Slavic and East European Review, The Quarterly Review of Economics and Business,* and various texts on economic theory and concepts. He is currently working on comparisons between different types of economic systems, specifically comparisons within non-capitalist countries.